BATTLE of BRITAIN
ATTACK OF THE EAGLES

BATTLE *of* BRITAIN
ATTACK OF THE EAGLES

13 AUGUST 1940 – 18 AUGUST 1940

DILIP SARKAR
MBE, FRHistS, FRAeS

BATTLE OF BRITAIN ATTACK OF THE EAGLES
13 August 1940 – 18 August 1940

First published in Great Britain in 2024 by
Air World
An imprint of
Pen & Sword Books Ltd
Yorkshire – Philadelphia

Copyright © Dilip Sarkar, 2024

ISBN: 978 1 39905 791 2

The right of Dilip Sarkar to be identified as Author of this work has been asserted by him in accordance with the Copyright, Designs and Patents Act 1988. A CIP catalogue record for this book is available from the British Library All rights reserved.

No part of this book may be reproduced or transmitted in any form or by any means, electronic or mechanical including photocopying, recording or by any information storage and retrieval system, without permission from the Publisher in writing.

Typeset by SJmagic DESIGN SERVICES, India.

Printed and bound in the UK by CPI Group (UK) Ltd.

Pen & Sword Books Limited incorporates the imprints of Archaeology, Atlas, Aviation, Battleground, Digital, Discovery, Family History, Fiction, History, Local, Local History, Maritime, Military, Military Classics, Politics, Select, Transport, True Crime, After the Battle, Air World, Claymore Press, Frontline Publishing, Leo Cooper, Remember When, Seaforth Publishing, The Praetorian Press, Wharncliffe Books, Wharncliffe Local History, Wharncliffe Transport, Wharncliffe True Crime and White Owl.

For a complete list of Pen & Sword titles please contact:

PEN & SWORD BOOKS LTD
George House, Units 12 & 13, Beevor Street, Off Pontefract Road,
Barnsley, South Yorkshire, S71 1HN, England
E-mail: enquiries@pen-and-sword.co.uk
Website: www.pen-and-sword.co.uk

or

PEN AND SWORD BOOKS,
1950 Lawrence Road, Havertown, PA 19083, USA
E-mail: uspen-and-sword@casematepublishers.com
Website: www.penandswordbooks.com

Contents

Author's Note and Glossary vi

Foreword x

Introduction xi

Map xv

ATTACK OF THE EAGLES:
A DIARY, 13 AUGUST 1940 – 18 AUGUST 1940

Chapter 1   Tuesday, 13 August 1940 2

Chapter 2   Wednesday, 14 August 1940 33

Chapter 3   Thursday, 15 August 1940 50

Chapter 4   Friday, 16 August 1940 129

Chapter 5   Saturday, 17 August 1940 176

Chapter 6   Sunday, 18 August 1940 181

Reflections 241

Acknowledgements 243

Bibliography 245

Other Books by Dilip Sarkar 256

Index 258

Author's Note and Glossary

The aviation-minded reader will notice that I have referred to German *Messerschmitt* fighters by the abbreviation 'Me' (not 'Bf', which is more technically correct), or simply by their numeric designation, such as '109' or '110'. This not only reads better but is authentic: during the Battle of Britain, Keith Lawrence, a New Zealander, flew Spitfires and once said to me 'To us they were just "Me's", "109s" or "110s", simple, never "Bf".'

In another attempt to preserve accuracy, I have also used the original German, wherever possible, regarding terms associated with the *Luftwaffe*, such as:

Adlerangriff	'Attack of the Eagles'.
Adlertag	'Eagle Day'.
Eichenlaub	The Oak Leaves, essentially being a bar to the Ritterkreuz.
Erprobungsgruppe	Experimental group, in the case of *Erprobungsgruppe* 210, a skilled precision bombing unit.
Experte	A fighter 'ace'. Ace status, on both sides, was achieved by destroying five enemy aircraft.
Freie Hunt	A fighter sweep.
Gefechstand	Operations headquarters.
General der Jagdflieger	General of Fighter Pilots.
Geschwader	The whole group, usually of three *gruppen*.
Geschwaderkommodore	The group leader.
Gruppe	A wing, usually of three squadrons.
Gruppenkeil	A wedge formation of bombers, usually made up of vics of three.
Gruppenkommandeur	The wing commander.
Jagdbomber ('Jabo')	Fighter-bomber.
Jagdflieger	Fighter pilot.
Jagdgeschwader	Fighter group, abbreviated JG.

AUTHOR'S NOTE AND GLOSSARY

Jagdwaffe	The fighter force.
Jäger	Hunter, in this context a fighter pilot or aircraft.
Kampfflieger	Bomber aircrew.
Kampfgeschwader	Bomber group, abbreviated KG.
Kanal	English Channel.
Katchmarek	Wingman.
Lehrgeschwader	Literally a training group, but actually a precision bombing unit, abbreviated LG.
Luftflotte	Air Fleet.
Oberkannone	Literally the 'Top Gun', or leading fighter ace.
Oberkommando der Wehrmacht (OKW)	The German armed forces high command.
Ritterkreuz	The Knight's Cross of the Iron Cross.
Rotte	A pair of fighters, comprising leader and wingman, into which the *Schwarm* broke once battle was joined.
Rottenführer	Leader of a fighting pair.
Schwarm	A section of four fighters.
Schwarmführer	Section leader.
Seelöwe	Sealion, the codename for Hitler's proposed seaborne invasion of England.
Seenotflugkommando	*Luftwaffe* air sea rescue organisation.
Stab	Staff.
Staffel	A squadron.
Staffelkapitän	The squadron leader.
Störflug	Harassing attacks, usually by lone Ju 88s.
Stuka	The Ju 87 dive-bomber.
Sturkampfgeschwader	Dive-bomber group, abbreviated StG.
Vermisst	Missing.
Wehrmacht	Armed forces.
Zerstörer	Literally 'destroyer', the term used for the Me 110.
Zerstörergeschwader	Destroyer group, abbreviated ZG.

Each *geschwader* generally comprised three *gruppen*, each of three *staffeln*. Each *gruppe* is designated by Roman numerals, i.e. III/JG 26 refers to the third *gruppe* of Fighter Group (abbreviated 'JG') 26. *Staffeln* are identified by numbers, so 7/JG 26 is the 7th *Staffel* and belongs to III/JG 26.

BATTLE OF BRITAIN ATTACK OF THE EAGLES

Rank comparisons may also be useful:

Gefreiter	Private 1st Class
Unteroffizier	Corporal, no aircrew equivalent in Fighter Command.
Feldwebel	Sergeant
Oberfeldwebel	Flight Sergeant
Leutnant	Pilot Officer
Oberleutnant	Flight Lieutenant
Hauptmann	Squadron Leader
Major	Wing Commander
Oberst	Group Captain

RAF abbreviations:

AAF	Auxiliary Air Force
AASF	Advance Air Striking Force
A&AEE	Aeroplane and Armament Experimental Establishment
AC1	Aircraftsman 1st Class
AC2	Aircraftsman 2nd Class
ACW1	Aircraftswoman 1st Class
ACW2	Aircraftswoman 2nd Class
AFC	Air Force Cross
AFDU	Air Fighting Development Unit
AHB	Air Historical Branch
AI	Airborne Interception radar
AOC	Air Officer Commanding
AOC-in-C	Air Officer Commanding-in-Chief
ARP	Air Raid Precautions
ASR	Air Sea Rescue
ATA	Air Transport Auxiliary
ATS	Armament Training School
BEF	British Expeditionary Force
CAS	Chief of the Air Staff
CFS	Central Flying School
CGS	Central Gunnery School
CO	Commanding Officer
DAF	Desert Air Force
DES	Direct Entry Scheme
DFC	Distinguished Flying Cross
DFM	Distinguished Flying Medal
DSO	Distinguished Service Order

AUTHOR'S NOTE AND GLOSSARY

E/A	Enemy Aircraft
FAA	Fleet Air Arm
EFTS	Elementary Flying Training School
FIU	Fighter Interception Unit
FTS	Flying Training School
GPC	Guinea Pig Club
ITW	Initial Training Wing
LAC	Leading Aircraftman
MC	Military Cross
MRAF	Marshal of the Royal Air Force
MSFU	Merchant Ship Fighter Unit
MTB	Motor Torpedo Boat
NCO	Non-Commissioned Officer
OR	Other Ranks
ORB	Operations Record Book
OTC	Officer Training Corps
OTU	Operational Training Unit
PDC	Personnel Distribution Centre
RAFVR	Royal Air Force Volunteer Reserve
RFS	Reserve Flying School
RN	Royal Navy
RNAS	Royal Navy Air Service
R/T	Radio Telephone
SASO	Senior Air Staff Officer
SHAEF	Supreme Headquarters Allied Expeditionary Force
SOO	Senior Operations Officer
SSC	Short Service Commission
TAF	Tactical Air Force
UAS	University Air Squadron
U/S	Unserviceable
WAAF	Women's Auxiliary Air Force
WDAF	Western Desert Air Force

Also:

'Angels' refers to height measured in thousands of feet, hence 'Angles One-Five' means 15,000ft. A 'vector' is a compass course, measured in degrees, a 'Bandit' is a confirmed enemy aircraft while a 'Bogey' and an 'X-Raid' are as yet unidentified but potentially hostile radar plots. 'Tally Ho!' was shouted when the enemy were sighted and the leader was ordering an attack.

Foreword

In this volume, Dilip Sarkar takes his deep research into the Battle of Britain in a manner which cannot fail to excite the reader. The daily record of engagements from both RAF and Luftwaffe side at the time when the Battle was soaring in intensity is fascinating. I, personally, have not read an account of the Battle of Britain which presents the opposing viewpoints so comprehensively. And as has been noted by Sir Stephen Dalton in his foreword to Volume 2, it often challenges accepted narratives.

But the author does not neglect the other British contributions. Both Bomber and Coastal Commands receive the attention they deserve, as, too, do the other armed Services. Their efforts, all, were crucial and courageous.

The Battle of Britain Memorial Trust is to be congratulated on its association with this remarkable collection of work on a subject which will, I hope, always be part of the syllabus at schools for the education of future generations.

ACM Sir Michael Graydon GCB CBE FRAeS
Past President, The Battle of Britain Memorial Trust

Introduction

During the last few days covered in the previous volume, *Battle of Britain: The Breaking Storm: 10 July 1940 – 12 August 1940*, it was clear that the enemy was no longer just focusing on convoys but had changed tack, attacking instead coastal radar installations and forward aerodromes. Although hundreds of reconnaissance sorties were flown over England, however, German intelligence had frequently misinterpreted the information collated. The *Luftwaffe* planners did not understand how Air Chief Marshal Dowding's System of Air Defence worked; although they had grasped the fact that radar was important, they did not understand how it fitted into the chain and how radar generated information was fed into the system. Moreover, the crucial significance of Sector Stations had not been appreciated, and the status of various airfields, such as those at Eastchurch, Lympne and Gosport – none of which Fighter Command bases – was wrongly interpreted. During that phase, the really heavy fighting began, although due to this poor intelligence picture the Germans would waste much time and resources attacking targets that were not of any particular significance to their mission: the destruction of RAF Fighter Command.

The initial phase had also suffered from Hitler's indecision and his delusional desire for Britain to seek peace terms through a diplomatic solution. Hitler knew that his navy was inferior to the Royal Navy, and his generals baulked at the prospect of a seaborne invasion and drawn out war with Britain. Nonetheless, while prohibiting attacks on inland targets, leading up to Hitler's 'last appeal to reason' of 19 July 1940, the air offensive against Britain saw increasingly large formations, and, indeed, Hitler's infamous Directive of 16 July 1940, promising to 'prepare and if necessary carry out a landing operation', was all bluff. Hitler had played a perfect game of brinkmanship before the outbreak of war, infamously pushing Europe to the edge over Czechoslovakia at the Munich Conference in 1938, and had been appeased by Britain and France.

Now, however, Hitler faced a very different prime minister to the appeaser Neville Chamberlain. Winston Churchill knew his history, and was convinced that states which meekly acquiesce to aggressors and dictators vanish from the record – but those which go down fighting rise again. Consequently, there was no question whatsoever of Churchill and his War Cabinet coming to terms with Hitler. Even after his 'last appeal' was initially ignored, and then publicly rejected in a broadcast by Lord Halifax – previously a close Chamberlain ally and appeaser – still Hitler dallied. Ultimately, Hitler was pushed to a point where he had no choice but to either back down or go ahead with preparations for a seaborne landing – Operation *Seelöwe*.

The reality, however, was that Hitler's service chiefs had no experience of such a grandiose combined operation, the army were used to river crossings – but not the English Channel. Differences of opinion between the German service chiefs, therefore, over virtually every aspect of the undertaking was inevitable. Plans were clearer by 31 July 1940, as was the fact that Churchill would not back down. On that day, Hitler conferred with his warlords at the Berghof, his mountain retreat, and decided that aerial supremacy over Britain was pre-requisite to a sea crossing, and that:

> The air war will start now ... If the results of the air war are not satisfactory, (invasion) preparations will be stopped. But if we gain the impression that the English are being crushed and that the air war is, after a certain time, taking effect, then we shall attack ... An attempt must be made to prepare the operation for 15 September [1940].

From this point onwards and until the invasion was ultimately postponed indefinitely, because air operations were now closely aligned to paving the way for an invasion, arguably the Battle of Britain, if we are to understand that it was fought to deny the Germans aerial superiority over southern England necessary to launch a seaborne invasion, actually began on this day, 31 July 1940.

By this time, Hitler also had firmly planted in his mind an invasion of Russia for spring 1941 – this also being part of his strategy to defeat Britain. Whereas his generals were reluctant to enter a drawn-out war with Britain, they were confident of defeating the Soviet Union in short order. Britain, Hitler believed, was pinning its hopes on either American intervention or the Russians changing sides, probably both. By conquering

INTRODUCTION

Russia and removing that option, isolationist and neutral America would be preoccupied with the advantage that provided Japan, territorially in the Far East, and much less concerned with Britain and Europe. So, in the first instance Hitler's strategy against Britain called for a quick decision forced by air power preceding a successful invasion, or a longer solution aimed squarely at Russia. Whatever happened, it was always part of Hitler's Nazi ideology to defeat the Bolsheviks and seize Russia as '*Lebensraum*' (living space) and this war with Britain was now an inconvenience preventing immediate pursuance of that primary objective.

Consequently, from 31 July 1940 – as far as Hitler was concerned – the way forward could only be decided by an aerial assault on Britain, and so the flamboyant and boastful *Reichsmarschall* Hermann Göring found his *Luftwaffe* centre-stage that fateful summer and autumn of 1940. After Hitler's decision of 31 July, the *Luftwaffe* regrouped and prepared for a renewed assault – starting on '*Adler Tag*', 'Eagle Day', scheduled for 13 August 1940, and on which date this book begins.

The Battle of Britain is a *huge* story, with so many concurrent and parallel threads, and this eight-volume narrative, to be sure, has been no insignificant undertaking to produce. My brief was not to produce a referenced academic text but a more accessible history, of use to researchers and historians, and to be enjoyed by enthusiasts and the 'general reader' alike. In so doing I have tried, wherever possible, to provide a flavour of life and times beyond the cockpit of a Hurricane or Spitfire – although, clearly, the air fighting is the central theme.

In that respect an early decision was made to review every single individual Fighter Command pilot's combat reports, and quote selectively thereof, and from squadron and station Operations Records Books, thereby enabling the combatants to speak to us today, all these years later, in their own words. However, going right back to British and German primary sources has in many cases rewritten history – although unhelpfully, and perhaps surprisingly, official records are often contradictory in respect of timings, and sometimes bear no semblance to reality at all. The records are also incomplete, in certain respects, so interpreting an accurate picture can be very time-consuming and complex.

Two things the reader must appreciate is that Fighter Command combat claims were frequently wildly exaggerated, there being an enormous gulf of difference between a claim and a confirmed enemy casualty. There are various reasons for this, mainly connected with the speed of combat often deceiving the human eye; the fog of war; the chaos of large numbers of aircraft engaged; and several pilots simultaneously attacking and destroying or damaging the same target, oblivious of each other, the enemy aircraft concerned consequently appearing more than once on the balance sheet. The second thing is that aircraft identification in combat was demonstrably and consistently poor – for example, Me 110s mistaken for Ju 88s (or vice-versa) and 'He 113s', which never entered operational service, frequently reported when they were, in fact, Me 109s. When researching and constructing a detailed narrative such as this, even from primary sources, nothing can be taken either for granted. The whole thing has to be carefully deconstructed and forensically analysed – and very often it is pointless trying to establish exactly who shot down who, because of the sheer volume of combat claims involved. My work, as a trained detective in a past professional life, and a trained historian, is evidence-based, the actual facts driving the narrative – not made to fit some preconceived or convenient notion or theory.

So, here we have the *Attack of the Eagles: 13 August 1940 – 18 August 1940* – as never before.

Dilip Sarkar MBE, FRHistS, FRAeS, BA (Hons), 2023

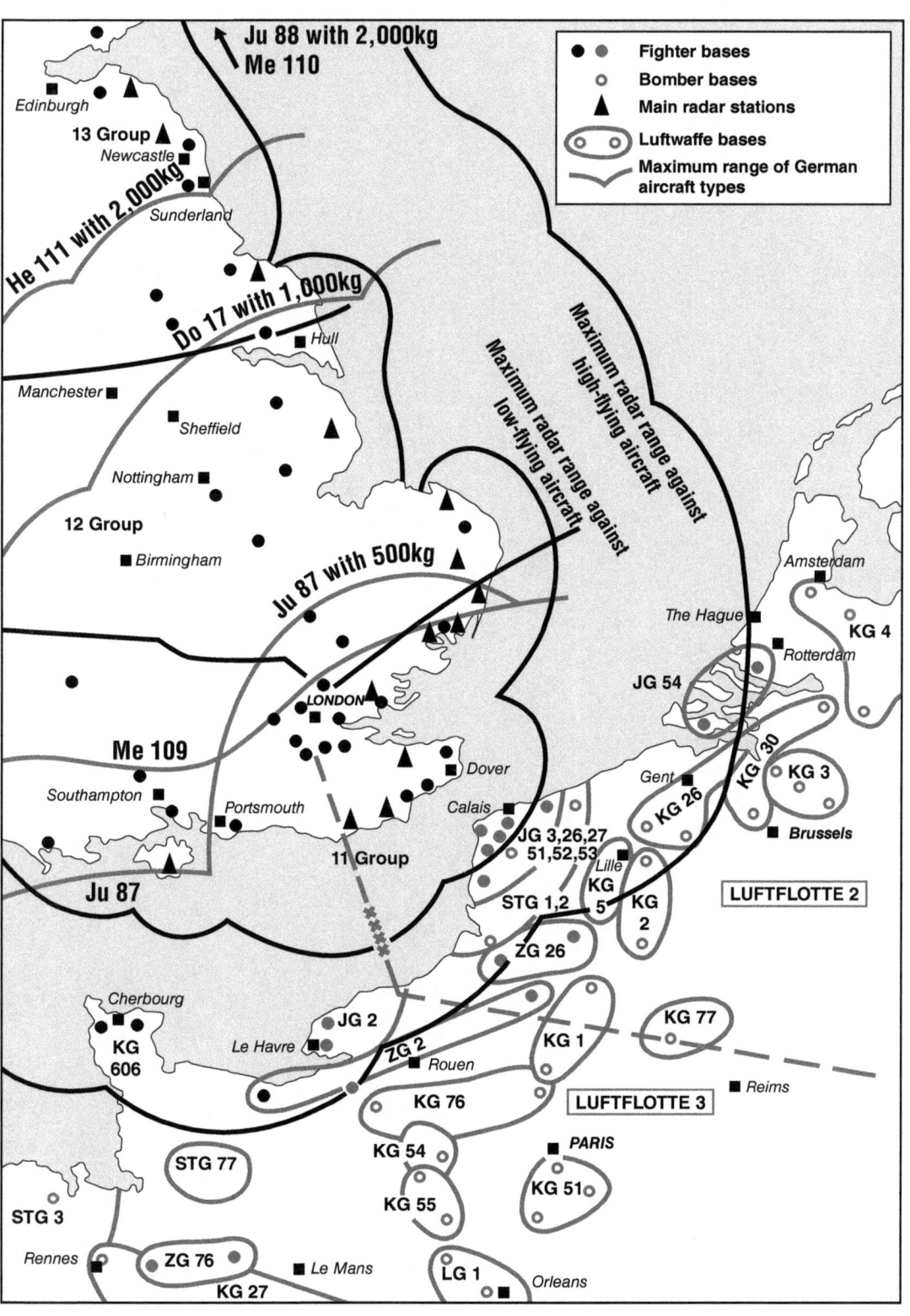

ATTACK OF THE EAGLES
A DIARY
13 AUGUST 1940 – 18 AUGUST 1940

Chapter 1

Tuesday, 13 August 1940

Early in the morning, the *Luftwaffe* Chief of Staff, *Generaloberst* Hans Jeschonnek, was aboard his personal train, codenamed 'Robinson', somewhere in the Pas-de-Calais, studying the day's first meteorological reports with *Generalmajor* Otto Hoffman von Waldau, head of the *Oberkommando der Luftwaffe* (OKL) *Operationsabteilung*, and the OKL intelligence chief, *Oberst* Joseph 'Beppo' Schmid. Although the previous day good weather had been predicted, enabling *Adler Tag* to proceed, overnight there had been a deterioration: the zone of high pressure over the Azores, which had promised a few days of fine and settled weather, had evaporated – so instead of the expected clear skies, the aerial battlefield was shrouded in low, 10/10ths, cloud. Nearby, in a tunnel at Le Coudray, *Reichsmarschall* Hermann Göring was aboard his command train, 'Asia' – and, exasperated, decided that the initial operations planned for 'Eagle Day' would have to be cancelled. Instead, the great 'Eagle Attack' would be launched later in the day, at 14.00 hrs, providing the weather had sufficiently improved.

The pressure was certainly on, because with 15 September 1940 scheduled for Operation *Seelöwe*, and with so much time during the short campaigning season having already been wasted by Hitler's delusional dreams of a negotiated peace, the *Luftwaffe* could not afford further delays. Time was tight, because the closer autumn approached, given the unpredictable British weather, conditions for a successful sea crossing could not be guaranteed – and mid-September was about as late as the invasion could realistically be launched. Time was now being lost at the start of this proposed great air offensive, and, over the course of the month ahead, during which Fighter Command's defeat was essential, what could be guaranteed was that more days would be lost to the weather. Consequently, the German aircrew was soon to learn that, as Edward Bishop wrote, 'like British farmers, they would have to work hard during the "bright intervals", and keep going as best they could between them'. Indeed, the German airmen on the *Kanalfront* described the worst of British weather as 'Four

TUESDAY, 13 AUGUST 1940

B' – because in the words of an English-speaking German, it was 'Four times worse than bloody awful'!

There was, however, an immediate problem for *Luftflotte* 2: seventy-four Do 17s of *Oberst* Johannes 'Papa' Fink's KG 2 *Holzhammer* were already airborne, en route to attack Eastchurch airfield and the nearby dockyard at Sheerness (both targets being on the Isle of Sheppey, located on the southern bank of the mouth of the Thames Estuary). Eastchurch, however, was a Coastal Command station, this being an early indication of just how poor *Luftwaffe* air intelligence was, in spite of countless reconnaissance sorties, leading to inappropriate target selection and wasted effort in attacking objectives unconnected with Fighter Command and Britain's defences. Indeed, this would become a common theme as both *Adler Tag* and the Battle of Britain generally progressed.

At 04.50 hrs (GMT), KG 2 had taken-off from Arras and St Leger, with the *Geschwaderkommodore*, Fink, leading I/KG 2, *Major* Paul Weitkus behind with II/KG 2, and *Major* Adolf Fuch's III/KG 2 bringing up the rear. For some unknown reason, the signal '*Angriff beschränken*', cancelling the raid, from *Generalfeldmarschall* Albert Kesselring's *Luftflotte* 2 field headquarters at Cap Blanc Nez, went unreceived by Fink – so KG 2 droned on to St Omer, there to rendezvous with *Oberstleutnant* Joachim Huth's escorting Me 110 fighters of ZG 26 *Horst Wessel*. Like something from a farce, Weitkus's radio operator did receive the signal, but misinterpreted it as '*Angriff ausfuehren*': attack to proceed. Then, Weitkus accidentally left his radio on transmit, jamming the airwaves. ZG 26, however, had received the cancellation signal, but from the bombers' purposeful direction of travel it was obvious to Huth that Fink had not. Consequently, the one-legged Me 110 *Kommodore* flew erratically around and towards the Do 17s in a desperate attempt to make Fink understand something was wrong, and to turn back. Huth's efforts, however, served only to confuse and irritate Fink, who maintained his course for England, and became even more bewildered when the fighters disappeared. Nonetheless, Fink, formerly the *Kanalkampfführer* in the battle's initial phase, pressed on, the worsening weather, ironically, concealing his approach. At 05.32 hrs (GMT), the Me 109s of Major Adolf Galland's III/JG 26 had also taken off, from Caffiers, before the cancellation order was transmitted, to sweep ahead of Fink's bombers. Whether or not Galland received the message is unknown, but this *Freie Jagd* was uneventful. No.11 Group's controllers, though, were firmly focused on KG 2's approach.

Between 05.30 hrs and 05.40 hrs, the defenders' RDF, or radar, had detected the big build-up of enemy aircraft assembling over Amiens – the first sign of trouble brewing. At 06.10 hrs this plot separated into two formations, each of thirty plus, which struck northwards, towards England. Simultaneously, a formation of over 100 enemy aircraft was indicated near Dieppe, and another of forty plus over Cherbourg. This early warning gave sector controllers time to order a substantial number of squadrons to intercept. By 06.15 hrs, North Weald's 151 Squadron was patrolling a convoy in the Thames Estuary; 111 Squadron was up from Croydon, over Hawkinge, and the newly promoted South African Squadron Leader A.G. 'Sailor' Malan led 74 Squadron from Hornchurch to cover Manston. Furthermore, sections of three other squadrons, 85, 43 and 238, were airborne and patrolling their respective bases (Debden, Tangmere and Middle Wallop).

Fink's Dorniers emerged from the bank of low cloud near Whitstable, and proceeded to Eastchurch at just 1,500ft – finding 74 Squadron ready and waiting.

Squadron Leader Malan reported that at 07.00 hrs:

> While leading the squadron into attack against enemy bombers in the Estuary I came across them in a vic formation on my beam.
>
> I closed to within 100 yards and raked them with machine-gun fire. I then swung into line astern and fired at No 3 of the formation. I fired at 150 yards, using four two second bursts. This machine burst into flame in mid-air and was last seen heading for the sea.
>
> I then attacked the leader of the formation and gave him a three second burst at 150 yards, and one of the engines was put out of action and bits and pieces fell off. This machine cannot possibly have reached home.
>
> I attacked the third of the section and used the last of my ammunition but did not see any result.
>
> No evasive action was taken by these machines.

Malan was credited with one Do 17 destroyed and a probable. In total, the Spitfires claimed the destruction of seven Do 17s, three 'probables' and three more damaged. Flight Lieutenant Stanislaw Brzezina claimed one of the bombers destroyed, but was hit by return fire, causing an explosion in his cockpit; the Polish pilot took to his parachute, and landed safely. Pilot Officer Henryk Szcesny, also Polish, was similarly shot-up; unable to lower his undercarriage, he crash-landed, unhurt, at West Malling.

TUESDAY, 13 AUGUST 1940

Malan's Spitfires were too small in number, however, to attack all of the Do 17s and prevent the target being bombed, although every Dornier in the rearmost KG 2 section was hit, and six bombers were definitely destroyed. The remaining two waves of fifteen Do 17s each, however, continued in vic formation and successfully attacked Eastchurch. Coincidentally, the previous day (see Volume 2), 'B' Flight of 12 Group's 19 Squadron and those of 266 Squadron had been temporarily deployed to Eastchurch, so there were a handful of Spitfires and their pilots under the bombs – among whom was Sergeant David Cox:

> I was awakened by the bombing at about 0730 hrs. 1 rushed out of my room, which was in a wooden hut, into a corridor where I met Flight Sergeant Tofts, who was in charge of servicing 'B' Flight's aircraft. He grabbed me by the arm and we ran into the only brick shelter available, a urinal, and Tofts pushed me onto the floor saying 'This is no time to be squeamish, lad!' Thirty odd people were killed in that raid, although fortunately none from our 19 Squadron.

The 19 Squadron ORB noted that Eastchurch had been 'Most thoroughly bombed'. According to the 266 Squadron ORB, over 100 high explosive and incendiary bombs were dropped by thirty Do 17s, which hit all hangars, destroying all ammunition and 'much equipment', in addition to damaging the water supply; sixteen airmen were killed and one Spitfire destroyed.

Although Eastchurch was not a Fighter Command airfield, it was used by Coastal Command for attacks on the E-boat bases and invasion preparations at Calais and Boulogne, and it may have become a target because the Germans were becoming increasingly concerned by these operations. As a result of the raid, neither 19 or 266 squadrons proceeded to support Coastal Command on such operations as planned, returning instead to their bases in 12 Group. Despite questionable target selection, the raid was successful – although the cratered runway was repaired and the station was once more operational by 16.00 hrs.

Meanwhile, the second of the KG 2 formations was intercepted by twelve Hurricanes of Squadron Leader John Thompson's 111 Squadron, up from Croydon,

> ordered to intercept an enemy raid from Hawkinge area. R/T touch was lost over Eastchurch and Squadron patrolled above

cloud owing to visibility. Just before 0700 hrs a formation of about ten Dorniers was sighted proceeding up the Thames Estuary. Squadron Leader Thompson instructed 'A' Flight to intercept while 'B' Flight engaged a further similar formation coming up from astern in vics of three. Head-on attacks were made on both formations by the entire Squadron. The enemy formation was broken up and a number of machines isolated. Green Section attacked three E/A which were damaged, pieces of engine cowling were observed to fall from one by Pilot Officer Hardman (Green 3). Flying Officer Ferriss DFC (Red 1) brought one Dornier down off Seasalter; most of the crew baled out, but some too late. Yellow 1 and 2 destroyed one E/A in the sea, NE of Herne Bay. Rear-gunner baled out and E/A was rapidly losing height with one engine completely out of action. Squadron Leader Thompson (Blue 1), Pilot Officer Walker (Blue 2), and Pilot Officer McKintyre (Red 3) each crippled Dorniers, the wreckage of these machines being found at Stodmarsh and Barham between 0700 – 0715 hrs.

'Treble One' had done well, for no loss, although both Sergeant William Dymond and Sergeant John Craig were badly shot up and returned to Croydon, and Pilot Officer Athol McIntyre crash-landed back at base with a damaged Hurricane. Fortunately, none of the pilots were injured.

Next into action were the Hurricanes of 151 Squadron, engaging the same enemy formation over Eastchurch. Pilot Officer Richard 'Dickie' Milne claimed two of the bombers destroyed, 'one of which broke up in the air, the other crashing in the vicinity of Christchurch [*sic*: should read Eastchurch]' (ORB). Sergeant Joseph Savill claimed a Do 17 shot down into the sea.

Interestingly, Flight Lieutenant Rod Smith claimed a Dornier 'probable' while flying an experimental Hurricane (L1750) armed with two 20mm cannon:

> I opened fire at 300 yards firing into the general mass, as the enemy were flying in exceptionally close formation. One immediately burst into flames, and another started smoking, when my windscreen's front panel was completely shattered by enemy fire, so I broke away downwards and returned to North Weald.

TUESDAY, 13 AUGUST 1940

Between them, 74, 111 and 151 squadrons had accounted for five KG 2 Do 17s destroyed, with a further seven damaged – most crash-landing in France or returning to base with wounded crewmen aboard. Back at Arras, a badly shaken *Oberst* Fink was apparently beside himself with rage, venting his spleen over the telephone to *Feldmarschall* Kesselring – who immediately travelled to see the bereft *Kommodore* in person, explaining that the cancellation order had been sent but not received by KG 2. Kesselring's apologies, however, could not conceal the fact that *Adler Tag* had almost immediately gone awry, emphasising the *Luftwaffe*'s inexperience of coordinating such large attacks. Worse would follow.

To the west, certain *Luftflotte* 3 units had also failed to receive Göring's cancellation signal. Consequently, at dawn, the Me 109s of *Oberstleutnant* Harry von Bulow's I/JG 2 took-off from Beaumont-le-Roger to support thirty-eight Ju 88s of I and II/KG 54 '*Totenkopf*', the bomber units' respective targets being the airfields at Odiham and Farnborough in Hampshire. Again, though, neither airfield was of any significance to Fighter Command: the former was home to the Royal Aircraft Establishment, the latter an army cooperation station.

At 06.20 hrs, Squadron Leader Hill Harkness, an Irishman, led 257 Squadron's Hurricanes up from Northolt with orders to patrol Canterbury. With the threat developing from Dieppe and Cherbourg, however, while en route the squadron was vectored south and Tangmere, where, above the clouds, at 06.40 hrs, it became the first to sight and engage the incoming enemy formations.

Flying Officer Lancelot Mitchell:

> I was Green 1 of 257 Squadron and when at 12,000ft over coast, South of Tangmere, I saw several He 111s [*sic*: Me 110s]. I climbed towards them and they also climbed. I ordered the section into line astern and climbed to get into the sun. At this time I noticed for Me 109s circling above and moving into the sun. I continued to try and get into the sun. The Me 109s came down and fired at us. We made a sharp turn and came in on their tails. The enemy section leader then left his section to take evasive action. He dived down to 5,000ft, turning to left and right. I closed up as he straightened up before going into cloud and gave him a long burst, which I believe found its mark at just under 400 yards range. I then lost him in cloud. On coming out of cloud I saw a Ju 88 in front of me with a

> Hurricane on its tail. The Hurricane broke away as smoke trails started from the E/A's engines. I closed in and opened fire from 300 yards and gave it two or three bursts from astern. Masses of smoke poured from the engines, the E/A being almost lost in smoke. He dived down to sea-level during the attack, going into the haze over the water. I broke away looking for enemy fighters and on turning back for the E/A I found that I had lost it in the haze. Being well out to sea at this time, I turned north and had a passing head-on shot at another Ju 88, but the range was too great for any result to be obtained.

Mitchell claimed a Ju 88 probably destroyed and another damaged, while Squadron Leader Harkness damaged a Ju 88 but submitted no claim. Sergeant Donald Hulbert returned to Northolt in a damaged Hurricane but was fortunately unhurt.

Five minutes before 257 Squadron had scrambled from Northolt, 43 Squadron's Hurricanes had been ordered up from Tangmere, engaging the incoming enemy, the bombers flying in two waves, 200 yards apart, at 06.45 hrs between the seaside town of Littlehampton, and Arundel, a few miles inland.

Flight Lieutenant Thomas Dalton Morgan:

> I engaged an E/A in the rearmost formation, delivering a head-on level attack. He burst into flames and Pilot Officer Woods-Scawen saw it dive steeply, enveloped in flames. I carried on through formation and tried to engage a second but he swerved away. I engaged a Ju 88 straggling behind the forward formation. As I fired, two other Ju 88s in front throttled back hard and engaged me from one side. My machine was hit in several places and caught fire. I hoped to make a forced-landing, descending to 6,000ft, when aircraft became so hot that I baled out and landed at Cocking Down on a tree stump, which, according to the Medical Officer, twisted my tendons and sprained my ankle. I am walking with the help of crutches.

Morgan was credited with a 'He 111' [sic] confirmed.

Sergeant Jack Mills:

> I was Red 3 ... sighted an Me 109 behind and rather lower than the bombers just approaching coast. I dived on his tail

TUESDAY, 13 AUGUST 1940

and he headed out to sea. He took evasive action by steep turns and half rolls but I managed to keep on his tail and fired as opportunity offered. After my third burst, smoke emerged and bits of aircraft dropped away and he started a steady dive, still out to sea. Still in this dive of about 30° he hit the sea and submerged immediately. Nothing was seen to float and just a little oil covered the water.

Surprisingly, there is no apparent Me 109 loss corresponding to this claim. Indeed, the only Me 109 down was *Oberleutnant* Paul Temme, adjutant of I/JG 2, who force-landed on Shoreham airfield and was captured. Previous accounts have accredited Temme's loss to Mills, but clearly that could not have been the case, given that Mills described his opponent as crashing into, and being consumed by, the sea. Collectively, 43 Squadron claimed '1 He 111, 1 Me 109, 3 Ju 88s, 1 Do 17 confirmed. 2 Ju 88s, 1 Do 17 probable. 1 Me 110, 5 Ju 88s damaged' (ORB). Pilot Officer Charles Woods-Scawen, in addition to Flight Lieutenant Morgan, was shot down, making a safe forced-landing near Midhurst.

The six Hurricanes of 601 Squadron's 'B' Flight had scrambled from Tangmere at 06.30 hrs, and also engaged the enemy at 06.45 hrs in the Midhurst-Arundel area. Among the 'Legionnaires' was the American Olympian volunteer, Flying Officer William Meade Lindsley Fiske,

> sighted E/A when at about 8,000ft above us on our right, up-sun, about five miles distant. Manoeuvred to attack in section vic formation. I attacked a Ju 88 on beam with good burst. He gave out a lot of white smoke from both motors and broke away from formation. Further Hurricanes came in on his tail so I continued across rear of E/A formation and attacked aircraft as it was going into cloud ... I put in a long burst and starboard propeller stopped. E/A broke away and dived straight from about 8,000ft through cloud to 2,500ft. I followed him all the way, firing in an attempt to put port engine out. Unsuccessful but E/A could not gain enough height to get back into cloud. He had no more ammunition, at least his firing ceased. I called for other 'Weapon' [radio callsign for 601 Squadron] aircraft over South Downs ... 'Weapon' Yellow 1 came up but was also out of ammunition. E/A last seen in gentle glide over Solent about 2,500ft, proceeding towards Bembridge with AA fire all around him.

BATTLE OF BRITAIN ATTACK OF THE EAGLES

Fiske was credited with a Ju 88 destroyed, 'B' Flight collectively claiming a further two Ju 88s destroyed and another shared between three pilots, six probables and two damaged, along with an Me 110 damaged – all without loss.

Under heavy attack and yet to reach their targets, the enemy formations received a recall signal and so turned about, heading back to the coast, homeward bound. The bombers' ordeal was far from over, however. Having left Kenley at 06.35 hrs, eight aircraft of 64 Squadron arrived on the scene at 07.00 hrs – minus Squadron Leader MacDonell, who was forced to return to base owing to undercarriage failure. Going into action over Chichester, the Spitfires harried the withdrawing enemy until well out over the Channel: 'Pilot Officer Jones damaged 1 Do 215 [*sic*] which Flying Officer Woodward later destroyed, confirmed. Pilot Officer Simpson, Pilot Officer Roberts, Flight Sergeant Laws, Flight Sergeant Gilbert damaged 1 Do 215 [*sic*] each. Pilot Officer Jones landed Tangmere and Pilot Officer Roberts at Gatwick' (ORB).

Earlier that morning, at 06.00 hrs, a section of 238 Squadron's Hurricanes, operating from Warmwell, patrolled to base and 'rose to 30,000ft, passing Isle of Wight, when E/A came into sight, being about thirty Me 10s which turned tail before an attack could be made' (ORB). At 06.30 hrs, presented with a further threat, the Middle Wallop Sector Controller scrambled Red, Yellow and Blue Sections of 238 Squadron – which were bounced by Me 109s, probably of II/JG 2 (two pilots of which each claimed a Hurricane destroyed at an unknown location and time, but no other known German combat claims appear to fit, and this was JG 2's area of operations), half an hour later, at 25,000ft south of the Isle of Wight. Fortunately, Sergeant Jack Mann, Blue 1, shouted a warning and the Hurricanes broke – hard – but, nonetheless, Sergeant Gordon Batt's aircraft was shot-up, forcing Yellow 2 to land in a field near Tangmere with a damaged oil tank. Meanwhile, Sergeant Eric Seabourne, Blue 3, 'made a most audacious attack on three E/A', claiming two of these destroyed before being 'brought down by the third' (ORB); Seabourne's Hurricane erupted into flame – but his sliding canopy jammed, preventing him baling out. Suddenly, the fighter rolled over and pitched forward, throwing the pilot and offending hood clear. Delaying deploying his parachute for 16,000ft, the badly burned pilot orally inflated his Mae West and dropped into the sea, several miles south of the Isle of Wight. Fortunately, the destroyer HMS *Bulldog* was patrolling nearby so rescued the wounded pilot, some of the crew, along with watchers on land, having witnessed the combat overhead. Apart from Seabourne's

TUESDAY, 13 AUGUST 1940

claim, none were made by the remainder of the squadron, who, having 'been attacked by a large formation of Me 109s and Me 110s were unable to attack in return as they were concerned in avoiding E/A' (ORB). There can be no doubt that with Sergeant Mann's warning, the Hurricanes would have come off much worse.

The final engagements of this confused early morning raid involved a section of Exeter's 87 Squadron, scrambled at 06.35 hrs, led by their previous CO and current Station Commander, Squadron Leader Johnny Dewar DSO DFC. At 07.35 hrs, twenty miles south of Bognor Regis, a lone, straggling, Ju 88 was sighted, flying East. Pilot Officer Trevor Jay reported that:

> Squadron Leader ordered line astern and attacked. Saw Squadron Leader dive and break away. I went left, Blue 2 went right and attacked. I delivered a quarter attack and subsequently three more attacks from astern ... E/A's starboard engine stopped and port engine was damaged. E/A hit the sea and sank. No one got out of aircraft except one who jumped before crash. After the fight I saw Blue 2, Flying Officer Glyde, behind me and leader, with white vapor issuing. When next looked, Blue 2 was not there.

Flying Officer Richard Glyde DFC, an Australian, had been hit by return fire from the Ju 88 and simply disappeared. This was a sad loss indeed for 87 Squadron; only the previous week, the 26-year-old had joined Squadron Leader Dewar and other 87 Squadron pilots at Buckingham Palace, where all received their gallantry awards from King George VI.

Like the punishment meted out to KG 2 further east, Fighter Command had taken a heavy toll of KG 54: four Ju 88s were destroyed with eleven more damaged, many of these also crash-landing in France with dead or wounded crewmen aboard. In responding to this attack on Odiham and Farnborough, four Hurricanes had been lost; three pilots were safe, although one was badly burned, but the fourth was missing.

After this hectic early morning action, things went ominously quiet. At 11.00 hrs, *Reichsmarschall* Göring personally ordered that further attacks were to be delayed until 14.00 hrs. This signal was received by KG 54, which had been tasked with a raid on Portland – but, in yet another communications failure, not the Me 110s of *Hauptmann* Horst Liensberger's V(Z)/LG 1. The original plan had been for the *Zerstörers* to bring defending fighters to battle and exhaust them before the bombers arrived. Although the Ventnor

BATTLE OF BRITAIN ATTACK OF THE EAGLES

RDF remained out of action after the previous day's attack, at 11.40 hrs the Germans' approach was still detected by the remaining Chain Home stations on the South Coast. At 11.50 hrs, 238 Squadron was scrambled from Warmwell with orders to patrol Portland at 25,000ft; five minutes later, 601 Squadron was ordered up from Tangmere and vectored to Swanage and Angels 20, and at 11.58 hrs 213 Squadron took-off from Exeter to patrol Portland at 15,000ft.

Hauptmann Liensberger's Me 110s had arrived over Portland and formed up into the *Abwehrkreis* defensive circle (later renamed the *Angriffkreis* or 'Attack Circle'), orbiting Portland and advertising their presence to lure up the British fighters. In this formation, the heavily armed Me 110s each protected the aircraft in front, thereby inviting attack when potentially holding the tactical advantage. The use of this *Abwehrkreis* had already proved most successful on several previous days, allowing the Me 110s to remain in a particular area while awaiting trouble, and in the process lay claim to a large part of the sky. The tactic had been born on the Western Front during the First World War, according to General Bruno Loerzer, a forty-four victory Great War ace now commanding *Luftflotte* 2's II *Fliegerkorps*, owing to a number of pilots in his unit, *Jagdstaffel* 26, having been peacetime footballers trained to 'back up' on the field. So it was that this tactic was absorbed by air fighting – and would become such a familiar sight in the summer of 1940.

Reichsmarschall Göring, also a First World War fighter ace, was an enthusiastic supporter of the twin-engine Me 110 'destroyer' concept, and had complete confidence in the type's destructive ability. Armed with two 20-mm MG FF cannon and four MG17 machine-guns, all nose-mounted, plus an aft-mounted MG15 operated by a rear-gunner, the Me 110's top speed was 336 mph at 19,685ft, so not far behind the Spitfire's 355 mph at 19,000ft, and faster than the Hurricane's of 324 mph at 15,650ft – although its acceleration was sluggish and turning circle far greater than the more-nimble single-engine fighters. So far, though, the Me 110 had already provided good service in more roles than any other *Luftwaffe* aircraft type: fighter, fighter-bomber and reconnaissance. In the aerial conflict ahead, however, too much would be expected of the Me 110 – not least owing to the work imposed upon their limited numbers due to Me 109's limited range. Nonetheless, on this day, Liensberger and his men still had every reason to feel highly confident, as they orbited Portland, hoping to attract Fighter Command's attention.

No.238 Squadron was first on the scene, going into action over Portland at exactly midday, led by Acting Flight Lieutenant David Hughes:

TUESDAY, 13 AUGUST 1940

> On reaching 16,000ft, 30+ E/A were seen flying north at 12,000ft. I ordered 'B' Flight to carry on climbing and intercept Me 109s flying at 25,000ft. I ordered 'A' Flight into line astern and dived to attack, out of the sun. I opened fire on one at 250 yards ... as soon as fire was opened they commenced to circle but the Do 17 [sic] I had attacked dived down. I followed on down, firing from 250–300 yards. The E/A's evasive tactics were 'S' turns and circling. I observed that the rear-gunner was out of action and closed to 20 yards and gave a deflection shot of two seconds. The starboard engine was smoking and as I passed over and across him, within a few feet, I observed the pilot climb out of his cockpit. The E/A crashed in the sea. I saw the pilot descending by parachute but did not observe where he landed.

For once, the Hurricanes had the height advantage, although aircraft identification was poor, Hughes's pilots claiming a mixture of Me 110s, He 111s and Do 17s destroyed, albeit without loss.

The Hurricanes of 601 Squadron then joined the fray at 12.15 hrs, 20,000ft over Portland, as reported by 'A' Flight's commander, Flight Lieutenant Sir Archibald Hope:

> As we approached Portland I saw about twenty – thirty aircraft going round in circles. We were at 20 grand and their highest aircraft was just below us. The squadron went into line-astern and I turned left towards the E/A which were still circling left-handed in a sort of spiral about 2,000–3,000ft deep. I went for the top Me 110 and fired a deflection 60° burst at it. It continued to turn and I followed on its tail, firing until it appeared to go down and I thought I had gone down far enough. It had continued to turn left and I was by now circling with the E/A, so I turned to go against their circle. I fired a short burst at one E/A head-on and as I passed it took another the same way. He tightened his turn and pulled straight up across me so that I could see all his pale blue underneath and I finished my bullets into his bottom in a full deflection shot.
>
> I then spiralled steeply down and watched the sea. I saw one parachute go in and circled it for a minute or two, until I saw a boat going straight for it. This was about ten miles east

of Portland. I flew west for about four miles and found another British pilot in the water and what looked like a dead German. I marked the place by the oil where an aircraft had gone in and went SW to where I found two more pilots in the water, one British and one doubtful. By this time I had been joined by Blue 1 and 2 and I left them to circle the last two while I went back to the others. In the end all were picked up, though we had considerable difficulty in showing the boat where the German was. The boat that picked up the first pilot went straight back to shore and I couldn't make it come towards the others. I took one look around Weymouth Bay without seeing any more and returned home as I was getting short of petrol.

The first pilot rescued, thanks to Flight Lieutenant Hope, was a fellow 'Legionnaire', the Australian Pilot Officer Howard Mayers, who was shot down and baled out, slightly wounded by shrapnel, over Weymouth Bay. Hope was credited with an Me 110 probable and another damaged.

Flight Sergeant Arthur Pond, Yellow 3:

We flew west and sighted a dogfight taking place over Portland between Me 110s and Hurricanes. I followed Yellow 1 climbing above and on the outside of the defensive circle. I attacked two head-on but saw no effect, so I climbed away into the sun and next attacked an Me 110 from astern and below. After a long burst his starboard engine stopped but it did not smoke or catch fire. We were then turning steeply to the right. The Me 110 then went into a much steeper turn. In trying to follow I span about two turns. My engine had stopped but came on again after a long dive through two cloud layers down to 6,000ft. I climbed back again and sighted a single-engine aircraft flying SW. I followed but discovered it was a friendly Hurricane returning to base. I climbed again to 18,000ft over Portland but saw no more signs of E/A. Control then recalled all Weapon aircraft to pancake. As I was nearing base Control called any Weapon aircraft in the air to intercept a bandit flying NE about four miles west of base at 10,000ft. I climbed to this height and flew NE until I received an order to orbit. While doing this I saw one Hurricane flying just above the cloud at 8,000ft. I reported this to Control and

TUESDAY, 13 AUGUST 1940

receiving no further instructions pancaked as I was running out of petrol.

Having already been in action earlier that morning, against KG 54, the American volunteer Pilot Officer 'Billy' Fiske was again successful, claiming two Me 110 probables and two damaged. His own aircraft was damaged, however, as was Pilot Officer Michael Doulton's Hurricane, although both pilots returned safely to base. During the engagement 601 Squadron claimed two Me 110s destroyed, six probables and six damaged.

With the enemy still over Portland, Squadron Leader Hector MacGregor and his 213 Squadron Hurricanes engaged at 12.30 hrs; the Canadian Pilot Officer Joseph Laricheliere:

> I saw the Section Leader dive towards an Me 110. I followed and saw a through an opening in the clouds a Ju 88. I immediately stalled, turned, and managed to get on its tail, giving him a short burst on the starboard engine, which began to emit black smoke. I followed and played hide and seek in the clouds for fifteen minutes, he always heading towards home, SE of Portland. Eventually I caught him up in a clear patch and put his port engine on fire as he dived straight into the sea. I could see small motor boats making towards the wreck. While I was looking at it, however, I was surprised by an Me 109. I immediately did a steep climbing turn to reach the clouds, thinking that I would not be followed there. Then I came back again through the cloud to find the Me 109 inspecting the wreck. I gave him a burst of about three seconds and saw him give a sudden upward flick, stall, and dive into the sea in flames about 500 yards from the Ju 88.

As no Ju 88s were involved in this Portland operation, it is possible that Laricheliere had stumbled upon a machine of III/LG 1 which failed to return from a raid on Andover – more likely, perhaps, is another case of misidentification, given that 213 Squadron's Sergeant Reginald Llewellyn also claimed a 'Ju 88' destroyed. All of 213 Squadron's aircraft returned safely to Exeter.

Without doubt, for those watching the whirling mass of duelling fighters from the cliffs around Weymouth Bay, it was quite a spectacle. Among them was Mrs Ivy Marshall, on the cliffs above the beautiful Kimmeridge Bay, who watched the damaged 15(Z)/LG 1 Me 110 crewed by *Unteroffizier* Werner Schümichen and *Obergefreiter* Otto Gugelhuber pass overhead 'like a blackbird shedding feathers'. The crew baled out, their aircraft crashing at Swalland Farm, close to Mrs Marshall's vantage point. At the time, Mr Anthony Marshall, the eye-witness's husband, was attending to his lobster pots a mile or so offshore, and now steered his small boat to rescue the downed airmen. Gugelhuber was devastated by their martial failure, and his pilot, a fluent English-speaker, could only mumble 'He was too young, too young, just a frightened boy.'

Oberleutnant Helmut Müller (13(Z)/LG 1) and *Oberleutnant* Joachim Glienke (13(Z)LG 1) each claimed a 'Spitfire' [*sic*] destroyed in this action, while *Oberleutnant* Emil Schnoor, *Leutnant* Altendorf and *Unteroffizier* Horst Hamann (all 15(Z)/LG 1), all claimed Hurricanes. As neither 213 Squadron or 238 Squadron suffered any loss, these claims doubtless correspond to the combat fought by 601 Squadron, which lost one Hurricane shot down, its pilot rescued from the sea, and two damaged. Both sides, therefore, overclaimed, but clearly this had been a successful action for the defending fighters, which had collectively claimed the destruction of eight enemy aircraft (of various types), seven probables and six damaged. In reality, five of Liensberger's Me 110's had been destroyed, their crews either killed, missing or captured, and five more aircraft returned to France damaged.

So far, this long-awaited day had been disastrous for *Reichsmarschall* Göring – and *Adler Tag* had not even officially begun – the operations flown thus far all being due to communications chaos. During the early afternoon poor bombing weather prevailed over southern England, but between 15.27 hrs and 15.40 hrs RDF detected three incoming enemy formations of 30+ over the Channel between St Alban's Head and St Catherine's Point; 30+ more were plotted fifteen miles north of Cap Gris Nez, and another of similar size to the north and west of the first formation. Clearly, as in the morning, elements of both *Luftflotte* 2 and 3 were making a simultaneous pincer attack.

At 15.15 hrs, *Erprobungsgruppe*'s Me 110 fighter-bombers had taken off from Calais-Marck to attack Rochford airfield, escorted by Me 110s fighters of *Hauptmann* Wilhem Makrocki's I/ZG 26. Crossing the Channel at 11,000ft, a full covering of cloud at 3,700ft prevented the intended attack going ahead, with bombs being dropped randomly in the Canterbury area instead. At 15.50 hrs, 56 Squadron had scrambled from Rochford and ordered to patrol over Manston at 10,000ft. At 5,000ft, the squadron was

TUESDAY, 13 AUGUST 1940

informed of the raid approaching Rochford, and after climbing through thick cloud found an enemy formation escorted by Me 110s, 8,000ft above. Flight Lieutenant 'Squeak' Weaver reported that the attack commenced at 16.15 hrs, while he was:

> leading 'A' Flight, which was in the rear of 'B' Flight ... Owing to our lack of height it was not possible to catch the bombers, so I climbed as fast as possible towards the Me 110s. These started breaking formation, some of them forming a defensive circle. My Number Three broke away towards a 110 which was above him and to the left. I then realised that a 110 was getting onto his tail, so I pulled up very steeply and tried to fire at this second 110, vertically, from underneath. Commencing fire, I saw Number Three (Pilot Officer Joubert) dive away with a glycol leak, and observed damage to the 110. I then stalled.
>
> I attacked another 110 from dead astern at about 200 yards, and fired at him for about five seconds. He turned sharply away and dived with glycol pouring out of one of his engines (I believe the port one). I did not continue the attack as there was a 110 on my tail. I broke sharply away and got on the tail of another 110. At about 150 – 200 yards I fired off the remainder of my ammunition (about six seconds), dead astern, and after a few seconds violent twisting and turning, he turned over on his back and went vertically downwards into the clouds with both engines on fire. I broke away and joined up with Yellow Three (Pilot Officer Wicks), who confirmed that this E/A was destroyed.

Weaver's victim was a 110C of 3/ZG 26, which actually exploded in mid-air over Warden Bay, Isle of Sheppey – the crew, *Oberleutnant* Karl Fuchs and *Unteroffizier* Willi Ebben were both killed.

The 56 Squadron ORB expands upon the action:

> In the action, F/O Weaver, P/O Sutton and P/O Mounsden each destroyed an Me 110 and F/O Weaver, F/Lt Gracie, P/O Westmacott, P/O Joubert, F/O Davies and Sgt Hillwood each damaged a 110, F/Lt Gracie also damaging a second. P/O Joubert, F/O Davies and Sgt Hillwood were all shot down and

baled out, the former being slightly injured and F/O Davies fairly severely burned. Sgt Hillwood was practically uninjured having delayed his jump from 12,000ft to 6,000ft and swimming 2½ miles to land. F/O Brooker's machine was wrecked when he forced-landed at Hawkinge.

Although several others were damaged, the 110 claimed by Weaver was the only I/ZG 26 machine destroyed – a poor return against the loss of four Hurricanes with two pilots wounded, one seriously. Indeed, this action indicates just how dangerous the Me 110 could be on occasions. For *Erprobungsgruppe* 210, however, *Adler Tag* must have been somewhat of an anti-climax, although *Hauptmann* Rubensdörffer's formation suffered no loss.

Meanwhile, all three *gruppen* of JG 26, led by the Olympian and 'Spaniard' *Major* Gotthard Handrick, were flying a *freie hunt* intended to divert the defenders' attention away from a raid, while simultaneously heading for the Coastal Command station at Detling. The Me 109s were led by II/JG2, which was engaged over the Channel at 16.00 hrs by the Spitfires of Kenley's 65 Squadron, operating that day from Manston, both flights of which having been ordered to combine in the air and make for the Dover Straits. Sergeant Joseph Kilner described how the Spitfires had the height advantage:

> The Squadron flying at 21,000ft towards Calais met enemy fighters which were 2,000ft below, and attacked. As Blue 2, I followed Blue 1 in line-astern and selected an Me 109 on his starboard. As the E/A did a gentle climbing turn to the left I gave one burst at 1½ rings deflection, and saw ammunition enter around the pilot's cockpit.
>
> Apparently out of control, probably due to injuries sustained by the pilot, the Me 109 dived vertically with a slight aileron turn and was not seen to recover before entering clouds 15,000ft below.

Kilner was awarded a probable, as was Flying Officer Tommy Smart, who also claimed another destroyed, while Flight Lieutenant Gordon Olive was credited with two Me 109s destroyed and a probable. Although *Leutnant* Karl Borris of 5/JG 26 claimed two 'Hurricanes' destroyed, 65 Squadron's Spitfires returned to base without loss. Their combat claims, however,

TUESDAY, 13 AUGUST 1940

were somewhat optimistic: the only Me 109 actually destroyed was that of *Unteroffizier* Hans Wemhöner, also of 5/JG 26, who baled out and was captured, his aircraft crashing at Denton, near Hawkinge.

While cloud had saved Rochford from *Erprobugsgruppe* 210, unfortunately this was not now the case for the Coastal Command airfield at Detling. While 56 Squadron was engaged over Rochford, and 65 off Dover, *Stukas*, escorted my Me 109s, slipped through between these two actions and, unmolested by RAF fighters, set about pulverizing Detling.

No.53 Squadron ORB:

> At 1600 hrs a heavy bombing and machine-gun attack was made on the aerodrome by Ju 87s and Me 109s. Five Blenheim aircraft of the squadron were destroyed after being set on fire by incendiary machine-gun fire.

The death-toll was grim: sixty-seven service and civilian personnel were killed, including Squadron Leader Dennis Oliver AFC, the CO of 53 Squadron. Runways, perimeter tracks and aircraft bays were cratered. Three messes were destroyed, in addition to all hangars and the Station Operations Block. Many more personnel were injured; as the 500 Squadron ORB recorded: 'casualties were numerous'.

This devastating attack once more emphasised how effective the Ju 87 dive-bomber was when either not intercepted by defending fighters or in circumstances of aerial superiority, such as during the Battle of France, when the *Stuka* became a terrifying icon of *Blitzkrieg*. It could have been so different: just fifteen miles to the north-east of Detling lay Eastchurch airfield which, although still suffering the aftermath of the morning's raid, still accommodated the Spitfires of 'B' Flight of 19 Squadron. With the incoming raid on Detling having been detected by RDF while approaching across the sea, and visually tracked inland by the Observer Corps, it is surprising that Squadron Leader Pinkham and his pilots were not scrambled before their take-off at 16.15 hrs. After an uneventful patrol of forty-five minutes, however, the frustrated pilots returned to Eastchurch for one more night, before flying back to their home base at Fowlmere. In his log book, Pinkham wrote: 'Terrific air battle in afternoon, which we rather missed'. That should not have happened.

While the foregoing action was occurring over Kent, Southampton and Portland was targeted by *Luftflotte* 3. A huge German formation was reported incoming at 15.30 hrs along a forty-mile-wide front. Some thirty

BATTLE OF BRITAIN ATTACK OF THE EAGLES

Me 110s of *Hauptmann* Christans' I/ZG 2 escorted 120 Ju 88s of KG 54 and LG 1, with JG 27's Me 109s providing the escort to nearly 100 *Stukas*, while the 109s of II/JG 53 swept ahead of this massive *Valhalla*. This was an enormous formation, comprising over 300 'bandits'. The state of anxiety in the Middle Wallop Sector Station Operations Room can only be imagined, as the Duty Controller, Wing Commander David Roberts, quickly scrambled all of the 10 Group fighters available to him.

At 15.00 hrs, ten Spitfires of 152 Squadron had already taken off from Warmwell to patrol Portland at 15,000ft, so were already well-placed to meet the Portland raiders:

> At this height, six miles south of Portland 25-30 Me 110s were encountered ... All sections of 152 Squadron climbed and delivered an attack in line-astern from above and out of the sun. Green 1 and Black 2 saw several Me 109s above the 110s ... The Me 110s adopted circling tactics, the 109s evidently counter-attacking from above. Owing to rapid movement, pilots were unable to determine effect of fire on individual E/A. It is confirmed that one Me 110 was destroyed and three 110s damaged. (152 Squadron combat report)

Pilot Officer Richard Innes, however, was shot-up by a JG 53 Me 109 and slightly wounded in an elbow; he returned his damaged Spitfire safely to Warmwell.

No.213 Squadron had scrambled from Exeter at 15.26 hrs and also engaged the enemy over Portland, at 16.00 hrs. Pilot Officer Alexander Osmand later reported on his combat, timed at 16.10 hrs:

> I was on patrol below cloud above Portland when a 'Tally Ho' was given from above cloud. Our section climbed up and contacted a circle of Me 110s, with attendant Me 109s. I dived on stray Me 109 and was soon the centre of five of these aircraft. One passed slightly in front of me at close range and I fired two bursts which resulted in black smoke pouring from his engine. The aircraft went down, apparently out of control. I followed it through cloud and found signs of three aircraft being shot down into the sea – two with signs of having fallen recently. This was about fifteen miles to the south of Portland.

TUESDAY, 13 AUGUST 1940

Osmand recorded his combat as 'inconclusive'.

In the same action, Pilot Officer Larichliere followed up his earlier success by claiming an Me 110 destroyed, as did Pilot Officer Harold Atkinson. Sergeant Philip Norris, however, was shot down and killed.

Having scrambled from Middle Wallop at 15.34 hrs, 238 Squadron 'patrolled Portland at 20,000ft, where an enemy formation estimated at 400+ was encountered, travelling north, Battle was joined and three Me 110s and 109 were destroyed, confirmed. Also four Me 109s were damaged' (ORB).

Two Hurricanes failed to return: Sergeant Ronald Little, who baled out and was rescued from the sea slightly wounded, and Sergeant Henry 'Tony' Marsh, who was never seen again. Of Marsh, the squadron diarist wrote that 'he was one of the early members of the squadron, and the leader of Yellow Section from the start. His quiet, painstaking personality made him popular, and his section efficient.'

Some of the raiders had been bound for Middle Wallop – which they reached, but unsuccessfully attacked, their bombs falling harmlessly at 16.00 hrs behind 238 Squadron's dispersal, close to Wallop village. At the same time 238 Squadron received a signal ordering a move to St Eval the following day – the squadron had fought hard during this early period of Battle and now needed to rest and refit.

Pilot Officer Michael Appleby, 609 Squadron:

> This was a very big raid, intercepted by various squadrons, 609 Squadron claiming many enemy aircraft destroyed without loss to ourselves. I did not personally claim any aircraft destroyed but I was credited with a Ju 87 and an Me 110 damaged. This was both a turning point for our Squadron, and a great success for our CO, George Darley, because of the tactics he had adopted in getting us in the right position at the right time, providing the information received from our radar people was reliable.

Having had a hard time of it previously, it was no wonder 609 Squadron was ecstatic:

> Thirteen Spitfires left Warmwell for a memorable tea-time party over Lyme Bay, and an unlucky day for the species Ju 87, of which no less than fourteen suffered destruction or damage in a record Squadron 'bag', which also included five of the escorting Me's.

BATTLE OF BRITAIN ATTACK OF THE EAGLES

   The enemy formations, consisting of about forty dive-bombers in four vic formations, with about as many Me 110s and Me 109s stepped up above them, headed Northwards from the Channel, was surprised by 609 Squadron's down-sun attack. All thirteen of our pilots fired their guns, the casualties claimed being as follows:

F/O P Ostaszewski	2 Ju 87s Probable.
P/O MJ Appleby	1 Me 109 and 1 Ju 87 damaged.
F/Lt JHG McArthur	1 Me 109 damaged.
F/O T Nowierski	1 Me 109 destroyed and 1 damaged.
P/O DM Crook	1 Me 109 destroyed.
F/Lt F Howell	2 Ju 87s destroyed.
F/O HM Goodwin	2 Ju 87s destroyed.
Sgt A Fearey	1 Ju 87 destroyed and 1 Me 110 damaged.
F/O J Dundas	1 Ju 87 destroyed and 1 Ju 87 damaged.
P/O CN Overton	2 Ju 87s destroyed.
PO RG Miller	1 Ju 87 destroyed, 1 probable.
PO ME Staples	1 Ju 87 destroyed, 1 Ju 87 damaged.

Pilot Officer Rogers Garland Miller's combat occurred five miles west of Dorchester:

   I was flying Yellow Two, 'A' Flight was scrambled to 17,000ft when Red Four saw E/A flying below us. Red Leader led us into the sun in line astern, and we dived down astern on the nearest formation which comprised about twenty Ju 87s in vics of thirteen and seven. I selected a vic of three on the starboard side, opening fire at 300 yards, firing for five seconds. The E/A did a steep climbing turn to the right then dived down with black smoke coming from its engine. Last seen diving in a wide spiral towards the clouds. I broke off to the right, diving, and did another stern attack on another formation below. I singled out three which were flying in extremely tight vics, opening fire at their leader at about 300 yards. As all three rear gunners were firing at me I yawed slightly from side-to-side, spraying all three. Before I broke away, the port E/A commenced a slight climbing turn to the right but was not smoking. As all my ammunition was expended, I pancaked.

TUESDAY, 13 AUGUST 1940

Before I made my attack I saw Yellow One shoot down one Ju 87 in flames.

I was sixth to go into the attack and before I opened fire I observed at least five E/A going down smoking heavily. Red Section completely demolished a section of three.

Interestingly, in his book *Spitfire Pilot*, 609 Squadron's Pilot Officer David Crook described his part in the action, which involved a fleeting engagement with the withdrawing escort:

At this moment 1 saw about five Me 109s pass just underneath us. I immediately broke away from the formation, dived on the last Me 109 and gave him a terrific burst of fire at very close range. He burst into flames and spun down for many thousands of feet into the clouds below, leaving behind a long trail of smoke.

I followed him down for some way and could not pull out of my dive in time to avoid going below the clouds myself. I found that I was about five miles north of Weymouth, and then I saw a great column of smoke rising from the ground a short distance away. I knew perfectly well what it was and went over to have a look. My Me 109 lay in a field, a tangled heap of wreckage burning fiercely, but with the black crosses on the wings still visible. I found out later that the pilot was still in the machine. He had made no attempt to get out while the aircraft was diving and had obviously been killed by my burst of fire. He crashed just outside a small village, and I could see everybody streaming out of their houses and rushing to the spot.

The record, however, proves that all three Me 109s of 5/JG 53 lost in this clash with 609 Squadron crashed in the sea. The wrecked enemy aircraft seen by Pilot Officer Crook could not, therefore, have been the Me 109 that he had shot down, but more likely one of the three *Stukas* which crashed in Dorset that afternoon. Among them was a Ju 87B of 5/StG2 which crashed and burned out at Grimstone viaduct, killing *Oberfeldwebel* E. Haack and *Unteroffizier* H. Haselmayer. Mr E.G. Read of Stratton remembered that afternoon:

My neighbours and I had been watching an aerial battle and machine-gun ammunition clips had fluttered down around us.

Suddenly there was a blood-curdling banshee wail – which was heart-stopping, as it approached us.

Right over our heads came the stricken plane, from the northeast. There was dense black smoke pouring from its starboard engine and two young airmen were clearly visible – they had just seconds to live. Later came the news that a German plane had crashed behind Grimstone viaduct [as the Ju 87 *Stuka* was single-engine aircraft]. We went there immediately on our bikes, but a sentry was there on guard with a fixed bayonet. Beneath two white parachutes were the crumpled bodies of the airmen.

The Hurricanes of 87 Squadron, up from Exeter, also joined in this action (although records are poor and the only combat claim arising clearly incorrectly timed at '1745 hrs'), Pilot Officer Denis David claiming a Ju 87 confirmed destroyed, and an Me 110 unconfirmed over Portland.

The *Stukas* faced fierce resistance and, owing to cloud at 3,000ft preventing dive-bombing, were unable to locate their targets – the airfields inland of Portland; they had little choice but to turn about and beat it for France. No.609 Squadron's combat claims were somewhat exaggerated, as five failed to get home, although several others were damaged. In his diary, General Wolfram von Richthofen, a cousin of the infamous 'Red Baron' and commander of VIII *Fliegerkorps*, wrote: 'Thanks to cloud our formations returned without releasing their bombs. The weather forecast had been false, and the attack ordered from "on high". It just couldn't be done. Thank goodness the English fighters came too late!'

The Ju 88s of III/LG 1 did make it to Andover, however, causing damage, but, yet again, this aerodrome had no connection to Fighter Command.

While this massive air battle went on over Weymouth Bay and Portland, the Ju 88s of I/LG 1 made it unhindered to Southampton, the afternoon's main target, which was accurately bombed: warehouses were set ablaze and a cold storage facility blown up – but the vital Supermarine factory at Woolston was clearly not even on the target inventory, no doubt because at this time *Luftwaffe* intelligence believed it to be producing bombers. This raid achieved nothing insofar as battering Fighter Command into submission went.

Between 16.00 hrs and 16.25 hrs, the Tangmere-based Hurricanes of 601 Squadron variously engaged the enemy between Winchester and Southampton/Portsmouth, mainly engaging the Me 110 escorts.

TUESDAY, 13 AUGUST 1940

The 'Millionaire's Mob' claimed two Me 110s destroyed, eleven probables, and a 109 damaged. Sergeant Leonard Guy had found an Me 110 inland of Southampton, attacking it from the blind-spot, below and behind – the pilot, *Leutnant* Wolfgang Münchmeyer baled out but broke both legs when colliding with his doomed machine's elevators; landing in a tree, the German was captured by the local Home Guard. His *Bordfunker* (Radio Operator), *Unteroffizier* Fritz Labusch, however, was killed. To the east, at 16.25 hrs, Flight Sergeant Pond encountered one of the Southampton raiders north of the port city, engaging and chasing it to Portsmouth, where the Ju 88 was last seen disappearing into cloud, pouring black smoke. It had been a successful engagement, even given the somewhat optimistic combat claims, and all of 601's pilots returned to safely Tangmere.

Still the RAF fighters harried the withdrawing enemy, which were now over the Solent, heading home. At 16.00 hrs, 43 Squadron had scrambled to protect Southampton, but only Sergeant Jim Hallowes engaged, claiming a 'Do 17' and a Ju 88 destroyed, and a Ju 88 damaged, over the north-west corner of the Isle of Wight. Similarly, 257 Squadron, also operating from Tangmere, encountered a lone Ju 88, returning from Andover, west of Selsey Bill at 16.35 hrs:

> Squadron Leader Harkness, leading the squadron, made the first attack on the bomber. After Pilot Officer Capon, Flight Lieutenant Beresford and several other members of the squadron attacked, the plane finally crashed in flames in a field. The claim for 1 Ju 88 destroyed was divided among the squadron ... The Squadron retuned to Northolt at 2030 hrs where they were met at Dispersal by Group Captain Vincent, the Station Commanding Officer. Having hearing the accounts of the air battles the Group Captain congratulated the squadron. (ORB)

The Ju 88, of 8/LG 1, crashed and exploded at Sidlesham, killing the crew.

At 16.35 hrs, the Dorchester Observer Corps post's log at Poundbury Camp, just north-west of Dorchester, recorded:

> Confirmed friendly and hostile pilots approaching the post. Much machine-gun and cannon fire. Fierce contest going on. Plane shot down, believed Me 110, another plane down, much confused sound-plotting and heavy firing for a considerable

period. One plane, believed friendly, flying low, East. Believed forced-landing this side of the Maiden Castle House and the neighbourhood of the Fever Hospital.

Finally, at 17.05 hrs, the daylight fighting concluded when Green Section of 92 Squadron, having been scrambled from Pembrey in South Wales and vectored towards Portland, engaged and destroyed a Ju 88 which crashed into the sea, two of the crew taking to a rubber boat, waving as their victor, Flight Lieutenant Robert Stanford Tuck orbited overhead; the victory was shared jointly with Pilot Officer William Watling and Flight Sergeant Ralph 'Titch' Havercroft. This Ju 88 may have been another of the Andover raiders, an aircraft of III/LG 1, which failed to return – but, if so, the two men in their dinghy were claimed by the sea.

On this day, Squadron Leader Alexander 'Sandy' Johnstone led his Spitfire south from Drem, first to refuel at Church Fenton, and then onwards to Westhampnett, Tangmere's satellite airfield. Although

> held up owing to poor weather ... fifteen Spitfires left at 1610 hrs as 11 Group anxious for us to get south owing to large amount of activity in the South. Squadron eventually arrived at Westhampnett 1720 hrs ... A large battle was in progress at the time but 602 were unable to take part as they were not on the correct R/T frequency.' (ORB)

Squadron Leader Sandy Johnstone:

> When I ... got the boys down, I began to wonder what we had let ourselves in for. On the centre of the field a Hurricane lay on its back while, from behind one of the boundary hedges, a thick pall of black smoke was rising lazily into the air ... Then an officer, his right arm in a sling, came forward and introduced himself as Johnny Peel, CO of 145 Squadron, whose outfit we'd come south to relieve ... He told me that 145 had taken a lot of stick and was now down to four aircraft and the same number of pilots. 'That,' he said, pointing to the Hurricane inverted on the field, '... is what's left of mine. I got badly shot up and had to land without ailerons. I stopped a bullet in the arm too; hence the sling. However, on a cheerier note, the smoke is coming from a downed Nazi.' He added that

TUESDAY, 13 AUGUST 1940

his four aircraft had already left, but that he had stayed on to see us in. If I had no objection he too would like to push off. So saying he climbed into his little sports car and with a final wave from his serviceable limb, drove away to join his lads at Drem ... The handover was presumably completed!

Pilot Officer Peter Parrott, 145 Squadron:

> Our feelings at being withdrawn were obviously relief, and some regret and sadness for those who had not survived – although we expected to be back south again soon, as soon as we had re-equipped and received replacement pilots. The groundcrews were also due for a rest. Apart from the slight lull in late June to early July 1940, they had been working day and night to carry out the rearming and refuelling under considerable pressure. The groundcrew establishment had not foreseen the number of hours flying, with a servicing requirement for the Hurricanes every ten, twenty-five, fifty and one hundred hours. The more hours flown, the greater the maintenance required, of course. They also had damaged and defective aircraft to see to, and the job of rearming and refuelling in between seven – fifteen minutes, two, three, or sometimes four times a day. 'Chiefy' Bannister will always be remembered for his high standards, and for his care for his crew.

As we have previously seen, pre-war Fighter Command tactics were found to be inappropriate in practice for modern air combat. It was a case of learning on the job, and there was a huge gulf of difference between chasing lone reconnaissance. Bombers or nuisance raiders in the North of England and over Scotland, compared to fighting Me 109s. Spitfire pilots had first discovered this over the French coast during the Dunkirk fighting, after which individual squadron commanders, prominent among them 'Sailor' Malan and Douglas Bader, began experimenting with their own formations and tactics. No.602 Squadron, however, had not previously served in 11 Group, so had no experience of meeting the single-engine German fighters. As Pilot Officer Peter Brown said, who had flown Spitfires with 611 Squadron at Dunkirk, 'The increased tempo of battle, owing entirely to the Me 109, was traumatic – and many squadrons new to the south had a hard time adjusting.' Those squadrons which had served in the front line, like 145 Squadron, had gained invaluable combat experience – but no process was in place for those squadrons to brief relieving units. Squadrons like 602, then, had to start from scratch.

There was much more to 'Eagle Day' than just daylight fighting involving Fighter Command though. As ever, there are events running in parallel to the main event.

Throughout the day, Coastal Command had flown the usual round of patrols, and Photographic Reconnaissance Unit (or PRU) Spitfires continued photographing the enemy coastlines. No.2 Group's daylight sorties were hampered by weather conditions, however, although the seaplane base at Brest, and the airfields there and at Morlaix, Caen and Waalhaven were all hit. For 82 Squadron, however, the day was disastrous. Four sections of the Watton-based squadron's Blenheims were briefed to attack Aalborg airfield in Denmark – but, in a virtually clear sky, owing to a navigational error, landfall was made over the southern, instead of northern, Danish coast. Consequently, the unescorted bombers had to fly northwards over the Danish mainland and – inevitably – were intercepted by Me 109s of *Hauptmann* Johannes Janke's I/JG 77 and battered by heavy flak on the target approach. All eleven Blenheims failed to return, and only nine of the thirty-three participating aircrew survived, all of whom were captured. It is astonishing that the 'Bomber Barons' continued to send unescorted bombers long distances in daylight, in spite of the losses and lessons which should have been learned. It was not so long ago, however, that British Prime Minister Stanley Baldwin had told the House of Commons that 'The Bomber would always get through', no matter what; the reality was clearly very different – unfortunately for 82 Squadron. Aalborg was an important German transport air base which would undoubtedly have played a part in ferrying enemy troops and matériel to Britain in the event of a seaborne invasion, so this raid is also yet another example of the part played by, and the unsung sacrifices of, Bomber Command in counter-attacking German invasion preparations and resources.

Under the cloak of darkness, Bomber Command sallied forth to attack German airfields in France, industrial targets in Germany and Italy, and undertake reconnaissance sorties. A Hampden of 44 Squadron failed to return from a Netherlands target, and the Whitley of 10 Squadron's Pilot Officer Parsons DFC was badly shot-up over his distant target: Turin's Fiat factory; having nursed his damaged aircraft all the way back to the Kentish coast, as the pilot prepared to crash-land near Lympne

TUESDAY, 13 AUGUST 1940

in the early hours of 14 August 1940, the Hampden plunged into the sea. Parsons and Sergeant Alfred Campion were killed, their remains later washing up on the French coast. Two sergeants, Chamberlain and Sharpe, escaped from their sinking aircraft and were fortunately rescued by a passing fishing smack, which was subsequently taken under tow by the lifeboat *Charles Cooper Henderson*, which was officially seeking the missing bomber crew. Watching these proceedings was Peggy Prince, an ARP ambulance driver based in Dymchurch – who was dissatisfied when the search for survivors appeared to be prematurely called off. *The London Gazette* reported a week later how Miss Prince, full of pluck and accompanied by a soldier, 'elected to go out again in a small canoe', picking up the Wireless Operator, Sergeant Marshall, who was found 'clinging to a buoy. Somehow the exhausted airman was got into a small canoe, and his rescuer paddled back to her home.' Miss Prince was made an MBE for her life-saving actions; clearly, as *The London Gazette* notice concluded, the airman 'undoubtedly owes his life to Miss Prince's courage and determination'. Indeed, it is such stories of courage way above and beyond, by 'ordinary' people, that confirmed Britain's resolute stand against Hitler that fateful summer.

By now, the Germans were well-aware of the importance of the Castle Bromwich Aeroplane Factory (CBAF), then producing the new Spitfire Mk II, even if the Supermarine works at Woolston were believed to be producing bombers. Stopping or reducing the flow of Spitfires and Hurricanes from the factories was a priority, but, intentionally on the defenders' behalf, the huge Castle Bromwich plant was far too deep inland to attack in daylight. And that is where *Kampfgruppe* 100 came in – after the sun had set on 'Eagle Day'.

Operating from Vannes, towards dusk, twenty-one He 111s of the soon-to-be elite and first *Pfadfinder* (Pathfinder) unit took off – heading for the CBAF – *Luftwaffe* target number 7,461 – and nearby Fort Dunlop. Flying in sections of three, thirty minutes apart, these special aircraft were uniquely assisted by the *X-Verfahren* (X-Procedure), and specifically *X-Gerät* (X-Apparatus) – essentially a radio navigation aid comprising beams guiding bombers to their invisible targets. In England, Professor R.V. Jones, the Assistant Director of Intelligence (Science), had been 'much excited' as early as March 1940 by a 'recorded fragment' of a conversation shared with him between two captured German airmen at Cockfosters, the London interrogation centre, discussing *X-Verfahren* and *X-Gerät*, which appeared to involve 'radio pulses'. Further snippets of intelligence were incoming but even by 'Eagle Day' the detail of this precision bombing aid remained a mystery to the British. For now, then, in the *X-Verfahren*, the *Luftwaffe* had a distinct advantage – even if at this stage it was only available to KGr 100. At 23.10 hrs, the first bombs hit CBAF.

Alex Henshaw, Vickers-Supermarine Chief Test Pilot, CBAF:

> The Germans seemed to find the factory ... every time and one got hardened to the sight of a direct hit on, say, the machine shop before all the employees had gone into the shelters; as day slowly dawned it was common to find bits of bodies mingled with valuable equipment blasted to small pieces and hanging gruesomely from what had been the roof. The spirit of the British people at that time was magnificent and quite irrepressible and within days there would be a temporary roof on, new machines would be moved in and back into production. One of the worst weapons of that summer was the delayed action bomb. These were scattered all over the place, particularly on the aerodrome and around the factory, and it was a little disconcerting when taking-off for one to suddenly explode nearby.

In that first raid by KGr 100, six civilian workers were killed and over forty more seriously injured. Among the dead was 39-year-old John Guest, of nearby Erdington, who worked as a driller at the CBAF, and left behind a widow, Beatrice, and daughter, Frances; as the Prime Minister rightly said: 'The front line runs through factories. The workmen are soldiers with different weapons but the same courage.' Churchill might also have referred to 'workwomen', because many females had taken the place of males now in the forces. The courage shown by all these civilian workers, who toiled long hours day and night, fully aware that they could be attacked at any time, is yet another inspirational thread of the overall Battle of Britain narrative.

Miss Megan Llewellyn worked in 'C' Block of the CBAF, making starboard wing sections:

> I remember going to work to start the 6 am shift one morning and 'D' Block had been bombed the night before. The clothes, shoes and gas masks of the workers from 'D' Block were piled in heaps between 'A' and 'C' Blocks. They were wet from the

TUESDAY, 13 AUGUST 1940

water used by the fire brigade to fight the fires. You could see bodies still in the girders of the roof of the factory. It is a sight that you never forget. It was after the bombing of 'D' Block that they altered the working hours to three shifts, 0600 hrs – 1400 hrs, 1400 – 2200 hrs, and 2200 hrs – 0600 hrs.

This was a successful attack, the first major raid on a British aircraft factory, which damaged various offices and buildings, but overall Spitfire production at the CBAF site was unaffected. It led, in fact, to the 'Shadow Factories', with various aspects of the manufacturing process being dispersed – often to the most unlikely places, including railway arches, garages and even furniture-making workshops. Consequently, there was never a chance of the enemy completely bringing Spitfire production to a standstill, no matter how successful raids were in future on the CBAF. For Professor R.V. Jones, however, this was only the start of what became known as the 'Battle of the Beams', as the race to combat *X-Verfahren* with counter-measures began.

So closed the long-awaited assault on 'Eagle Day'. But what had it achieved? The airfields at Detling and Eastchurch were unconnected with Fighter Command, and the fighter airfields of Hawkinge and Manston remained operational, while Rochford and Middle Wallop were untouched. None of the damage caused to airfields, therefore, affected Fighter Command's capacity one iota. The initial confusion of *Luftwaffe* communications would have been farcical had men's lives not been lost as a consequence, but the two-pronged, simultaneous assaults during morning and afternoon by *Luftflotten* 2 and 3 on both 10 and 11 groups' areas was a new feature of operations – which was well-conceived and became a common feature of the fighting. Certainly, the attack on Southampton had caused some damage, but this, again, was disproportionate to the losses sustained and had no effect on the defences, and the failed attempts to bomb both Farnborough and Odiham airfields were pointless. Moreover, considering the previous day's successful attack on Ventnor, it is difficult to fathom why other Chain Home stations were not made priority targets on 'Eagle Day', to be pressed by a maximum effort – but none were damaged.

According to Bekker:

> Despite the bad weather and delayed start, 484 bombers and dive-bombers and some 1,000 fighters of both kinds had

crossed the English coast. Nine enemy airfields were reported to have been attacked, 'five of them to such good purpose that they could have been put out of action'.

Clearly, then, the OKL was equally misinformed regarding the actual damage and effect of the 'Eagle Attack' on this supposedly great air offensive's first day. In the twenty-four-hour period of 'Eagle Day', the *Luftwaffe* flew 1,485 sorties and lost forty-five aircraft – the Ju 87 *Stuka* suffering particularly badly. Fighter Command flew 700 sorties in daylight and a further twenty-seven at dusk or after dark, losing thirteen aircraft – seven pilots of which were safe. To the OKL, those thirteen RAF fighters became 134, with Bekker writing that both Kesselring and Sperrle were 'satisfied with this success'.

The reality, however, was very different: 'Eagle Day' had been a complete failure.

Chapter 2

Wednesday, 14 August 1940

Daily Home Intelligence Report:

> Morale is high: there is general satisfaction over the results of raids on our ports. There are some indications that people are beginning to believe these intensified attacks are preliminaries to a more general attack or invasion. On the other hand, verbatims show a scepticism found on previous false alarms, e.g. 'News. I never listen to it. When the Germans come over I'll start thinking about invasion.'

Despite the shaky start, the *'Adler Angriff'* was no 'false alarm' however, although having flown so many sorties the previous day, enemy air activity was somewhat reduced, to less than 500 sorties, partially owing to ongoing unfavourable weather. The early morning saw low cloud, down to 2,000ft, and drizzle – further vexing the *Reichsmarschall* eager to deliver his knockout blow against Fighter Command. Inevitably, German reconnaissance aircraft were active from the off, the first combats involving these snoopers.

At 09.10 hrs, unusually, Sergeant Reginald Llewellyn of Exeter's 213 Squadron was scrambled solo to patrol the south-west coast between Seaton and Bridport; thirty minutes later, while below cloud at 1,800ft some two miles off Seaton, the lone Hurricane pilot sighted a Do 17, which he managed to open fire at from long-range – 600 yards – before the bomber disappeared into cloud, its starboard engine smoking.

At 11.40 hrs, the Dover and Pevensey RDF detected German formations assembling over the French coast. Five minutes later, 11 Group scrambled a flight of 151 Squadron's Hurricanes from Rochford to intercept any incoming raid around the North Foreland. Earlier that morning, 615 Squadron had gone down from Kenley to Hawkinge, from where, at 11.50 hrs, the squadron was scrambled to protect Dover. In addition to these

Hurricanes, the Spitfires of 65 Squadron, operating from Manston, were scrambled to patrol base (take-off time unrecorded), and those of Biggin Hill's 610 Squadron were sent up from Biggin Hill and vectored first to patrol over Manston, thence to Hawkinge.

Some eighty *Stukas,* of II/StG 1 and IV/LG 1, were approaching Dover, possibly intending to bomb Hawkinge, with both I and III/JG 26 as close escort while II/JG 26 flew a supporting *freie hunt,* there being around 100 Me 109s airborne. Furthermore, the Me 110s of 1/*Erprobungsgruppe* 210 were up from Calais-Marck and briefed to attack RAF Ramsgate, Manston's satellite airfield, while 2nd *Staffel* were to hit the Manston Sector Station.

On 5 August 1940, the Canadian Squadron Leader John Gordon had succeeded the exhausted 'Teddy' Donaldson in command of 151 Squadron, and now, at 11.50 hrs on 14 August 1940, the new CO led Red and Yellow sections up from Rochford with orders to intercept enemy aircraft over Manston at 20,000ft. Five minutes previously, Sergeant George Atkinson and Sergeant Leonard Davies, comprising Green Section, had taken off to patrol a convoy east of Southend, but given the incoming threat, they were ordered to join the other two sections, with Atkinson leading.

Squadron Leader Gordon reported that:

> Red Section, followed by Green, arrived over Manston at about 12,000ft and sighted about fifteen Me 109s about 3,000ft above. We climbed to attack and engaged them. I got on the tail of one E/A and dived down to the North. I gradually closed and fired a burst of about 1,600 rounds at about 300 yards. At about 2,000ft the E/A started to smoke. I broke away and when I had turned towards him again an aircraft had just gone into the sea and the pilot was floating down by parachute.

In this combat, Pilot Officer James Johnston, another Canadian, claimed a 109 damaged, while Sub-Lieutenant Henry Beggs, an FAA pilot, destroyed another. It is probable that the Me 109s engaged were from II/JG 52, which lost three fighters on operations over Canterbury area this day on what was a diversionary sweep. Sergeant George Atkinson, Green 1, however, was shot down and baled out; fortunately he was rescued from the sea and admitted to Manston Hospital suffering from shock. Atkinson's was the only British fighter down in this engagement, and at the material time, *Leutnant* Franz Beyer of 8/JG 3, claimed his first aerial victory: a Hurricane.

WEDNESDAY, 14 AUGUST 1940

Meanwhile, while 151 Squadron mixed it with the Me 109s, 1/*Erprobungsgruppe* 210's attack on Ramsgate airfield had been thwarted by barrage balloons, and so these Me 110s joined 2nd *Staffel*'s attack on Manston. Owing to varying degrees of 7/10ths cloud at 3,000–4,000ft, 151 Squadron had engaged the Me 109s, blissfully unaware of the carnage below.

RAF Manston ORB:

> The station was again attacked by nine Me 110s. They were heavily engaged by ground defences and two E/A were destroyed – one by a Royal Artillery (RA) post (Bofors) and one by a RAF post (Hispano). Two hangars on the east camp were partially wrecked and damage was caused to a Bellman and Bessonneau hangar. One large crater made in centre of aerodrome.

The hangars belonged to the auxiliary 600 'City of London' Squadron, a night-fighter unit equipped with the Blenheim Mk IF. Squadron Leader David de Brassey Clark, the CO, became the only casualty when a stone ricocheted off his Adjutant's steel helmet during the attack and blacked his eye.

This time, 2/*Erprobungsgruppe* 210 did not escape unscathed: the Me 110 flown by *Leutnant* Heinrich Brinkmann was one of the two hit by AA fire, the aircraft immediately exploding, killing the pilot and his *Bordfunker*, *Unteroffizier* Richard Mayer. *Gefrieter* Ewald Schank was *Bordfunker* of the second aircraft hit, flown by *Unteroffizier* Hans Steding, and later recalled:

> At a height of about 3000 m. the *Staffel* began a diving attack in order to hit the target. After the bombs had been dropped, we pulled our machine higher. In the same instant, our aircraft received a heavy blow from below, probably a hit from the Flak. Because of this, the aircraft was damaged and crashed. I was thrown out of the machine, but remained attached to the aircraft by a boot. Without thinking, I freed myself from the boot. When I was free of the aircraft, I operated my parachute. Shortly after the parachute opened, I landed heavily on the hard-red tarmac. I quickly released my parachute, as it was pulling me towards a large fire. When I stood up, I realised

that I was missing a boot, and was wounded in the head. As I looked around, I noticed pieces of aircraft, undercarriage, a wheel, and bits of the fuselage. The rest of the aircraft was smashed into the red tarmac not far away.

I dragged myself through the wreckage to search for the pilot, but could see nothing. As I was all alone and helpless on the runway, three men in blue uniforms came. I did not know, or understand, any English words at that time. I said to the soldiers in German: 'My friend is in the aircraft.' They took me in their midst and led me to a shelter, in which there were soldiers in brown uniforms and steel helmets, with guns. A soldier spoke to me in German, but I no longer recall what he said. I asked him: 'When will I be shot?'

'You will not be shot,' he replied. 'You will go to a prison camp with many others.'

I probably said: *'Ich bin glücklich, dass mich Gott gerettet hat'* (I am lucky that God has saved me). I fainted shortly afterwards. (Reproduced with permission of John Vasco.)

Meanwhile, a huge dogfight had developed over Dover, involving somewhere approaching 150 fighters. The first RAF fighter squadron on the scene was 65, which had initially been ordered to patrol 'Charlie Three' – Manston – but then, ironically, diverted to Dover. At 12.20 hrs, 65 Squadron engaged Me 109s off Dover; among the Spitfire pilots was the celebrated Supermarine test pilot Flying Officer Jeffrey Kindersley Quill, who had, to his great credit, volunteered to fly in combat in order to gain essential experience flying the Spitfire operationally. On this day, the gallant Quill claimed an Me 109 'Destroyed – probable. Mid-Channel':

I was leading Yellow Section and hen about 12,000ft near Dover we saw evidence of E/A who were attacking balloons. The Squadron headed for a quantity of aircraft which were circling there and which I assumed to be Me 109s, but which turned out to be Hurricanes. We were now in line astern when I sighted an Me 109 below my starboard wing and passing underneath me. I immediately turned onto his tail – he was going quite slowly and flying straight and I do not think he saw me. I opened fire at about 200 yards and he made no evasive action. I gave three bursts, the final one at about 50 yards and

WEDNESDAY, 14 AUGUST 1940

then formed the opinion that the pilot was probably dead, because he still took no evasive action and was going very slowly, in a gradual descent.

I then turned round and proceeded towards Dover where I believed the rest of the squadron was engaged. I saw some single Spitfires and climbed and circled for a time but as no further E/A were observed I returned on R/T instruction to Rochford.

Quill's success was shared with Yellow 2, Flying Officer John Nicholas. Similarly, Flight Sergeant Robert MacPherson and Sergeant Michael Keymer shared the destruction of a 109, while Flight Lieutenant Gordon Olive probably destroyed another. Flying Officer Lee Pyman claimed a 109 destroyed off Dover – but in turn, his Spitfire was 'hit by six cannon shells in the wing and fuselage', although Pyman 'effected a successful forced-landing and the machine was only temporarily unserviceable' (ORB).

Originally, this raid had been plotted as '30+', but as it approached Folkestone RDF reports indicated that it was much stronger. At 12.30 hrs the enemy formation crossed the coast at Folkestone, and was reported by the Observer Corps to be '100+' as the raid proceeded towards Dover. A number of Me 109s attacked and destroyed eight of Dover's barrage balloons, their deflated carcasses dropping on the town, the heavy cables dragging along behind, causing minor damage to property – Beaconsfield Road was blocked by one for two hours, although fortunately there were no casualties in the town. The raid then swept inland to Ashford, only dropping eight bombs inconsequentially on St Margaret's at 12.45 hrs, after which the enemy began retiring. As the main raid had approached Folkestone, however, some units became detached and attacked the Folkestone lightship.

The Hurricanes reported by Quill were those of 615 Squadron. Pilot Officer John Gayner later reported being attacked by an Me 110, returning his damaged fighter to Kenley while the other two members of Yellow Section took evasive action. Red Section, however, became separated by cloud, Pilot Officer Sydney Mable patrolled uneventfully below cloud, while Flying Officer Peter Collard and Pilot Officer Cecil Montgomery ventured above – where they were ambushed and shot down by Me 109s. Back at base, no one knew for sure what had happened to them, although Pilot Officer Keith Lofts reported having seen a Hurricane crash into the sea five miles south-west of Dover. Some days later, however, the remains of both pilots washed up on the French coast and were interred at Oye-Plage. Nine days after he was reported missing, Collard's DFC was gazetted, accrediting him with six aerial victories; this, then, was an experienced pilot that Fighter Command could ill-afford to lose.

Blue and Green sections of 615 Squadron:

> Saw Ju 87s attacking Folkestone lightship and engaged them. Pilot Officer Lofts shot down one which crashed into the sea half way to Gris Nez ... He also damaged another one. Flying Officer Eyre and Sergeant Porter attacked the third section and both saw pieces fly off. When they finished there were no signs of this aircraft at this spot. Flight Lieutenant Sanders saw three aircraft crash into the sea ... Pilot Officer Roger's aircraft was damaged on landing at Hawkinge, his undercarriage collapsing. (ORB)

Ron Spearpoint witnessed the attack on the *Folkestone Gate* lightship:

> On this particular morning I was in Folkestone town (probably on leave after a motor launch that I'd been aboard was bombed).
>
> I decided to walk through Holmesdale Terrace on to the Leas to look down on my father's old home, 6 Marine Crescent, and see what was happening in the Channel. While leaning on the wooden rustic fence, I saw the lightship below me. It was moored just west of Victoria Pier and about a mile out. It seemed strange and somewhat eerie for, as far as I could see, I was the only person on the Leas.
>
> Suddenly, the quiet was broken by the screams of four *Stuka* dive bombers that appeared out of the clouds from the west. When almost over the beach they banked right, headed seaward and bombed the lightship across the beam.
>
> As the planes continued toward France, almost at sea level, three or four Hurricanes or Spitfires (not certain, as I ducked!) zoomed over the Leas pavilion. They flew out just above the roof tops, guns blazing as they pursued the *Stukas*. I think the tail-end *Stuka* was shot down as great plumes of smoke appeared from the sea.
>
> When the spray subsided, the crew of the lightship – all, I hoped – took to the lifeboat. It seemed a matter of only

WEDNESDAY, 14 AUGUST 1940

minutes before a high-speed rescue launch from Dover was on the scene. It picked them up and headed back to Dover.

The lightship finally began to founder. Shaken, I made a quick retirement to the *East Kent Arms* and swiftly downed a couple of beers.

Even in wartime, hazards of the sea such as dangerous shoals and rocks still had to be marked, hence the presence of the unarmed lightship. On 29 January 1940, the *East Dudgeon* light had been sunk by a He 111, and the *East Goodwin* followed her to the seabed on 18 July 1940. The *Folkestone Gate*, therefore, was the third light to be sunk – but would not be the last.

The Spitfires Ron Spearpoint had seen belonged to 610 Squadron:

> Red, Yellow, Blue and Green Sections ... engaged E/A over Folkestone at 15,000ft. The E/A were in hundreds: Ju 87s, Me 109s and Me 110s. Pilot Officer Norris attacked a formation of Ju 87s, fired at one which went down in flames – then attacked, over Dover, a formation of about fifty Ju 87s and Me 110s – fired at one Ju 87 which went down in flames – attacked a third Ju 87 which went down smoking heavily. Sergeant Hamlyn fired at an Me 109 and saw his bullets going in and clouds of smoke pouring from E/A. Sergeant Else attacked one of two Me 109s which were attacking a Spitfire, fired a long burst, saw E/A disappear emitting clouds of smoke. Sergeant Ramsey got separated from the squadron, fired two bursts at an Me 110 in mid-Channel and E/A disappeared emitting clouds of smoke, after turning on his back and one of the crew baling out. Sergeant Chandler attacked an Me 109 as it was climbing and E/A went down in flames. Sergeant Parsons attacked one of twelve Ju 87s and saw it go down in flames, broke off engagement to deal with an Me 109 coming for him, saw his bullets hit E/A which disappeared into cloud, skidding sideways. Sergeant Corfe shot down an Me 109. Pilot Officer Rees damaged a Ju 87. Sergeant Gardner forced-landed at Wye after causing a He 113 [*sic*] to crash in the Channel. (ORB)

The next RAF fighter squadron to intercept 'Raid 34' over Dover was 32, scrambled from Hawkinge at 12.30 hrs and soon embroiled with Me 109s covering the Ju 87s' withdrawal.

BATTLE OF BRITAIN ATTACK OF THE EAGLES

Pilot Officer Rupert Smythe:

> I was leading Yellow Section and sighted about nine Me 109s above us on the port quarter, circling to attack. I called the Squadron Leader and turned in towards them. Some more Me 109s appeared behind and my section split up. However, two Me 109s were still in front of me so I chased them and caught up just behind Dover. The one I fired at started to break up, turned on his back and went down vertically; the pilot baled out. Then some more Me 109s attacked me and got my glycol. I ... went straight for the nearest cloud. Eventually landed at Hawkinge, just as my engine was starting to burn.

In this engagement, RAF pilots claimed five Me 109s destroyed, three probables and three damaged; six Ju 87s destroyed, three probables and one damaged, and an Me 110 destroyed. Five Me 109s, of JG 3, JG 26 and JG 52 were lost, with only one of these – the aircraft destroyed by Smythe – crashing on land, at Coldred; the pilot, *Unteroffizier* Gerhard Kemen of I/JG 26 was wounded and captured. Only one Ju 87, of 10/LG 1, was destroyed – its crew missing – and another of the same unit damaged. There is no record of an Me 110 being destroyed. Equally, the Me 109 pilots' claims were exaggerated: six Hurricanes and ten Spitfires were supposedly destroyed, when in reality only two Hurricanes failed to return and two more were damaged. The Spitfires suffered no loss, excepting Pyman's shot-up 65 Squadron machine. This was another poor result for the Germans, with just a few bombs randomly dropped on St Margaret's and a lightship sunk. If the raid was a diversion for *Erprobungsgruppe* 210's attack on Manston it succeeded, but if the intention was for the *Stukas* to bomb Hawkinge, it failed in the face of strong fighter opposition.

All went quiet after the enemy's withdrawal, excepting various enemy reconnaissance sorties. At 16.50 hrs, Squadron Leader John Badger was up from Tangmere, patrolling the Isle of Wight area with 'B' Flight of his 43 Squadron, when the Hurricanes, flying just below cloud at 8,000ft, were ordered to seek a bandit:

> I detached Green 2 to have a look above (cloud). Almost immediately he gave 'Tally Ho' and one bandit was seen coming through cloud in NW direction. He saw us and turned away, diving very steeply. I put both sections in line-astern and

WEDNESDAY, 14 AUGUST 1940

carried out astern attacks. I saw all aircraft go in and deliver attack. Clouds were almost down to sea-level but very thin. Just before he reached this layer the starboard engine emitted clouds of smoke and appeared to be on fire – it practically stopped. He turned back towards the Isle of Wight and jettisoned eight bombs which exploded in the sea. Attacks were sustained intermittently as opportunity offered. I followed aircraft in cloud layers and saw him hit sea ... Twenty miles SW St. Catherine's Point.

This Ju 88, an aircraft of I/LG 1, was shared equally between 'B' Flight.

The morning's effort on Kentish targets had been mounted by *Luftflotte* 2, and now the focus switched to *Luftflotte* 3. Between 15.44 hrs and 16.05 hrs, RDF reported four enemy formations off the Normandy coast, heading for England. Instead of these being the usual large '*Valhallas*', the formations were small, the largest only '9+'. At 17.30 hrs, 'B' Flight of 87 Squadron, however, up from Exeter, encountered a mixed formation of some '70+' Me 110s and Ju 87s, five miles south of Portland. Just Pilot Officer Harry Mitchell managed to engage the enemy:

E/A sighted in large numbers at 6,000–8,000ft. Climbed to 11,000ft ... fired at Me 110 using full deflection from vertical astern, blew his tailplane off. Pulled round in steep turn with another Me 110 in sights. Gave him full deflection and saw tracer go into him but didn't stay to watch results. Saw Ju 87 doing nothing in particular below me. He dived away into a thin layer of cloud but I caught him in a clear patch and shot him down from dead astern.

Mitchell was credited with both an Me 110 and a Ju 87 destroyed, and an Me 110 damaged. No losses appear in German records apparently attributable to this combat, however.

The strange thing is that the Ju 87s do not appear to have attacked any target, so whether they were seeking shipping or, as the largest formation deployed by *Luftflotte* 3 that afternoon, intended simply to draw RAF fighters to battle, remains a mystery. Certainly, according to the KG 55 history (see Bibliography) operations this day were intended 'to constantly challenge and wear down the British fighter force'. Airfields, though, were the target for other small formations.

BATTLE OF BRITAIN ATTACK OF THE EAGLES

Pilot Officer David Crook of Middle Wallop's 609 Squadron:

> The day was very cloudy, and soon after lunch the air raid warning sounded at Wallop, and we all dashed out of the Mess and went down to the dispersal point where our Spitfires were.
>
> There were no orders for us to take off, though three of our machines were already in the air and circling the aerodrome.
>
> So we sat in our aircraft and waited. A few minutes later we heard the unmistakable 'ooma-ooma' of a German bomber above the clouds. I immediately signalled to my ground crew to stand by, as I did not intend to sit on the ground and be bombed! I kept my finger on the engine starter button and waited expectantly.
>
> Almost immediately the enemy bomber – a Junkers 88 – broke out of the cloud to the north of the aerodrome, turned slightly to get on his course and dived at very high speed towards the hangers. At about 1,500ft he let go four bombs – we could see them very distinctly as they plunged down – and a second later there was an earth-shaking 'Whoom' and four great clouds of dust rose. All this happened in a matter of seconds only, but by this time everybody had got their engines started and we all roared helter-skelter across the aerodrome. Why there were no collisions I don't know, but we all got safely into the air and turned round to chase the enemy.

Yellow Section, Flying Officer John Dundas and Sergeant Alan Feary, were already airborne, patrolling nearby Boscombe Down at 15,000ft. A Ju 88 briefly appeared out of cloud and was fired upon by Dundas before it disappeared again. Feary immediately dived into the cloud, hoping to intercept the bomber as it emerged from this layer, descending to 8,000ft when, at 16.50 hrs the Spitfire pilot,

> Saw to starboard a Ju 88 which was bombing Middle Wallop. I gave chase and closed to 250 yards astern and gave a long burst and saw E/A commence to dive steeply. I closed up again and gave further burst which finished my ammunition. I followed the E/A down and saw it crash and burst into flames.

This aircraft, which was also attacked by Sergeant Michael Boddington of 234 Squadron, the Spitfires of which having moved to Middle Wallop the

WEDNESDAY, 14 AUGUST 1940

previous day, belonged to I/LG 1 and crashed at Turf Hill, North Charford, at 17.05 hrs; One crewman was captured unhurt but the second survivor died of wounds the following day; two others were killed in the crash.

Across the Channel, the airfield at Villacoublay was home to elements of *Oberst* Alois Stoeckl's KG 55, and that afternoon the *Kommodore* took off with three He 111s of his *Stabstaffel* (staff flight) and set course for Liverpool. An engine of Stoeckl's aircraft, G1 + AA 'Anton-Anton', was not running properly, however, so after rendezvousing with the rest of his formation over Paris, he had no option but to relinquish the lead. Two other aircraft of his *Stabskette* (staff section) remained with him and the three bombers continued towards England – intent upon attacking Middle Wallop instead, being nearer the South Coast. Stoeckl's small formation found their target, as the 609 Squadron diary recorded:

> Middle Wallop Station was raided by three twin-engine enemy bombers, who scored direct hits on our hangar, and made a shambles of the offices. While attempting to close a hangar door, Corporal R.W. Smith, LAC H. Thorley and LAC K. Wilson were killed, and Corporal F.H. Appleby admitted to hospital, injured.

Various small enemy formations were in the Middle Wallop area and harried by 609's Spitfires. Pilot Officer Crook and Flying Officer Dundas caught Stoeckl, as the latter reported:

> Met one Ju 88 [*sic*] three miles west of base, flying south. The E/A was already damaged and as I attacked I saw its undercarriage coming down. I gave him the rest of my ammunition at close range from dead astern, saw a black puff of smoke come from his starboard engine and saw him crash and break up on the munitions store about five miles SW of the aerodrome.

In German aircraft the navigator was the captain – in this case Stoeckl, whose pilot, *Oberleutnant* Bruno Brossler had prepared for a crash-landing which went badly wrong: He 111 'Anton-Anton' had crashed and exploded at the Royal Naval Armaments Depot at Dean Hill, Eastdean. Stoeckl and Brossler died in the crash, along with *Oberst* Walter Frank, V *Fliegerkorp*'s Chief of Staff, who incredibly, had joined the crew for this sortie as the air gunner. *Feldwebel* Heinz Grimmstein, the *Bordfunker*, and *Feldwebel* Jonny Thiel, the flight engineer, were both badly wounded but survived to become prisoners of war, being repatriated early, in 1944, owing to their injuries. *Oberst* Stoeckel was a popular commander, whose loss was keenly felt by KG 55. Indeed, the damage to Middle Wallop was hardly worth the loss of an experienced *Geschwaderkommodore* and a senior staff officer. *Oberstleutnant* Hans Korte succeeded Stoeckel – and going forward KG 55 would find itself heavily engaged throughout the Battle of Britain.

No.609 Squadron, however, had a missing pilot: Flying Officer Henry MacDonald Goodwin, who simply disappeared. Pilot Officer Crook expressed surprise, given that all of the combats had taken place over land, near the airfield, and had not involved enemy fighters. It was assumed that 'Mac' had pursued an enemy aircraft out to sea and been jumped by fighters, but no German fighter pilot claimed a British fighter in this area that afternoon. Ten days later, Goodwin's body washed up on the Isle of Wight, so it is likely that he fell victim to return fire from one of the bombers. 'Mac' was taken home to Chaddesley Corbett, Worcestershire, and buried at St Cassian's – next to his younger brother, Pilot Officer Barrie Goodwin, killed in a flying accident on 24 June 1940 while flying Hurricanes with 605 Squadron.

He 111s of KG 27 were also prowling about over England; of which Pembrey's 92 Squadron's dashing Flight Lieutenant Robert Stanford Tuck took a heavy toll – although even fighter aces misidentified their quarry:

> [17.30 hrs] Ordered to patrol Barry, 16,000ft. On arrival approximately in patrol position above 10/10ths cloud, Blue 3 indicated bogies behind and on my right. Did a quick turn towards them and identified them as Ju 88s flying in close formation at 16,000ft, heaving NW. I broke up my section and we carried out two or three beam quarter and astern attacks with little apparent effect. E/A maintained formation and steady height and course. I then called up my section and instructed them both to carry out head-on attacks, but owing to heavy R/T interference they did not hear this order. I proceeded well ahead and on the same level of E/A formation and then turned back, head-on to them. I got in a dead steady burst of two seconds head-on to the E/A. When I had passed directly over him at 50ft I pulled vertically upwards and looked backwards, downwards, and saw that No 3 E/A had broken away quickly from the main formation and was losing height with a lot of heavy smoke pouring from both

WEDNESDAY, 14 AUGUST 1940

engines. He disappeared into the cloud, losing height, heading south or SW. The other two aircraft still maintained height and formation so I carried out exactly the same head-on attack on the leading E/A. After pulling up vertically and looking back I saw that precisely the same had happened to this aircraft as No 3 E/A. I followed this E/A down through the cloud, heading SSW, but had great difficulty in stopping behind it as apparently its engines were out of action, alternatively I had hit the pilot. I lost this E/A in cloud and eventually came out below, fifteen miles south of Weston-Super-Mare. While I was looking for the E/A I had fired at, I came down through cloud and saw a stick of five bombs land on the railway midway between Highbridge and Glastonbury. I quickly looked round the sky and saw what appeared to be a He 111. As soon as I turned towards him he climbed into cloud and I lost him. I then returned to base to refuel and rearm.

The other members of Tuck's Blue Section, namely Pilot Officer William Watling and Sergeant 'Titch' Havercroft, also scored against the bombers, as did Pilot Officer Desmond Williams and Flying Officer Alan Wright. No.92 Squadron was actually responsible for bringing down three 9/KG 27 He 111s: one, engaged by Tuck, crashed at Charterhouse, near Cheddar, at 18.00 hrs; the second, attacked by Tuck and Watling after the attention of Wright and Williams, crashed and burned out at Puriton five minutes later; the third, shot down by Tuck, went into the sea at Bridgewater Bay. It was quite a result and yet another example of how vulnerable unescorted bombers were, even in cloudy conditions.

Over the 11 Group area, 'A' Flight of 615 Squadron was scrambled from Kenley to intercept a bandit, and despite low cloud over Dungeness, all three pilots of Red Section, engaged a 'Ju 86' at 18.30 hrs, which was last seen disappearing into cloud with damage. At 19.15 hrs, Green Section of Tangmere's 43 Squadron intercepted a He 111 forty miles south of Beachy Head; the enemy aircraft escaped but not before shooting down Sergeant Herbert Montgomery, who was killed. Then, the final daylight action over the 10 Group area occurred at 19.40 hrs, six miles south of Lyme Regis; Pilot Officer Harold Atkinson was Green 2 of Exeter's 213 Squadron:

I saw three He 111s fly NW, just below, in and out of cloud. I called to Green Leader and turned. I attacked No 3 of the formation from astern, getting in three attacks as best I could between clouds. After my first burst on the port engine it started smoking. I had to break away upwards owing to possibility of losing E/A in cloud if I broke downwards. The undercarriage fell down and the whole E/A caught fire. The crew of four jumped and were picked up in the sea. The E/A crashed four miles south of Lyme Regis. My aircraft was fairly shot about and I had splinters in my left arm.

This was an 8/KG 27 He 111, although only two of the crew were rescued and captured – two others drowned and a fifth was never found, probably killed or incapacitated by Atkinson's attack and therefore unable to bale out. This enemy formation was carrying out an armed reconnaissance of Liverpool, during the course of which the remaining two aircraft attacked the training base at RAF Sealand in Flintshire. Approaching from the west, below 1,000ft, the first He 111 dropped eight HE bombs and an incendiary device on the airfield but no serious damage was caused, the bomber raking the target with machine-gun fire as it passed overhead, causing only slight damage to two Miles Master trainers. The second Heinkel then attacked from the South, dropping five HE bombs and an incendiary from 3,500ft in the area of the base occupied by 30 Maintenance Unit. The Sergeants' Mess was extensively damaged by a direct hit, which also blew in the windows of adjacent buildings. One airman was killed and nine more injured. The raiders did not escape unscathed, however. Three miles to the south-west of Sealand lay Hawarden aerodrome – home to the 7 OTU Spitfire conversion unit – and one of the raiders was engaged by pilots from there, namely Wing Commander J. Hallings-Pott, Squadron Leader J. McLean and Pilot Officer Peter 'Decoy' Ayerst. The He 111 was shot down, the pilot crash-landing at Border House Farm near Chester at 21.00 hrs. Although these three pilots saw action during the Battle of Britain, like Pilot Officer Alec Bird (see 25 July 1940, *The Breaking Storm*) their names will not be found among those of the Few, having been serving with a training unit at the time.

So ended the daylight fighting on what was a strange day. The attack on Manston was successful, the appended fighter sweep understandable, the *Stukas* foray to Folkestone and Dover puzzling. Over the 10 Group area the number of bombers active was commensurate with the size of previously deployed mass formations, but these were operating in many small formations across a broad front. If these tactics were intended to reduce casualties they failed: eighteen *Luftwaffe* aircraft were lost on these operations against just

WEDNESDAY, 14 AUGUST 1940

six RAF fighters and four pilots. Various RAF airfields had been hit, the most important being Middle Wallop, and apart from Manston, none of the other aerodromes were connected to Fighter Command. Railways had also been targeted, but only traffic on the Southampton line was halted due to debris. Yet again, none of the damage caused adversely affected Fighter Command's defensive capability. What the defenders did not know, of course, was that the enemy was planning a maximum effort for the following day, which also explained the lack of nocturnal activity.

The day had seen a change in enemy strategy in that for the first-time mainland Britain came under daylight attack proper, as opposed to shipping and coastal targets. The fighting was almost exclusively over the 10 Group and 11 Group areas, frustrating 12 Group's pilots who stood idly by, playing patience and awaiting the scramble call that never or rarely came. To the irrepressible Squadron Leader Douglas Bader, commanding 242 Squadron at Coltishall in Norfolk, it was inconceivable that he and his Canadians should play a lesser role in the historic battle taking place further south.

Pilot Officer Denis Crowley-Milling:

> Naturally Douglas wanted to get us of 242 Squadron into the action. He used to say 'Why don't they get us airborne when the Germans are building up over the Pas-de-Calais?' He felt that we could then proceed south and meet the enemy formation at combat altitude head on.

Fighter Command's strategy, however, had been clearly thought out by wiser and infinitely more experienced men than Squadron Leader Bader – and 12 Group's obligation was to defend the industrial Midlands and North, in addition to patrolling 11 Group's airfields while Air Vice-Marshal Park's fighters were engaged further forward. Unfortunately this would soon become an issue, as we will explore in due course.

For Coastal Command, 14 August 1940 saw various sorties cancelled owing to the unfavourable weather. Nonetheless, over forty routine patrols and searches were completed, and an Oban-based 210 Squadron Sunderland flown by Flight Lieutenant Parry Jones had a lucky escape many miles out to sea; having taken off at 11.30 hrs to escort a convoy of fourteen merchantmen and two escorts:

> At 1335 hrs passed over SS *Brittanic*. At 1338 hrs an E/A attacked from astern, being sighted from the amidships gun

position. The gunner opened fire and gave the alarm signal. The E/A opened fire with cannon, one shell entering the starboard mainplane and exploding on entry and penetrating the starboard middle tank and pipelines. The tail gunner returned fire and tracer bullets were seen to enter the fuselage. The E/A passed overhead, making off in a southerly direction, the nose turret opening fire on the retreating aircraft. The E/A was a Focke-Wulf 'Condor'. At 1413 hrs course set for home, at 1508 hrs passed one aircraft carrier and three destroyers, arrived Oban and moored up 1555 hrs.' (ORB)

The bravery and tenacity of these Coastal Command crews must not be overlooked. Flying long and uncomfortable hours on patrols many miles from land, they performed an essential function that often went without recognition.

The weather also reduced 2 Group's intended operations, but the airfields at Morlaix, Dinard and St Omer were still attacked. By night, thirteen 2 Group Blenheims raided more airfields, but two Wyton-based 40 Squadron aircraft and an 18 Squadron Blenheim from West Raynham failed to return. Wellingtons, Whitleys and Hampdens attacked a variety of targets, airfields, factories and inland waterways, in France and Germany, and the Italian Caproni aircraft factory in Milan. Tragically, the only losses were two Whitleys of Dishforth's 51 Squadron which collided with barrage balloon cables, one near Langley, Buckinghamshire, the other near Eastleigh, Hampshire; both five-man crews were killed.

On this day, there was a clear indication of what lay in store for Britain if Operation *Seelöwe* succeeded. On 2 August 1940, Hitler personally appointed the Nazi *Gauleiter* Gustav Simon as Chief of Civil Administration in Luxembourg. Four days later Simon transferred all police powers from the Luxembourg *Gendarmerie* to German units, and on 14 August 1940 suspended the Grand Duchy's constitution. All existing political parties were abolished, and, in due course, Simon dissolved the Luxembourg Parliament and Council of State. By August 1942, Luxembourg was annexed to the German Reich, ceasing to be a state in its own right, and Luxembourger males in their early twenties were subjected to mandatory conscription. A general strike broke out in protest and was ruthlessly put down with martial law by Simon; twenty strike leaders were executed, 2,000 people were arrested and 290 student activists were deported to 're-education' camps in Germany. German became the official language exclusively, while Simon

WEDNESDAY, 14 AUGUST 1940

set about reducing Luxembourg's population of 3,500 Jews. At first, Jews were encouraged to voluntarily emigrate and by October 1941, only 750 remained in the country – but then deportations, first to ghettos, then to extermination camps, began. Of 634 Jews deported, only thirty-six survived, and throughout the war some 2,000 of Luxembourg's Jews perished. There can be no question that had Britain fallen, a similar fate lay in store.

Indeed, in June 1940, SS-*Oberführer* Walter Schellenberg, a high-ranking officer of the Nazi security service, the *Sicherheitsdienst des Reichsführer*-SS (SD), had been tasked with compiling the *Informationsheft* GB, a plan for the occupation of Britain post-*Seelöwe*. This handbook, which included information on British culture and institutions, included a sinister supplement: the *Sonderfahndungsliste* GB, or 'Special Wanted List GB', the infamous so-called 'Black Book', listing 2,300 prominent British citizens, including politicians, clergymen, academics and philanthropists, to be arrested immediately.

This, then, was what was at stake should the RAF, including all commands, falter or fail during this summer of summers – and it must never be lost sight of. Hitler was not bluffing. On this day, the *Führer* met with his eight new field marshals, presenting batons. Of *Seelöwe*, Admiral Raeder later recalled Hitler's words:

> I do not intend to carry out an operation whose risk is too great. I take the view that Britain's defeat does not depend upon invasion alone. It can be achieved by other means. But I want to continue the threat of an invasion. Preparations must, therefore, go ahead.

This was no deception operation, however: Hitler made clear that day that preparations must be genuine and completed by mid-September 1940.

Chapter 3

Thursday, 15 August 1940

The quiet night and start belied what was about to happen – which would go down in *Luftwaffe* history as 'Black Thursday'. If ever there was justification for Air Chief Marshal Dowding's strategy and deployment of Fighter Command, the events of this day provided it. Also, friction between 11 Group and 12 Group erupted into a full-scale row – which would ultimately have far-reaching and negative consequences for both Air Chief Marshal Dowding and Air Vice-Marshal Park. This was, therefore, a 'day of days' for more than one reason.

The previous evening ambitious plans had been revealed for large-scale raids by *Luftflotten* 2 and 3, synchronised, for the first and only time, with a major aerial assault on north-east England by *Generaloberst* Hans-Jürgen Stumpff's Norway-based *Luftflotte* 5 – which so far had played no significant part in the battle. The meteorologists, however, predicted unfavourable weather over England which was unlikely to clear, meaning that, as with 'Eagle Day', this massive attack would have to be postponed. Indeed, the much trumpeted 'Eagle Attack' had achieved little so far – incensing *Reichsmarschall* Göring. Given the predicted adverse weather reports, Göring summonsed the senior commanders of *Luflotten* 2 and 3 for a post-mortem conference at his opulent country residence, Carinhall, a large hunting estate north-east of Berlin in the Schorfheide forest. Consequently, the air fleet top brass were absent from the Channel coast at what would prove a crucial time.

Göring issued the following orders after the conference:

1. The fighter escort defences of our *Stuka* formations must be readjusted, as the enemy is concentrating his fighters against our *Stuka* operations. It appears necessary to allocate three fighter *Gruppen* to each *Stuka Gruppe*, one of these fighter *Gruppen* remains with the *Stukas*, and dives with them to the attack; the second flies ahead over the target at medium altitude and engages the fighter defences; the

THURSDAY, 15 AUGUST 1940

third protects the whole attack from above. It will also be necessary to escort *Stukas* returning from the attack over the Channel.
2. Night attacks on shipping targets are only fruitful when the night is so clear that careful aim can be taken.
3. More importance must be attached to cooperation between members of individual aircrews. Seasoned crews are not to be broken up except in cases of utmost urgency.
4. The incident of V/LG 1 on 13 August shows that certain unit commanders have not yet learnt the importance of clear orders.
5. I have repeatedly given orders that twin-engine fighters are only to be employed where the range of other fighters is inadequate, or where it is for the purpose of assisting our single-engine aircraft to break off combat. Our stocks of twin-engine fighters are not great, and we must use them as economically as possible.
6. Until further orders, operations are to be directed exclusively against the enemy Air Force, including the targets of the enemy aircraft industry allocated to the different *Luftflotten*. Shipping targets, and particularly large naval vessels, are only to be attacked where circum-stances are especially propitious. For the moment, other targets should be ignored. We must concentrate our efforts on the destruction of the enemy Air Forces. Our night attacks are essentially dislocation raids, made so that the enemy defences and population shall be allowed no respite. Even these, however, should where possible be directed against Air Force targets.
7. My orders regarding the carrying out of attacks by single aircraft under cover of cloud conditions have apparently not been correctly understood. Where on one afternoon fifty aircraft are despatched without adequate preparation on individual missions, it is probable that the operation will be unsuccessful and very costly. I therefore repeat that such sorties are to be undertaken only by specially selected volunteer crews, who have made a prolonged and intensive study of the target, the most suitable method of attack, and the particular navigational problems involved. By no means all our crews are qualified to undertake such tasks.
8. KGr100 (bombers) is also in future to operate against the enemy Air Force and aircraft industry.
9. It is doubtful if there is any point in continuing the attacks on radar sites, in view of the fact that not one of those attacked has so far been put out of operation.

10. The systematic designation of alternative targets would appear frequently to lead to certain targets being attacked which have absolutely no connection with our strategic aims. It must therefore be achieved that even alternative targets are of importance in the battle against the enemy Air Force.
11. The Commanders-in-Chief of the *Luftflotten* are to report to me on the question of the warnings to be given during enemy air penetrations over the Reich. At present, the warnings are causing a loss of output whose consequences are far graver than those caused by the actual bomb damage. In addition, the frequent air raid warnings are leading to nervousness and strain among the population of Western Germany. On the other hand, we must take into account the risk of heavy loss of life should an attack be launched before a warning has been given.

These orders were clear: instead of attacking the 'lightship off Dover', the *Luftflotten* were to prioritise the destruction of the RAF and the British aircraft industry. Issues concerning inappropriate deployment of the Me 110, and limited numbers thereof, are highlighted in addition to indications that the *Stuka* was proving extremely vulnerable to RAF fighters. The *Luftwaffe* chief was also critical of the previous day's deployment by *Luftflotte* 3 of so many unescorted lone bombers, leading to heavy losses. That attacks on RDF sites were to be suspended, however, provides firm evidence that the vital importance of radar to the defenders was still not fully appreciated – and this was definitely too hasty considering that Ventnor had, in fact, been taken offline by the attack on 12 August 1940. This, however, was a clear fault of *Luftwaffe* intelligence – not Göring's. Popular narrative often presents the *Reichsmarschall* as an incompetent, flamboyant, buffoon, but these sensible orders, taking aside the RDF issue, contradict that caricature.

Inevitably, the day's first interception was a reconnaissance snooper, a Do 17, probably of 3(F)/31, which 'B' Flight of 602 Squadron, recently arrived at Westhampnett from Church Fenton, engaged at 07.40 hrs fifteen miles south of Portland and sent into the sea off Ventnor; there were no survivors.

By mid-morning the conditions over southern England suddenly changed: blue skies prevailed and high pressure foretold of fine weather. With *Luftflotte* 2 chiefs Kesselring and Lörzer, and *Jagdfliegerführer* Osterkamp all away at Carinhall, executive authority had been entrusted to *Oberst* Paul Deichmann, the II *Fliegerkorps* Chief-of-Staff. Deichmann was of the opinion that Göring's reluctance to launch this massive assault was

THURSDAY, 15 AUGUST 1940

only because of the poor weather – which no longer applied. Surprised by the improving conditions, Deichmann signalled all units, which had already been brought to readiness as planned, despite the weather, that the proposed attacks would now go ahead. The intention was to saturate the British defences on a vast front, from Exeter to Newcastle: target RAF airfields. Poor intelligence, however, once more led to questionable target selection, given that, as usual, certain of the airfields selected for bombardment were unconnected with Fighter Command. Nonetheless, Deichmann's order had supercharged the three *Luftflotten* with heavy activity from Cherbourg to Aalborg. Having sent his signal, Diechmann then hasted to the 'Holy Mountain', *Luftflotte* 2's underground bunker beneath Cap Blanc Nez, where the operations officer, *Oberstleutnant* Herbert Rieckhoff, had just received a signal from Berlin cancelling offensive operations owing to bad weather. It was too late, though, as *Luftwaffe* units were already taking-off, and in view of the improved weather, Deichmann refused to recall the formations. The attack was on – and on a scale hitherto unseen in aerial warfare.

Between 10.45 hrs and 11.10 hrs, RDF detected a formation of '30+' assembling over Cap Gris Nez and moving north across the Channel. This was actually sixty *Stukas* of *Hauptmann* Anton Keil's II/StG1 and *Hauptmann* Bernd von Brauchitsch's IV(St)/LG 1 (a son of *Feldmarschall* Walther von Brautchitsch, Commander-in-Chief of the German army), escorted by the Me 109s of, among other units, II and III/JG 26. The dive-bombers' targets were the coastal airfields of Hawkinge and Lympne.

In response, between 11.05 hrs and 11.10 hrs, the Biggin Hill Sector Controller scrambled eleven 501 Squadron Hurricanes, led by Flight Lieutenant George Stoney, from Hawkinge with orders to patrol base at varying heights; at 11.18 hrs, twelve Spitfires of 54 Squadron were ordered off from Manston, with the 'order "patrol behind Dover and engage enemy fighters" becoming as familiar as the old convoy patrols' (ORB). With the Spitfires operating further forward, at 11.20 hrs 56 Squadron's Hurricanes went up from Rochford to cover Manston; at 11.25 hrs 615 Squadron was scrambled from Kenley and vectored to Dungeness.

The two formations of *Stukas* crossed the coast north of Dungeness at 11.29 hrs, then turned North. A minute later, south of Folkestone, 501 Squadron went into action. Pilot Officer Robert Dafforn:

> E/A were first sighted five miles south of Folkestone (twenty Ju 87s and six Me 109s) heading towards Hawkinge.

> I singled out a Ju 87 and did a No 1 Attack from rather below. E/A started to smoke and dived and I dived away. I was unable to see what happened to E/A.
>
> I then singled out another Ju 87 and did a No 1 Attack from dead astern. Eleven second burst from 300 yards gradually closing. E/A started smoking and diving. I broke away but was unable to see what was happening to E/A.
>
> My ammunition was now finished but I noticed two pilots in the sea, three miles south of Folkestone, so I attracted the attention of a boat in Folkestone Harbour and then circled the two pilots. The latter were eventually picked up by MTBs from Dover. I returned to base and pancaked.

According to the 501 Squadron's ORB, 'The enemy formation was broken up and fourteen E/A were destroyed or damaged.' Me 109s of II/JG 51, however, counter-attacked, falling on the Hurricanes from high above, shooting down Flight Lieutenants John Gibson and Alan Putt, both of whom baled out, and damaging the aircraft of the Polish Flying Officer Stefan Witorzenc, who returned safely to Hawkinge.

Although 'A' Flight of 615 Squadron patrolled over Dungeness and 'saw nothing but Spitfires' (ORB), at 11.40 hrs, Pilot Officer Keith Lofts, Blue 3 of 615 Squadron, was with nine other Hurricanes of 'B' Flight patrolling over Folkestone at 11,000ft, flying north-east:

> I noticed six Me 109s diving down from the sun onto Green Section who were behind. I gave the 'Tally Ho' and broke left with Blue Leader (Flying Officer Anthony Eyre) and noticed an Me 109 following down a Hurricane which was throwing out smoke. I got on the tail of the Me 109 and gave him a continual burst until ammunition was expended. He pulled up from dive and burst into flames. I then broke away and looked to see if any more E/A were on my tail. During the attack Blue Leader also attacked this E/A from my right and confirms this report. The above Me 109 is shared with Flying Officer Eyre.

Eyre reported having seen the Me 109 'burst into flames', the pilot 'baled out as the aircraft started to spin. I circled him in the sea but several others were doing the same so I returned and rearmed at Hawkinge … The parachutist was picked up by a rowing boat from shore.'

THURSDAY, 15 AUGUST 1940

The enemy pilot was *Feldwebel* Otto Steigenberger of 5/JG 51, who was captured. The smoking Hurricane was that of Pilot Officer Anthony Truran, whose aircraft was damaged by Steigenberger, being hit by:

> A cannon shell in fuselage which caught alight and fortunately went out and one shell in wing, near petrol tank. He managed to land his machine safely at Kenley in spite of shrapnel wounds in his leg. Flying Officer Eyre and Pilot Officer Lofts brought down the aircraft which had attacked Pilot Officer Truran. (ORB)

Pilot Officer David Evans' Hurricane was also shot-up, although he 'landed at Hawkinge with bullet holes through his glycol tank' (ORB). Sergeant Derrick Halton, who was shot down by an Me 109 and crashed into the sea (not 'Seal', as reported elsewhere); the 21-year-old had been married less than a year, and remains missing. Although Steinberger was unable to return to France and file a combat claim, *Hauptmann* Horst 'Jacob' Tietzen, *Staffelkapitän* of 5/JG 51, claimed two Hurricanes destroyed over Folkestone during this action, and *Unteroffizier* Rudolf Helber recorded his first victory.

No.54 Squadron engaged the enemy between 11.18 hrs and 12.15 hrs, over Dover and Folkestone:

> Large formations of Me 109s scattered before the squadron's approach over Dover; proceeding to Hawkinge further He 113s [*sic*] were met; their tactics of 'milling' and 'circling' did not bring our pilots into the trap set for them. Sergeant Norman Lawrence showed his genuine hatred for the Ju 87 by shooting down three of them in flames before himself falling victim to an enemy fighter. He had a fortunate escape when his machine crashed into the sea, taking him down with it. Rescued by the Navy he is now in Dover Hospital, suffering from shock. Sergeant Wojiech Klozinski (Polish), our other casualty, was shot down near Ashford, but is making progress in hospital there. For these loses we claim four E/A destroyed (including a new type, Ju 87, to our list) and three damaged. Flight Lieutenant Al Deere claimed an Me 109 destroyed Flying Officer Desmond McMullen, Flight Lieutenant George Gribble and Pilot Officer Pelham Hopkin were responsible for the damaged E/A. (ORB)

During the attack, bombs were dropped on Dover, Hythe and Folkestone; RAF Hawkinge ORB:

> A Bombing attack, 1135 to 1145 hrs by about twenty Dorniers, Heinkel IIIs [*sic*] and Junkers 87 flying at various heights from 300 to 2,000ft. Attack came from all angles. Ground defence guns fired as follows: V.1. 27 rounds, 1 hit claimed; V.2. 23 rounds, 2 hits on Heinkel III's claimed; L.M.G. 160 rounds; V.3. 2 rounds, gun jammed; V.4. 18 rounds; L.M.G. 4 rounds. One 'plane hit and seen falling, believed Dornier, and the hit was confirmed by V.1. About twenty bombs were dropped, two of the heaviest (about 250 Kilos) hit hangars, and smaller (25 or 50 Kilos) on aerodrome surface. One small barrack block destroyed. There were no casualties. (ORB)

Manston was also hit, according to the Station ORB, at 12.10 hrs:

> The station was again attacked by nine Me 110s. They were heavily engaged by ground defences and two E/A were destroyed – one by a RA post (Bofors) and one by a RAF post (Hispano). Two hangars on the east camp were partially wrecked and damage was caused to a Bellman and a Bessonneau hangar. One large crater made in the centre of the aerodrome.

The only serious damage was to Lympne airfield, where hangars were damaged and the paint store destroyed; power and water services were severed and the station sick quarters suffered a direct hit. Yet again, this had no effect on Fighter Command, however, and the station was operational again forty-eight hours later.

No.56 Squadron, patrolling further to the north-east, over Rochford, saw no action.

For the next two hours small formations of enemy aircraft prowled about the Channel, three RAF fighter squadrons being scrambled as insurance against an attack developing – which it did not. These feints may well have been to divert attention from the huge raid about to be made on north-east England by *Luftflotte* 5 – if so, this confirms how little *Luftwaffe* intelligence understood regarding Britain's air defences: *Luftflotte* 2 had the attention of 11 Group, certainly, but *Luftflotte* 5's intended targets were of

THURSDAY, 15 AUGUST 1940

no concern to Air Vice-Marshal Park, being the responsibility of Air Vice-Marshal Richard Saul's northern 13 Group – to which the day's events now memorably shifted.

According to *Luftwaffe* air intelligence chief *Oberst* 'Beppo' Schmid in May 1939, Fighter Command's defensive system only provided for the aerial protection of London, leaving the remainder of the country open to attack. On 16 July 1940, Schmid – an ambitious and astute officer – reported that both the Spitfire and Hurricane were inferior to the Me 109, but conceded, somewhat surprisingly given his penchant for telling the *Reichsmarschall* what he wanted to hear rather than the actual facts, that the Me 110 was superior to the Hurricane but not the Spitfire. In the same report, Schmid – surely the worst air intelligence officer of all time, stated the Hampden to be Britain best bomber, when it was actually the most obsolete type in service with the RAF. On 8 August 1940, Schmid had informed all *Luftflotten* and *Fliegerkorps* that:

> As the British fighters are controlled from the ground by R/T their forces are tied to their respective ground stations and are thereby restricted in mobility … Consequently the assembly of strong fighter forces at determined points and at short notice is not to be expected. A massed German attack on a target area can therefore count of the same considerations of light fighter opposition as in attacks on widely scattered targets.

Schmid believed, therefore, that Fighter Command would be swamped by mass attacks, and this view informed tactical decisions on 15 August. Having failed to properly understand the benefits of radar, Schmid missed the point: owing to RDF, the assembly of large formations was actually easier to detect and guide defending fighters to intercept. Schmid was also, of course, unaware of ULTRA – and decrypts now in the public domain confirm that from German signal traffic, Air Chief Marshal Dowding was aware that on 15 August, *Luftflotte* 5 was to attack the north-east, and that seven raids in total were planned for that day over a broad front. Schmid also overestimated Fighter Command's losses, so *Luftwaffe* chiefs believed that despite certain setbacks, Fighter Command was already well on the way to annihilation – during the period 12–19 August, for example, Schmid believed 644 RAF fighters had been destroyed, when in reality that figure was 141. The failings of Schmid's *Luftwaffe* air intelligence department, *Abteilung* 5, were about to come into sharp focus for *Luftflotte* 5.

BATTLE OF BRITAIN ATTACK OF THE EAGLES

The first threat to 13 Group materialised at 12.08 hrs, when RDF forewarned of 20+ over the North Sea, opposite the Firth of Forth. Two more formations were soon indicated, all three flying south-west and heading for the north-east coast above Tynemouth, between Acklington and Blyth. This overall formation was much bigger than shown on the radar screen: sixty-three He 111s of *Oberstleutnant* Hermann Busch's I and *Major* Günther Wolfien's III/KG 26, all based at Stavanger/Sola, escorted by twenty-one Me 110s of *Hauptmann* Werner Restemeyer's Stavanger-Forus-based I/ZG 76, bound for RAF airfields at Dishforth and Linton-on-Ouse. Owing to the distance of nearly 400 miles between Stavanger and Dishforth, with additional flying time for take-off, assembly, attack and landing, and allowances for any navigational errors, it was impossible for Me 109s to escort the bombers, and even Restemeyer's Me 110s had to be fitted with auxiliary '*Dakelbauch*' (Dachshund) fuel tanks to make the trip. In an attempt to confuse the British RDF, Restemeyer's 'Dora' was also fitted with a radio jamming device operated by his back-seater for this trip, none other than *Fliegerkorps* X's chief signals officer, *Hauptmann* Hartwich. Given subsequent events, it is likely that other Me 110s also carried jamming devices.

At Drem, Flight Lieutenant Archie McKellar's 'B' Flight of 605 Squadron was 'available' when scrambled, hurrying into the air ten minutes later, at 12.05 hrs, to patrol Acklington-Tyneside. At 12.20 hrs, ten Spitfires of 72 Squadron, led by Flight Lieutenant Ted Graham, were ordered into the air from Acklington to investigate the raid now approaching the Farne Islands. At 12.42 hrs, the Hurricanes of Acklington's 79 Squadron were also scrambled to patrol the Farne Islands, followed by the Spitfires of Catterick's 41 Squadron at 12.45 hrs which were ordered to patrol ten miles north of base. If the approaching enemy aircrews expected to meet little or no fighter opposition, based upon Schmid's assessment, they were about to receive a sharp shock – although arguably the use of radio counter-measures suggests that a strong defence was anticipated.

No.72 Squadron was first to shout 'Tally Ho!', at 12.45 hrs, as Flight Lieutenant Ted Graham recalled: 'I was leading 72 Squadron, and the German formation was quite a sight, something I will never forget, and I must confess to have reported the enemy in a rather excited manner!'

Graham officially reported that

> The squadron, with a leading section of three aircraft, another of four and a rearguard of four more protecting the rear and

THURSDAY, 15 AUGUST 1940

flanks encountered over 100 E/A, He 111, Ju 88 [*sic*] and Me 110 types, thirty miles east of Farne Islands. The squadron was flying at 22,000ft on course 020° with the enemy well below, flying west in mainly vic formations, line abreast and line astern. I decided to attack the enemy of his right flank, which was approx. three miles northward. Circling the flank I warned the rearguard of escort fighters and then ordered the squadron to attack, leading my Blue Section in a No 3 Stern Chase onto three He 111s which were flying behind and slightly above the enemy preceding vics. I opened fire at 250 yards, closing to about 30 yards, and saw smoke burst from the fuselage and port engine. Intense return fire was encountered but this was inaccurate. On diving away from he I spotted an Me 110 circling above me, so I dived straight for the clouds, 900ft below.

Pilot Officer Douglas 'Snowy' Winter:

I was Green 4 acting as rearguard in the squadron formation. As E/A were sighted Blue and Red Sections prepared to attack ... in turn and Green 1 and 2 were then on the port side of the E/A. They then attacked, and I was left on my own – Green 3 having attacked himself by then. Still acting as rearguard I flew back and forth over the combats then taking place, looking for more fighters which did not appear.

Then I decided to attack myself at the same time seeing a He 111 with its wheels down gliding seawards. I followed it for a while until I saw it hit the sea and disappear. Climbing up again I saw about 2,000ft below me at 16,000ft a circle of six Me 110s with a Spitfire in the circle. I waited until one Me 110 was detached a little from the circle on the Spitfire's tail and dived to attack. I waited until I was about 100 yards from it and opened fire. I saw bullets entering pilot's cockpit. The E/A turned onto its back and dived seawards, eventually crashing in the sea. I observed no return fire.

Climbing up again I found another ring of six Me 110s with three Spitfires in the circle; one of the Me 110s flew to one side and I again dived to attack. In the first burst I opened at about 150 yards and the port engine started to smoke. I fired two more bursts which entered pilot's cockpit. The E/A dived vertically for the sea. I followed it through the cloud and saw it crash into the sea. No return fire was observed.

One of the Me 110s destroyed by Winter was also attacked by Flying Officer Oswald St John Pigg, a 'Geordie' defending his home coastline:

I followed him down to the cloud layer at 9,000ft, where I temporarily lost him. I continued on through the clouds and was just in time to see the E/A dive almost vertically into the sea on my port side. I immediately dived onto his splash mark and exposed my cine-camera in order to confirm enemy loss. I then climbed up again through the clouds, but as I did not contact any further E/A, I returned to base and landed.

In this hectic action, for no loss 72 Squadron claimed eleven enemy aircraft destroyed, three probables and one damaged.

As 72 Squadron withdrew to rearm and refuel, the enemy formation droned onwards towards Seaham and Barnard Castle, over which it was engaged by the Spitfires of 41 Squadron at 13.00 hrs. The Spitfires were led by Pilot Officer George Bennions, who sighted the enemy over Bishop Auckland in a

mass arrowhead formation of fifty bombers, massed in the arrowhead, escorted by forty fighters 500 yards astern and 400ft above. Yellow 1 detailed Green Section [1: Pilot Officer Edward Shipman; 2: Flying Officer Ronald 'Wally' Wallens, and 3: Sergeant Frank Usmar] and later Blue Section [1: Flying Officer Tony Lovell; 2: Sergeant Isaac Howitt, and 3: Pilot Officer Gerald Langley] to attack escort fighters, to allow Yellow [1: Pilot Officer Bennions; 2: Flight Lieutenant Norman Ryder; 3: Pilot Officer Oliver Morrogh-Ryan, and 4: Pilot Officer Robert Boret] and Red [1: Flying Officer John MacKenzie, a New Zealander; 2: Sergeant Roy Ford, and 3: Pilot Officer Eric Lock] sections to get at the bombers. Although this was done, the escorting fighters maintained formation and Red and Yellow Sections were forced to carry out a dummy attack from the beam. Yellow and Red broke away underneath and climbed behind main formation of enemy fighters. Went

THURSDAY, 15 AUGUST 1940

in to attack rearguard or three aircraft and our formation split up and a dogfight ensued with the escort fighters and a few stragglers from the bombers.

Bombers maintained formation apart from rearguard fighters. Fighters made no attempt to attack our aircraft, or dummy attack, and even when attacked from astern only aircraft actually attacked attempted to engage our aircraft ... All pilots report E/A fast and used 12lbs boost to catch them.

Blue 1 saw three Me 110s turn round in line astern and attacked the last of the three, No 1 Attack, 250 yards, One burst, seven seconds, terrific explosion and flames obviously from tank with partial disintegration of E/A. Attacked another Me 110. Many pieces fell away and E/A seemed out of control.

Blue 2 followed Blue 1 and went for second of three Me 110s. Gave three short bursts from astern. After third burst saw smoke from starboard engine and E/A fall away to starboard. Blue 2 broke away and went after another Me 110 – gave a full ring deflection shot.

Blue 3 did not fire, he spun off a turn and did not get back into combat.

Green 1 followed Blue in line astern but section of five E/A turned and came straight for Green Section, head-on. Green 1 fired for 2 seconds, head-on, 400 yards. E/A broke away to port. No noticed effect. Then attacked another E/A with several deflection shots – very short bursts, no apparent result. Then got on tail of another Me 110 and fired rest of ammunition, one burst putting E/A starboard engine out of action. Engine was smoking and stopped. E/A broke away rapidly to port and dived into cloud, apparently out of control.

Green 2 ... saw the three aircraft described by Green 1. Gave a burst of two seconds at 100 yards from astern of Me 110. Saw fire enter E/A but did not stop to observe effect. Turned and climbed and saw another E/A below and did a diving quarter attack, giving up to two rings deflection, pulling through E/A from tail to nose. Burst was about seven seconds. Saw smoke and bits fly from E/A which then went into cloud layer.

Green 3 saw Green 2 first attack and saw an Me 110 cross to attack Green 2. As E/A passed across sights at fifty yards range, Green 3 gave short burst but was unable to observe effect as an He 111 was coming straight for him. Gave very quick burst and E/A blew to pieces and three Green 3 about 40ft into the air. Another Spitfire then came past as if it had attacked same E/A, but no other pilot remarks on attack on He 111. Green 3 then came down to 7,000ft and saw Do 17 [*sic*] come out of cloud and did a beam attack, firing short burst at 80 yards. E/A went into cloud and was lost – although Green 3 went above cloud. (41 Squadron composite combat report)

Among 41 Squadron's pilots was Pilot Officer Eric 'Sawn Off' Lock (Red 3), a Salopian known as such for his short stature and who recorded his first combat success in this action:

Red 3, after dummy attack went in with Red 1 and 2, sighted an Me 110 and fired at it, 400 yards, one second burst from dead astern. No effect. About to break away but managed to get another burst of three seconds at 200 yards into E/A. Starboard engine caught fire and E/A went down to port. Followed E/A down, firing three bursts of one second. Could see rear gunner of E/A firing, but this soon ceased and port engine caught fire. E/A went into cloud on fire. Red 3 suffered two hits in port wing: one in main spar, one in aileron.

Given that Lock soon became one of Fighter Command's top-scoring pilots, it was a historic occasion.

So the fighting continued, with 41 Squadron ultimately claiming four enemy aircraft destroyed, five probably destroyed and four damaged, all for no loss.

The Hurricanes of 79 Squadron also engaged, according to the AHB narrative, at 13.00 hrs, although no combat reports appear to have survived:

Controller reported large raid approaching base. About sixty bombers were seen flying South over the sea off Amble, and several Me 110s which were attacked, two being shot down and one probable. The Squadron split up but rejoined over

THURSDAY, 15 AUGUST 1940

Blyth and when ordered to patrol Usworth at 10,000ft about sixty Do 215s [*sic*] were seen approaching Newcastle and two squadrons of Me 110s. Our fighters attacked and one Do 215 was believed to be shot down near Newcastle. Pilot Officer Millington attacked a formation of sixty to eighty He 111s, alone, and shot down three. (ORB)

The (anonymous) Catterick Intelligence Officer later submitted the following report to the 13 Group Intelligence Officer:

> Pilot Officer Millington attacked He 111. E/A emitted black smoke and burst into flames. Went down through clouds out of control. Attacked a second He 111 after a few short bursts. E/A burst into flames and large pieces flew off E/A, which turned sharply to starboard and vanished through cloud in steep dive. Attacked a third He 111. Large quantity of black smoke emitted by E/A. E/A last seen in shallow dive heading through clouds. This claim seems to be for two confirmed and one possibly damaged. Flying Officer Lord Guisborough at present interrogating pilots of 79 Squadron ['Gizzy' was 41 Squadron's Intelligence Officer].
>
> Pilot Officer Millington states that AA fire ceased when he attacked E/A and that AA officer giving a talk on the raids stated that his battery ceased fire on the approach of our fighters. Pilot Officer Millington suggests that this might be the same battery as he observed to cease fire and that they might be able to give conformation.

The outcome of this investigation into Pilot Officer William Millington's combat is unknown; an Australian later decorated with the DFC, the 23-year-old pilot would not survive the Battle of Britain. In this combat, Millington was badly shot-up but returned safely to base.

For 605 'County of Warwick' Squadron of the AAF, it would also be, the squadron diarist noted, 'A red letter day ... Big air battle off Newcastle', the Hurricanes engaging at 13.15 hrs. Flight Lieutenant Archie McKellar:

> I was Blue 1, Commander of 'B' Flight which left Drem at 1205 hrs and patrolled Acklington–Tyneside area at

10,000–20,000ft. Owing to lack of orders from Control I kept my Flight patrolling round Newcastle as I considered it to be the most vulnerable and important target for the enemy. At 1310 hrs Blue and Green Sections observed large formations of E/A approaching Tyneside from the SE at 12,000–14,000ft. I ordered Blue and Green Sections into line astern and to follow me up into the sun to do a diving attack on the large formation. I also called up Poldar [Sector Control] and informed them about the E/A and that Cockle [radio callsign of 605 Squadron] 'B' Flight were going in to engage the large formation, and did a dive attack in formation on last E/A of the first formation, which was stepped-up in box formation. I gave a three second burst from 250 yards and the E/A dropped off in a spiral dive. While carrying out this attack I was hit in the wings by the rear E/A from behind. By then we were now over Newcastle so I ordered 'B' Flight to make individual attacks as I considered harrying tactics to be the best way of breaking up the formation and defeating the object of the enemy which appeared to be the bombing of Tyneside. I accordingly climbed up and noticed a Hurricane engaging in a stern attack with two E/A of the second formation. I accordingly attacked with full beam attack, giving a two to three second burst without other visible result than chasing the E/A away from the Hurricane which turned out to belong to 607 Squadron. I then climbed up again into the sun and engaged the leader of the second formation with a full beam attack following No 2 of the formation with a quarter attack, giving an eight second burst from 400ft on the No 1, twenty-five yards on No 2 and breaking through the formation. As a result of this attack I saw greyish white smoke issuing from the engines of the E/A. Both E/A probably crashed into the sea, but I had no time to follow their downward course as I was breaking through the formation. After breaking and climbing I saw that the second formation now appeared to be three straggling aircraft which were trying to join up with the main formation, at the same time I could count seven E/A all spinning down into cloud and into the sea. I accordingly again climbed up into the sun and engaged

THURSDAY, 15 AUGUST 1940

the last straggler in a beam quarter attack from 100 – twenty yards with a three second burst, probably killing the top gunner. I saw grey smoke coming from the starboard engine of the E/A and as I was hit by the top gunner with cannon in my engine and wing roots, I flew west at 180 IAS and after twelve minutes flying made a landfall six miles south of west Hartlepool.

McKellar claimed one He 111 destroyed and three probables. Pilot Officers Christopher 'Bunny' Currant and Cyril Passy both claimed He 111s destroyed, and Currant shared another with Pilot Officer Ian Muirhead. In addition to McKellar's slightly damaged aircraft, Passy's Hurricane was also shot-up by return fire, as a result of which he crash-landed near Usworth but was safe. So too was Pilot Officer Kenneth Schadtler Law, who forced-landed his similarly damaged Hurricane on Hartlepool golf course, wounded and suffering from concussion.

At 13.15 hrs, 607 'County of Durham' Squadron of the AAF was scrambled from Usworth, near Newcastle, and went into action just a few miles from base, over Seaham:

> Five sections of Squadron in combat with about 40/60 He 111 and Do 17 [*sic*] E/A at sea eight miles east of Tyne. Casualties inflicted on enemy: confirmed six He 111, two Do 17; probable: five He 111, one Do 17. Damaged: four He 111, one Do 17. Unit aircraft and personnel loses: nil. (ORB)

Again, no individual combat reports appear to have survived, but as 605 Squadron's Flight Lieutenant McKellar went into action off Tyneside at 13.15 hrs and identified a 607 Squadron Hurricane, so 607 must have engaged minutes after take-off. Among 607's pilots that day was Pilot Officer Harry Welford, who later remembered:

> At 1230 hrs we of 607 Squadron were going off duty for 24 hours leave when the whole squadron was called to readiness. We heard from the Group Operations Room that there was a big 'flap' on, that is a warning of imminent enemy action along the NE coast. We waited out at dispersal points, at Flights, for half an hour, then scrambled in squadron formation. I was in a feverish state

of excitement and we quickly took off and climbed to our operational height of 20,000ft, ready to patrol the coast. We kept receiving messages over the R/T of forty or fifty plus bogeys approaching Newcastle from the north. Although we patrolled for over half an hour, we never saw a thing. Just as I was expecting the order to pancake, I heard the senior flight commander shout 'Tally Ho!', and 'Tally Ho' it bloody well was! There, on our port side at 9,000ft, must have been 120 bombers, all with swastikas and German crosses as large as life, having the gross impertinence to cruise down Northumberland and Durham's NE coast. These were the people who were going to bomb Newcastle and Sunderland, where our friends and families lived, we being an auxiliary unit raised from that local area.

I'd never seen anything like it. They were in two groups, one of about seventy, the other about forty, like two swarms of bees. There was no time to wait and so we immediately took up station and delivered No 3 attacks in sections. As only three Hurricanes at a time, flying along nicely in formation, attacked a line of twenty bombers, I didn't see how their gunners could miss us. We executed our attack, however, and despite the fact that I thought it was me being hit all over the place, it was their machines which started dropping out of the sky. In my excitement, during the next attack I only narrowly missed one of our own machines while doing a 'split-arse' breakaway – there couldn't have been more than 2ft between us! Eventually, spotting most of the enemy aircraft dropping down with only their undercarriage damaged, I chased a He 111 and filled the poor devil with lead until first one, then the other, engine stopped. I then enjoyed the sadistic satisfaction of watching the bomber crash into the North Sea. With the one I reckoned to have damaged with my first attack, these were my first bloods, and so I was naturally elated.

Once more, it had all gone wrong for the Germans. He 115 seaplanes had first flown a feint towards Montrose, intending to confuse the defences and divert attention from the main attacks, but this only served to alert 13 Group to the main threat. After first intercepted by 72 Squadron, the raiders had actually separated into two formations, one of which crossed the coast north of the Tyne – representing a serious navigational error, given that the intended targets were much further south. Strangely, the Me 110s made no attempt to cross the coast and some RAF pilots remarked on their impotency, making little effort to counter-attack, leading to a supposition that rear-gunners had been sacrificed to save weight for extra fuel. Under heavy attack, the He 111s largely dropped their bombs in the sea. The southerly force, apparently comprising bombers only, similarly bombed to no effect around Seaham Harbour, the only major damage caused being to civilian properties in Sunderland. Neither formation reached its intended target, and, in any case and yet again, neither Dishforth or Linton-on-Ouse were Fighter Command aerodromes – the irony being that even had they been successfully bombed Britain's defences would have remained unaffected.

Although RAF combat claims arising were wildly exaggerated, KG 26 lost eight He 111s while ZG 76 lost seven Me 110s – including the *Kommandeur* of I/ZG 76, *Hauptmann* Restemeyer, whose aircraft, it will be remembered, was fitted with a radio jamming device. In such a hectic combat involving so many aircraft, it is often impossible to ascertain who shot down who, but as Restemeyer's aircraft is known to have substantially caught fire, or possibly exploded, it appears likely that he was shot down by Flight Lieutenant Tony Lovell of 41 Squadron at 13.00 hrs; interestingly, 79 Squadron reported that 'R/T was very bad due to German interference which was present throughout the *whole* [my italics] of the engagement' (ORB) – so it appears that other aircraft also carried radio disrupting devices.

The defenders had achieved a remarkable victory, considering that no military objectives were hit and no RAF pilots were lost. Indeed, in the words of Basil Collier in the official history *The Defence of the United Kingdom*, '13 Group and the 7th Anti-Aircraft Division, commanded respectively by Air Vice-Marshal R.E. Saul and Major-General R.B. Pargiter, could justly claim to have fought one of the most successful air actions of the war.'

Meanwhile, ninety miles further south, another major action was in progress, as *Luftflotte* 5 attempted to overwhelm the defences. From Aalborg-West, fifty unescorted Ju 88s of *Oberstleutnant* Walter Loebel's KG 30 sallied forth to attack the RAF aerodrome at Driffield – another Bomber Command station in Yorkshire, situated in Fighter Command's 12 Group area of responsibility. At 12.39 hrs, RDF indicated a raid first estimated at 6+ but soon upgraded to 30+ heading for the coast below Scarborough. Forewarned, therefore, the 12 Group Controller brought 73 Squadron at Church Fenton to a state of readiness at 12.57 hrs, scrambling 'A' Flight five minutes later (according to Form 540, but 1245 hrs in Form 541) with orders to patrol Convoy *Arena* off the Humber. At 13.00 hrs the Spitfires of 616 'South Yorkshire' Squadron were scrambled to patrol east of Flamborough Head. Then, between 13.05 hrs and 13.10 hrs, the Defiants of 264 Squadron were sent up from Kirton-in-Lindsey, also ordered to patrol over *Arena*.

Oberleutnant Rudolf Kratz, *Stab*/KG 30:

> The weather was dreadful, so bad that one wouldn't have put a dog out in it. It rained, it poured down ... Against all expectations the rain stopped falling. Some engines were running already when the crews arrived at their aircraft in their cumbersome flying overalls and boots for a mission against the enemy. They all knew their target but what would the next hours bring them?
>
> Now our aircraft was ready to take-off. Exactly on time the engines roared away and drew us and our load of bombs into the sky, leaving the airfield behind us. One by one the rest of the aircraft took-off until behind us a string of aircraft followed at regular intervals. Slowly they got closer together and soon the formation had been established. The changing landscape was worth looking at, but not now, perhaps on the way back. We did not have the time for that at this point in the mission; our thoughts were set on course, altitude, weather and the like. The machine guns were readied for action. A few shots into the water? The coast had already left behind – and yes, it still shot all right, why shouldn't it?
>
> 'FT klar' [wireless transmitter all right] reported the wireless operator and things were cosy on board the aircraft. There wasn't any drama – no stick or machine gun 'convulsively gripped' and no 'sharp profiles of energetic men' as the correspondents would lead one to believe. The many missions we had flown together, the many battles fought together made talking unnecessary. We understood each other, through a simple gesture, through a smile.

THURSDAY, 15 AUGUST 1940

The land had disappeared some time ago and the white caps of breaking waves also vanished. Seen from above the sea had a strange sense of immobility. The intense cold, a sign of high altitude, made us think about oxygen.

'All right, masks on.' Unfortunately with masks donned one could no longer whistle or play tunes on the mouth-organ, but we made do with a murmured song. Time went by slowly.

'How long till the English coast?'

'Twenty minutes.'

The ammunition drums for the machine guns were placed within reach. Everyone was more attentive now. English fighters might appear from anywhere.

Visibility had become poor. The water and the sky merged into each other without a trace of horizon. It was misty. Any moment now the English coast would appear below. Had our navigation been correct? Nothing to be seen yet. Aircraft upon aircraft were flying with us. They wobbled up and down, carrying death. Our target: an English airfield.

What would it look like? We knew its layout accurately from the aerial photos taken during reconnaissance fights – every hangar, every barracks. But was it a sun-drenched field, with aircraft standing in front of the hangars, groundcrews busy as ever? Did they know we were on our way? Maybe the fighters had already taken-off, and shells were already being loaded into the barrels of the AA guns?

'The coast. The initial point.' No time left for thinking – there lay England, the lion's den. But the eagles were going to attack the lion in his lair and wound him grievously.

'Fighters to starboard ...' Three specks overflew us, disappeared to the rear and, after a diving turn, hung behind us.

'Your turn now'. The words disappeared in the rattle of our machine guns. In short bursts the volleys flew towards the first fighter. He turned away and the second one took his place. This one's fire was ineffective as well and both passed below and were shot at by our ventral gunner. Like hornets they swooshed through our formation, the roundels on their fuselage looking like eyes.

'Five fighters to port above,' reported the wireless operator calmly.

'Dammit,' the pilot said, but did not get agitated. We kept on flying towards our target. Staring before us we tried to locate the airfield amid the ragged clouds.

The fighters were the Spitfires of 616 Squadron, the pilots of which were about to fight their first major action of the war, engaging KG 30 at 13.15 hrs over the sea, five miles east of Flamborough Head. Among them was Group Captain Sir Hugh 'Cocky' Dundas, then a pilot officer, who later recalled:

> As we of 616 Squadron were having lunch and at thirty minutes notice to fly, we really thought that the Controller had taken leave of his senses, but he was insistent, all the time the Controller becoming increasingly insistent and excited. A phone call to the Officers' Mess, where we were dining, sent us running to our cars, and as we sped around the perimeter track we saw our groundcrews urgently preparing our Spitfires for flight. Disembarking, we ran to our aircraft and took off urgently. The Controller's still excited voice ordered us to head out to sea and intercept a big raid incoming south of Flamborough Head. I have to say that the whole scenario appeared most unlikely, but we welcomed anything that broke the monotony of convoy patrols.
>
> We flew at top speed, not as a squadron or even in flights or sections, but individually we raced across the coast and out to sea. About fifteen miles out to sea I saw them, to our left front and slightly below, twin-engine German bombers, flying in a loose and scattered formation towards our coastline. I switched on my reflector sight, setting the range for 250 yards, and turned the gun button to fire. I curved towards the nearest bomber, the rear gunner of which fired at me but this stopped after my first burst. The bomber fell back, gushed black smoke and fell steeply towards the sea. All around Spitfires were jockeying for position to fire at enemy aircraft, jostling each other out of the way to get in a shot. I then chased a damaged bomber, which was heading out to sea, but by the time I shot it down I was a long way out and the sky was empty. As I was running low on ammunition by that time, hot and elated I decided to return to Leconfield.

THURSDAY, 15 AUGUST 1940

Pilot Officer Lionel 'Buck' Casson:

> About ten miles SE of Flamborough the section was ordered into line astern to attack Ju 88 approaching coast. This aircraft had already been attacked by No 3 of Blue Section when the leader of Green Section went into attack. As I received no further orders I broke from line astern into echelon starboard as the E/A started a diving turn to the right. The aircraft appeared to be severely damaged and I broke away completely after giving it two short bursts, but my leader followed it right down below the cloud. I then returned inland and was just crossing the coast about two miles north of Flamborough when I saw a Ju 88 making out to sea at about 5,000ft. I turned and gave him two bursts of about three seconds, opening fire at about 300 yards, in quarter attacks. The enemy then commenced to dive steeply until about 1,000ft above the sea. I followed down and gave him further series of short bursts until the rear-gunner ceased fire and the aircraft dived to about 150ft above the sea. At this stage another Spitfire joined in [Pilot Officer Dundas] and when I had used up all my ammunition I broke off and he continued to fire until his ammunition was also expended. The aircraft appeared to be severely damaged and it is doubtful if it would return to its base safely as the rear-gunner had ceased firing completely and just before we returned to our base to rearm, the E/A's port engine was seen to be smoking badly.

Without loss, 616 Squadron claimed the destruction of eight Ju 88s destroyed, four probables and two damaged in what forever after became known as the 'Junkers Party'.

While 73 Squadron's 'A' Flight patrolled Hornsea, the Hurricanes were ordered to reinforce 616 Squadron over Flamborough Head, joining the battle at 13.20 hrs, three minutes after the raiders crossed the coast. Sergeant Alexander McNay reported:

> We intercepted about fifty – sixty Ju 88s. I selected one and fired a burst at about 800 yards. He turned out of formation. I closed to about 400 yards and fired another long burst. He

> jettisoned his bombs into the sea. My next burst caused bits to fly off and his starboard engine to smoke rather badly. The panel blew off my port machine-guns and I lost control for a few seconds. I was heading back to Leconfield from Flamborough for a new panel when I saw another Junkers at about 50ft. I fired a longish burst from abeam which appeared to rake his wings, engines and pilot's cabin. Coming round on his tail I fired about half a dozen short bursts. He had meantime lost so much height that he broke some 'phone wires. I pursued him for about five miles west of Hornsea to about ten miles east of it, where he suddenly struck the sea, appearing to explode. All this action was going on at heights varying from fifty to 5ft over the sea. I returned west and at the same point as before, five miles west of Hornsea, I met another Junkers travelling on the tree tops. I came round on his tail and fired two short bursts into him. My next burst was longer, about two seconds, which I fired at about 200 yards. My ammunition was finished so I broke off the attack, climbing up to his starboard. When I last saw him he appeared to be doing a very gentle side-slip. When I straightened out he had disappeared. I returned to my 'drome as there were a number of enemy machines about and I was defenceless. Later that day the wreckage was found by some of our pilots and civilians gave them details indicating that it was my target.

McNay was credited with two Ju 88s destroyed, the aircraft brought down over land being one of 3/KG 30 which crashed at Hamilton Hill Farm, Barnstown, near Bridlington; the crew were captured unhurt.

Pilot Officer Donald Scott, seven miles south-east of Flamborough Head:

> E/A on seeing us kept straight on. I carried out a stern attack on one E/A which I followed over land, giving him three bursts. E/A then turned as if he was making east again and just before he dived into cloud I gave him three further short bursts. No effect from my first three bursts but as he went into cloud a parachute came out of the top of the cabin and became entangled in the tail unit. I then turned on another

THURSDAY, 15 AUGUST 1940

E/A going east. Carried out stern attack, firing two bursts. E/A dived very steeply toward cloud. Gave three more bursts as he entered cloud. When I came out of cloud I followed down and saw E/A blow up on ground. A flash and black smoke. Then saw pieces of E/A spread over ground, scars on the ground and what appeared to be two craters. Also an open parachute nearby. E/A fired at me, probably from top gunner. Two hits on my port wing and one just below glycol pump on an engine-bearer strut [serial number of Hurricane unrecorded, as is this damage anywhere else; known to have been TP-D].

This Ju 88, of 4/KG 30, crashed and burned out at Hunmanby, killing the crew. Pilot Officer Scott and Sergeant John Griffin later inspected the wreckage of the Ju 88 destroyed by McNay, and this one, in which they 'Found ammunition and Very pistol dated June 1940, and number plate off engine.'

Pilot Officer Peter Carter reported sighting the raiders at 13.08 hrs:

Flying westward in very open formation at 270 mph. Usual crosses on E/A, with very dark green camouflage. E/A came straight on after sighting us. I made a stern attack on one E/A, giving him three bursts at 350 yards. I immediately noticed both propellers stopping and E/A started to glide down. I then broke away satisfied that the E/A was finished. E/A fired a long burst which went wide of me. I then made a stern attack on another E/A below me. I gave him two or three short bursts which silenced his rear-gunner who had been firing at me with no effect. I gave E/A two further short bursts as he went down towards the sea and followed him to 1,000ft when I saw him cartwheel into sea about four miles from the coast and six miles south of Flamborough Head. At same time I saw another E/A crash in sea. Previously I had seen Red 1 break away from him. I climbed back to 5,000ft above clouds which were then 7/10ths. I attacked another E/A from underneath with deflection and gave long burst exhausting all my ammunition. His port engine caught fire. His left wing went down and last I saw was E/A disappearing into cloud in steep spiral. I then broke away.

In total, 73 Squadron claimed seven Ju 88s destroyed, three probables and three damaged. All pilots returned safely the only aircraft damaged being Scott's, and that was of a minor nature. That evening, the squadron was sent a congratulatory message by Air Vice-Marshal Leigh-Mallory, the 12 Group Commander, on a 'wonderful performance' (ORB).

Nonetheless, some thirty of the Ju 88s managed to reach and bomb Driffield, including *Oberleutnant* Kratz:

> 'There, the field, below us!'
>
> The target at last – the fighters were beginning to be a real nuisance. The time had come now. I did not give one single Pfennig for the life of those below – drop the bombs, away with the blessing! The aircraft went into a dive, speed rapidly building up, and the wind roared and howled around us. The hangars grew and grew. They were still standing. The AA guns were firing away at us, but they were too late.
>
> A jolt – the bombs were free, the steel bodies whistling down. Below all hell was let loose. Like an inferno, steel hit steel, and stones. Bomb upon bomb exploded, destroying and tearing apart what they hit. Hangar walls and roofs crumpled like tin sheets, pieces flying through the air. Aircraft were shattered by a hail of splinters. Barracks tumbled down, enormous smoke and dust clouds rose like mushrooms. Here and there explosions and flames shot up. The airfield and the hangars were already badly hit but bombs kept falling from the bombers that followed us, kept raining down, a horrible shower. Fire from exploding ammunition burst like torches. The English AA artillery had been eliminated, their firing positions turning to craters.

It was estimated that at 13.20 hrs, 100 bombs were dropped during the attack on 4 Group's Driffield aerodrome, commanded by Air Commodore Henry Hunter MC, at which the Group's Towing Flight, and 77 and 102 squadrons of Bomber Command were based. Ten Whitley bombers were destroyed on the ground and four hangars were badly damaged, and buildings and shelters were strafed. Worse, seven RAF personnel were killed, including 19-year-old ACW2 Marguerite Hester Hudson. The first of three WAAFs killed during the Battle of Britain, the teenage casualty was the daughter of Claud and Elizabeth Hudson of Wadsley, Sheffield, who took their daughter

THURSDAY, 15 AUGUST 1940

home and buried her in the town's Wisewood Cemetery. Ten airmen, including three junior officers, were killed in the attack.

At 13.10 hrs, fourteen Blenheims of 219 Squadron had been scrambled and as the enemy retired back across the North Sea, these twin-engine fighters attacked them, in what was the only such multiple interception in daylight by Blenheims throughout the Battle of Britain.

Flying Officer Thomas Harnett:

> At 1325 hrs ... 219 Squadron intercepted a flight of about forty E/A at Filey Bay. Squadron broke formation and attached. I, Yellow Leader, chased a Ju 88 out to sea about 160 miles, never getting closer than 600 yards. Gave two short bursts, in return was attacked by one Ju 88 at 500ft from the front. Rear gunner gave several long bursts, 2,000 rounds. I turned and gave chase, giving about five long bursts at about 300 yards, at this time E/A was at sea-level and was out of range (by tracer shots all seemed to hit E/A amidships).

Harnett was credited with a Ju 88 damaged, as were Flight Lieutenant Edward Wolfe, who also shared another with Sergeant John Topham, and Pilot Officer Donald Lake and Pilot Officer William Lambie. Flight Lieutenant Henry Goddard, commander of 'B' Flight, claimed a 'Do 17' [*sic*] destroyed, and Sergeant Oswald Dupree a 'He 111' [*sic*] – who was badly wounded by return fire and only able to crash-land his crippled aircraft at Driffield with help from his air gunner, Sergeant Thomas Bannister. Both men were subsequently awarded the DFM, gazetted on 24 September 1940, their citation reading thus:

> Sergeant Dupee and Sergeant Banister were the pilot and air gunner respectively, in an aircraft which attacked a Heinkel 111K. Shortly after commencing the attack the return fire from the enemy aircraft ceased, but as Sergeant Dupee was about to continue his attack at short range the Heinkel's dorsal gun again opened fire severely wounding him in the arm and causing damage to his aircraft. Sergeant Banister thereupon crawled forward, assisted Sergeant Dupee from his seat and took control of the aircraft. Despite failing strength, through loss of blood, Sergeant Dupee gave directions to Sergeant Banister who, although untrained as a pilot, was enabled to fly

the aircraft until compelled to force land. This was carried out on a strange aerodrome with the undercarriage retracted and only slight damage was caused to the aircraft.

Meanwhile, *Oberleutnant* Katz returned safely to Aalborg:

> The sun shone into our cabin. The enemy fighters had been got rid off. Below us lay the wide sea. How beautiful the Earth can be. Hands loosened their grip on the machine guns. What happened just a few minutes ago lay behind us and we relaxed. The engines were running evenly, we were flying home.
>
> The seemingly endless expanse of water and the regular beat of the engines heightened the impression of unworldliness. Earthly worries seemed far away and ridiculously small. A kind of soothing weariness left room only for the most simple thoughts but could not drive away the steady attentiveness. Minutes crawled by. The nearer we came to our base, the more we felt the need to express our impressions. A burning question was the one about our comrades, their aircraft, their results.

Eight of KG 30's Ju 88s were not so lucky and failed to return from the raid, their wreckage either scattered over Yorkshire or lying at the bottom of the North Sea. In response, Sergeant Dupree's 219 Squadron Blenheim had been badly shot-up, the pilot wounded, and 73 Squadron's Pilot Officer Donald Scott's Hurricane suffered minor damage. Although according to *Oberleutnant* Kratz, in an account written for personal amusement and not propaganda purposes, 'The airfield didn't exist anymore; that was the result. The camera held proof thereof.' The fact was that Driffield, damaged though it was, had not been destroyed – and again, the base was unconnected with Fighter Command, so in terms of eroding Britain's defences the raid achieved nothing.

The situation was well summarised by Air Chief Marshal Dowding:

> The sustained resistance which they were meeting in south-east England probably led them to believe that fighter squadrons had been withdrawn, wholly or in part, from the north in order to meet the attack … the contrary was soon apparent, and the bombers received such a drubbing that the experiment was not repeated.

THURSDAY, 15 AUGUST 1940

It was another excellent result for the defenders and 12 Group's first major action of the Battle of Britain on a day which really saw the defeat of *Luftflotte* 5. These two raids on north-east England cost *Generaloberst* Stumpff an eighth of his total bomber strength and a fifth of his long-range fighters. Never again would Stumpff attempt such raids; on this day, *Luftflotte* 5 was effectively neutralised.

During the afternoon, the focus shifted to *Luftflotte* 2, which was to mount three major attacks.

At 14.14 hrs, the first indication of another threat appeared on the RDF screens: 30+ assembling over Calais, and 15+ (later upgraded to 50+) over St Omer. At 14.28 hrs, another formation was estimated at 20+ north of St Omer, and increased to 50+ as it crossed the east coast at Felixstowe. At 15.00 hrs a plot approaching Orfordness, initially estimated at 3+, became 30+, and similarly, another raid became not 3+ but 50+ when incoming over Deal at 15.08 hrs. Clearly this was another major attack with multiple formations and targets – and equally apparent was that the 11 Group Controller was going to be busy.

At 14.14 hrs, nine Hurricanes, Red, Yellow and Green sections of 1 Squadron, left Northolt to operate from North Weald and first patrol the Clacton area. Between 14.30 hrs and 14.45 hrs, Nos. 32, 266, 64 and 151 squadrons were ordered off to patrol between Hawkinge and Manston, the indication at this time being that the incoming threat was directed at Dover, while at 14.54 hrs, the whole of 111 Squadron scrambled from Croydon to patrol Beachy Head, and between 15.10 hrs and 15.35 hrs, ten Hurricanes of 501 Squadron went up from Hawkinge and vectored towards Dover.

This enemy force approaching was substantial: all three *Gruppen* of KG 3 '*Blitz*', based at Antwerp-Deurne and St Trond, comprising eighty-eight Do 17s led by *Oberst* Wolfgang von Chamier-Glisczinski and his *Stab*, up from Le Culot, who flew at the head of *Hauptmann* Otto Pilger's II/KG 3. The bombers' targets (*Stab* and II/KG 3) were the airfield at Rochester – home of the Short brothers aircraft factory, producing the new four-engine Stirling bomber, which had yet to enter service – and the Coastal Command airfield at Eastchurch. Supporting this effort was literally masses of Me 109s: II and III/JG 26 swept over Kent in advance of the raid, while 130 Me 109s of JGs 51, 52 and 54 provided close escort.

Simultaneously, there was another threat incoming ...

At 14.20 hrs, *Oberleutnant* Otto Hintze led his Me 109s of 3/*Erprobungsgruppe* 210 up from Calais-Marck, rendezvousing with the Me 110s of *Stab*, 1 and 2 *Staffel* – target the RAF Martlesham Heath, the North Weald satellite near Woodbridge in Suffolk. The Hurricanes of 17 Squadron were operating from Martlesham that day, the sections of which were engaged on convoy protection patrols off the east coast, including Red Section, comprising Flight Lieutenant William Harper, Pilot Officer Geoffrey Pittman and Sergeant Desmond Fopp, which took off on such a sortie at 14.50 hrs. At the same time, having been requested to send reinforcements by the 11 Group Controller, 12 Group scrambled six Spitfires of 66 Squadron; at 15.00 hrs, a section of 242 Squadron's Hurricanes from Coltishall followed and, also at 15.00 hrs, thirteen Spitfires of 19 Squadron from Fowlmere, all vectored towards Martlesham, both airfields being fifty miles away.

With typical dash, *Erprobugsgruppe* 210 attacked Martlesham at 15.10 hrs, and were unopposed. According to the AHB account:

> Attack by Ju 87 [*sic*] and Me 110 'Jaguar' dive-bombers with an above guard of Me 109s; Ju 87s [actually Hintze's Me 109s] concentrated on an uncompleted Signals Station two miles to the west of the aerodrome and the Jaguars on the aerodrome. Signals Station suffered broken windows and a burst water tank. The bombs were widely dispersed. Two craters were filled in by 1900 hrs. Two bombs fell on the main camp and wrecked the Guardroom, coppersmith's and joiner's shops, and burst the water main. Two bombs severely damaged the Officers' Mess. A visiting Fairey Battle, carrying 1,000lbs of bombs, was set on fire and blew up. The explosion rendered two hangars completely unserviceable and the Watch Office and Night Flying Equipment sheds were completely destroyed. The attack lasted approximately five-minutes.

As the attack was in progress, Flying Officer David Hanson, Pilot Officer Leonard Stevens and Sergeant Leonard Bartlett of 17 Squadron, all managed to take-off, but were unable to intercept the raiders.

Flight Lieutenant Mike Crossley and ten Hurricanes of 32 Squadron had scrambled from Hawkinge at 14.30 hrs, ordered to intercept 'Raid 20' off Harwich. Thirty minutes later, Hurricanes were at 11,000ft off Harwich and engaged Me 109s; the Polish Pilot Officer Boleslaw Wlasnowalski reported:

> I was flying 3 of Red Section when I saw nine Me 109s above me in vic formation. I climbed up and attacked one of the Me 109s

THURSDAY, 15 AUGUST 1940

> from astern, we circled round each other then the 109 dived away. I got in a short burst and the Me 109 burst into flames and dived down towards the sea. I turned towards the other Me 109s but could not catch them. My glycol temperature was too hot so I force-landed in Essex. The machine is temporarily unserviceable as my undercarriage was smashed owing to the bad surface of the landing field.

Wlasnowalski, who forced-landed at an unrecorded location in Essex, was credited with an Me 109 destroyed. Pilot Officer Douglas 'Grubby' Grice DFC, however,

> was attacked by aircraft, unobserved type, and was shot down in flames about fifteen miles north of Harwich; he baled out, landing in the sea. He was picked up after ten minutes by a MTB and taken to RN Hospital Shotley suffering from burns to face and wrists. (ORB)

Grice was lucky to be rescued from the sea so soon, and had nearly drowned having been unable to release his parachute because of his wounds, which would keep him out of the battle until 14 October 1940.

While patrolling Clacton, 1 Squadron, led by Flight Lieutenant Mark 'Hilly' Brown, a Canadian, was vectored to Martlesham Heath, and arrived over the airfield just as *Erprobungsgruppe* 210 was retiring.

Pilot Officer Harold Mann, 'A' Flight, 1 Squadron:

> I was Yellow 2 ... I was attacked by Me 110s which came in from behind and above and lost the squadron through taking evasive action. I noticed the cannon fire from the E/A going wide. I then chased five or six bombers out to sea and I was diving so fast that I could not get my sights onto the E/A. Ten miles out to sea this became a stern chase but the E/A drew away. I turned away, being unable to catch up with the E/A, and was fired at by an Me 109. I steep-turned to the left and came in behind the E/A as it was climbing for height and got a direct shot at the whole plan of the E/A. The E/A went straight down in a dive but when at 5,000ft I was again shot at by another Me 109 which must have hit my petrol tank. I turned and fired at this one but with no visible effect. I was again fired

at by three more Me 109s but my main petrol tank ran out and switching over to the reserve I landed at Martlesham. The Me 109s had yellow wing tips.

Mann was awarded an Me 109 destroyed; the damage to his machine, however, went unrecorded excepting in the pilot's personal combat report (the Form 541 confirms Mann's aircraft as Hurricane P3395).

Pilot Officer John 'Tim' Elkington engaged the Me 109s:

> The enemy aircraft started to climb and turn to the left, but I turned sharp left and came in behind him, giving a short burst with no noticeable effect. I again fired at the enemy aircraft from astern as it straightened out and went into a steep climb. I gave him a two second burst from astern and above. The engine belched fumes and it turned over on its back, staying there for about three seconds, and then turned over and dropped like a plummet into the sea. I circled round but saw no one get out.

Elkington was awarded an Me 109 destroyed, years later recalling:

> We were patrolling when vectored towards Harwich, which was being bombed. I attacked an Me 109, which I believe I hit, and last saw diving away, trailing smoke, disappearing through cloud. I don't know whether it was destroyed or not, but I certainly frightened it! The first time you actually saw an aircraft with a black cross on it was quite a moment – they looked deadly, sinister. I also saw another twelve 109s going out over the coast, but wasn't in a position to attack them.

Flying Officer Peter Matthews, also of 1 Squadron, 'Sighted a large number of E/A over Martlesham and that the aerodrome was being bombed. He attacked three aircraft and a Ju 88 [*sic*] was damaged, the starboard engine being fired, but the bomber was lost to sight in the steep dive.' (ORB)

Although 1 Squadron's pilots' combat reports record the action over Martlesham as having occurred at '1445 hrs', this was guesswork on behalf of the squadron's Intelligence Officer. We know that the airfield was bombed at 15.10 hrs, and Flight Sergeant Fred Berry's Yellow Section (Pilot Officer Birch and Pilot Officer Elkington) did not leave North Weald until 15.00 hrs.

THURSDAY, 15 AUGUST 1940

As the raid lasted five minutes, 1 Squadron therefore intercepted at 15.15 hrs. Afterwards, though, all three Hurricanes of Red Section were missing.

Flight Lieutenant Brown, Red 1, was shot down by an Me 109 and baled out over the sea, wounded in the hands and face; fortunately, he was rescued by a passing trawler. Neither Pilot Officer Dennis Browne nor Sergeant Martin Shanahan, however, were ever seen again. There was also another damaged Hurricanes, details of which went unrecorded by the 1 Squadron diarist but were noted in the personal flying log book of Pilot Officer Elkington: 'Sergeant Clowes' "B" full of holes.'

While *Erprobungsgruppe* raced back to the French coast, Red Section of 17 Squadron, having taken off at 14.50 hrs to patrol a convoy, was flying towards Martlesham at 14,000ft at 15.20 hrs when the high-flying Me 109 escorts were sighted at 20,000ft, also heading home. Red 1, Flight Lieutenant Harper, reported:

> Tally Ho given and section climbed to 22,000ft and approached out of the sun. Two Me 109s were sighted away from the rest and I called up sections to see if they were with me. Red 3 was still in position so I attacked rear Me 109 from beam. Tracer appeared to go into E/A. Two second burst only was given as E/A was obviously shaken. He carried on clumsily and went down. I turned sharply to starboard to get onto the first Me 109, who was attempting to get on tail of section. This aircraft, however, overshot section and was chased down by Red 3. While I circled watching Red 3's tail and taking stock of situation I had my engine stopped by enemy action and was incidentally shot through the leg. I dived down to sea-level, past destroyers, for protection, and glided on to pancake on marshland by Felixstowe. My face was cut during my landing as nose of aircraft struck a ditch in the field and I was thrown forward.

Although Harper claimed an Me 109 damaged, according to the 17 Squadron ORB, he was accredited with one 'confirmed'; having crash-landed at Laurel Farm, his Hurricane was damaged but repairable. This was 17 Squadron's only claim and casualty in this action.

It was another successful attack by *Erprobungsgruppe* 210, although by the evening of the following day the telephone line was restored and water mains reconnected. Moreover, this was not an all-important Sector

Station and so no harm came to an operations room. Nonetheless, in those terrifying five minutes, *Erprobungsgruppe* 210 certainly made a mess of Martlesham – and escaped unscathed. Air Vice-Marshal Park was furious, blaming 12 Group for having failed to protect the airfield as requested. Conversely, 12 Group complained that they had been called for too late. This was, however, a lightning-quick and well executed surprise attack on a coastal airfield, giving the 11 Group Controller little time to react – and even less for 12 Group's fighters to scramble and cover the distance to Martlesham.

Sergeant David Cox, 19 Squadron, Fowlmere:

> The attack on Martlesham Heath, near Ipswich, was brilliantly executed by Erich Rubensdörfer, *Erprobungsgruppe* 210's approach going completely undetected until just a few minutes from the target. Considering the distance from Fowlmere to Martlesham, sixty air miles, our chances of contacting the enemy were nil. Even taking into account an *optimistic* speed for our Spitfires of 300 mph, it would take twelve minutes from take-off to reach Martlesham Heath. In any case, at our altitude, 2,000ft, I doubt that our cannon-armed Spitfire Mk IBs were capable of that speed, as its maximum speed was not achievable until 19,000ft. I would therefore suggest that 280 mph was the most likely maximum speed for height, but even at 300 mph 19 Squadron could not achieve the impossible.

Cox makes a good point well: as far as Fighter Command was concerned nobody was to blame, but it was the first clash between 11 and 12 groups in what would soon become a sorry and bitter tale – as we will in due course see.

As the 111 Squadron ORB noted, this particular afternoon 'heralded a period of intense activity from large formations of enemy aircraft' – and while *Erprobungsgruppe* 210 successfully 'pranged' Martlesham, the KG 3 formation had split, crossing the coast at 15.08 hrs over Deal, Felixstowe, Harwich and Ordfordness. Already, at 14.55 hrs, the Spitfires of Squadron Leader Don MacDonell's 64 Squadron had clashed with the Me 109 escorts off Dover, as the CO reported:

> I was Red 1. The squadron was ordered to patrol a position behind Dover at a height of 20,000ft. On nearing the coast I approached Dover from west in order to use the sun to our

best advantage. At a height of 22,000ft, while patrolling mid-Channel I saw the Dover defences open fire. I manoeuvred the squadron and approached from the west, at the same time sighting about twenty Me 109s on the same level, crossing the Channel ahead of us from south to north. Another formation of about twenty or more Me 109s approached and attacked from astern on our starboard quarter. We engaged as soon as possible. The squadron, with the exception of the last section, were in close formation with me. The last section were about ½ mile astern. I engaged four Me 109s and opened fire on the leader at a range of 250 yards in a climbing turn. The E/A turned sharply towards France and was joined by about five others with yellow painted wingtips. I gave three long bursts from below and astern. The E/A turned quite slowly onto its back and then dropped inverted. A moment later a part of the starboard wing came away from the E/A which developed an extremely high spin and struck the sea.

Two Me 109s engaged me at a height of about 800ft. I concentrated on one and opened fire from the quarter with four or five short bursts. The E/A appeared to have been hit in the engine and slowed up rapidly, with bursts of black smoke coming from it. I closed again and opened with a short burst from the port quarter. My ammunition was then exhausted. I followed E/A in a tight-spiral towards the sea but was unable to observe the result of my engagement. A formation of six to ten Me 109s then attacked me, so I returned to base. These aircraft did not pursue me over our own coast.

Squadron Leader MacDonell – the Laird of Glengarry and known to his pilots as 'Bonnie Prince Charlie', was credited with one Me 109 destroyed and another damaged. Me 109s destroyed were also claimed by Pilot Officer James O'Meara and Flight Sergeant Adrian Laws; Flight Sergeant Ernest Gilbert claimed a probable, and Flying Officer Alexander Laing one damaged. This was not, however, without loss. Flying Officer Christopher Andreae disappeared without trace, and Pilot Officer Ralph Roberts, who had become disorientated and mistook the French for the English coast, was shot down over Calais-Marck by *Leutnant* Gerhard Müller-Dühe of 7/JG 26; safely crash-landing in a beet field near the airfield there, Roberts was captured.

BATTLE OF BRITAIN ATTACK OF THE EAGLES

To the defenders, it must have seemed as though the whole *Luftwaffe* was up over the south-eastern Kentish coast. KG 3's Do 17s had already separated into two formations: I and II *Gruppen* heading for Rochester airfield while III/KG 3 turned north-west and made for Eastchurch. Meanwhile, *staffel*-strength formations of Do 17s from KG 1 and 2, escorted by Me 110s of *Major* Hans Trubenbach's I/LG 2, attacked various targets in Kent, including Maidstone, Dover, Rye and the Foreness Chain Home Low RDF station. RAF Hawkinge was also attacked:

> Second hostile attack at 1525 hrs by aeroplanes at considerable height, lowest 8,000ft ranging up to 20,000ft. Too high for light AA. Twenty to Thirty small bombs were dropped over an area, a few on the aerodrome surface. These aircraft were engaged by three AA [guns]. The attack lasted ten minutes. There were no casualties. No record of hits by ground defences were recorded. The detachment of RE's immediately after the raid commenced work on the aerodrome surface which has not been seriously damaged.

Nine Hurricanes of 151 Squadron had scrambled from Rochford at 14.45 hrs to patrol west of Dover at 20,000ft, on what was, the squadron diarist recorded, 'a busy day', engaging the enemy off Dover at 15.40 hrs.

Pilot Officer Kenneth Debenham:

> The Squadron was patrolling in line-astern at about 18,000ft when it was attacked by a number of Me 109s. Observed a large number of Dorniers and Me's approaching the English coast, and was engaged by an Me 109. I got on his tail and he started twisting and turning his way towards France. I got in a second burst which seemed to have no effect until he crossed the French coast when he turned on his side, dived into the ground and blew up about a mile east of Calais.

Having chased his opponent and destroyed him over France, Debenham beat a hasty retreat back to England. Pilot Officer John Ellacombe also destroyed an Me 109 over the French coast, returning safely to base with a damaged radio aerial (pilot's combat report refers; previous accounts having wrongly stated that Debenham's aerial was damaged, but not so).

Flying Officer Richard 'Dickie' Milne:

THURSDAY, 15 AUGUST 1940

Red Section had just refuelled after a patrol. We had reached 16,000ft and were over the coast west of Dover when we sighted large formations of E/A in the Channel. We continued climbing and the enemy turned and approached Dover. When at 19,000ft we were attacked by a formation of Me 109s from above. I was leading Blue Section and was unable to catch up an Me 109 which passed immediately above me. Turning, I saw in front a 109 attacking one of our Hurricanes. The Hurricane turned violently and evaded the 109, which turned right away and dived steeply towards the sea and France. I followed and it took me some time to catch the E/A, which was now at 1,500ft, still diving. He flew quite straight and I closed to 150 yards before firing. I held my fire for about six seconds and at 500ft the E/A emitted a trail of white smoke and continued in a dive, striking the sea. Flying Officer Blair saw the crash from higher up.

I now turned and climbed and saw the Dorniers turning over land. When at 10,000ft I was attacked by many Me 109s and had to half-roll violently to avoid being hit. I climbed again and as attacked once more by Me 109s at 13,000ft. Being alone, I never had a chance to close with the Dorniers. I saw Me 109 formations all over the sky and was once more attacked by several from the starboard quarter. After final evasive tactics I returned to land. All the Me 109s had their wing-tips orange. They were at all heights and obviously there to attack fighters long before we reached the bombers.

I saw several columns of smoke from woods and one from the village where aircraft had crashed.

The Polish Mieczlaw Rozwadowski also claimed an Me 109 destroyed, but JG 51 had successfully prevented 151 Squadron from attacking the bombers.

According to the 501 Squadron Form 541, between 15.10 hrs and 15.35 hrs, ten Hurricanes took-off, from Hawkinge, on an unspecified 'Active Operations Patrol', the Form 540 adding that 'Two further engagements took place at 15.15 hrs and 17.25 hrs, eight aircraft were destroyed or damaged.' Although both the Polish Sergeant Anton Glowacki and Sergeant James 'Ginger' Lacey are credited in various secondary sources with Do 17s damaged at 15.35 hrs in the 'Maidstone-Rochester' area, along with three more damaged by 'unknown pilots', none of these combat reports appear to have survived. Owing to the lack of primary source material available, we must rely upon the AHB narrative for an account of 501 Squadron's activities:

> There remained the seven Hurricanes of 501 Squadron, which did not take off from Gravesend until 1515 hrs, two more aircraft following later but being unable to find the rest of the squadron. They were directed to intercept behind Dover, first at 8,000ft then at 10,000ft. They were then told by the controller that the enemy was at 3,000–5,000ft and they consequently dived down over Dover. As they did this, they saw enemy aircraft above them at 15,000ft and were then aware of what they estimated to be 150 Dorniers near Dungeness, flying north-west to cross the coast near Folkestone. The Hurricanes, now at 4,000ft, consequently climbed until they were a thousand feet above the enemy, and then at 1530 hrs delivered a beam attack on the second wave of bombers. They claim that they broke the enemy formation, and that they were able to pursue detached aircraft into the Thames estuary, and to the Maidstone-Chatham area.

With the Do 17s heading for Rochester and Eastchurch, 111 Squadron, which was patrolling from Beachy Head to Dover and over the latter, was urgently 'vectored in a north-westerly direction, Red and Yellow sections fought an action in the Dover area and following a north-westerly course' (ORB).

No.111 Squadron was based at Croydon alongside 1 (Fighter) Squadron of the RCAF, the third Canadian unit to arrive in England and commanded by Squadron Leader Ernest 'Archie' McNab, who was attached to 'Treble One' to gain operational experience. On this day, McNab was Blue 2, at 15.30 hrs engaging 'Do 215s' at 5,000ft:

> Two enemy bombers ... were sighted flying in close formation and I did a stern attack on them, firing a short burst with no apparent effect before breaking off. On my next attack after the first burst the rear-gunner ceased firing and the E/A started to lose height. I followed him down, firing. His engines began to smoke and he crashed in some marshy ground just west of

THURSDAY, 15 AUGUST 1940

Westgate-on-Sea. As my ammunition was used up I returned to base and refuelled.

Strangely, McNab has always been accredited with having destroyed a Do 17Z-2 of 6/KG 3 which crashed into the sea a mile east of Reculver at 15.30 hrs, but his combat report specifically states: 'he crashed on some marshy ground just west of Westgate-on-Sea'. While there is no German casualty apparent on land, there is no doubting that this happened; Squadron Leader John Thompson:

> In company with Squadron Leader McNab and Sergeant Wallace, I attacked two Do 215s [*sic*] in Thames Estuary at 16,000ft. I saw Squadron Leader McNab shoot his down and at the end of my second attack, from 200 yards astern, I finished my ammunition and saw both engines of the Dornier emitting smoke and flame and going down. Being aware Me 109s were somewhere in the vicinity I dived down and returned to base. Confirmed by Squadron Leader McNab.

Thompson had, it is believed, shot down a Do 17Z-2 of 6/KG 3 which crashed into the sea between Ramsgate and Deal, the crew of which were captured.

Sergeant William Dymond reported engaging 160 'Do 215s' in waves of twelve to eighteen aircraft at 15.30 hrs, ten miles south of Detling:

> Yellow Section followed Red Section into a head-on attack, and attacked the second wave of bombers. Two starboard E/A were seen to be hit and broke away from formation and flew east. I turned and engaged a Do 215 [*sic*] which I attacked from dead astern and set fire to the rear-gunner's cockpit on breaking away. I then attacked a vic of three in succession and the port E/A was seen to be hit. Cowling broke away. Ammunition expended, I landed at West Malling to rearm but owing to damage sustained to my aircraft had to return to Croydon by Magister.

Dymond added that his Hurricane, R4195, was 'damaged by gunfire'.

In total, for no loss, 111 Squadron claimed three 'Do 215s' destroyed, four probables and three damaged, in addition to a damaged Me 109.

Flight Lieutenant Henry Ferriss DFC was among those claiming a bomber probably destroyed, but was shot-up himself during the action, landing his damaged Hurricane, trailing white glycol smoke, at Hawkinge.

With only 111 and 501 squadrons having managed to attack the Do 17s, the hordes of Me 109s clearly made for an otherwise impregnable fighter screen. Unfortunately, the RAF fighters had to break off before the enemy bombed their targets, which went ahead unopposed by reinforcements.

Between 15.40 hrs and 15.58 hrs, some eighteen Do 17s bombed Rochester airfield, causing major damage to the Short Brothers' hangars and, to a lesser extent, the adjacent Pobjoys aircraft factory. A direct hit on the Finished Parts Store caused a great blaze, and many Stirling components were destroyed, along with various engineering drawings and jigs. Seven Stirlings, which had been approaching completion, were destroyed, although, fortunately the workforce had taken shelter; just one civilian was mortally injured: 28-year-old John Gordon Oakley of Dartford, a Pobjoys carpenter, who died in St Bartholomew's Hospital the next day. The Rochester site was so devastated that Stirling production was put back by a year, and Short Brothers moved their operation to Belfast.

II/KG 3 reported that 'Aero-engine works repeatedly hit ... copious flame and smoke...'

Rochester was, however, another questionable target insofar as the destruction of Fighter Command was concerned, given that it had no connection with Britain's defences – but German civilians would in due course be thankful that this long-range bomber programme was delayed. By the time the Stirling finally entered service, the huge, lumbering, four-engine bomber was already virtually obsolete and easy prey for the German night defences, which were well-advanced by then.

In addition to the damage at Rochester, and that caused by *Erprobungsgruppe* 210 at Martlesham Heath, thirty-eight enemy aircraft bombed West Malling airfield from high-altitude, damaging new buildings, living quarters and cratering the runway. The damage was such, in fact, that the important coastal aerodrome was out of action for five days. The raid on Eastchurch wrecked the gas contamination centre and damaged the runway, but being in no way connected to the System, this was again inconsequential.

In this latest assault, six RAF fighters had been destroyed, three pilots killed, one captured, three wounded and five aircraft damaged. The Germans appear to have lost at least three Me 109s destroyed, with one pilot captured, two missing, and two Do 17s destroyed with crew-members variously

THURSDAY, 15 AUGUST 1940

killed, captured, wounded or missing, while six more crash-landed back in France, five with wounded aircrew aboard. The day's fighting, however, was still far from over.

The previous day, Squadron Leader Rodney Wilkinson's 266 Squadron, formerly based at Wittering and temporarily operating from Eastchurch, was moved to the Hornchurch Sector Station. On the morning of 15 August, 266 Squadron's Spitfires flew to Manston, from where nine aircraft were scrambled at 16.00 hrs to intercept a bandit, a He 115 seaplane, seven miles south of Deal, at 500ft.

Pilot Officer Robert Roach:

> We were all together when I Tally Ho'd the E/A. We were at 2,000ft. The E/A was proceeding in the direction of Deal at approximately 180 mph. E/A made straight for home on seeing us, making steep turn to the right. I did a shallow dive towards him from astern, giving him a five second burst at 300–250 yards, but saw no effect. I broke upwards for a second attack – head on – giving him a seven second burst, breaking upwards. E/A dived but still no effect. As I was attacking again from beam E/A crashed into the sea. All my ammunition was expended, so I returned to base.

No He 115 loss corresponds to this engagement, although an Arado 196 floatplane, which was searching for downed aircrew, was shot down over the Channel with the loss of both crewmen. The aircraft crashed into the Channel eight miles south-west of Dunkirk – but a Spitfire was lost in the process: Sergeant Frederick Hawley was hit by return fire, crashed into the Channel and was never seen again.

After all this hectic mid-afternoon action over the Channel, Thames Estuary and Kent, there was an ominous lull for about two hours – it was not to last. At 17.00 hrs and for the next twenty minutes, information began coming in from RDF stations regarding seven large enemy formations heading for the South Coast. Half of these plots appeared Portland bound, the rest the English coast between the Needles and Selsey Bill. These raids were to be dealt with by a combined force of fighters from both 10 Group – which had so far played no part in the day's fighting, and 11 Group. Indeed, this defence represented seven of Air Vice-Marshal Brand's 10 Group squadrons, and the same number of Air Vice-Marshal Park's 11 Group units – numbering some 150 RAF fighters, the most fighters deployed by Fighter Command to date.

BATTLE OF BRITAIN ATTACK OF THE EAGLES

No.10 Group scrambled the following fighters:

17.00 hrs: Spitfires of 152 Squadron from Warmwell, vectored to Portland.

17.05 hrs: Spitfires of 234 Squadron's Spitfires from Middle Wallop to patrol Swanage (having arrived from the much quieter St Eval sector only the previous day).

17.05 hrs: 'A' Flight of 601 Squadron's Hurricanes from Tangmere, to patrol the coast.

17.15 hrs: Hurricanes of 213 Squadron from Exeter, vectored to Portland.

17.20 hrs: A section of 249 Squadron's Hurricanes from Boscombe Down were sent up to patrol Ringwood (having moved from the quiet Church Fenton sector of 13 Group only the day before).

17.25 hrs: Hurricanes of 87 from Exeter, vectored to Portland.

17.35 hrs: Spitfires of 609 Squadron from Middle Wallop, scrambled upon approach of enemy aircraft.

17.35 hrs: Blenheims of 604 Squadron, as above.

No.11 Group:

17.05 hrs: Hurricanes of 601 Squadron from Tangmere to patrol base before meeting the incoming threat over the Isle of Wight.

17.05 hrs: Hurricanes of 111 Squadron from Croydon to patrol Shoreham.

17.08 hrs: Hurricanes of 43 Squadron to patrol base then meet raid approaching Isle of Wight.

17.20 hrs: Hurricanes of 32 Squadron from Biggin Hill, to patrol Horsham before intercepting enemy off Selsey Bill.

17.25 hrs: Hurricanes of 501 Squadron from Gravesend to patrol over base and the coast.

THURSDAY, 15 AUGUST 1940

17.37 hrs: Hurricanes of 1 Squadron from Northolt to patrol Guildford.

17.50 hrs: Spitfires of 602 Squadron from Westhampnett to patrol inland of Tangmere.

This robust response by Fighter Command was as swift as it was strong, because by the time the first enemy aircraft crossed the coast at 17.20 hrs, eight fighter squadrons were already airborne.

These incoming raids were all mounted by *Luftflotte* 3. Sixty Ju 88 crews of *Generalmajor* Alfred Bülowius's LG 1, based at Orleans, were briefed to attack both the Middle Wallop Sector Station – a vital cog in the 10 Group defences – and nearby Worthy Down, at that time an FAA base. Close escort was provided by *Hauptmann* Erich Groth's II/ZG 76 Me 110s; based at Le Mans, these fighters were operating from Rennes and using auxiliary fuel tanks to extend their range and increase the time available for combat over southern England. This airfield attack was to coincide with another large raid: Ju 87s of *Hauptmann* Paul-Werner Hozzel's I/StG 1 and *Hauptmann* Walter Eneccerus's II/StG2, a combined force of fifty Lannion-based dive-bombers attacking Portland. The *Stukas* were to be escorted by a great number of fighters: Me 109s of JG 27, commanded by the somewhat elderly 44-year-old *Oberst* Max Ibel, and those of *Major* Hans-Jürgen von Cramon-Traubadel's JG53, in addition to Me 110s of *Hauptmann* Horst Liensberger's V(Z)/LG 1 and those of *Hauptmann* Karl-Friedrich Dickoré's III/ZG 76. It must be said that for the *Jagdflieger*, escorting *Stukas* was their least popular mission. This was because the *Stukas* low cruising speed of 200 kph meant that the faster fighters had to weave to and fro, to remain with their slower charges, thereby using so much fuel that upon reaching the target the fighters had to turn about with little or no fuel reserves for combat. This especially applied to the Me 109, which, like the Spitfire and Hurricane, had not been designed, or intended, as a long-range escort or offensive fighter, a role to which it was unsuited, but now having to fulfil.

According to the AHB narrative, the first RAF fighter squadron to contact the incoming Germans was 152 Squadron, at 17.20 hrs. According to the Form 540, the ORB monthly summary, on the day in question, however, the unit carried out 'Several patrols, no combats'. In what has to be among the worst ORBs of the period, which is missing the Form 541 daily records, this entry appears for 13 August 1940 – which, in fact, refers to the engagement about to take place over Portland:

> While on patrol over Portland, Flight Lieutenant Boitel-Gill led an attack on a large formation of Ju 87s. He fired on one which broke up on the air. He then attacked two Me 110s, both of which burst into flames. His own machine was extremely badly damaged. His bringing it back to base was undoubtedly a magnificent effort.

Ray Johnson was an armourer at Warmwell with 152 Squadron, and recalled the incident:

> The squadron's duties were in defence of the Portland naval base, Southampton docks, Yeovil aircraft factory etc, and throughout 152 Squadron managed to give a good account of itself, accounting for fifty or sixty confirmed victories. They were certainly hectic days, from dawn to dusk we were at dispersal. It seemed as though we were always at readiness, rearming, refuelling, daily inspections of aircraft all seemed to follow each other without pause. It was certainly thrilling to see your aircraft return with its gun ports in the wing leading edges open and black streaks down the underside of the wings, indicating that it had been in action. Very often there was a victory roll before the undercarriage was lowered and the pilot brought it in to land. Sometimes, though, your aircraft did not return, and you were left wondering what had happened to it. Sometimes a Spit would land badly shot-up. One such incident occurred when Flight Lieutenant Boitel-Gill crashed his Spitfire right into the corner of the airfield. The aircraft was absolutely riddled, we counted more than seventy holes, that is points of entry, and lost count. His undercarriage could not be lowered and neither could his flaps. Boitel-Gill was one of those unflappable types, he never rushed, always appeared casual. He was an inveterate cigarette smoker, using a long cigarette holder, that he always carried. This time, after alighting from the wreck, he calmly placed the cigarette in the holder and said 'I thought I'd better put it in the corner, out of the way' – a really cool customer.

THURSDAY, 15 AUGUST 1940

The 152 Squadron Form 540 continues (incorrectly entered on 13 August 1940 in the ORB):

> Pilot Officer Hogg carried out three attacks on this same formation but without apparent result. Sergeant Shepherd then attacked this same formation but without visible result. He then attacked a single machine from another formation, which was damaged and had broken away. He could not say if it was definitely destroyed. Sergeant Barker also attacked this formation and he reports that fire ceased from the rear-gunner of the machine he attacked. He then attacked an Me 110 and it went into a steep spiral dive with smoke coming from both engines. He did not see it hit the sea. Pilot Officer Marrs attacked a Ju 87 and saw his Perspex splinter and the machine went down from formation. He followed it down but was then attacked and his machine was so much damaged and his rudder jammed, he returned to base. Sergeant Robinson attacked an Me 109 which he followed down and saw burst into flames and crash in a wood near Abbotsbury.

Unfortunately, however, none of 152 Squadron's pilots' combat reports survive in relation to this engagement, and there is no record of an Me 109 crashing at Abbotsbury on this day – but more of this later. No.152 Squadron's Sergeant Ralph 'Bob' Wolton was shot down in this action and ditched his Spitfire in the sea off Chesil Beach before swimming to a nearby buoy from which he was rescued; like Flight Lieutenant 'Bottle' Boitel-Gill, Sergeant Harold Akroyd returned to Warmwell with a damaged Spitfire, his rudder having been jammed when the aircraft was hit by enemy fire, and Pilot Officer Eric 'Boy' Marrs similarly landed a damaged machine back at base. Fortunately, none of 152's pilots were hurt.

At 17.05 hrs, Flight Lieutenant Sir Archibald Hope led 'A' Flight of 601 Squadron up from Tangmere, the Hurricanes running into the advancing enemy, twelve Ju 88s heading for Worthy Down, at 17.30 hrs over Spithead, pursuing the bombers inland to Bishops Waltham.

Pilot Officer Michael Doulton was leading Green Section, astern of the squadron:

> Green Section followed Red Section closely into a quarter attack on the enemy bombers. No enemy fighters appeared to follow the bombers inland. The E/A were in a tight and level

> vic of eleven, with one straggler 1,000ft below and ½ mile astern. Although we were slightly above the formation it was necessary to use full throttle to gain slowly on them. The formation wheeled right during my first attack and my sighting was upset by slipstream effect. Some of the right-hand bombers jettisoned their bombs. Three or four Ju 88s broke formation and dived. I got onto the tail of the last of these. He dived very steeply but I got in a steady burst dead astern. We both pulled out near Southampton balloons. He then started evasion which were really steep dives and climbing turns. My next bursts were slight deflections on both sides of the fuselage. Oil poured from the engines and covered my windscreen.
>
> During the next burst at 100 yards range streams of dense white smoke poured from the wing tips. I imagined this was done purposely to make the fighter think that the aircraft was burning. After my final burst he dived steeply and landed in a stubble field on a hill south of Winchester. Just before landing he jettisoned incendiary bombs. Four of the crew were seen walking round the crashed aircraft. I circled low and fired several white and red Very cartridges to call the attention of people on the ground. Flying Officer Clyde assisted in shooting down this E/A and witnessed the landing. I landed at Tangmere 1820 hrs.

This 4/LG 1 Ju 88 crashed at Twyford, its crew captured unhurt. Flight Lieutenant Carl Davis destroyed another, which crashed in flames at West Tisted, killing the crew. Flight Lieutenant Hope and Flying Officer Gordon Cleaver shared another, and Hope shared a second with Sergeant Leonard Guy. Flying Officer William Clyde also claimed a probable, in addition to sharing Pilot Officer Doulton's kill, and Flight Sergeant Arthur Pond and Sergeant Norman Taylor both damaged Ju 88s. That morning, 601 Squadron's Pilot Officer John McGrath was notified that he had been awarded the DFC, but during this action he was shot-up and crash landed, fortunately unhurt, at Selsey. Pilot Officer Cleaver was also shot down, baling out over Winchester and admitted to hospital with serious facial injuries.

At 17.30 hrs, 43 Squadron also engaged, between Emsworth and Selsey; Pilot Officer Charles Woods-Scawen:

> I was Yellow 1, the rear section of 43 Squadron, flying at 15,000ft when the E/A were sighted. I remained up above

THURSDAY, 15 AUGUST 1940

> them, in the sun, when our Squadron engaged them. Seeing that the enemy fighters weren't going to play, I attached myself to four He 111s flying South at 17,000ft, where I was joined by Yellow 2 [Pilot Officer Roy Lane], who had just engaged a Ju 88. We attacked simultaneously just after crossing the coast at West Wittering, employing small deflection tactics at close range and firing at front E/A. The majority of my attacks were directed at the port aircraft which shortly afterwards crashed into the sea with a trail of thick white smoke issuing from it (Yellow 2 witnessed this). I then attacked the opposite flank aircraft, together with my No 2 and when I ran out of ammo the He 111 was obviously damaged, the port engine issuing intermittent dense black smoke and flying in a see-saw fashion, though this may have been evasive action. The two rear-gunners had long since ceased fire and E/A had been left behind by remainder of formation. I called up Yellow 2, telling him to return to base with me, since we were uncomfortably far out to sea ... We landed at base safely. On the whole, the rear-gun fire from the He 111s was inaccurate.

This was already becoming a confusing air battle, with various enemy formations wandering around in addition to the big 'Valhalla'. It is likely that the He 111 shot down into the sea by Woods-Scawen was an aircraft of II/KG 53 which ditched in the Channel with two dead and three wounded crewmen. Pilot Officer Lane claimed a He 111 damaged, while Squadron Leader John 'Tubby' Badger led the remaining Hurricanes into attack the unescorted Ju 88s, the squadron claiming three destroyed and a probable for no loss.

After its earlier action, 111 Squadron had returned to Croydon and 'scarcely refuelled when a further scramble was given' (ORB). At 17.05 hrs, ten Hurricanes took off, led by Squadron Leader John Thompson, to patrol Shoreham, although the CO was forced to abort the sortie and return to base suffering engine trouble. Vectored to Thorney Island, the Hurricanes engaged the a 'very large formation', according to Sergeant Thomas Wallace, a South African, of Me 110s:

> Blue 2 was following Section Leader and I stayed above to balk fighters providing escort for Ju 88s, which remainder of the squadron attacked from below. I was attacked by an Me 110 and took evasive action in a head-on position. I held

my fire until about 400 yards and gave a burst of two seconds. I was attacked by an Me 109 and returned with Blue 1 to base. Blue 1 confirmed E/A crashed.

Flight Lieutenant Stanley Connors DFC claimed a Ju 88 destroyed and one damaged; Sergeant John Craig somewhat optimistically claimed three Ju 88 probables, and Wallace was credited with an Me 110 destroyed. Flying Officers Basil and Antony Fisher, brothers from Kensington and both Old Etonians, shared in the destruction of a Ju 88 – Antony watched his younger brother get shot down in flames. Basil Fisher baled out, but his parachute harness was so badly damaged by flames that he fell clear of the life-saving silk umbrella, falling to his death in a pond near the Selsey gasholder (just how traumatic this was for Antony Fisher can only be imagined – but he would go into action once more before the day was out. On 24 August 1940, however, he was posted away from 111 Squadron, going into training, and never flew operationally again). Pilot Officer Athol McIntyre, a New Zealander, was more fortunate: shot down by an Me 110, he safely landed his badly damaged aircraft at Hawkinge; his wounds, however, would keep him out of the battle for over two months.

At 13.00 hrs on 15 August, Squadron Leader John Grandy's 249 Squadron, which had only arrived at Middle Wallop from Church Fenton the previous day, was ordered to be available for take-off at fifteen minutes notice. Two hours later, 'A' Flight was brought to immediate readiness while 'B' Flight remained at fifteen minutes. At 17.15 hrs, the whole squadron was brought to readiness. At 17.12 hrs, Squadron Leader Grandy and Flight Lieutenant James Brindley Nicolson scrambled with 'A' Flight to patrol the sector's forward airfield of Warmwell at 15,000ft. At 17.19 hrs, the Canadian Flight Lieutenant Robert Barton led 'B' Flight off, Squadron Leader Eric 'Whizzy' King, attached to the squadron as 'supernumerary' before commanding one of his own, taking off solo a minute later. Luck would favour 'B' Flight, which got its first glimpse of a massed enemy formation: the sixty Ju 88s of LG 1, escorted by forty Me 110s of ZG 2. Over Ringwood, at 17.35 hrs, Barton's Hurricanes attacked. Back at Boscombe Down, for no loss, the Hurricane pilots claimed the destruction of five Me 110s. The lone Squadron Leader King encountered and attacked twelve Ju 88s, leaving one trailing smoke from its port engine. For no loss, it was an encouraging start to the squadron's tour of duty in 11 Group – but the bombers, nonetheless, droned on towards Middle Wallop.

At 17.15 hrs, RAF Exeter's Station Commander, Wing Commander Johnny Dewar DSO DFC, led twelve Hurricanes of 213 Squadron up to

THURSDAY, 15 AUGUST 1940

patrol Portland at 20,000ft. While the Ju 88s struck inland, at 17.35 hrs Dewar's pilots met the incoming raid of 100+ Me 109s, Me 110s and Ju 87s five miles south of Portland Bill.

Pilot Officer Joseph Laricheliere:

> As we were approaching Portland our Section Leader gave us the warning of E/A presence. Immediately on my left and below I saw an Me 110 and dived after it, getting on his tail and giving him a short burst on the port engine which immediately started to emit black smoke. The Me 110 dived, I saw the hood fly off and airmen jumping out. I followed the Me 110 down and saw it crash in the sea in mile or so south of Portland. Immediately, I climbed again and as I was going through a thin layer of clouds at approximately 4,000ft I noticed Ju 87 trying to escape towards the south-east. I immediately flattened out and after a few minutes of dodging in and out of the clouds I finally took position on its tail at about 150 yards and gave him two bursts. I saw all kinds of bits flying about and the Ju 87 started to spin. I followed it and saw it crash into the sea very near the coast east of Portland. For the second time I dived again at 7,000ft and met another Me 110. After quite a lot of dodging I suddenly found myself immediately below an Me 110 at less than thirty yards. I pulled up in a very stiff climb and gave him long bursts in the engine and centre section. Half the wing blew up and the 110 seemed to cartwheel spin and finally crash into the sea, again very near the coast of Portland. This last burst had exhausted all my ammunition so I returned to base.

To destroy two Me 110s and a Ju 87 within a few minutes was exceptional shooting indeed from this Canadian pilot.

The Belgian Pilot Officer Jacques Philippart reported:

> Leading Yellow Section above Portland Bill I made an attack on the last Me 110 of a formation; after a little burst he made a flick roll and continued spinning into the sea. I had been attacked from astern by four Me 110s. Seeing tracer bullets coming from astern I made a quick turn and got onto his tail. After two bursts the starboard engine fired and he went in a slow gliding turn. I then made a beam attack on the second

aeroplane in an echelon formation of Me 110s. The third of that formation turned over on his back and went into an inverted dive, pieces falling away. I then engaged a single Me 110 and had a dogfight with him. I first stopped his starboard engine; he dived into the clouds; I remained just above the clouds which were in patches, and when he reappeared the rear-gunner fired at me when I engaged him. I followed him beneath the clouds. As the rear-gunner was silent I came closer to him but had no more ammunition. Flight Lieutenant Sing observed his port engine smoking badly and running spasmodically. I returned to base where they discovered a bullet in my starboard tank and a second in the cockpit.

Excellent shooting again, with Phillipart – who had clearly had a lucky escape himself – claiming three Me 110s conclusively destroyed and another 'inconclusive'.

In his log book, Pilot Officer Alexander Osmand wrote:

Patrol Portland at 20,000ft – but ran into E/A at 15,000ft. Saw about sixty Ju 87s, sixty Me 110s and several Me 109s. We went for the 110s – I got in a good head-on burst at one – a long deflection shot at another – then lost the fight chasing a 109 into cloud (on this show 'A' Flight got ten and 'B' Flight nine – with only one lost!).

It was an enormously successful interception, 213 Squadron exacting great execution on the Me 110s in particular, claiming some fourteen destroyed, and five Ju 87s. The squadron had a missing pilot, however: Pilot Officer Maurice Buchin, a free Belgian, was shot down over the sea and never seen again.

Squadron Leader Terence Gunion 'Shuvvel' Lovell-Gregg, a New Zealander from Picton, Marlborough, had succeeded Johnny Dewar in command of 87 Squadron on 12 July 1940, but, conscious of lacking operational experience, the new CO sensibly allowed his two seasoned flight commanders, Flight Lieutenants Ian 'Widge' Gleed and Roderick 'Roddy' Rayner to lead in the air until he felt ready to take the helm. According to the 87 Squadron ORB, ten Hurricanes, led by Gleed and Rayner with Lovell-Gregg in the formation, took off from Exeter with 213 Squadron in what had been a 'panic take-off' to defend Portland. 'What was described as the fiercest dogfight yet experienced then took place.'

THURSDAY, 15 AUGUST 1940

No.87 Squadron engaged the enemy at 17.45 hrs, seven miles south-east of Portland. Flight Lieutenant Gleed claimed two Me 109s destroyed and a 109 probable in this sharp and fast combat. In his 1942 memoir *Arise to Conquer*, Gleed wrote:

> Over the wire comes: 'Patrol Portland. You are to fix the escort fighters.' I slam the receiver down and run like hell.
> 'Start the bloody thing, you fools!'
> 'A's' prop, is still only turning slowly over; it kicks into life just as I reach it. 'B' Flight are already taxi-ing out.
> 'Quick, help me with my parachute.'
> I swing up into the cockpit. Good show! all the boys are started.
> I strap my helmet on, taxi a few yards, then open up full for the take-off, just behind 'B' Flight's last man. I glance behind; all the boys are screaming off the deck. I throttle back for a second. Oh, good show, boys! Dickie and Dennis are in position, tucked in close to me already.
> 'Shuvvel' has done a complete circuit to give me a chance to get into position. I swing in behind 'B' Flight, who are in close formation, climbing hard.
> 'Crocodile calling Suncup leader. Are you receiving? Over.'
> Clearly comes 'Shuvvel's' voice, 'Hullo, Crocodile! Suncup leader answering. Receiving you loud and clear. Over.'
> 'Hullo, Suncup Leader! Patrol Portland. Over.'
> 'O.K., Crocodile. Listen out.'
> I glance at the altimeter. 5,000ft. Hell! a long way to go yet. We clamber upwards. I turn on the oxygen. Dennis grins at me through his Perspex roof. Dickie the other side makes rude gestures with his hands. I give them both a thumbs-up. Behind and slightly above, Yellow section is flying in perfect formation. We are going much too fast to weave.
> At 15,000 I give Dickie the two-fingers sign, that means, 'Open to search formation.' Dennis and Dickie swing out to about two spans; Robbie's boys follow suit. Below me 'B' Flight have opened out. The long finger of Portland Bill stretches out into the sea in front of us. 'Blast! the sun is from the sea – that means they'll come out of the sun.'
> Far below us I catch a glimpse of another Squadron – 213, I suppose. At last, we reach 25,000; it has taken us fifteen

minutes – not bad. 'Shuvvel' has throttled back. I pull the throttle back to O boost. Dennis and Dickie weave; Robbie weaves his section behind me. I peer seawards. 'Blast the sun! Can't see a thing.'

Faintly on the R.T. comes: 'Crocodile calling Suncup Leader. Bandits are just south of Portland now, heading north. Heights are from fifteen to twenty-five. Over to you – over.'

'Suncup Leader answering. Your message received and understood.'

We head seawards. I open my glasshouse. I'm sweating like a pig. I strain my eyes looking seawards. I wonder what Pam is doing at this moment. 'Hell! there they are.' I speak on the R.T. 'Hullo, Suncup Leader. Tally-ho! Bandits just to our right. Line astern, line astern, go.'

I slam my glasshouse shut. 'Christ! It's worse than a Hendon air pageant. A horde of dots are filling the sky; below us bombers flying in close formation – JU. 88s and 87s. Above them, towering tier above tier, are fighters – 110s and 109s.

The mass comes closer. 'Now steady; don't go in too soon – work round into the sun.' The bombers pass about 10,000ft below us. I start a dive, craning my neck to see behind. A circle of 110s are just in front of us; they turn in a big circle.

Suddenly the white of the crosses on their wings jumps into shape. I kick on the rudder; my sights are just in front of one. 'Get the right deflection.' Now I press the firing-button – a terrific burst of orange flame; it seems to light the whole sky. Everything goes grey as I bank into a turn. 'Ease off a bit, you fool, or you'll spin.' I push the stick forward-white puffs flash past my cockpit. 'Blast you, rear-gunners!' I climb steeply, turning hard. Just above me there is another circle of 110s; their bellies are a pale blue, looking very clean.

'Look out! look out!' Oh God! a Hurricane just in front of me is shooting at a 110; another 110 is on its tail. Hell! it's too far for me to reach. The 110 goes vertically downwards, followed by the Hurricane. – 'Hell, you bastards!'

A stream of tracer from behind just misses my right wing. I turn hard to the left; two splashes appear in the calm sea; already it is dotted with oily patches. For a second, I get my sights on another 110. He turns and gives me an easy full deflection shot. I thumb the trigger; a puff of white smoke comes from his engine. Almost lazily he turns on to his back and starts an inverted, over the vertical, dive. I steep turn. Down, down he goes – a white splash. At the same time two other splashes and a cloud of smoke go up from the beach. Four 'planes have hit the deck within a second.

'Keep turning,' a voice inside me warns; and sure enough a second later I spot three 110s behind and just below. 'You fools! You'll never turn inside me; turn and turn.'

About twenty 'planes are around me: black crosses seem to fill the sky. About half a mile away I can see the greenish camouflage of another Hurricane.

'Hell! where have the boys got to? Blast these rear-gunners! Oh God, my arm is getting tired.'

For a fleeting second, I am on the tail of another. I give him a burst, then turn frantically as a stream of tracer goes over my head. 'Damn! We're getting out to sea.'

Below me the bombers are now heading seawards, no longer in their tight formation, but in ones and twos. 'Hell! this is too hot.' I over-bank, stick right in the bottom right-hand corner. 'Down, down.' The altimeter whirls round; 400 mph shows on the clock. I go flashing by 110s. Now I am below them I straighten out and head for the finger of Portland. The voice inside me again: 'Turn, turn.'

Rat-tat-tat, rat-tat-tat. 'Christ! 109s cannon; you silly b------!' One is past me – overshot. Sights on, I thumb my firing-button. Brrrrrrmmmmmm. A long burst from about fifty yards, a splash of oil hits my windscreen. Rat-tat-tat. 'Yank back on the stick.'

Nearly dead behind me is another 109, with two others just behind it. 'Oh God, get me out of this.' Once more I aileron. Down, down, down. The sea rushes up to meet me. I pull out and scream towards the pebbly beach about a mile away. The 109s are far above me, heading for the south. I pull up into a turning climb. The sea now seems littered with odd bits of aircraft and splodges of oil. On the cliff-tops smoke rises lazily from several wrecks.

I weave gently, and throttle back. My engine has been flat out for about fifteen minutes. I glance at the instruments; the temperatures are high, but not in the danger mark. The sky seems empty. I climb to 5,000ft. Nothing. Faintly on the RT comes, 'All aircraft return to base and land.' Thank God for that! I open the lid. The country looks very lovely beneath me. I dive. Oh God, I wonder if the boys are OK I dive down low.

People are standing in the streets of a tiny village; they wave to me from under the eaves of thatched Devon cottages. I wave back; I am happy – my clothes feel dripping with sweat, but I am happy. I roar along, low-flying towards the 'drome; my wings look free of bullet-holes. 'Good old A! you have knocked down seven Jerries now definitely, and probably two more.' The red earth round the 'drome looks very warm and friendly. I roar round low over the dispersal points. Already most of the 'planes are in. I turn in and do a bouncy landing, taxi quickly in to the dispersal hut.

Like 213 Squadron, 87 Squadron had done well, and 'less than half an hour from leaving the ground the first Hurricanes were returning' (ORB).

Eight Me 110s were claimed destroyed along with two probables and four damaged, plus two Ju 87s and an Me 109 destroyed. Having been seen to shoot down an Me 110 into the sea, 19-year-old Pilot Officer Peter Comely, however, was attacked by another Me 110 and followed his victim into the sea; he was never seen again. Sergeant James Cowley was shot-up and slightly injured, making a forced-landing at Symondsbury, near Bridport, and likewise Pilot Officer Trevor Jay came off second best in a duel with an Me 109 – fortunately unhurt, he brought his damaged Hurricane down at Field Barn Farm, Radipole. Squadron Leader Lovell-Gregg, however, had been killed, the ORB commenting that the loss was 'a bitter blow. In the short time he was with us he had become very well-liked and respected. He had never been in combat before this occasion but for days had been impatient to get his first chance.' But what had befallen 87 Squadron's popular Kiwi leader?

His Hurricane having been hit, Squadron Leader Lovell-Gregg was wounded and seen by eye-witnesses on the ground to recover control and descend, in a glide, apparently intending to crash-land near The Fleet Lagoon at Abbotsbury, on the Dorset coast west of Portland. Approaching a suitable field, Lovell-Gregg was too low to avoid a small wood; the Hurricane stalled, hit an oak tree and caught fire. 'Shuvvel' was thrown clear and lay on the ground.

William Dunfold was an Abbotsbury schoolboy and on the scene:

THURSDAY, 15 AUGUST 1940

> With another schoolboy I ran to the spot where the pilot had fallen. He was badly shot about and burning. We put out the flames with two buckets of water. About two hours later a truck came from Warmwell and we were then told the flier's identity. Though he had those wounds, I am sure, had he made it to belly-land on the shallow waters of The Fleet, he would have made it.

In this hectic action over Portland, given the volume of combat claims, it is impossible to say with any certainty who was responsible for Squadron Leader Lovell-Gregg's demise. One sentence, however, stands out in the 152 Squadron ORB and is specific: 'Sergeant Robinson attacked an Me 109 which he followed down and saw burst into flames and crash in a wood near Abbotsbury.' No Me 109 crashed near Abbotsbury that day, nor anywhere else in Dorset, so the possibility of Lovell-Gregg being the victim of 'Friendly Fire' cannot be discounted. As we have repeatedly seen, aircraft identification in combat was frequently poor, and given the speed of combat, mistakes caused by the confusion and fog of war were not uncommon. Whether that was the case in this instance we will never know for sure, but the description of Sergeant Robinson's combat and facts surrounding it are potentially significant.

Meanwhile, the Ju 88s had reached Middle Wallop, as Pilot Officer David Crook described:

> Through some delay on the part of the Operations Room, we got off the ground only a few minutes before they arrived at the aerodrome, and were unable to intercept them or even to see them until they were practically over the aerodrome, as they dived out of the sun, dropped their bombs and then streamed back towards the coast as hard as they could go.

Flight Lieutenant Frank Howell:

> I found one serviceable aircraft after 'B' Flight had taken off. As I took off, salvo of bombs fell on the hangars. I climbed into the sun and saw eight E/A flying from Middle Wallop towards Warmwell. I easily caught one Ju 88 doing 320 mph, which dived for cloud. I followed through and fired a ½ second burst just before he entered. No sign of E/A in front, so climbed up

into sun. E/A appeared below so attacked again from above. E/A entered cloud. Climbed again into sun, attacked again for two seconds, and then eight seconds approx. Fire appeared from wings of E/A, which dived below cloud. R/T talk in German was very loud indeed ... one voice was speaking the whole time in a very excited manner. Machine-gun and cannon bursts clearly audible between what sounded like almost hysterical orders or swearing. This completely drowned all orders from 'Bandy' [Middle Wallop Control].

Howell was credited with a Ju 88 destroyed.

The German formation leader, *Hauptmann* Wilhelm Kern, who later mistakenly reported having bombed Andover, however, had misjudged his bomb release by two seconds; his formation followed his lead and dropped their payloads simultaneously. Consequently, the majority of bombs fell wide of the aerodrome, although two hangars were hit, three Blenheims of 604 Squadron destroyed on the ground and another damaged (ORB).

The Spitfires harried the retreating enemy; the Polish Flying Officer Piotr 'Osti' Ostaszewski-Ostoja reported:

While flying at 10,000ft I was alone, having taken off independently of my section. I saw a circus of about seven Me 110s doing left-hand circuit. I turned and made a circuit right-handed outside them. One machine broke away to try and engage me. I turned inside him and opened fire from the quarter at about 300 yards. I gave him a two or three second burst, and this E/A dived steeply, making 'S' turns. I followed him down, we went through the balloon barrage at Southampton. He pulled out just above the ground and started hedge-hopping. I gave him several short bursts, closing from 300 to 100 yards. The E/A flew low across Southampton Solent and on to the Isle of Wight. I saw another Spitfire, which was also chasing and firing at him. After several short bursts I noticed both engines smoking and stop. The E/A then made a crash-landing and burst into flames. The Me 110 struck the side of a road, skidded across it and came to rest, burning on the other side of the road. He crashed on the Southside of the Isle of Wight, a few hundred yards from the sea.

THURSDAY, 15 AUGUST 1940

By sheer coincidence, the other Spitfire was also flown by a Pole, namely Pilot Officer Jan Zurakowski of 234 Squadron, with whom 'Osti' shared the kill. The Me 110 belonged to 6/ZG 76; the pilot, *Feldwebel* Jakob Birndorfer was killed in the crash but his *Bordfunker*, *Unteroffizier* Max Guschewski, was captured.

No.609 Squadron's Flight Lieutenant James McArthur claimed two Me 110s destroyed in this action, one of which crashed and exploded at Plaitford Common, near Romsey, killing the crew. Flying Officer Alexander Edge claimed another, while Flying Officer John Newberry claimed two Ju 88 probables, and Squadron Leader Horace Darley was accredited with one Ju 88 probably destroyed.

When the Spitfires of 'B' Flight took off, however, a twin-engine Blenheim Mk IF fighter of 604 Squadron was returning to Middle Wallop from a training sortie; Pilot Officer David Crook describes what happened next:

> This occasion was the now famous one when I shot down one of our own machines – a Blenheim!
>
> There was a Blenheim fighter squadron stationed at Wallop, they are not fast enough for day fighting but are used a lot for night work as they are fairly large and can carry some of the bulky equipment which is now used for night fighting. Incidentally, they are twin engine machines and very similar in appearance to the Junkers 88.
>
> One of these Blenheims happened to the doing some practice flying near the aerodrome when the attack started and in a fit of rather misguided valour, he fastened himself on to the German formation as it ran for the coast, and started attacking the rear machines.
>
> I was rapidly overhauling the Germans and when in range opened fire at the last machine on the line, which happened to be the Blenheim. I hit both engines and the fuselage, one engine stopped immediately, and he made a crash landing at Wallop. Fortunately, the pilot had been saved by the armour plating behind him, and the rear gunner had a bullet through his bottom which doubtless caused him considerable discomfort and inconvenience, but was not serious.
>
> Nothing was said about this mistake as it was certainly not my fault, and equally the Blenheim pilot could scarcely

be blamed for his desire to engage the enemy, even though it was rather unwise since his machine was so similar to the Germans.

The Blenheims had sometimes got in our way before, and we had often remarked jokingly 'If one of those blasted Blenheims gets in our way again, we'll jolly well put a bullet through his bottom.' And now it had come to pass and everybody was very amused (except possibly the rear gunner).

The whole story became very well-known and I was ragged about it for a long time afterwards.

It was a very easy mistake for Crook to have made, so similar were the Blenheim and Ju 88 in appearance; fortunately Sergeant Cyril Haigh and Sergeant George Evans survived the experience.

At 17.05 hrs, 234 Squadron, newcomers to Middle Wallop, had also been scrambled and patrolled Swanage uneventfully for an hour before meeting the retiring Middle Wallop raiders over the sea, south-west of Swanage. Having previously flown in the infinitely quieter St Eval sector, 234 Squadron had yet to adjust to the increased tempo of combat, and especially the presence of Me 109s. As Pilot Officer Bob Doe put it:

We did everything wrong that we could possibly do wrong. We formed into four sections of three, in tight formation, with sections astern, so that the only person not concentrating on formation flying was the CO. We flew to the same height that we had been told the enemy were flying and proceeded to patrol up and down the sun. After one such turn, we found that there were only nine of us left.

Around 18.15 hrs, 234 Squadron was jumped by Me 109s. Over the coast, just east of Swanage, *Feldwebel* Karl Schulz of 9/JG 27 and 7/JG 27's *Gefreiter* Werner Rethfeld both claimed Spitfires, and at which point two of 234 Squadron's fighters went down: the Polish Sergeant Zygmunt Klein's aircraft was severely damaged, the pilot making a forced-landing at Twyford; Pilot Officer Cecil Hight, a New Zealander, however, was shot down and baled out. Sadly, the 22-year-old former car salesman from Stratford was apparently too badly wounded to deploy his parachute and fell dead in the garden of 'Hambledon', a house in Leven Road, Bournemouth. Two other 234 Squadron pilots were also missing, however …

THURSDAY, 15 AUGUST 1940

For one, Australian Pilot Officer Vincent Parker, this was his first taste of combat; the other, Pilot Officer Richard 'Dick' Hardy, had inconclusively engaged a lone Dornier off Falmouth a week before – but this scenario, with so many aircraft engaged, was entirely different. For both of these Spitfire pilots, the afternoon of 15 August 1940 represented their baptism of fire.

Pilot Officer Hardy, Red 1, was leading Red Section, with Pilot Officer Parker being his Red 2. Pilot Officer Edward Mortimer-Rose was Red 3, and reported that at 18.15 hrs:

> On sighting the enemy on our port flank, 2,000ft below, the Squadron Leader gave the order to attack. Red Section was somewhat behind at the time and Red 1 and 2, who were together, appeared to lose the enemy in the haze, so being well behind I followed the bombers and carried out an attack on a pair of 110s in the centre of the formation, slightly below. They went into line astern and I followed through a series of turns. I closed to fifty yards and fired all my ammunition. His starboard engine burst into flame, rear-gunner ceased fire and before breaking for home I saw him drop away to the left. By then I was in the middle of the formation but noticed no attack and dived for home.

Mortimer-Rose's combat occurred at 11,000ft, twenty-five miles southwest of Swanage; the Spitfire pilot was credited with an Me 110 destroyed.

Pilot Officers Hardy and Parker pursued the enemy back to France – but neither would return to base. What, though, happened to them?

Unteroffizier Willy Lehner, the *Bordfunker* of *Leutnant* Siegfried Hahn, *Stab* II/ZG 76, claimed a Spitfire destroyed at 18.30 hrs (GMT) '30 km vor Cherbourg: 3,000m'.

Pilot Officer Vincent Parker: 'After two combats with Me 110s, which I shot down, my engine gave up and I had to bale out from 900ft over the English Channel.'

Parker makes no mention, however, of having been hit by return fire from one of the Me 110s he engaged, or provides an explanation as to why his engine 'gave up', but it is likely that it was he who Lehner hit.

As Parker also explained in his PoW debrief upon repatriation:

> After almost four hours in the water, a German speedboat picked me up and took me to Cherbourg. I was flown to Dulag Luft (Oberusel) in a Ju 52 on 16 August. Here I was

interrogated and given false Red Cross forms to fill in, but gave only number, rank and name. I was kept in the cells for three days and then put into the main camp.

Parker would prove a thorn in the Germans' side during captivity, making several determined escape attempts leading to his incarceration at Oflag IVC – the notorious Colditz Castle, where he was ultimately liberated by American forces on 19 April 1945.

Far out to sea that afternoon of 15 August 1940, Pilot Officer Richard Hardy – having already patrolled over Swanage for an hour before the engagement – was jumped by Me 109s off the French coast and shot-up by *Oberleutnant* Georg Claus, III/JG 53's Technical Officer. As we have seen, RAF pilots pursuing the withdrawing enemy far out to sea, and even over France, was not altogether uncommon – but unfortunately some paid the price for their keenness. According to *Oberleutnant* Hans von Hahn, *Staffelkapitän* of 8/JG 53, Claus caught Hardy's Spitfire:

> In the middle of the Channel, the 'Tommy' made off to the South. Claus improved each of his turns with a brief burst of tracer fire. So it went all the way to Théville, JG53's forward airfield near Cherbourg. There 'Tommy' lowered his undercarriage and luckily the 20mm flak failed to hit him. Then he landed safely and taxied in.

Critically low on fuel and with a damaged Spitfire, like 64 Squadron's Pilot Officer Roberts earlier in the day, Hardy had no choice but to land in France – wheels down because he was landing on an airfield, the forward base of I/JG 53 (and not making a forced-landing in a farmer's field, as had Pilot Officer Roberts, wheels-up, that morning).

Leutnant Karl Leonhard, 3/JG 53:

> The English pilot slid back the cockpit hood and immediately raised his hands – he obviously expected to be shot. He was just as surprised when I asked him to lower his hands and instead climb out and come to the pilots' mess to have a glass of champagne with the pilots of I/JG53.

In 1974, British historian Alfred Price (see Bibliography) suggested that the damage behind Hardy's cockpit, clearly seen in several photographs,

THURSDAY, 15 AUGUST 1940

was caused by the pilot having activated the demolition charge and blown up 'secret IFF equipment' – but as the IFF aerial wires, running from the fuselage to tailplane, on both sides, are missing in photographs, clearly IFF was not fitted – although 'Pip-Squeak' may have been (see Volume 1, *The Gathering Storm*). Either way, the standard radio set would provide the enemy useful intelligence, and so needed to be destroyed. According to *Leutnant* Leonhard, however, Hardy was captured while still in his cockpit, and therefore the damage must have been caused by *Oberleutnant* Claus's fire, which appears to have been delivered from above and astern. Certain other accounts attribute the damage to flak, but clearly *Oberleutnant* von Hahn's account discounts this. One recent account claimed that Hardy received a back wound, but no evidence is cited or can be found to substantiate this, which, considering the sheets of armour plate behind the pilot's seat and head seems unlikely. Considering the shrapnel which must have been flying around inside the Spitfire from Claus's 20mm cannon round, and shards of Perspex from the smashed canopy, it is, however, possible that this could have caused some superficial wounds. Over the years, however, there have been various completely unsubstantiated rumours that Hardy defected, deliberately delivering his Spitfire to the Germans, which was evaluated by the *Erprobungsstelle* research and development unit based at Reclin. So too was Pilot Officer Roberts' K9964, and various other captured Allied aircraft, so this was hardly a unique occurrence – and nor was RAF fighter pilots pursuing enemy aircraft back to France and finding themselves consequently in trouble. With insufficient fuel to regain base, a damaged aircraft, possibly wounded, and sixty miles of sea separating him from home, what else could Hardy do but land in France? Any allegation, therefore, that Hardy was a traitor is baseless and defamatory.

No.234 Squadron's first encounter with a large enemy formation was not all one-sided, though; the Australian flight commander Flight Lieutenant Pat Hughes, and Pilot Officer Bob Doe each claimed an Me 110 destroyed and shared another; Pilot Officer Edward Mortimer-Rose and Pilot Officer Janusz Zurakowski also claimed Me 110s destroyed, the latter's shared with 609 Squadron's Flying Officer Ostaszewski-Ostoja, and Pilot Officer Kenneth Dewhurst damaged a 109.

Although Middle Wallop had been hit the damage was not bad, and the attack on Worthy Down was largely unsuccessful, with only a handful of bombers reaching the target. Indeed, *Luftflotte* 3's results on this raid were poor with no advantage gained – and losses were high, even if Fighter Command combat claims were somewhat wildly optimistic.

Nonetheless, if the Me 110s had intended to repeat their successes of previous days over Weymouth Bay, they were disappointed. II/ZG 76 lost eight Me 110s with eleven aircrew killed or missing, and three more wounded. III/ZG 76 lost four Me 110s, including that of the popular *Gruppenkommandeur*, *Hauptmann* Karl-Friedrich Dickoré. LG 1 lost seven Ju 88s destroyed, and at least four Ju 87s failed to return. Offset against this execution, three Spitfires were destroyed and three more damaged, with one Spitfire pilot killed and two captured along with one repairable aircraft; five Hurricanes were also destroyed and four damaged; three Hurricane pilots had been killed, another was missing and three were wounded. It had been a successful interception and the balance sheet was firmly in the defender's favour. The sun had yet to set on the day-fighting on this day of days – the focus of which had already returned to 11 Group and south-east England.

With the fighting over the south-west coast and Channel still ongoing, at 17.53 hrs RDF indicated that *Luftflotte* 2 was preparing to mount further attacks on the south-east. By 18.15 hrs, some 70+ bandits were being tracked by radar approaching the Kentish coast between Dungeness and Dover. Again, the enemy intended to confuse and disrupt the defences by simultaneously attacking two targets, while formations of Me 109s both swept ahead of the bombers and escorted them. *Erprobungsgruppe* 210, escorted by JG 52's Me 109s, was to attack Kenley airfield, while various formations of Do 17s struck out for Biggin Hill Sector Station.

At 17.25 hrs, 501 Squadron had scrambled from Gravesend to patrol 'Hellfire Corner', and an hour later sighted '200+' incoming near Dungeness. Near Gatwick the Hurricanes attempted to attack strangling bombers but were fended off by the fighter escort and, short of fuel, forced to retire without achieving any results.

At 18.20 hrs, Squadron Leader Wilkinson led seven of his 266 Squadron Spitfires up from Manston to patrol base. At 18.40 hrs, while flying at 15,000ft, 266 Squadron also sighted '200+', Me 109s and Ju 88s, and went into action ten miles south of Dover.

Sub-Lieutenant Henry la Fone Greenshields was an FAA pilot flying Spitfires with 266 Squadron, and reported:

> I was Green 2 in a section of two, but became separated from my leader before engaging the enemy. I attacked six Me 109s but was fired at by another Me 109 (colour light grey or green with black crosses which had white edges – the

THURSDAY, 15 AUGUST 1940

> 109 which I was attacking had dark camouflage with yellow roundels on wing tips) before coming in range of my target; having evaded the 109 behind by closing my throttle and turning sharply, I again attacked the dark 109 and gave it a short burst while it was turning steeply, but tracer showed me my shots were going behind although I used 'full ring' deflection, so I waited till he straightened up and then gave two more bursts of three seconds each, which seemed to be accurate. The 109 dived vertically from 1,500ft into the sea – thinking that he was still trying to evade me (since his engine appeared to be going flat out) I followed him down and gave several more bursts from dead astern. When my air speed had passed 500 mph, indicated, I pulled out in sight of land (probably Dover) and climbed back to 1,500ft, but was unable to locate E/A.

Greenshields was credited with the Me 109 destroyed, although he had a lucky escape himself: 'Two machine-gun bullets passed from behind, through the trailing edge of the wing fairing and into the cockpit under my seat. It did not affect the handling or performance of my machine.'

Some of 266's pilots managed to penetrate the fighter screen and attack the bombers, among them Flight Lieutenant Dennis Armitage and Sergeant Arthur Eade, as the latter reported:

> With my Section Leader two No 1 Attacks were carried out on a Ju 88 in rear of the main formation. I attacked immediately after my Section Leader and encountered fire from rear top turret. Tracer bullets passing to the right, clear of my aircraft. In this attack I fired a burst of five seconds duration, enemy fire ceased, and I observed wreckage leaving the E/A around the fuselage. Enemy steered straight course, gradually losing height. I carried out a second No 1 Attack behind my Section Leader, as the Section Leader broke away the port engine of E/A took fire. No fire was experienced from rear guns. I fired burst of five seconds duration, wreckage fell from E/A, its wheels were lowered and it lost height rapidly, and disappeared into haze, the port engine still on fire.
>
> I was then attacked by an Me 109, receiving a bullet in my radio set, I lost the 109 in the haze and returned to base.

Armitage and Eade shared the bomber as a 'probable', while Squadron Leader Wilkinson claimed a Ju 88 destroyed, and Pilot Officer Robert Roach damaged a 109. Back at Hornchurch, however, Spitfire N3168 and Pilot Officer Francis Cale, an Australian, were missing. Later, it transpired that the 25-year-old from Perth had been shot down by a 109, possibly by *Leutnant* Hans Götz of 1/JG 54, and baled out, his aircraft crashing into the bank of the river Medway at Teston, near Maidstone. Unfortunately the pilot landed in the river and was drowned, his body being recovered the following day.

At 18.45 hrs, 151 Squadron had scrambled from North Weald with orders to patrol Manston, but were diverted to Dover. West of Dover 'a large force of Me 109s were again encountered.' The Hurricanes had, in fact, run into *Hauptmann* Adolf Galland's III/JG 26, up on a *Freie Jagd*, the Me 109s being so numerous that Sergeant Irving Smith, a New Zealander, found it 'impossible' to estimate numbers. Smith was the only 151 Squadron pilot to make a combat claim in this action: 'Three five second bursts. I followed Me 109 down from about 20,000ft to about 4–5,000ft. I then broke away. The Me 109 was spinning slowly at a speed in excess of 400 mph and going down vertically.'

III/JG 26 lost no 109s, however, but claimed three of the Hurricanes destroyed – which under-estimated the casualties inflicted: Pilot Officer James Johnston baled out off Dymchurch but was picked up dead; Sub-Lieutenant Henry Beggs, an FAA pilot, was shot-up and crash-landed, wounded, at Shorncliffe; Squadron Leader John Gordon, a Canadian, returned to base with a damaged aircraft and was wounded, and the Polish Pilot Officer Mieczyslaw Rozwadowski was never seen again. During the combat, Pilot Officer John Ellacombe had used his emergency boost excessively, causing his engine to fail and necessitating a forced-landing near Ashford. As the 151 Squadron ORB recorded: 'In this action we fared badly' (ORB).

More RAF fighters were hurrying to intercept the Germans as they pressed on inland, searching for Biggin Hill. At 18.28 hrs, twelve Spitfires of 54 Squadron, led by Squadron Leader James 'Prof' Leathart DSO scrambled from Manston and vectored towards Maidstone, while at 18.43 hrs Flight Lieutenant William Warner, a 21-year-old auxiliary and Old Malvernian, led seven 610 Squadron Spitfires up from Biggin Hill with orders to intercept the approaching raid.

No.610 Squadron was first to engage, at 18.50 hrs:

> About ten miles to the SE they met about twenty-five Do 215s escorted by many Me 109s. The bombers flying at 14,000ft and the

One Luftwaffe Unit that earned itself respect from friend and foe alike during this phase was *Erprobungsgruppe* 210 – which began specialising in low-level and dive-bombing attacks. Equipped with the Me 110 and Me 109, this is a Me 110C-6 of 1/*Erprobungsgruppe* 210, which is armed with a 30mm cannon under the nose. (John Vasco)

Leutnant Horst Marx with an *Erprobungsgruppe* 210 Me 110D – he was shot down flying a Me 109 on 15 August 1940 and captured. (John Vasco)

Erprobungsgruppe 210's brilliant *Kommandeur*, *Hauptmann* Walter Rubensdörffer – killed in action after a raid on Croydon, 15 August 1940. (John Vasco)

The grave of *Hauptmann* Walter Rubensdörffer and his radio operator/ air gunner, *Obergefreiter* Ludwig Kretzer at the German war cemetery at Cannock Chase in Staffordshire.

Above: *Hauptmann* Rubensdörffer was succeeded in command of *Erprobungsgruppe* 210 by *Oberleutnant* Martin Lutz, seen here whilst commanding 1/*Erprobungsgruppe* 210 and in conversation on 30 July 1930 with *Generalfeldmarschall* Albert Kesselring, commander of *Luftflotte* 2. (John Vasco)

Right: The grave in Sheffield of the first of three WAAFs killed during the Battle of Britain: 19-year-old ACW2 Marguerite Esther Hudson, a victim of the bombing of RAF Driffield on 15 August 1940. (Mark Gregory)

The well-kept grave of the American Pilot Officer Fiske at Boxgrove Abbey, near Tangmere in West Sussex.

The only American volunteer to die fighting with the RAF during the Battle of Britain was Pilot Officer William 'Billy' Meade Lindsley Fiske III (right), an Olympian and wealthy international banker. Flying Hurricanes with 601 Squadron at Tangmere, Fiske was shot down and crash-landed back at base on 16 August 1940 – but died of shock and burns the following day.

Pilot Officer Martyn Aurel King, the youngest of The Few, aged 18, who was one of a section of 249 Squadron Hurricanes patrolling Southampton and led by Flight Lieutenant James Brindley Nicolson on 16 August 1940. The section was bounced by *Hauptmann* Heinz 'Pietzsch' Bretnütz, *Staffelkapitän* of 6/JG53, who shot down Nicolson and King. The latter's parachute, however, was so badly damaged by shrapnel in the attack that the canopy collapsed during King's descent – he died in the arms of a Sotonian in a suburban garden.

Above left: Pilot Officer King's grave at All Saints, Fawley, Hampshire.

Above right: For his 'signal act of valour' over Southampton on 16 August 1940, Flight Lieutenant Nicolson, pictured here with his wife, Muriel, and new born son, was awarded the Victoria Cross – becoming the only RAF fighter pilot to receive the highest award for valour throughout the entire Second World War. He failed to return from an operation in the Far East in 1945.

Hauptmann Heinz 'Pietzsch' Bretnütz, *Staffelkapitän* of 6/JG53, who shot down Flight Lieutenant Nicolson and Pilot Officer King over Southampton on 16 August 1940.

Above left: Leading German ace Major Helmut Wick – who shot down No.1 Squadron's Pilot Officer Elkington over the Solent on 16 August 1940. Wick would be reported missing after a combat off the Isle of Wight on 28 November 1940.

Above right: Pilot Officer J.F.D. 'Tim' Elkington – who believed had he not been shot down by Major Wick and hospitalised, he would never have survived the Battle of Britain. Tim also owed his survival to Flight Sergeant Fred Berry, who used the slipstream from his Hurricane to blow the unconscious pilot's parachute towards land. This was successful and Tim came down on the beach at West Wittering – but had no opportunity to thank Berry who was killed soon afterwards.

Alexander Osmand was a Pilot Officer flying Hurricanes with 213 Squadron at Exeter during the Battle of Britain, and is pictured here as a sergeant before having received his coveted pilot's 'wings'. Sadly, he would perish fighting the Japanese in the Far East in 1943, leaving behind a widow and young son. (Tony Osmand)

YEAR 1940		AIRCRAFT		PILOT, OR 1ST PILOT	2ND PILOT, PUPIL OR PASSENGER	DUTY (INCLUDING RESULTS AND REMARKS)
MONTH	DATE	Type	No.			
—	—	—	—	—	—	— TOTALS BROUGHT FORWARD
AUG	16	HURRICANE	P3113 "!!!"	SELF	—	PATROL AT 10000 FT — FIRST TO START POINT, THEN 10 MLS SOUTH. VECTORED TO PORTLAND AT 15000 FT — 10 MLS TO SEA, AGAIN — THEN ON TO RINGWOOD AT 20000 FT. DIVED ONTO "SPITFIRES" VERY MUCH TO THE BOOK! (TO BASE WITH LITTLE FUEL).
AUG	17	HURRICANE	N2630 "E"	SELF	—	PATROL SIDMOUTH 15000 FT — ON TO PORTLAND. NO SIGN OF E.A. — ONLY "SPITFIRES".
AUG	18	HURRICANE	N2630 "E"	SELF	—	PATROL BASE — 10000 FT.
AUG	18	HURRICANE	N2630 "E"	SELF	—	PATROL PORTLAND — 15000 FT. ON TO ST CATHS PT — WHERE I WAS ATTACKED BY 3 x ME 109'S, WHICH TRIED TO PICK ME OFF REAR OF SQUADRON. HEAD ON — GOT BURST IN WINDSCREEN — GLASS IN MY EYES !

GRAND TOTAL [Cols. (1) to (10)] 247 Hrs. 45 Mins. TOTALS CARRIED FORWARD

A page from Pilot Officer Osmand's log book, succinctly describing some of the action in August 1940.

A Spitfire of 64 Squadron at Kenley during the Battle of Britain.

The crew of a He 111 pointing out bullet holes after crash-landing their bomber following a raid on England. They were lucky to get home: many did not.

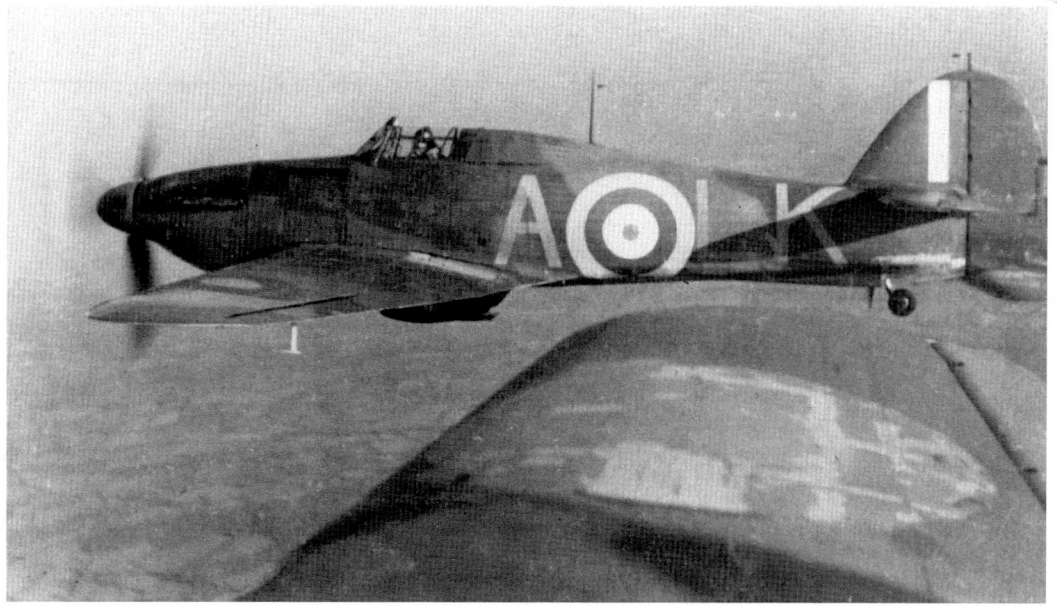

Flight Lieutenant Ian 'Widge' Gleed DFC leading 'A' Flight of 87 Squadron, temporarily based at RAF Bibury in Gloucestershire, on patrol over the West Country.

The Polish Sergeant Anton Glowacki makes out his report to 501 Squadron's Intelligence Officer, complete with 'Battle Bowler'.

The Me 109 of *Oberleutnant* Gerhard Schöpfel of III/JG26 camouflaged at Caffiers in the Pas-de-Calais.

Hurricane pilots of 501 Squadron at Hawkinge. From, left, seated, are: Pilot Officer Robert Dafforn; Sergeant Paul Farnes; Pilot Officer Kenneth Lee; Flight Lieutenant John Gibson and Sergeant Hugh Adams. Those standing are, from the left: Pilot Officer Stefan Witorzenc (Polish), Flight Lieutenant George Stoney, and Sergeant Anton Glowacki (Polish). Stoney would be killed in action on 18 August 1940, Adams on 6 September 1940, whilst Dafforn and Glowacki lost their lives after the Battle of Britain but before the Second World War ended.

Oberleutnant Gerhard Schöpfel of III/JG26, who achieved a hitherto unprecedented feat on 18 August 1940, when he shot down four 501 Squadron Hurricanes in half as many minutes over Canterbury.

Dornier 17s of 9/KG76 skimming the waves and passing Beachy Head en route to RAF Kenley on 18 August 1940.

Kriegsberichter Rolf von Pebel was aboard one of the 9/KG76 bombers and photographed 64 Squadron's dispersal being strafed as the Dorniers roared overhead.

Although overgrown, the same blast pen survives today at Kenley, the airfield now used for gliding and as a common.

Right and below: Wrecked hangars at Kenley on 18 August 1940.

A wrecked Hurricane of 615 Squadron at Kenley on 18 August 1940.

Seen from St Andrew's, Coulsdon, smoke billows over Kenley airfield following the heavy attack on 18 August 1940.

An artist's impression of WAAF Sergeant Joan Mortimer, after already having maintained her switchboard during a heavy raid on Biggin Hill, 18 August 1940, marking UXBs – for which courageous action she would receive the Military Medal.

Flying Officer Franciszek Gruszka of 65 Squadron. Reported missing on 18 August 1940, Gruszka was not recovered from the wreckage of his Spitfire until it was found buried in marshes near Canterbury in 1974. He was the first Polish Spitfire pilot to die in the Battle of Britain.

Flying Officer Gruszka's grave at Northwood Cemetery.

Unless otherwise indicated, all photographs are from the Dilip Sarkar Archive.

THURSDAY, 15 AUGUST 1940

> fighters at 15,000ft. Flight Lieutenant Warner attacked an Me 109 and gave it three long bursts, smoke came from the fuselage as it dived down vertically. Sergeant Arnfield fired several bursts at an Me 109 which began to smoke badly. Pilot Officer Cox fired three short bursts at an Me 109, the tracer appeared to hit him about the rear of the fuselage and wings. (ORB)

For no loss, 610 Squadron claimed one Me 109 destroyed, a probable and two damaged – but were unable to penetrate the enemy fighter screen.

For 54 Squadron it would be the day's second engagement against a large German formation, and before take-off the New Zealand ace Pilot Officer Colin Gray – who was awarded the DFC on this day – told his fellow Kiwi, the indomitable Flight Lieutenant Al Deere DFC, that he had 'had enough for one day', and hoped that the Germans would let the squadron 'return in peace' that evening to its home base at Hornchurch. No sooner had Gray expressed this sentiment that the scramble bell rang – setting 'Hornet Squadron's' pilots running for their Spitfires. A few minutes later, the Spitfires engaged the raiders over Maidstone.

Flight Lieutenant Al Deere:

> I saw a large formation of enemy bombers heading towards London, and about 150 fighters in front of them and about 4,000ft above. I warned the rest of the squadron and climbed to engage the fighters – He 113s [*sic*] – at 19,000ft. I managed to get in a short burst at one before I had to break away. I then followed two He 113s [*sic*] and after a long chase caught up with them. This was at 17,000ft and I had to use 12lbs boost.

So engrossed in the chase had Deere become, however, that he 'hadn't realised we had crossed the Channel. It was only when I broke through the cloud behind the Hun that I saw with horror the coast of France directly below.'

Nonetheless, the Spitfire pilot attacked:

> I fired at the first one from 300 yards. I do not think the E/A could have seen me, because it took no evasive action. My burst must have killed the pilot, because the machine went straight down into the sea, glycol and smoke pouring from it. I attacked the second one in a similar way and again glycol

and smoke poured from it – but I did not actually see it crash although it stood little chance of getting back. The cloud was 10/10 all over the Channel and when I came through it, I found I was over Calais-Marck aerodrome. At the same time, five He 113s [*sic*] appeared from nowhere and chased me back across the Channel. They were very fast and must have been within range most of the time as my instrument panel and hood were shot about, and the machine probably sustained other damage. I was only 800ft above the sea when the E/A left me at Folkestone. I continued inland, but my engine stopped and the plane began to catch fire. I managed to gain a little height, up to 1,500ft, when I baled out. I just felt the jerk of my parachute opening when my fall was broken by some tall trees. My machine crashed fifty yards away from me. My only injury was a sprained wrist.

Deere's clinical combat report, however, only tells half the story; in his post-war memoir *Nine Lives*, he elaborated on baling out on this occasion – which must have been terrifying even for him, a hero straight out of the pages of the *Boys' Own Paper*, or so it seems:

I wasted no time in making a decision to abandon the aircraft, it was the only safe way of escape in the circumstances. I rolled the aircraft on to its back ... having first released my Sutton harness, and pushed the control column hard forward. Immediately I shot out of my seat only to be caught by my parachute fouling some part of the cockpit when I was almost clear of the aircraft. Before I could get back into the cockpit, which I tried to do, the nose of the aircraft dropped alarmingly and it was then I realised that I hadn't put the actuating trimmer fully forward, a necessary precaution when attempting to bale out of an inverted aircraft as it tends to keep the nose up. Frantically I struggled to get free, but the increasing airflow over the cockpit was forcing me backwards against the fuselage. With the aircraft almost vertical, and the ground alarmingly close, I at last broke loose and was hurled backwards against the tailplane which struck my right wrist a crushing blow. The parachute responded immediately to the pull of the rip-cord, and a matter of seconds later I hit the

THURSDAY, 15 AUGUST 1940

ground not a hundred yards from where my burning *Kiwi* had exploded in a sheet of flame.

For Deere, this was another one of his nine lives used up. After the combat he was credited with one 'He 113' [*sic*] destroyed and another damaged.

While 54 Squadron's Flight Lieutenant George Gribble and Flying Officer Desmond McMullen also tangled with the German fighters, claiming an Me 109 destroyed and another damaged, Gribble, Sergeant Robert Robbins and Pilot Officer Colin Gray managed to attack and damage several bombers, as the latter reported:

> The squadron engaged enemy bombers (Do 17s) at 16,000ft. I got in a shot at two, but broke away when we were attacked by enemy fighters. After this, I saw a single bomber (Do 17) in the distance and pursued it at 10,000ft to Dungeness, where I caught it up and gave it a fairly long burst from astern, range 300 yards, closing to 200 yards. Large pieces fell off this machine but in spite of this damage it would probably get home. E/A took no evasive action, relying on speed to get home. Owing to the speed of the aircraft I am of the opinion that it may have been an Me 110 but I cannot confirm the type as I was firing from dead astern.

The bombers, however, got through – but not to Biggin Hill; in what was a navigational error, thirty-eight Do 17s bombed RAF West Malling, an airfield five miles west of Maidstone and nearly twenty miles due east of Biggin Hill. West Malling, although operational, was still being constructed, several new buildings and the Men's quarters being damaged during the raid, which also cratered the runway, rendering the aerodrome unserviceable for five days; two airmen of 26 Squadron, a Lysander-equipped army cooperation unit, Corporal George Bage and LAC Gorge Hulse were killed. Both were taken home for burial, Corporal Bage, a married man, to South Shields, and LAC Hulse to Wolverhampton, his parents choosing the following epitaph for his headstone: 'Rest On Dear Son Who Lived Life So Well, Yet Gladly Gave it When Duty Called'; he was 24.

Damaged though West Malling was, it was not an all-important sector station like the intended target of Biggin Hill – and another navigational error was simultaneously costing the Germans dear in the adjacent Kenley sector.

BATTLE OF BRITAIN ATTACK OF THE EAGLES

At 18.15 hrs, *Erprobungsgruppe* 210 – which was rapidly earning a reputation as an elite precision bombing unit – took off from Calais-Marck, led once more by the brilliant *Hauptmann* Walter Rubensdörffer. This strike force consisted of fifteen Me 110 and eight Me 109 fighter-bombers, escorted by Me 109s of JG 52: target Kenley aerodrome. At 18.35 hrs the formation crossed the English coast over Dungeness, unopposed by 11 Group's fighters which were either occupied with the West Malling-bound raiders or on the ground refuelling. Striking inland, however, the fighter escort, flying 200 metres above Rubensdörffer's formation, became detached and disappeared back to base, probably having lost their charges owing to haze flying into the setting sun, and, given their limited fuel, wisely decided not to hang around. This decision by the Me 109 commander would have significant ramifications for *Erprobungsgruppe* 210 in the minutes ahead. At this time, Hitler still expressly forbade attacks on Greater London, the whole area marked as a no-go zone on *Luftwaffe* air maps; indeed, the *Führer*, as supreme German war lord, reserved the sole right to order an attack on Britain's historic capital. Somehow, Rubensdörffer found himself over South London, so turned east to approach Kenley – or, at least, what the Swiss-born *Kommodore* thought was Kenley.

At 18.50 hrs, an 'Air Raid Warning Red' was received by RAF Croydon, putting the station and defences on full alert. Immediately, Squadron Leader John 'Tommy' Thompson scrambled with eight other Hurricanes, with orders to patrol base at 10,000ft. At the same time, 32 Squadron was scrambled from Biggin Hill and vectored to Croydon and 'Raid E'. Having only landed half an hour before from the combat off Selsey Bill, Squadron Leader John Worrall, who had other commitments, had placed the squadron in the hands of Flight Lieutenant Mike Crossley – but as the Hurricanes raced into the air, Worrall raced after them, slotting into formation behind Crossley. Equally hurriedly, Acting Squadron Leader Humphrey 'Humph' Russell and Pilot Officer John 'Polly' Flinders also took off, in Hurricanes belonging to the squadron's Training Flight, hastening after 32 Squadron. Consequently, a combined force of twenty Hurricanes was now bearing down on *Erprobungsgruppe* 210. According to *Leutnant* Otto Hintze, leading 3/*Erprobungsgruppe* 210, he heard base call up cancelling the attack – but, at 19.00 hrs, Rubensdörffer responded 'Too late, we're attacking' – and dived. Hintze would later recall that owing to the haze it was 'very difficult to decide whether this aerodrome was Kenley or Croydon'. It was, in fact, Croydon, the Kenley Sector Station's less important satellite airfield.

THURSDAY, 15 AUGUST 1940

Down below, having seen the Hurricanes of 111 Squadron scramble, Croydon civilians were unperturbed, as this was a frequent sight, the fighters engaging the enemy much further away – although according Brian Haines, then a schoolboy living in Hamilton Way, just west of the aerodrome, when the aircraft returned:

> You always knew if they'd been fighting because of the black holes in the fabric in front of the gun muzzles. They were usually covered with undoped fabric which was a bright terracotta colour. This time the aircraft took off to the west and that was it, so far as I was concerned, show over.

The 'show' was far from over, however.

Margaret Cunningham was in Pine Ridge, Carshalton, and earning extra pocket-money mowing the front lawn when she heard machine-gun fire and assumed it to be a training exercise – albeit a major one as spent shell cases clattered all around her. She was standing in the garden 'enjoying the scene and completely oblivious to the danger', when her father suddenly pulled her inside, to safety. From the vantage point of her bedroom window, the teenager saw,

> minute objects drop … then came the 'crump' as each bomb exploded and palls of rubble and smoke rose into the sky. The curtains at the open windows jerked upwards as if unseen hands had pulled at them and released them quickly, as the blasts from the bombs came across from Purley Way. I stood fascinated and without fear – the excitement was too great!

The airfield was hard hit: the Terminal Building, of what was previously a civilian airport, was damaged, the Armoury suffering a direct hit which completely destroyed it, the Control Tower was strafed, and while both 'A' and 'D' hangars were hardly damaged, 'C' hangar and the aircraft within were destroyed. Five airmen belonging to 111 Squadron were killed and another from station HQ, and two civilian telephone operators and a Canadian airman were hospitalised. It was beyond the perimeter fence, on the Croydon Airport industrial estate, that most damage was caused however. The soap department of the Bourjois cosmetics factory in Waddon Way was hit, with loss of life; the blast also damaged the Central Electricity Generating Board's (CEGB) stores across the road. Ironically, it was the

Nuremburg Schraube Fabrik – better known as British NSF Ltd – factory that suffered the most, thirty-five workers were killed there, including the Works Manager, Robert Hutchings, and his secretary, Bessie McGrattan, who were meeting in the Board Room; 16-year-old factory worker John Ford was the youngest fatality.

No.111 Squadron's ORB:

> At 1900 hrs aerodrome at Croydon base was attacked by Me Jaguar dive-bombers ... Enemy aircraft about fifteen in number approached aerodrome from east and dived low towards hangars, dropping a number of HE bombs in a stick and destroying part of the main buildings and some civilian aircraft factory hangars on the north side of the aerodrome. Fires started in the Canadian squadron armoury also in the main building block, and a quantity of ammunition was exploded by the fire, which was under control and out in thirty minutes. The hangars on the northside of the aerodrome burned for a considerable time.

Crowds flocked to the scene, as Ernest Jones remembered, who had survived the attack in the damaged CEGB premises: 'we saw the crowds of sightseers. There must have been hundreds and hundreds of them, the fire brigade had a job to get up the road ... They had to call the police to shove them back.'

Brian Haimes:

> We went along Stafford Road ... and there were thousands of people. They had come out of their houses, great crowds, and I remember thinking 'If the Germans come back they're really going to cause some slaughter'... the air-raid sirens went off and I thought 'My God, are they coming back again?' But, no, it was the warning for the air-raid we'd had.

While RAF Croydon had received a warning minutes before the attack, there was no wider alert to the local civilian population – a not untypical scenario and a controversial matter of some angst frequently mentioned in Daily Home Intelligence Reports, in fact.

At the tail-end of the attack, having managed to reach 5,000ft, 111 Squadron's Hurricanes attacked Croydon's assailants, as Squadron Leader John Thompson reported:

THURSDAY, 15 AUGUST 1940

> At 1900 hrs the squadron engaged Me Jaguars dive bombing base. I ordered my section into line astern and went into attack. I fired a 5 second burst at a Jaguar climbing vertically from astern and observed bits of cowling, fuselage etc flying off in all directions. This was observed by Pilot Officer Walker, No 2 of the section. This aircraft was probably destroyed, but I was forced to break away owing to my low speed. I was unable to climb up to the Jaguars again but observed a Hurricane below me chasing a 109 and a 109 chasing him. I engaged this 109 with a deflection attack from about 200 yards and observed my bullets bursting on his wings and fuselage. I broke off when I observed the black smoke and glycol pouring out of the enemy aircraft.

During the 1950s, the pioneering Battle of Britain historian Francis K. Mason was serving in Fighter Command and wrote in his updated edition of *Battle Over Britain* (1990 – see Bibliography) that back then he had watched certain surviving wartime cine-gun films, including Thompson's from this particular combat. According to Mason, because the enemy aircraft involved was flying south with the evening sun low in the west, as Thompson attacked on the starboard side with the sun behind him, the film's clarity was exceptional – so much so that the Me 110's fuselage codes were clearly visible: S9 + AB: Rubensdörffer's aircraft. Although Thompson was credited with the Me 110 destroyed, he had not seen the enemy aircraft crash, although a handwritten note on his otherwise typed combat report adds 'Jaguar confirmed ground observations'. None of *Erprobungsgruppe* 210's aircraft crashed in the vicinity of Croydon, however – but Rubensdörffer's Me 110 had been gravely damaged by Thompson. Together with his *Stabschwarme*, Rubensdörffer headed south-west, accompanied by the Me 109 of *Leutnant* Horst Marx – who the *Kommandeur* called up on the R/T and reported that he was wounded and his *Bordfunker, Obergefreiter* Ludwig Kretzer, was dead.

Sergeant William Dymond was leading 111 Squadron's Yellow Section when the enemy were engaged over Croydon:

> Yellow Section engaged the attacking aircraft from head-on at the bottom of their dive. I then climbed, having lost the rest of my section. I attacked two Me Jaguars from head-on while they were flying in a defensive circle. One aircraft broke

and headed due south. I engaged it two miles north of Redhill aerodrome – he crashed in flames on that 'drome'.

This same Me 110, that of the *Gruppe* Adjutant, *Oberleutnant* Horst Fiedler, and his *Bordfunker*, *Unteroffizier* Johann Werner, was also pursued and attacked by Sergeant Leonard Pearce of 32 Squadron, which had also arrived over Croydon and was setting about the raiders:

> I selected a Do 17 [*sic*] flying south from Croydon district and when about 600 yards from it saw another Hurricane level with me. I dived and came up below it [the enemy aircraft], firing into the front fuselage mainly, while the other Hurricane attacked from astern. Port engine caught on fire and the aircraft dived on fire, probably at Redhill.

Fiedler would later die in hospital from injuries sustained in the crash; Werner survived and was captured.

Flight Lieutenant Humphrey 'Humph' Russell, also of 32 Squadron, had joined the southerly pursuit of Rubensdörffer's *Stabschwarme* and attacked the rearmost Me 110 from out of the sun, fifteen miles north of Bexhill:

> I fired three bursts of one second each and the E/A wobbled badly and the starboard engine smoked badly. I broke away to port and then steep-turned back and attacked the same E/A from astern again. I fired three more bursts of one second and the E/A turned on its side, began to smoke very badly and lost height rapidly and I last saw it one-mile south of Bexhill, turning inland about 1,000ft off the water. A searchlight site confirm this as having crashed at Pevensey … The searchlight site identify this E/A as an Me 110.

This was another of the *Stabschwarme*, *Leutnant* Karl-Heinz Koch, the *Gruppe* Technical Officer, and his *Bordfunker*, *Unteroffizier* Rolf Kahl, who forced-landed at School Farm, Hooe. Koch was captured unhurt by the LDV, but Kahl was so severely wounded that he would later be repatriated.

When the attack began on Croydon, 111 Squadron's Flight Lieutenant Connors DFC was leading Green Section and fired a short burst at three Me 110s before breaking away owing to being attacked himself. The third Me 110, however, the Hurricane pilot gave 'a very long burst and a great

THURSDAY, 15 AUGUST 1940

deal of smoke started to come from the starboard motor. Green 2 went in and fired at E/A which dived straight into the ground, bits falling off it on the ay down. E/A crashed south of Redhill.'

It was not Connors' 'Green 2', but the South African Sergeant Thomas Wallace, Blue 3:

> Followed Blue 1 and found E/A making a circle after completing bombing attack. I picked off one, fired four bursts from below on several aircraft. I could see my tracer entering E/A. I followed one Jaguar that broke away from the right. He dived slightly. I gave two short bursts from astern and he went straight into the ground. I returned towards base and intercepted another Me Jaguar, I gave a long burst from 250 yards when I left him with both engines smoking, flying low, eastwards. I intercepted a third Jaguar and attacked him from astern with one long burst, followed him at point-blank range without experiencing any return fire, and left him flying low towards the coast.

Wallace claimed one Me 110 destroyed and two damaged. The aircraft that had crashed, at Broadbridge Farm, Horley, was that of 1 *Staffel Leutnant* Erich Beudel and *Obergefreiter* Otto Jordan, both of whom were killed.

Over Croydon, 32 Squadron's charge was led by Flight Lieutenant Mike Crossley:

> I attacked a Do 17 [*sic*] from astern and opened fire at 200 yards, setting the port engine on fire. I broke away and Red 2 (Squadron Leader John Worrall) closed in and knocked some pieces off it. He then gave way to Red 3 who also hit it. We followed and the fire appeared to go out, giving place to two streams of white. Red 2 and 3 then went in and knocked it about so badly that it crashed east of Sevenoaks, the pilot escaping by parachute.

Who 'Red 3' was is not known, but clearly all three pilots of Red Section were responsible for this Me 110's demise – although only Crossley and Worrall were credited with half a kill each. The enemy aircraft concerned was a 2 *Staffel* machine, which crashed at Ightham, just east of Sevenoaks, killing the *Bordfunker*, *Obergefrieter* Berhard Lohmann. The parachutist was indeed the pilot, *Leutnant* Helmut Ortner, who was captured.

2/*Erprobungsgruppe* also lost another Me 110 to the Hurricanes of 32 and 111 squadrons, that of *Leutnant* Alfred Habisch and *Unteroffizier* Ernest Efner, who were shot up over Croydon, the former being the pilot who was shot through the right hand by a single round. While fleeing southwards, the Me 110 began shaking violently, leaving Habisch no choice but to crash-land at Hawkhurst, where both enemy airmen were captured.

But what of Rubensdörffer?

With his *Bordfunker* killed, himself wounded and his aircraft damaged over Croydon by Squadron Leader Thompson, and escorted by Marx's Me 109, *Erprobungsgruppe* 210's *Kommodore* vainly continued flying south with *Leutnant* Marx's close protection. What exactly happened next remains unclear, but an indisputable fact is that *Hauptmann* Walter Rubensdörffer's *Bordfunker*, *Obergefreiter* Ludwig Kretzer, had been killed in Thompson's attack – and the *Kommandeur* himself was killed when his Me 110 crashed at Bletchingly Farm, Catts Hill, Rotherfield, south of Royal Tunbridge Wells.

At 17.25 hrs, five Hurricanes of 501 Squadron, including Pilot Officer Ron Duckenfield, were scrambled from Gravesend on an unspecified 'Active Operations – Patrol' (ORB, Form 541). Five minutes later, the CO, Squadron Leader Harry Hogan, took off with three other Hurricanes to 'Patrol Hawkinge' (ORB, Form 541). According to the ORB Form 540, 'engagements took place at 1515 hrs and 17.25 hrs'. As we have seen, 501 Squadron was engaged over Maidstone mid-afternoon – but there was no combat involving these Hurricanes at 17.25 hrs and, unusually, no further detail is provided regarding any combat claims the squadron may have filed after that evening's patrol. Indeed, no such combat reports exist. Writing nearly forty years after the event, Group Captain Duckenfield (as he became) recalled 15 August 1940 and stated that 501 Squadron arrived on the scene after Croydon was bombed and *Erprobungsgruppe* 210 was fleeing home. Finding a 'Do 215' [*sic*] in a shallow dive heading south, according to Duckenfield he caught the enemy aircraft up, which was 'weaving pretty violently', into which he emptied his remaining ammunition. The raider then crashed near Tunbridge Wells. If this is so, it is surprising that there is no mention of such a victory in 501 Squadron records, or, indeed, a combat report – although, as we have seen, there are gaps in the preserved records. Two other things must be taken-into account: the Group Captain's memory was recorded a long time after the event, and what of *Leutnant* Marx?

Marx, who we are to understand by his own account had remained with his *Kommandeur*, was shot down. No.32 Squadron's Pilot Officer John Humpherson and Pilot Officer John Pain, an Australian, each claimed

THURSDAY, 15 AUGUST 1940

an Me 109 probably destroyed near Croydon – but neither saw their targets crash or reported a parachute. Pilot Officer 'Polly' Flinders, however, claimed an Me 109 destroyed. Having seen Croydon bombed, Flinders:

> Flew in that direction and saw two Ju 88 [*sic*] on my right and 3,000ft above me flying in a south-easterly direction about four miles away. I gave chase and was catching them up when an Me 109 came towards me from the starboard side. I throttled back completely and he passed in front of me and into my sights. I fired for about two seconds and a stream of white smoke came from his engine. The aircraft dived towards the ground, I realised that he could not get home and continued to chase the bombers. A minute later I saw a parachute open at about 6,000ft, south of Sevenoaks. By now the Ju 88s were about six miles ahead, and as I was still a long way out of range when I reached the coast, I returned to my base.

Flinders had shot Marx down, and his Me 109 crashed at Lightlands Farm, Frant, East Sussex; Marx himself, who suffered just a cut left thumb, landed nearby, at Mark Cross and was captured. Frant is some five miles north-east of Rotherfield, where Rubensdörffer crashed. According to Marx's own account, he surrendered to a police car hastening to the scene of Rubensdörffer's crash, so clearly Marx was shot down only minutes afterwards. If, then, he had remained with his *Kommandeur* in the air, it is surprising that he did not mention Rubensdörffer having been decisively attacked by a Hurricane just before he himself was shot down by Flinders. The question that cannot be conclusively answered is: did Squadron Leader Thompson so badly damage Rubensdörffer's Me 110 that the wounded pilot flew on until the aircraft became uncontrollable and crashed, or did Pilot Officer Duckenfield deliver the final blow, as he described thirty-nine years later?

In one of Rubensdörffer's pockets was found a telegram from *Generalfeldmarschall* Kesselring praising his courageous leadership and congratulating him on the award of the Iron Cross, First Class. Four days later the popular Swiss-born Rubensdörffer was posthumously awarded the Knight's Cross. However, 15 August was a dark day indeed for *Erprobungsgruppe* 210, which not only lost its beloved leader, but the whole of its *Stabschwarme* – among a total of six Me 110s and an Me 109 destroyed, while another Me 110 made it back to Calais-Marck resembling a colander. The wrong target had been attacked – which, being within the prohibited London area, incensed *Reichsmarschall* Göring who, according to Bekker, ordered a court martial. The man responsible, however, had paid the ultimate price for his error and was succeeded as *Kommandeur* by *Oberleutnant* Martin Lutz. *Erprobungsgruppe* 210 would see no more action until 20 August 1940.

So ended the daylight fighting on 15 August 1940. Never again would the *Luftwaffe* mount such a major attack, from Portland to Newcastle – a front of over 500 miles – and, significantly, no further daylight attack would be made by *Luftflotte* 5. The Germans flew nearly 2,000 sorties in total, a unique effort, and Fighter Command just under 1,000. Inevitably, combat claims by both sides were exaggerated, given the numbers of aircraft engaged and confusion of battle; RAF pilots claimed over 180 German aircraft destroyed, the actual figure being nearer seventy-five. When the Air Minister questioned Dowding regarding the accuracy of these figures, his response was succinct: 'If the German claims were correct, they'd be in England by now.' Conversely, the *Jagdwaffe* claimed 108 RAF fighters destroyed, of which eighty-two were believed to be Spitfires and Hurricanes – the reality was twenty-five of both types were lost, and at least twenty-seven damaged, although most were repairable. Seventeen Spitfire and Hurricane pilots had been killed or were missing, however, although this was less than on 11 August 1940, which saw the most Spitfire and Hurricane pilots lost in a single day (twenty-five), twelve wounded and three captured. In addition, one Blenheim had been damaged in action and crash-landed with two wounded aircrew aboard, and another had been damaged by a 'friendly fire' incident, wounding a crewman.

Notwithstanding the inflated combat claims of Fighter Command, the *Luftwaffe* had suffered a grievous blow. Indeed, as the historian John Vasco commented, 'It was, by far, the worst day in the operational history of the Me 110.' Twenty-seven Me 110s were either destroyed or written-off owing to severe damage, and six more damaged to a lesser extent. Forty-six Me 110 aircrew – including the highly respected *Hauptmann* Rubensdörffer – were either killed, wounded or made prisoner, with a further nine wounded. The shortcomings of the *Stuka* for these operations were also brought into sharp focus, which did not bode well. The day also highlighted, once more, the folly of sending bombers against England by day, either unescorted or with inadequate fighter escort. Considering the enormous effort involved, the damage achieved was comparatively inconsequential and the *Luftwaffe* was no closer to achieving its aim: the destruction of Fighter Command.

THURSDAY, 15 AUGUST 1940

Inevitably, target selection was faulty, none of the airfields hit being all-important sector stations, and some, as usual, were not even Fighter Command stations. The sector stations of Kenley and Biggin Hill escaped damage owing to navigational errors, and what damage there was to the lesser airfields hit was not serious. Moreover, the great assault on north-east England confirmed that the enemy did not understand how Britain's aerial defences were aligned. Indeed, the routing of *Luftflotte* 5 completely vindicated Dowding's resolve to maintain an effective force throughout the land, and not simply concentrated in the south-east, which is what the enemy wanted. Of Dowding's victory, Churchill wrote:

> The foresight of Air Chief Marshal Dowding ... deserves high praise, but even more remarkable have been the restraint and the exact measurement of formidable stress which had reserved a fighter force in the North through all these long weeks of mortal conflict in the South. We must regard the generalship here shown as an example of genius in the art of war.

On this day of days, Churchill had actually watched events unfold and personally witnessed the high tension and drama from the vantage point of the observation gallery in Air Vice-Marshal Park's underground Operations Room at 11 Group's Uxbridge HQ. The Prime Minister was there with his chief staff officer, General Hastings Ismay, and was deep in thought as the pair were driven back to Chequers, the Prime Minister's country house in Buckinghamshire. 'Don't speak to me,' Churchill told his companion, 'I've never been so moved' – having actually witnessed what was really the greatest day of the entire Battle of Britain. Churchill then said, spontaneously, 'Never in the field of human conflict was so much owed by so many to so few' – which, in a few days' time would be part of a long speech to the House which would launch a legend.

In spite of the day's intense enemy air activity, eighty-seven Coastal Command aircraft flew sixty-one sorties, escorting convoys, searching for U-boats, reconnaissance and 'anti-invasion' patrols. By night, 53 Squadron struck at Den Helder and Willemsoord, claiming direct hits, while Swordfish laid mines off the Dutch coast and a 206 Squadron Hudson destroyed a He 59 seaplane off Borkum. The Blenheims of 2 Group, however, had to abandon operations against oil facilities in Western Germany, and enemy airfields, owing to unfavourable weather conditions, but De Kooy airfield was bombed by an aircraft returning from Germany. It is actually inconceivable, however, that despite all the losses to unescorted bombers by day, it was intended to send these bombers as far as Western Germany by day and without fighter protection. That night, 2 Group's Blenheims successfully attacked various enemy airfields in the Netherlands and France, and the long-range artillery sites near Calais, the latter without result. Wellingtons and Hampdens bombed German industrial targets, and four Whitleys from Driffield hit the Turin aircraft factory and Caproni aircraft factory at Milan. A 15 Squadron Blenheim failed to return from attacking a Pas-de-Calais airfield and was never seen or heard of again, and a 10 Squadron Whitley was hit by flak on the Milan raid, one of the crew being killed while three were captured.

On the evening of this greatest of days, an RAF chaplain, the Reverend J.H.K. Dagger, was driving towards RAF Exeter, where he had been posted. Meandering towards the sea, the cleric stopped to buy a paper at a small town: 'It was a bit like any other August evening in England peaceful and secure, as I switched off the engine it felt a peaceful place where a tired traveller could rest forever and forget the war' – which was rather a juxtaposition, considering the day's intense violence. Arriving at Exeter and stepping within the Officers' Mess:

> Someone seized my arm and I found myself in the bar. Like lightning, a glass of beer was in my hand and I was saying 'Cheerio' to a dozen officers who moments before had been complete strangers. A tall man stood with his back to the bar with unbrushed hair and a worn flying jacket hanging untidily open, he was my new Station Commander [Wing Commander Johnny Dewar DSO DFC]. That night I learnt that what the newspaper had been saying was true, because I slept in a room that had been occupied by a Squadron Leader who had been shot down over the coast while I was driving peacefully through England [Squadron Leader Terence Lovell-Gregg].
>
> Having known RAF Exeter in later times, it is pleasant to remember those exciting summer days of 1940, when the Station Commander flew before breakfast, when there were few files and no runways, and Hurricanes took off in all directions during flaps with never a red rocket. The Ops Room worked informally; groups of friends studied the table and passed the information to less pushy friends who stood outside: 'Fifty plus coming in this direction.' In those days

THURSDAY, 15 AUGUST 1940

station HQ officers lounged at dispersal points as our aircraft returned most often with open gun ports.

To me it seemed like some exciting game played with Hurricanes, Dorniers and Heinkels, but at that time I had no personal friends among those who flew.

Things would soon change for Reverend Dagger.

Just as Bomber Command were active over Germany that night, regardless of their huge daylight effort, German bombers were equally active, continuing the relentless pressure on both defences and the British population. Up to 100 aircraft were involved in these raids, including seventeen Ju 88s of I/LG 1 briefed to attack various targets connected with the British aircraft industry. One of these crews later recorded having dropped three SC250KG, one incendiary and five SD50KG bombs on a factory plant at Worcester airfield, some thirty-five miles south of Birmingham in the West Midlands, noting hits on the nearby railway track system. That night, bombs did fall – harmlessly – on playing fields at Tunnel Hill, Worcester, adjacent to the railway, but this was a mile away from the airfield at Perdiswell – which was not hit. Moreover, there was no factory at this airfield, which was simply home to the Tiger Moths of 2 EFTS – another example of poor target selection. The Bristol Aeroplane Company at Filton was hit but apparently not damaged, although considerable damage was caused to Singer Motors at Small Heath, Birmingham. Mine-laying took place between Dover and the Isle of Wight, the Thames and Humber estuaries and Liverpool Bay, but most activity was over the Bristol Channel and South Wales.

The night was significant because the Boulton-Paul Defiant turret-fighter, which had been massacred by day on 19 July 1940, was starting to be used as a stop-gap night-fighter – and at 23.30 hrs, Pilot Officer David Whitley and Sergeant Robert Turner, of Kirton's 264 Squadron, made the type's first nocturnal interception:

> At 2330 hrs ordered to intercept Raid 75, discovered enemy two miles south of North Coates at about 6,000ft. E/A illuminated by searchlights intermittently but tried to hide in clouds, guns and machine-guns in action, but ceased on fighter's approach. E/A opened fire but without effect. Fighter raced up to attack, getting three good bursts but E/A lost in clouds. Consider our recognition light being kept on gave away our position to enemy. Landed at 0007 hrs.

Sergeant Turner, the air-gunner involved, reported that his tracer fire was 'blinding', and that although in between bursts the pilot could see the enemy, the gunner 'could see nothing'. It was therefore suggested that in future 'only ball and armour-piercing ammunition should be used' (ORB). Although a report was later received of an aircraft down in the sea near where the combat had occurred, and a dinghy was possibly seen paddling along the coast, which was reported to the Worcestershire Regiment at Withernsea, this claim cannot be confirmed. The night battle ahead, however, would cause Dowding great anxiety, especially before AI radar was perfected in dedicated night-fighting machines like the Bristol Beaufighter – but until then all single-engine fighters, and Blenheims, would find themselves contributing to the night-fighter role. For all its shortcomings as a day-fighter, at night the Defiant would contribute sterling service until the cavalry arrived – and this combat was the beginning of that story.

Daily Home Intelligence Report:

> The passing of 'August 15th' is reported to have had a tonic effect and there is evidence that the date has become well planted in people's minds.

And so it might. The report from Tunbridge Wells, however, concerned somewhat more domestic matters:

> There is a shortage of eggs, and poorer families have had none for a week; preserved eggs are not to be obtained.

So ended the 'Greatest Day'.

Chapter 4

Friday, 16 August 1940

Considering the huge effort made by both sides the previous day, 16 August 1940 was perhaps surprisingly another day of intense fighting – even for elements of the battered Me 110 force, although therein lies an unresolved mystery, as we will discover.

By 04.00 hrs, Britain's skies were at last clear of the nocturnal nuisance raiders and things remained quiet until 09.00 hrs. For the next two hours various lone German aircraft, or small formations, flew reconnaissance sorties. According to the daily report on the '*Luftlage*' (air situation) of *Luftflotte Kommando* 3 intelligence officer *Hauptmann* Genst, these reconnaissance flights began at 09.03 hrs (GMT), when two Ju 88s of 3/(F) 123 took off to photograph '*Flugpatz* [airfield] Pembroke', which presumably meant either the Coastal Command seaplane base at Pembroke, or perhaps Pembrey, the home of 92 Squadron, the other side of Bae Caerfyrddin. Either way, according to Genst's report, 'Further execution of the order was not possible owing to strong fighter defence. The second Ju 88 aborted due to engine failure.' None of these snoopers were intercepted, however, owing to cloud cover.

By 11.45 hrs, it was clear that a big attack was to be made somewhere in the Dover area. By midday, a formation of 30+ was identified by RDF six miles south-west of Cap Gris Nez, another of 30+ was four miles to the north-west of the Cap, while a third of 12+ was half way between Dover and Calais, and 20+ were just a few miles east of the South Foreland. Earlier that morning, ten Hurricanes of 111 Squadron had flown from Croydon to operate from Hawkinge, and at 11.52 hrs were scrambled to patrol the airfield at 10,000ft. A minute later, Squadron Leader Rodney Wilkinson took off from Hornchurch with his 266 Squadron to patrol Manston, and at noon, 56 Squadron's Hurricanes took-off from Rochford to patrol base. A few minutes after take-off, 56 Squadron was attacked by unknown assailants, probably Me 109s on a *Freie Jagd*; Pilot Officer Leslie Graham, a South African, was shot down and baled out, slightly wounded. Pilot Officer

Maurice Mounsdon was also shot up, but landed safely back at North Weald. The main action about to happen, however, was south of the Thames Estuary, so 56 Squadron played no further part in repelling this latest assault.

Orbiting Hawkinge, Squadron Leader Thompson and 111 Squadron were vectored to Dungeness, where, at 12.10 hrs, Do 17s of KG 2 and KG 76, escorted by Me 109s, were incoming over the coast. Within Thompson's formation was Flight Lieutenant Gordon McGregor (who, having been born in 1901, is believed to have been the oldest Canadian fighter pilot throughout the entire war). McGregor was actually a flight commander in 1 (RCAF) Squadron, which shared Croydon with 111, to which he was attached in order to gain operational experience with Thompson's seasoned Hurricane pilots. Now, the comparatively elderly Canadian followed his Section Leader, Flight Lieutenant Henry Ferriss DFC, in a head-on attack on the enemy, estimated at 200 strong. With the German bombers having glazed noses and large glazed canopies their crews were vulnerable to this frontal attack, of which Flight Lieutenant Gerry Edge (605 and 253 squadrons) was an enthusiastic exponent:

> They didn't like that head-on attack, you know, but you had to judge the break-away point exactly right. If you left it to the last 100 yards then you were in trouble, due to the fast closing speeds, but once you got the hang of it, a head-on attack was a piece of cake. When you opened fire you would kill or badly wound the pilot and second pilot. Then you'd rake the whole line as you broke away. On one attack, the first Heinkel I hit crashed into the next.

On this occasion, Red and Blue sections of 111 Squadron, attacking head-on, partially broke up the raid. One Do 17 was shot down in flames by Squadron Leader Thompson, south of the Tunbridge to Ashford railway line, and Sergeant John Craig claimed another over Tunbridge Wells. Flight Lieutenant Henry Ferriss, Red 1, attacked a Do 17 but was hit by return fire and collided with the bomber. Ferriss was killed when his Hurricane crashed at Sheephurst Farm, Marden. The Do 17, of 7/KG 76, came down at Moatlands, Brenchley, Paddock Wood, killing the crew. Red 2, Flight Lieutenant McGregor, fired his guns in anger for the first time but without noticeable effect. Flight Lieutenant Stanley Connors DFC, whose Hurricane was damaged by an Me 109, and Sergeant William Dymond and Sergeant Thomas Wallace, all damaged Do 17s, the latter chasing:

FRIDAY, 16 AUGUST 1940

> His back to the French coast and was attacked by six Me 109s on the way back. He took evasive action by steepening gentle turns, and five of the E/A returned towards France. Sergeant Wallace made a head-on attack on the remaining Me 109 and shot it down into the sea. (ORB)

Pilot Officer James Walker also claimed an Me 109 destroyed, but Sergeant Ralph Carnall was shot down, baling out 'suffering from slight burns' (ORB).

This was rather an understatement: Carnall's burns were sufficiently severe to see him become a patient at the Royal Victoria Hospital, East Grinstead, where he was treated by the pioneering plastic surgeon Sir Archibald McIndoe. He was in hospital for a year.

The loss of Flight Lieutenant Ferriss, a successful fighter pilot and popular flight commander however, was a bitter blow to 111 Squadron. Pilots could be replaced, but experience could not, as Squadron Leader Thompson explained:

> During August, our squadron was suffering casualties at a rapid rate. At one stage our squadron strength was down to nine pilots. We were sent replacement pilots, young and straight from OTU and most had had very limited training on Hurricanes or Spitfires. It was normal for us to give new pilots a form of simulated combat training, something they really should have got at OTU, but all they got there was how to fly the aircraft, combat training was left to us fellows on the operational squadron that they had been posted to. In most cases, especially when operations were at their height there was no time for this, and many a time new pilots would arrive in the morning only to be thrown into combat at midday. Needless to say, quite a few of them did not return from that first combat experience. It was sickening and disheartening and sometimes you get to wonder what chance do these young recruits have of survival.

Eighteen of the Do 17s intercepted by 111 Squadron did make it to their target, and bombed West Malling airfield at 12.30 hrs, which remained non-operational as a result of the previous day's raid. Incendiaries and HE bombs were dropped, destroying an aircraft on the ground, but the damage did not significantly worsen the airfield's condition. For 266 Squadron, however, a tragedy was about to unfold. At 12.20 hrs, the Spitfires clashed with Me 109s of II/JG 26 at 22,000ft over Canterbury, a running battle developing lasting some ten minutes or so and extending to the west of Margate.

Pilot Officer Robert Roach:

> I was Blue 2 of 'B' Flight. On sighting E/A, I broke from the rest of the squadron and attacked from astern a lonely Me 109. At a range of 250 yards I opened my fire. After a three second burst, white smoke appeared from the port side of its engine. I again opened fire, whereupon the E/A did a half-roll and pulled out, I did a steep right-hand turn and caught him coming up with white smoke still coming from his engine. I gave him another burst, when black smoke appeared from the engine and the E/A then dived for the ground, disappearing through cloud. The E/A were in line astern formation, appearing to be going round in a large circle. The weather was hazy.

Roach was credited with a probable.

Pilot Officer Richard Trousdale:

> I was Red 2 'A' Flight and first sighted E/A about 1230 hrs just west of Margate. Attacked Me 109 from astern and fired bursts which eventually caused petrol to issue from the fuselage. The Me 109 then dived towards Margate. At about 6,000ft the machine poured out quantities of black smoke. A few seconds later, the nose lifted and it rolled onto its back, apparently out of control. I last saw it at about 1,000ft, still diving on its back, leaving a trail of black smoke and petrol. About this time, Sergeant-Pilot Gretton at Manston saw a pall of black smoke appear from the ground in the direction of Margate.

Trousdale was also awarded a probable, as was Sergeant William Jones. II/JG 26 summoned assistance from *Major* Adolf Galland's III/JG 26, which was also up on a *Freie Jagd* but unable to locate the ongoing battle. In the skirmish, II/JG 26 lost its third *Kommandeur* in as many months, *Hauptmann* Karl Ebbighausen, who simply disappeared. The II/JG 26 *Stabschwarme* claimed two Spitfires destroyed – but the combat became a massacre when the Me 109s of II/JG 51 appeared on the scene. Squadron Leader Wilkinson

FRIDAY, 16 AUGUST 1940

is believed to have collided with *Unteroffizier* Ernest Bruder of 4/JG 51, who baled out over Faversham and was captured; Wilkinson was killed when his Spitfire, R6768, crashed at Eastry Court, just north of Deal. Sub-Lieutenant Henry la Fone Greenshields, 266 Squadron's FAA pilot, pursued Me 109s across the Channel but was shot down over Calais and killed, and Pilot Officer Nigel Bowen was shot down in flames and killed, his Spitfire crashing at Adisham. The Spitfire of commander of 'B' Flight, Flight Lieutenant Sydney Bazley, was also set on fire, forcing him to bale out over Canterbury with burns and minor wounds. Pilot Officer John Soden was shot-up and slightly wounded, forced-landing near Oare, and Sergeant Arthur Eade's aircraft was severely damaged, although he made it back to base and was unhurt. For 266 Squadron what had begun as a successful action degenerated into a disaster. Of the ten Spitfires involved, only four returned home unscathed. The CO and two other pilots had been killed, two pilots wounded, five Spitfires written-off and one damaged. All of the II/JG 51 pilots responsible for 266 Squadron's losses were aces: *Hauptmann* Horst Tietzen, *Oberleutnant*s Josef 'Pips' Priller and Josef 'Joschko' Fözö, *Leutnant* Erich Hohagen and *Oberfeldwebel* Johann Illner. In five days' time, 266 Squadron would be pulled out of 11 Group.

At 12.15 hrs, Squadron Leader John Worrall led ten 32 Squadron Hurricanes into the air from Biggin Hill with orders to patrol Dover at 10,000ft. Fifteen minutes later, Pilot Officer Peter Gardner destroyed an Me 109 three miles north of Folkestone:

> I was Green 1 and was doing a rearguard action when I saw nine Me 109s coming down to attack us. I shouted over the R/T and turned to attack them. Three set on us but I managed to get away from them with a damaged tail wheel [Hurricane P3679]. They had rather extraordinary markings: yellow wingtips with a double cross.
>
> I then heard over the R/T that there was a low raid coming in over Ramsgate. So I went there but saw nothing except one Me 109 6,000ft above, running for home. I kept underneath him until he reached my level of about 200ft and then tipped him into the sea just east of the Goodwins.

Flight Lieutenant Mike Crossley and the Belgian Pilot Officer Count Rudolpe Ghislain Charles de Hemricourt de Grunne also claimed Me 109s destroyed. All of 32 Squadron's aircraft returned safely to Biggin Hill.

BATTLE OF BRITAIN ATTACK OF THE EAGLES

At the same time 32 Squadron scrambled, so too did eight Spitfires of 54 Squadron from Manston, and five minutes later eight more Spitfires of Squadron Leader Don MacDonell's 64 Squadron took off from Kenley to patrol base. As the latter formation climbed, a Do 17 was sighted over Kenley at 30,000ft, so MacDonell despatched Blue Section to engage it and led the rest of the squadron on a sweep to Dungeness. MacDonell reported that:

> One formation of E/A was sighted NE of Dover at 24,000ft and another formation of about twenty Me 109s was approaching 1,000ft below our formation on the starboard beam. I ordered sections into line astern and turned south, passing over the enemy. Our formation then half-rolled onto the enemy and engaged. I opened fire at one Me 109 when I attacked from quarter deflection astern. E/A damaged and seen to be hit by my No 2 (Pilot Officer Simpson). I engaged second Me 109 over mid-Channel and opened fire astern and above, with two long bursts. E/A shook violently and flicked into dive, and struck the sea directly beneath me. This aircraft had yellow wingtips, the colour being so disposed as to make the wingtip appear rounded as opposed to square.
>
> I then saw a Spitfire diving on the tail of an Me 109. Spitfire opened fire. E/A turned over and dived inverted. Spitfire broke away. I closed with E/A, which had recovered and was diving vertically. I fired one long burst into tail of E/A but it dived into sea. This aircraft was undoubtedly hit by Spitfire (Pilot Officer Simpson).
>
> I engaged Me 109 which was circling above me. E/A turned behind me. I stall-turned and found E/A ahead and above me. I opened fire from beneath E/A's tail with two long bursts. E/A went down towards French coast in shallow dive. Several bits came away from the region of the cockpit and dive became very steep. No black smoke. I returned to 11,000ft and flew back towards Dover. Over mid-Channel I encountered one Me 109 which got on my tail and fired cannon over me. I manoeuvred for several minutes and got two long bursts from beneath and astern. E/A turned, diving beneath me in direction of Dover. I had exhausted ammunition but followed at 5,000ft. On approaching Dover I saw a sudden splash in the sea about

FRIDAY, 16 AUGUST 1940

four miles SE of Folkestone. On investigation this appeared to be the wreckage of an aircraft. There was a large patch of oil and a piece of aircraft, which appeared to be yellow. I flew low around the spot and then over Folkestone, but there was no sign of a survivor. I then returned to base.

Squadron Leader MacDonell claimed one Me 109 destroyed, a probable and one damaged. Pilot Officer Peter Simpson was awarded a 109 destroyed and Flying Officer Alexander Laing claimed a probable. No.64 Squadron's only casualty in this engagement was Sergeant Jack Mann, who was shot-up, slightly wounded and crash-landed his damaged Spitfire at Hawkinge.

Neither 32 Squadron or 64 Squadron, though, had managed to get at the German bombers. According to Pilot Officer Colin Gray DFC, however, 54 Squadron's Spitfires engaged 'forty Do 215s, forty Me 109s and He 113s', east of Hornchurch and over the coast', the bombers flying at 16,000ft, and their fighter escorts between 19,000 and 25,000ft. Gray claimed a 'Do 215' damaged:

> They were in a 'herring bone' formation and I managed to get in a short burst at close range. I saw pieces falling off the Do 215, but had to break away owing to the presence of enemy fighters on my tail. I climbed to about 30,000ft in the Dungeness area. I headed north and saw two Me 109s at 25,000ft between Dover and Deal. I dived to attack these. The first one I attacked I gave a fairly long burst from fifty yards range. The Me 109 turned over on its back, glycol streaming out and executing the turns of a machine completely out of control. The second Me 109 I treated in similar fashion. This behaved in exactly the same way and I followed this one down from 25,000ft and saw it crash in the Channel. There was no sign of the first one, which must have gone into the sea somewhere near.

Gray, a New Zealander and an exceptional fighter pilot, claimed both Me 109s and the Dornier damaged. Pilot Officer Desmond McMullen destroyed a 109, and Flying Officer George Gribble damaged another, but the only bomber hit in addition to Gray's was one damaged by Flight Sergeant Phillip Tew. Whether it was this formation of Do 17s, or the other detected at 12.45 hrs east of Tilbury, that had bombed Northfleet at 13.00 hrs cannot be ascertained, but much damage was caused to domestic property, the railway line and a paper mill. It is believed that owing to poor visibility, Northfleet had been bombed in error, the intended target having actually been Tilbury Docks. Given the inconsequential damage caused to West Malling, little was achieved by these raids. Once more, the weather had favoured the defenders, cloud cover being the reason, according to Bekker, why the bombers involved that morning, of II/KG 76, II/KG 1, III/KG 53 and I/KG 2, had been unable to locate such targets as the 'salient fighter bases at Debden, Duxford, North Weald and Hornchurch'.

Up in 12 Group, however, Air Vice-Marshal Leigh-Mallory's pilots remained frustrated at the lack of action. At 12.25 hrs, 19 Squadron was scrambled from Duxford's Fowlmere satellite, patrolling until 13.55 hrs; in his log book, the CO, Squadron Leader Phillip Pinkham AFC, wrote: 'Interception patrol after forty-four Huns which failed to materialise. Landed at Coltishall.' There, the pilots remained at readiness – bored. As Flight Lieutenant Brian Lane DFC, commander of 'A' Flight wrote: 'still we had no action. The *Blitz* had begun down south, and we were beginning to wonder if we were going to miss it.'

While the raids were in progress over Kent, however, RDF indicated enemy formations assembling over Cherbourg as early as 12.30 hrs. In anticipation of another simultaneous attack being launched, 11 and 10 Groups scrambled a number of squadrons to await the enemy. At 12.20 hrs, 1 Squadron's Flight Lieutenant Harry Hillcoat scrambled with the other five Hurricanes of his 'B' Flight from Northolt, to patrol Tangmere at 1,500ft, followed ten minutes later by the CO, Squadron Leader David Pemberton, with 'A' Flight. From Tangmere five Hurricanes of 601 Squadron raced into the air at 12.25 hrs, and at 12.45 hrs, Squadron Leader John 'Tubby' Badger also took off from there with like orders, leading six of his 434 Squadron Hurricanes – five more following at 13.20 hrs.

Further west, 10 Group was also deploying fighters: Squadron Leader Hector MacGregor led all of his 213 Squadron's Hurricanes up from Exeter to patrol Portland, and at an unspecified time, but certainly by 12.45 hrs, 152 Squadron's Spitfires were up from Warmwell, and at 13.05 hrs, twelve Hurricanes of 249 Squadron, led by Flight Lieutenant Robert 'Butch' Barton, a Canadian, scrambled from Boscombe Down to patrol the Southampton to Poole line.

This raid of over 100 enemy aircraft reached The Nab at the eastern tip of the Isle of Wight at 13.00 hrs, and with the firing of signal flares from the lead aircraft, the threat separated into four formations: twenty-nine

FRIDAY, 16 AUGUST 1940

Ju 87s of I/StG2 headed for Tangmere; twenty Ju 87s of III/StG1 went for the FAA base at HMS *Daedalus*, Lee-on-Solent; eight more of the same unit made for the Ventnor RDF station, and twenty-two Ju 87s of I/StG3 were briefed to attack '*Flugplatz* Portsmouth', or more specifically, the Coastal Command airfield at Gosport. Escort was provided, as also detailed in *Hauptmann* Genst's daily situation report, by seventy-four Me 109s of JG 27, seventy-eight of JG 53, sixty-two of JG 2, and forty-three Me 110s of ZG 2 along with eleven of V(Z)/LG 1. Unfortunately, Genst did not record which raid was escorted by which fighter unit.

No.1 Squadron were the first to engage 'Raid 47' off Selsey Bill, where the Hurricanes were bounced by the Me 109s of 3/JG 2. What followed would be traumatic for Pilot Officer 'Tim' Elkington:

> We were operating from Northolt when vectored towards Portsmouth. I was in Flight Sergeant Fred Berry's section, flying as top weaver, above the squadron. Tangmere was being heavily bombed by Ju 87s, but I saw nothing of it; because my radio was out of action, I received no instructions. I looked down one second and the squadron was there. Looked again – and as so often happens – the sky was empty. I suddenly saw enemy aircraft heading for Portsmouth so gave chase. As I straightened out – BANG – and my starboard fuel tank blew up. I tried to get out but forgot to disconnect my radio and oxygen leads. Did so and fell out at 10,000ft. I had been hit in the face and legs by shrapnel. No pain, just blood. I was floating down by parachute over the sea but hadn't inflated my Mae West. Then I passed out. Had I landed in the sea, I would have drowned, but, although being unconscious I saw nothing of it, Fred Berry used the slipstream of his Hurricane to blow me towards land.
>
> I came to in a field at West Wittering, being attended to by a pretty, freckle-faced, nurse who was cutting my trousers and pants off – all very embarrassing and, as my face was a bit of a mess, unsurprisingly my charm offensive failed miserably! I was taken by ambulance to West Sussex Hospital – from where my silk parachute was pinched!
>
> My mother and stepfather lived in the area, in fact, at Hayling Island. Mother was on the balcony, watching proceedings with my stepfather's naval glasses. I was admitted to Royal

West Sussex Hospital a few minutes later, from where staff telephoned my mother, incorrectly addressing her as 'Mrs Elkington'; she knew immediately, therefore, that the call involved me, and was unsurprised to discover that it was her son who she had watched descending by parachute.

That day, Flight Sergeant Berry, a veteran of the Battle of France, reported that:

> I was leader of Green Section of 1 Squadron, which formed the fourth in line astern on the frontal attack on the second formation of He 111s. After the first burst of three to four seconds at number eight of the second vic, it fell out of formation and glided away south, in the opposite direction, towards 10/10ths cloud. I climbed again and made a fresh attack from in front and below, in rather a steep climb. I gave a burst of two to three seconds, to number two of the third vic. The ammunition appeared to enter just behind the undercarriage. The E/A glided to the right, and I half-rolled and lost sight of him. The third attack was steeper still, from below and in front, with no apparent result. My number three mentioned that I was fired at, but I did not notice it; nor did I notice any fire from the lower gunners of the E/A that I attacked.

Berry claimed two He 111 probables.

Years later, Wing Commander Elkington (as he ultimately became after a long post-war career) recalled:

> Sadly, I never had the opportunity to thank Berry, who was killed on 1 September 1940, before I returned to the squadron. I later learned that American fighter pilots used a similar technique to deflect Japanese balloon bombs, and wonder whether Berry's use of the technique to save me was the first occasion. Much more recently I had the opportunity to meet Fred Berry's family, who confirmed the story, I, as explained, having seen nothing of it at the time. Another interesting thing is that more recently the 'Uncles' of 1, 43 and 601 Squadrons, the squadrons involved that day, worked out that I had almost certainly been the eighteenth victim of none other than

FRIDAY, 16 AUGUST 1940

Oberleutnant Helmut Wick, *Staffelkapitän* of 3/JG2, as he was then – who was himself killed over the Channel a few weeks later.

I remained on leave at my grandparents' in Cornwall until 16 September 1940. Quite honestly, I think I could have been bandaged up and flown again very soon afterwards, but remained on leave. Apart from holes in my face, and bigger ones in my legs, I felt okay, so could have called up and tried to get back to the squadron. But it just didn't occur to me. I had not yet developed a sense of responsibility.

I didn't fly again until 2 October 1940, by which time 1 Squadron was at Wittering, in 12 Group. That provided the opportunity for more training flights, although we did a number of operational patrols. I have no doubt that considering my comparative inexperience, had I not been shot down and removed from the fighting for what proved to be some intense weeks of fighting, I would not have survived the Battle of Britain.

During the combat, 1 Squadron recorded no successes, but Pilot Officer Elkington was the only casualty.

As the *Stukas* of the Cherbourg-based I/StG 2 '*Immelmann*' approached Tangmere, and while 1 Squadron occupied the Me 109 fighter escort, at 12.55 hrs 43 Squadron intercepted them between 13,000 and 15,000ft, off Selsey Bill.

Sergeant Jim Hallowes:

> I was Green 2 and took off with the squadron at 1245 hrs and landed at 1310 hrs. Large numbers of E/A sighted ten miles south of Selsey at 1255 hrs, approx., flying in sections of vic formations at 13,000ft reaching to 18,000ft. In the first attack, head-on, I observed my target go down with smoke coming from it – after falling a few hundred feet the E/A exploded and fell to pieces. I then managed to get on the tail of another which fell into the sea in flames. Sighting one Ju 87 attempting to get on my tail, I did a steep stall turn and got in two or three bursts, after which the E/A dived for the sea. Just before the aircraft crashed in the sea it jettisoned its bombs. I fired at one more E/A with no apparent results. The first Ju 87 which I shot down was observed by Green 3.

BATTLE OF BRITAIN ATTACK OF THE EAGLES

Pilot Officer Reginald Du Vivier:

> I was Blue 2 ... at 1245 hrs we sighted the E/A just above us. I hit two aircraft. The first I gave three bursts from behind in one attack, closing slowly and opening fire at about 200 closing to sixty yards. I followed E/A all the way down and saw him hit the sea. I then climbed back up and where I had come from and attacked another Ju 87. I gave him one deflection burst from the beam at right angles to his direction but missed. Got on his tail, gave him a burst which expended my ammunition. He smoked badly from his engine but I could not follow to see what happened as I found two E/A on my tail and had to shake them off. I got one bullet through the tip of my starboard mainplane which passed right through. Landed Tangmere 1310 hrs.

No.43 Squadron claimed an astonishing 'bag' – 'Seventeen Ju 87s destroyed, four Ju 87s probable, six Ju 87s damaged' (ORB) – which was somewhat wildly optimistic considering that I/StG2 actually lost five *Stukas*, with three more returning to base damaged. Pilot Officer Charles Woods-Scawen was shot down by an Me 109 and crashed, slightly wounded, at Parkhurst on the Isle of Wight, and Pilot Officer Hamilton Upton forced-landed his similarly damaged Hurricane on Selsey Beach, while Pilot Officer David Gorrie returned his safely to base. Unfortunately, however, 43 Squadron's intervention was not enough to prevent the dive-bombers reaching and pulverising Tangmere.

RAF Tangmere's ORB:

> Tangmere bombed between 1300 hrs and 1330 hrs by approximately seventeen Junkers Ju 87s and Messerschmitt Bf 110s. Following casualties were sustained: Ten service personnel, three civilians and twenty personnel injured. The following buildings were destroyed: all hangars, workshops, stores, sick quarters, pumping station, Y-hut Officers' Mess, and Salvation Army hut. Many buildings damaged, but promptly made fit for habitation. The following services were temporarily out of action: Tannoy-broadcasting system, all lighting, power, water and sanitation. The following aircraft were destroyed or damaged: three Blenheims (written-off), three Blenheims, seven Hurricanes, and one Magister (repairable at contractor's works). Six Merlin engines damaged but repairable.

FRIDAY, 16 AUGUST 1940

> Seven Motor Transports and thirty private cars damaged beyond repair. A large amount of equipment etc. was buried under debris and salvage work was put in hand immediately and ninety per cent recovered. The discipline at this station, and after, the attack was exceptionally good. During the attack, twenty-five enemy aircraft were brought down between this station and the coast. The depressing situation was dealt with in an orderly manner, and it is considered that the traditions of the RAF were upheld by all ranks.

This was the most successful raid on an airfield so far, and Tangmere was an all-important Fighter Command Sector Station with an operations room and therefore vital to the defences. The damage was clearly substantial, so this line in the Station ORB is incomprehensible: 'In conclusion, it must be considered that the major attack launched on this station by the enemy, was a victory for the RAF' – although the claims of RAF fighter squadrons engaged at the time suggested a greater toll of the raiders than was actually the case.

As the *Stukas* rained their bombs down on Tangmere, the Hurricanes of 601 Squadron also attacked them, claiming 'eight destroyed, two probables and three damaged' (ORB). Whatever the actual figures of 601 Squadron's victories, sadly this was not without a significant loss. During the battle, the Hurricane of Pilot Officer William 'Billy' Meade Lindsley Fiske III suddenly approached Tangmere to land.

Squadron Leader The Hon. Edward Ward, CO of 601 Squadron:

> The pilot approached the aerodrome while bombing by enemy aircraft was in progress. He did not fly over the aerodrome to see if there were any bomb craters on the aerodrome surface, which made it appear he was probably in trouble.
>
> He made a perfect landing, although it was across wind, and when he had just completed his landing run his aircraft caught fire.
>
> The ambulance was out by the aircraft almost immediately and the Corporal in charge helped to get the pilot out.

Corporal G.W. Jones and AC2 C.G. Faulkner had lifted Fiske from the blazing Hurricane, extinguished his burning clothing, and conveyed him to the station sick quarters, which had just received a direct hit.

BATTLE OF BRITAIN ATTACK OF THE EAGLES

Squadron Leader Ward continued:

> It would appear from the burns all over the pilot's legs and hands that the aircraft was alight in the cockpit prior to landing, although this was not evident from the ground.
>
> The aircraft burned out completely and therefore it is not possible to ascertain the cause of the accident. From the foregoing, it is thought that the aircraft must have been damaged in combat.

According to Ward, Fiske was 'immediately removed to hospital'. The significant thing about this particular pilot is that he was an American volunteer.

Born in Chicago into a wealthy family of international bankers, Fiske, like other members of 601 Squadron, the so-called 'Millionaires' Mob' and the most socially elite unit of the entire AAF, enjoyed a privileged lifestyle and was of independent means. A gifted sportsman, in the Winter Olympics he had set a new Cresta Run record and was a member of the Gold Medallist US bobsled team in 1928, aged just 16, and in 1932 led the team to victory as driver; he boycotted the Nazi games in 1936. During the early 1930s, Fiske studied at Cambridge, later learning to fly privately; as a member of the exclusive London-based White's Club, he met members of 601 Squadron and became an auxiliary himself. In 1938, Fiske, a confirmed Anglophile, married Rose Bingham, Countess of Warwick, although the couple initially set up home in America. When war was declared, the Fiskes returned to England and Billy, as he was universally known, was among the first foreign nationals to volunteer – which, as an American citizen, contravened the US neutrality laws. Circumnavigating the legal issue meant fabricating Canadian nationality, hence RAF personnel records state his place of birth as being 'Montreal'. Having met auxiliary members of 601 Squadron before the war, and having been commissioned into the RAFVR on 23 March 1940 after service flying training, Pilot Officer Fiske was posted to 601 Squadron at Tangmere on 12 July 1940.

Given his playboy image, there were initially concerns about Fiske on 601 Squadron, but his Flight Commander, Flight Lieutenant Sir Archibald Hope, paid tribute to the 29-year-old American:

> Unquestionably Billy Fiske was the best pilot I have ever known. It was unbelievable how good he was. He picked

FRIDAY, 16 AUGUST 1940

things up so fast ... he was a natural as a fighter pilot. He was also terribly nice and extraordinarily modest and fitted into the squadron very well.

On 17 August 1940, Pilot Officer Fiske died of burns and shock at the West Sussex Hospital, Chichester, earning a unique place in history as only one of nine American volunteers who fought with the RAF in the Battle of Britain to die during the 'Spitfire Summer' of 1940. Three days after his death, Fiske was buried in a highly publicised military funeral at Boxgrove Priory, near Tangmere. On 4 July 1941, Sir Archibald Sinclair, unveiled a plaque commemorating Pilot Officer Fiske's sacrifice at St Paul's Cathedral, saying that 'Here was a young man for whom life held much. Under no compulsion he came to fight for Britain. He came and he fought, and he died.' The plaque, which can still be seen today, reads: 'An American citizen who died that England might live.'

Returning to the bombing of Tangmere, Squadron Leader Sandy Johnstone's recently arrived 602 Squadron was 'released' – but suddenly scrambled, without warning, at 12.58 hrs – as the pilots ran to their ever-ready Spitfires, they saw the *Stukas* diving on Tangmere, the air aloud with the roar of their engines, bombs exploding and Bofors guns banging away in response. With no time for an orderly take-off, Johnstone's pilots raced off from Westhampnett from all directions – miraculously, none collided. South of the airfield, at 13.05 hrs, Flight Lieutenant Robert Boyd took off and engaged a Ju 87 almost immediately, at 300ft just south of the airfield – shooting it down before landing minutes later, having had no time, according to Squadron Leader Johnstone, to retract his undercarriage! Although 602 Squadron lost no pilots in this engagement, Pilot Officers Thomas Ritchie and Henry Moody were both shot-up and returned to base with damaged Spitfires.

That evening, Squadron Leader Johnstone would drive over to Tangmere, finding the base,

> a shambles, with smoke still rising from damaged buildings ... groups of airmen wandered around, many dazed and still deeply affected by the pounding they'd taken ... the remains of Billy Fiske's Hurricane still smouldered on the airfield ... Some were numbed by the enormity of it while others, often those least likely to be heroes, seemed spurred to greater action ... Such a man is our MO, 'Doc' Willey, who never left

his post throughout the raid and was instrumental in saving many lives.

Further west that fateful lunchtime, the raiding forces bound for the RDF station at Ventor on the Isle of Wight, and the airfields at Lee-on-Solent and Gosport, near Portsmouth, approached the eastern side of the Isle of Wight. A *Kriegsberichter* (War Reporter) in a *Propaganda Kompanie* (PK), Curt Strohmeyer was aboard one of the *Stukas* attacking Ventnor:

> When the *Kommandeur* was right over the target he put his aircraft into a dive and slowly the machine nosed down. All the other aircraft of the unit followed close behind him. I watched the *Kommandeur's* bombs disappearing in the middle of a large building – probably the machinery room and seconds later an immense smoke cloud erupted from it. Then our bombs were falling away. After flattening out I could still see, for a moment, the cruel and yet beautiful sight. Nothing was to be seen of the wireless station. Where only minutes before it had stood, only dense smoke was to be seen. I saw the last bomb crashing down right beside a wireless mast. The mast was lifted bodily and then fell into the smoke cloud above what had once been a wireless station [the reference to Ventnor being a 'wireless station' suggests the true significance of the Chain Home system was still not properly appreciated by the Germans].
>
> We hugged the ground on our way back to the Channel. There – English Spitfires and Hurricanes! The German fighters covering us attacked at once and a wild dogfight developed. Spitfires swooped through our formation followed by our Me 109s. Here and there a Spitfire escaped from its pursuer and I watched two of them attack the Ju 87 that was flying behind me. One of the two machines was turned away by the well-aimed fire of the wireless operator, but at the same moment the other Spitfire reached an excellent shooting position and fired a volley into the Stuka's fuel tanks. The *Stuka* burned fiercely and shortly afterwards crashed into the sea. The crew, however, was able to bale out. But the Englishman wasn't able to enjoy his success for long; at the same moment the *Stuka* disappeared beneath the waves, an Me 109 was on the

FRIDAY, 16 AUGUST 1940

Spitfire's tail and despite violent attempts to escape from his enemy by weaving, the German fighter put him in the Channel half a minute later. Just then I got a Spitfire in my gunsights. After a few bursts I saw that I'd hit him. A long thin smoke trail followed his aircraft but I lost sight of him in the general mêlée.

The English coast disappeared behind us and the enemy fighters, which only minutes ago were on our tails, did not seem to be particularly aggressive. They turned away and soon vanished over the horizon. Slowly the enormous tension ebbed away and only now could we feel happy about the successful attack on the wireless station. The fight against the English had lasted minutes – ten or fourteen of them had been shot down. All but one of our 'Jolanthes' (Ju 87) returned. The fighters zoomed past, waggling their wings. We waved back. The fight had lasted minutes but once again it was a memorable meeting with our unknown bold comrades of the fighter arm.

The attack on Ventnor had begun at 13.00 hrs, the same time as the attack on Tangmere, and lasted six minutes. Seven HE bombs were dropped, adding to the previous raid's damage and leaving only the Diesel House, R Block and underground buildings serviceable. Fortunately, there were no personnel casualties.

Strohmeyer's account was exaggerated in respect of losses and claims: four Ju 87s of III/StG 2 were destroyed, and four more damaged in the attacks on Ventnor and Lee-on-Solent that afternoon, and the RAF fighters involved were the Spitfires of 152 Squadron, having scrambled from Warmwell at 12.40 hrs to patrol over the Isle of Wight at 15,000ft, suffered no loss. According to the 152 Squadron Intelligence Report, 'A' Flight failed to contact the enemy, but '"B" Flight encountered a very large number of Me 110s escorted by Me 109s. The Flight was attacked and evasive action was so rapid that no pilot had any chance of opening fire or visualising the field of combat.'

Flying Officer Stephen Beaumont, Green 1 of 152 Squadron's 'B' Flight, did engage the enemy, however, and reported that at 13.40 hrs, 20,000ft five miles east of the Isle of Wight:

> We were at 18,000ft near Ventnor, heading west. I noticed about twelve Me 109s above us and called up Blue 1. As

they approached and circled on our tails I broke away right and climbed up. I then saw three Me 109s 1,000ft above me, proceeding south-west. I pursued underneath and climbed up behind the third, who was soon some way between the other two. I closed into range and opened fire. Black smoke poured out and the aircraft slowly turned on its back and went down vertically. The other two immediately dived towards France, and I followed one in the dive, gradually gaining, and eventually came into range and opened fire. The Me 109 staggered and bits came off. I broke away at 2,000ft as my speed was off the clock and the Me 109 continued down and must have crashed into the sea. I climbed up and came back to base.

Beaumont claimed two Me 109s destroyed.

Given the timing of this combat, if correct – just five miles east of the Isle of Wight at 13.40 hrs – and considering that the bombing of Tangmere was over by 13.10 hrs, these German fighters were doubtless a fighter screen positioned to cover the withdrawal of the four raiding parties. We know from *Hauptmann* Genst that forty-three Me 110s of ZG 2 and eleven more of V(Z)/LG 1 contributed escorting fighters – but we do not know for sure which specific raids these escorted. Given that 152 Squadron encountered 'a very large number of Me 110s escorted by Me 109s', the logical conclusion is that these Me 110s were those of ZG 2's larger formation.

HMS *Daedalus* reported having been heavily dive-bombed at 13.00 hrs, several hangars being destroyed and other buildings damaged, and around the same time, RAF Station Gosport was also attacked, for ten minutes. There, a hangar was destroyed and two others suffered damage; three airmen and a civilian unconnected with the base were killed, and an airman and a civilian employee died of their injuries the following day. Unlike Tangmere, however, neither aerodrome belonged to Fighter Command, so again the damage caused failed to undermine or weaken Britain's aerial defences. Over Portsmouth, III/JG 53 had destroyed nine '*Sperrballone*' (barrage balloons), and III/JG 27 one more, but this was hardly damaging to Fighter Command.

Way off to the west, at 12.45 hrs, the whole of 213 Squadron, led by Squadron Leader Hector MacGregor, scrambled from Exeter with orders to patrol Portland at 15,000ft. At 13.35 hrs, Blue Section, patrolling at 12,000ft between Swanage and St Catherine's Point, on the Isle of Wight's southern

FRIDAY, 16 AUGUST 1940

coast, were jumped by three Me 109s. Pilot Officer Harold Atkinson DFC was the only 213 Squadron pilot to react, and succinctly reported: 'I broke upwards and followed one with a red spinner and after damaging him and giving him three bursts he went straight down into the sea with black and white smoke pouring from the fuselage. The other two got away.' Not so lucky was the Canadian Pilot Officer Joseph Laricheliere, who disappeared, never to be seen again.

At Boscombe Down, 'B' Flight of 249 Squadron was at a state of readiness, while 'A' Flight was 'available'. At 13.05 hrs, however, twelve Hurricanes of both flights, led by the Canadian Flight Lieutenant Robert 'Butch' Barton, had scrambled to patrol the Southampton–Poole line, with Flight Lieutenant James Brindley Nicolson, the Commander of 'A' Flight (Red One, GN-A, P3576), leading Red Section, comprising Squadron Leader 'Whizzy' King (Red Three, P3870) and Pilot Officer Martyn Aurel King (Red Two, GN-F, P3616). Red Section would meet the enemy at 13.45 hrs, 17,000ft over Romsey, just inland of Southampton.

What happened next was described by Squadron Leader John Grandy, 249 Squadron's CO, when writing his initial casualty report – before personally speaking to Flight Lieutenant Nicolson:

> Flight Lieutenant Nicolson was leading a section of three aircraft in a squadron patrol east of Southampton. The section was engaged with an unknown number of Me 109 fighters and Flight Lieutenant Nicolson's aircraft was hit and set on fire. He managed to aim a short burst at one Me 109 fighter before being forced to invert his aircraft and bale out owing to flames in the cockpit. The aircraft crashed at Map reference U 8038 near Nursling, and Flight Lieutenant Nicolson landed near Eastleigh Aerodrome. He was shot at and injured by an LDV during the last part of the descent. Flight Lieutenant Nicolson is at present in the Royal South Hants Hospital, Southampton, suffering from burns and gunshot wounds. The Medical Officer in charge states that this Officer should be fit for flying within two-months.

Significantly, this initial report refers only to Me 109s. Furthermore, Nicolson's Hurricane actually crashed at Rownhams School, a mile or more from Nursling, and he did not land 'near Eastleigh Aerodrome', but some six miles to the SSW, at Millbrook, Southampton. That extra, or more accurate detail, would emerge when 249's CO interviewed Nicolson himself. Indeed, Flight Lieutenant Nicolson's personal combat report would be subsequently recorded by Squadron Leader Grandy at Southampton and South Hampshire Hospital: 'I was leading Red Section in a squadron formation – saw three E/A some distance to left – informed Blue 1 who was leading squadron, who ordered me up to investigate. Twelve Spitfires, however, engaged this formation before I got into range.'

This could only have been the Spitfires of 152 Squadron. Nicolson's report continues:

> I turned to rejoin Squadron, climbing from 15,000–17,500ft. I heard 'Tally-Ho' from Yellow Leader and immediately after was struck in cockpit by four successive cannon shells damaging hood, firing reserve tank and damaging my leg and thigh.
>
> I immediately pulled my feet up onto the seat and at the same time I put nose down and dived, steep-turning right. Saw Me 110 diving at same angle and converging – opened fire at approx. 200 yards and fired till I could bear the heat no more.
>
> I then abandoned the aircraft with difficulty and after dropping some 5,000ft pulled cord – I was shot in buttocks by LDV just before landing.
>
> Reflector sight was on but cannot swear firing button was at 'safe' or 'fire'.
>
> Eye-witnesses on the ground state that the Me 110 zig-zagged and dived steeply after Hurricane opened fire.
>
> This report is submitted on Flight Lieutenant Nicolson's behalf.

Nicolson elaborated further on his experiences in a subsequent morale-boosting BBC radio broadcast:

> Our squadron was heading towards Southampton on patrol from Boscombe Down, flying at 15,000ft, when I observed three Ju 88 bombers about four miles away, moving across our bows. I reported this to our commander and he replied 'Go after them with your section.' Breaking away from the Flight, I led my section of three Hurricanes round towards

FRIDAY, 16 AUGUST 1940

the bombers and chased hard after them, but when we were about a mile behind I saw the 88s fly straight into a squadron of Spitfires. I used to fly Spitfires myself and guessed it was 'curtains' for the *Junkers*. I was right, and they were all shot down in quick time, with no pickings for us! I must confess that this was very disappointing since I had never fired at a Hun in my life and was longing to have a crack at them. So, we swung round again and started to climb to 18,000ft over Southampton to rejoin the squadron. Our section was still a long way from them when suddenly, very close and in rapid succession, I heard four bangs, the loudest hit I have ever heard. They were made by an Me 110, which hit my machine.

There were no 'Ju 88s' involved in these raids, however, and considering how questionable pilots' aircraft recognition was throughout the Battle of Britain, and taking into account that this was Nicolson's first action, the question is: which aircraft had Nicolson seen? The Ju 88 is a twin-engine aircraft, so had he really seen (as he estimates the number of twin-engine aircraft at eighteen) the smaller Me 110 force of eleven V(Z)/LG 1 Me 110s? Clearly, the whole thing is ambiguous – but, as the Parachute Regiment's Brigadier Maurice Tugwell famously observed: 'Confusion in battle is what pain is in childbirth – the natural order of things.'

Nicolson's BBC broadcast continued:

The first shell tore through the hood of my cockpit, sending splinters into my left eye, one splinter I discovered later almost severed my eyelid. I couldn't see through the eye for blood. The second cannon shell hit my spare petrol tank, setting it on fire, while the third shell crashed into the cockpit and tore off my right trouser leg. The fourth shell struck the back of my left shoe, shattering the heel and making quite a mess of my foot, but I didn't know anything about that either.

The instantaneous effect of the shells was to make me dive away to the left in order to avoid further enemy action, then I started to curse myself for my carelessness. I thought 'What a fool!'

I was thinking of abandoning the aircraft when suddenly an Me 110 whizzed underneath me, in full view of my gunsight. Fortunately, no damage to my windscreen and foresights, so

I began to chase the 110, setting everything for a fight. When the Hun was in range I pressed the gun button, he was taking violent evasive action by twisting and turning to get away from my gunfire so I pushed the throttle wide open.

Both of us must have been doing 400 as we went down together in a dive. First, he turned left, then right, then left again, finally turning right. I remember shouting at him when I first saw him, 'I'll teach you some manners, you Hun!', and I shouted other things as well! I knew I was scoring hits on him all the time I was firing, and by this time it was pretty hot in the cockpit from the effect of the burst petrol tank. I couldn't see much flame but knew it was there alright. I remember once looking at my left hand which was keeping the throttle open, it seemed to be on fire itself and I could see the skin peeling off it yet could feel little pain. Unconsciously I had drawn up my feet under my parachute on the seat, to escape the heat, I suppose. Well, I gave him all I had and the last I saw of him was when he was going down with his left wing lower than the right one, and I gave him a parting burst.

As he disappeared, I then started thinking about saving myself and decided that it was about time I abandoned the aircraft and baled out, so I immediately jumped out of my seat but hit my head on the framework of the hood, which was all that was left. I again cursed myself for a fool and pulled the hood back – and wasn't I relieved! It slid back beautifully. I jumped up again, but again I bounced back into my seat for I had forgotten to undo the straps holding me in. One of them snapped so I had only three to undo, and I left the machine.

I suppose that I was about 12–15,000ft when I baled out and immediately started somersaulting downwards, and after a few turns like that I found myself diving headfirst for the ground. After a second or two of this I pulled the parachute ripcord, the result was that I immediately straightened up and began to float down. Then an aircraft, a Messerschmitt I was later told, came tearing past me and I decided to pretend that I was dead by hanging limply on the straps. The Messerschmitt came back once more and I kept my eyes closed but I didn't

FRIDAY, 16 AUGUST 1940

get the bullets I was half expecting. I don't know if he fired at me, the main thing is I wasn't hit. While descending I had a look at myself. The burns on my left hand left the knuckle showing through, and for the first time I discovered that my left foot was wounded, blood was oozing out of the lace-holes, and my right hand was pretty badly burned too. I decided to try my limbs and see if they would work – and thank goodness they did.

The oxygen mask was still covering my face but my hands were in too bad a state to remove it. I tried but I couldn't manage it. I found too that I had lost a trouser leg and the other was badly torn. My tunic was just like a lot of smouldering, torn, rags, so I wasn't looking very smart! Then after a bit more of this dangling down business I began to ache all over and my arms and legs began to hurt a lot. When I got lower, it was apparent that I was in danger of coming down in the sea and I knew that I wouldn't stand an earthly if I did as I would have been unable to swim a stroke with my hands like that. I managed to float inland and noticed I was heading for a high-tension cable, but fortunately floated over it towards a nice open field. When I was about 100ft from the ground I saw a cyclist and heard him ring his bell. This surprised me as I realised my descent had been in total silence. I bellowed at the cyclist but don't think he heard me.

Finally, I touched down in a field – and fell over. Fortunately, the day was very calm and my parachute floated down without taking me along the ground, as they sometimes do. I had a piece of good news almost immediately. One of the people who had come along and witnessed the combat said they had seen the Messerschmitt dive straight into the sea – so it hadn't been such a bad day after all!

Fortunately, among the first on the scene at Millbrook was a doctor and nurse, who were in the area on their rounds. The cyclist is believed to have be a local butcher's boy on his delivery round, who physically assaulted the LDV sergeant responsible for shooting the already wounded pilot. Only the arrival of the Hampshire Constabulary's PC Eric Coleman stopped the violence, and, as folklore has it, the ambulance summoned for the pilot actually took away the battered sergeant first – how true this is, however, has never been ascertained. What we do know is that later, Brigadier Hodgson, commander of the Southampton Garrison, disciplined the two soldiers who had opened fire on the descending pilot, and, also according to the same Army Council report to the Air Council of 7 February 1941, 'the members of the Home Guard were severely warned by the Officer Commanding, Home Guard Battalion'.

Speaking with the Constable at the scene, Flight Lieutenant Nicolson's first concern was dictating a telegram to his expectant wife, Muriel, confirming that he had been shot down but was safe – correcting the officer for misspelling his name with the more common 'h'. By now, a lorry had arrived on the scene, into which 'Nick' was stretchered. The driver then made haste for Royal South Hampshire Hospital in Southampton, PC Coleman riding the footplate ensuring no delays along the way. Upon arrival, the Hurricane pilot was given twenty-four hours to live, such were his injuries, the worst being to his hands, most of the flesh of which having been burned away.

As the 249 Squadron ORB noted, however, 'Red Section unfortunately bought it'.

The Hurricane of Squadron Leader King, who was attached to 249 Squadron as a supernumerary squadron leader to gain experience of operations and administration on a fighter squadron, was hit several times, but he was fortunately able to return safely to Boscombe Down, landing at 14.10 hrs. Pilot Officer Tom Neil was there and remembered:

> Squadron Leader 'Whizzy' King was among us. Excited. Garrulous. Hurrying about. His face creased by sweat and lines of his oxygen mask. Yes, he'd been hit and damaged. No, he wasn't wounded but the others had gone. Both shot down. In flames. The blighters had come down and caught them unawares. Down from behind. Me 110s. 'Whizzy' was in a highly emotional state and kept talking about tactics. We'd have to do things differently. Talking quickly and gesticulating.

Pilot Officer Martyn Aurel King, however, the youngest of The Few, aged 18, was dead. His Hurricane destroyed by cannon fire, Pilot Officer King had baled out – but his parachute collapsed and the teenage pilot plunged into the garden of 30 Clifton Road, Southampton – dying in the arms of Fred Poole, a local man. According to 249 Squadron records, this tragedy was caused because 'his parachute had been severely damaged by a

FRIDAY, 16 AUGUST 1940

cannon shell' – but eyewitnesses reported that the teenage pilot had been machine-gunned by a German fighter during his descent. On 19 August 1940, however, Squadron Leader Grandy reported that Flight Lieutenant Nicolson's Red Section,

> was engaged with an unknown number of Me 109 fighters. Pilot Officer King's aircraft was struck by enemy fire and crashed ... There is no evidence that it caught fire in the air. Pilot Officer King baled out and eye-witness accounts state that he was seen to descend normally by parachute but that when at approximately 2,000ft his parachute appeared to collapse. Pilot Officer King fell to the ground and was killed.
>
> The parachute was collected and on examination it was found that a bullet or bullets or metal fragments had passed through the pack before it had been pulled. This apparently damaged the canopy which, however, opened but did not hold for long enough.

The circumstances of Pilot Officer King's demise actually remained under investigation as late as 17 April 1941, when Squadron Leader (as he was by then) Nicolson, in response to an Air Ministry request for further information, reported under the title 'Shooting of personnel during parachute descents':

> I am not in a position to state whether Pilot Officer M.A. King, 249 Squadron, was shot in his parachute after leaving his aircraft or not. The report which was given to me in Hospital was that Pilot Officer King descended normally to 2,000ft when his parachute caught a balloon cable and collapsed. Squadron Leader J. Grandy, who was OC 249 Squadron at the time, told me that one or two bullets had punctured the pack before the rip-cord was pulled and made several holes in the canopy. I did not see Pilot Officer King after we were engaged by the enemy.
>
> I was informed from several sources that an aircraft believed to be German had made two attacks on me after the opening of my parachute at approximately 10,000ft (I had delayed pulling the rip-cord for approximately 5,000ft). It would appear, however, to be beyond the realms of possibility to check whether the aircraft was an enemy one shooting badly or a friendly one investigating my condition, although I heard

an aircraft which might easily have been a friendly fighter pass me at close quarters.

That fateful afternoon of 16 August 1940, the Hurricanes of Flight Lieutenant Nicolson's Red Section had, in fact, been well and truly bounced by Me 109s, *Hauptmann* Heinz 'Pietzsch' Bretnütz, *Staffelkapitän* of 6/JG 53 claimed the two Hurricanes shot down, chalking up his eleventh and twelfth aerial victories.

While Flight Lieutenant Nicolson recovered in hospital, on 26 October 1940, Wing Commander Victor Beamish, Station Commander at North Weald, where 249 Squadron was then based, recommended 'Nick' for a DFC:

> During an engagement with the enemy on 16 August 1940, in the neighbourhood of Southampton, Flight Lieutenant Nicolson's aircraft was hit in the cockpit by four cannon shells; he was wounded by two of the shells, while another set fire to his gravity tank. Just as he was going to bale out he sighted another enemy aircraft, an Me 110, which he attacked and shot down into the sea. As a result of staying in his burning aircraft Flight Lieutenant Nicolson sustained serious burns to his hands, face, neck and legs.
>
> Flight Lieutenant Nicolson has always shown great enthusiasm for air fighting, and this incident shows that he also possesses courage and determination of a high order.

Beamish had not personally spoken to Flight Lieutenant Nicolson, but would, of course, have read the combat report recorded from the pilot by Squadron Leader Grandy. In that report, Nicolson did not claim to have destroyed the aircraft he attacked, and nor did he in his BBC broadcast – everyone, it seems, was becoming very confused about exactly what really did happen over Southampton on the day in question. Squadron Leader Grandy's initial casualty reports concerning both Flight Lieutenant Nicolson and Pilot Officer King refer only to Me 109s being involved in the action – but Nicolson's personal combat report mentions an Me 110, and anecdotal evidence, albeit recorded many years later, from Wing Commander Tom Neil, recalled Squadron Leader 'Whizzy' King's return to Boscombe Down talking about Me 110s. There were, however, no Me 110s lost in the area at the time, and nor did any Me 110 pilots make any relevant combat claims.

FRIDAY, 16 AUGUST 1940

Nicolson himself, though, never claimed to have personally seen the enemy aircraft he attacked crash. While no Me 110s of V(Z)/LG 1 were lost in the area, we cannot be 100 per cent certain that one did not somehow get caught up in the action, given the fog of war.

On 29 August 1940, however, Air Vice-Marshal Gossage, Air Member for Personnel, had written to the Commanders-in-Chief of all three RAF home commands, including Air Chief Marshal Dowding, informing them that the King had expressed surprise that no fighter pilots had been awarded the Victoria Cross in the Second World War to date. With that in mind, upon receipt of Beamish's recommendation, Dowding approved it – adding his own view that 'I consider this to be an outstanding case of gallantry and endorse the Recommendation for the award of the Victoria Cross'. On 7 November 1940, the Secretary of State confirmed the award.

Convalescing at Torquay's Palace Hotel with other wounded airmen, Nicolson was astonished to receive a telegram informing him that he had been awarded his nation's highest award for bravery. The bemused recipient cabled his wife, about to give birth to their first child, a boy, also James: 'Darling. Just got the VC. Don't know why. Letter follows. All my love. Nick.'

Among the fighter pilots also recuperating at the Palace Hotel was Pilot Officer William Walker: 'A telegram arrived for Nick, whose response was simply "Well, what d'ya make of that?"'

When gazetted, the VC citation read:

> During an engagement with the enemy near Southampton on August 16th, 1940, Flight Lieutenant Nicolson's aircraft was hit by four cannon shells, two of which wounded him while another set fire to the gravity tank. When about to abandon his aircraft owing to flames in the cockpit, he sighted an enemy fighter: This he attacked and shot down although as a result of staying in his burning aircraft, he sustained serious burns to his hands, face, neck and legs.
>
> Flight Lieutenant Nicolson has always displayed great enthusiasm for air fighting and this incident shows that he possesses courage and determination of a high order by continuing to engage the enemy after he had been wounded and his aircraft set on fire. He displayed exceptional gallantry and disregard for his own life.

Clearly, Wing Commander Beamish's recommendation formed the basis for this citation – not Nicolson's own combat report.

Pilot Officer William Walker:

> At first, 'Nick' refused to wear the VC ribbon, saying he was embarrassed as he didn't deserve it. Then he got a dressing down so stitched the maroon ribbon to his tunic accordingly. He was genuinely puzzled, and not a little embarrassed, that of the hundreds of brave deeds performed by RAF fighter pilots that summer, his had been singled out for this very great honour.

On 25 November 1940, Flight Lieutenant Nicolson, in the company of his wife, mother and two sisters, received the VC from King George VI at Buckingham Palace. It would be the only supreme award to a fighter pilot throughout the whole of the Second World War. The problem was that 'Nick', having been shot down in his first combat, felt he did not deserve the medal and now had to earn it. This would profoundly influence the rest of his, perhaps inevitably comparatively short, life. Having recovered from his burns and resumed operational flying, the VC was posted to India, flying Beaufighters against the Japanese, for which he was awarded a DFC. In April 1945, Wing Commander Nicolson was on the staff of HQ RAF Burma, and on 2 May 1945, he was a passenger on a 355 Squadron Liberator bombing Rangoon. Over the Indian Ocean, 130 miles south of Calcutta, an engine fire caused the aircraft to crash into the sea. There were two survivors, but Wing Commander Nicolson was not among them – reported missing, he is remembered on the Singapore Memorial.

Returning to the events of 16 August 1940:

> By 1400 hrs, Hampshire and the Solent were devoid of enemy aircraft, and a lull lasting two hours ensued. At 1600 hrs, however, RDF indicated 30+ over Dunkirk, and at 1609 hrs the same number over St Omer and 15+ inland of Boulogne. Then another over St Omer of 20+. While the other formations temporarily remained over France, at by 1629 hrs the Dunkirk formation was in mid-Channel, and a smaller force was off Dover. This was clearly another attack developing on Kentish targets, while in the central Channel by 1641 hrs there were 50+ heading north from Le Havre, a formation of indeterminate

FRIDAY, 16 AUGUST 1940

size flying north from Cherbourg, and 30+ thirty miles South of St Catherine's Point, also heading North.

To deal with the raids heading for Kent and possibly Essex, the 11 Group Controller responded robustly:

16.15 hrs: Squadron Leader John Ellis DFC led the whole of 610 Squadron up from Hawkinge to patrol base and the Dungeness area.

16.20 hrs: Squadron Leader Joe Kayll DSO DFC and six Hurricanes of his 615 Squadron scrambled from Kenley to intercept 'a large raids approaching Brighton from the South' (ORB).

16.29 hrs: Squadron Leader Sandy Johnstone and 602 Squadron from Westhampnett ordered to patrol base.

16.35 hrs: Squadron Leader David Pemberton and five Hurricanes of 1 Squadron scramble from Northolt to patrol Guildford.

16.40 hrs: Squadron Leader Mike Crossley DFC, who had succeeded Squadron Leader John Worrall DFC in command of 32 Squadron this day, scrambled from Biggin Hill to intercept a raid in the Biggin Hill area.

16.51 hrs: Flight Lieutenant Steve 'Squeak' Weaver scrambled from Rochford leading 56 Squadron over the Thames Estuary.

16.55 hrs: Squadron Leader Harry Hogan and 501 Squadron's Hurricanes scrambled from Hawkinge to patrol base.

17.00 hrs: Flight Lieutenant Gordon Olive, an Australian, took off from Manston with five other Spitfires of 65 Squadron's 'A' Flight to patrol Deal.

17.40 hrs: Squadron Leader Don MacDonell led six of his 64 Squadron Spitfires from Kenley towards north-east Kent.

According to *Hauptmann* Genst of *Luftflotte Kommando* 3, *Gruppe* Ic, from the German perspective the day featured 'Attacks on English ground organisation between Southampton and Portsmouth, second between

Portsmouth and London.' The RDF plots now showing, therefore, represented the second wave of attacks, which were detailed by Genst as follows:

Fliegerkorps IV (German *Sommerzeit*, one hour ahead of British Summer Time):

16.29 hrs: 10 Ju 88s of I/LG 1 take-off against Hendon airfield.

16.33 hrs: 18 He 111 of I/KG 27 and 16 He 111s of III/KG 27 between 1615–1618 hrs, against Benson airfield.

16.44–16.50 hrs: 18 Ju 88s of III/LG 1 against Northolt.

Fliegerkorps V:

16.20 hrs: 15 Ju 88s of I/KG 51 against Redhill airfield.

16.28 hrs: 22 He 111s of I/KG 55 *Greif* and 28 He 111s of II/KG 55 and 25 of III/KG 55 take off at 1617–1622 hrs against Heston, Heathrow and Feltham airfields.

16.30 hrs: 18 Ju 88s of III/KG 51 against Gatwick.

16.30 hrs: 12 Ju 88s of I/KG 54 and 6 Ju 88s of II/KG 54 took off against Croydon.

Although not mentioned by Genst, we also know, from subsequent enemy losses, that 3/KG 2 were sent to attack Hornchurch, and from losses and combat claims that the fighters escorting these formations included Me 109s from JGs 51, 53 and 54, and II/ZG 2 and all of ZG 76, the Me 110s escorting the He 111s of KG 55.

Inevitably, target selection was again poor. Although the focus of attacks was airfields, only Croydon and Hornchurch belonged to Fighter Command. Clearly, the strategy was to attack multiple targets on a broad front, essentially a scatter-gun effect, instead of concentrating effort at fewer but more critical targets.

So far as 65 Squadron's records go, timings are contradictory: according to the Form 541, Flight Lieutenant Gordon Olive led his 'A' Flight up from Manston at 17.00 hrs – but pilots' combat reports state that their engagement occurred at 16.45 hrs. The later time, however, does appear more likely, because 65 Squadron's Spitfires met a large and mixed formation of over 150 enemy aircraft incoming off Deal. Supermarine Test Pilot Flying Officer Jeffrey Quill was leading Yellow Section:

FRIDAY, 16 AUGUST 1940

when a stray force of bombers was seen proceeding towards the coast at 16,000ft. Behind these were escorting fighters in several formations ranging from 20,000ft upwards. I climbed in company with the rest of the squadron in the direction of bombing force. It appeared impractical to attack the bombers, owing to the strength of the escort, and we therefore engaged some Me 109s in company with several other Spitfires.

I got on the tail of an Me 109 and opened fire at about 250 yards closing to point blank range during an instantaneous burst of about five seconds. A cloud of white smoke came from behind the engine and some occasional puffs of black smoke and flame. The aircraft fell away in a gradual turning dive. I then broke away to evade some Me 109s approaching my tail – and succeeded in getting the deflection burst across the circle on one of these aircraft but was unable to observe any results. I then broke away from the action having almost exhausted my ammunition.

Later, Quill wrote:

I was pleased with that little episode, partly because I was damn sure that the first 109 would not get home, and, secondly, because I was now absolutely sure the Spitfire Mk I could readily out-turn the 109, certainly in the 20,000ft area and probably at all heights.

Pilot Officer Lee Pyman, a Cambridge engineering graduate, failed to return, however.
Jeffrey Quill:

He was a quiet and thoughtful fellow but extremely aggressive as far as attacking the *Luftwaffe* was concerned. He was very prone, however, to trail off on his own and expose himself to getting picked off (I had already scooped him out of one such incident) but once onto a target he would pursue it regardless of his own vulnerability. He had been peppered full of holes on 14 August, so it seemed just a matter of time before the inevitable happened.

The Channel gave up 23-year-old Pyman's body and the *Luftwaffe* buried him with full military honours alongside Sub-Lieutenant Henry La Fone

Greenshields of 266 Squadron, who had been killed earlier on the same day, at Calais Southern Cemetery.

In total, 65 Squadron claimed 'Four destroyed, two probables, two damaged' (ORB).

At 16.55 hrs, 602 Squadron found 'Sixty Me 111s and thirty Me 110s' (ORB) just inland of Worthing at just 2,500ft. 'A' and 'B' flights had become separated owing to the weather, the latter's pilots finding themselves above the clouds. The 'B' Flight Commander, Flight Lieutenant Robert Boyd (Blue 1) reported:

> Sighted E/A approx. 1,000ft above and coming towards us. Blue 1 did climbing turn and delivered beam attack followed by Blue 2, who stopped one motor. Successive attacks were delivered by section until E/A crashed on waste ground approx. four miles north of Worthing.

Flying Officer Paul Webb was Blue 2:

> Sighted E/A 1,000ft above us flying in opposite direction. Did climbing turn onto E/A's tail and closed in to 100 yards. E/A dived, making a turn to port. Opened fire, closing to fifty feet when E/A crashed in a field near Arundel. This was confirmed by Blue Leader.

This was actually *Oberleutnant* Urban Schlaffer, the *Staffelkapitän* of 9/ZG 76, who was captured with his *Bordfunker*, *Obergefreiter* Obser, after their forced-landing at Lee Farm, Clapham.

No.610 Squadron, at 17.00 hrs, as Pilot Officer Donald Gray reported:

> Flying No 3 in Red Section, took off to patrol Hawkinge. We then received several vectors and encountered formations of Ju 88s and Me 109s south of Dungeness at 20,000ft. I followed Squadron Leader Ellis in an attack on a formation of Ju 88s, and delivered a short burst to evade one or more 109s, which dived on me. I fired a burst at a 109, which turned over and went into a dive, engine smoking. I saw five Me 109s diving on me and started a steep climbing turn to the right but received hits by two cannon shells, one of which struck the machine at the root-end of the wing at the trailing edge, the other hit the

FRIDAY, 16 AUGUST 1940

> radio housing, wrecking the set and blowing the panel off the other side, and the machine became uncontrollable. I regained control at 3,000ft and found I had no pressure, rendering the guns unusable. I flew north and reached the coast and followed a railway home. Machine appears to be completely unserviceable.

Gray was credited with a probable; his Spitfire was actually repaired. No.610 Squadron interception occurred at 20,000ft:

> Squadron Leader Ellis attacked a Ju 88 and after a four second burst at 200 yards saw E/A emitting clouds of smoke from the vicinity of engine and wing roots. Sergeant Arnfield fired at an Me 109 and saw his bullets going into cockpit and mainplane ... Visibility was very hazy, 10/10ths cloud at 3,000ft. (ORB)

The haze would, in fact, confound the raiders, although 610's successes were not without loss: Acting Flight Lieutenant William Warner, the commander of 'B' Flight, was shot down over the sea and remains missing.

Although records are incomplete, it would appear that 501 Squadron engaged the same enemy formation off Dungeness, Sergeant James 'Ginger' Lacey claiming an Me 109 probably destroyed, while Squadron Leader Hogan, and Pilot Officers Duckenfield and Dafforn all damaged Do 17s.

At 17.10 hrs, 1 Squadron attacked the same enemy formation over the South Downs, as Squadron Leader David Pemberton (Red 1) reported:

> I led the squadron alongside the bomber formation and when level with the first wave I turned and led the squadron in line astern into a frontal attack on the second wave. My first burst at the front of a He 111 sent the bomber down in flames. I dived to break away and came up again to make a second attack. Immediately afterwards my engine caught fire, and as I got ready to abandon the aircraft the flames subsided and I brought my aircraft back to base. Subsequent examination showed that two armour-piercing bullets had penetrated the top cowling and then scored the camshaft to a depth of approx. 1/16th of an inch. Possibly the fire was caused by oil fumes igniting then burning out.

Pilot Officer Peter Matthews was Red 2 and lost Squadron Leader Pemberton after the second attack, so he,

> climbed to 20,000ft behind the enemy formation and saw one Hurricane being attacked by five Me 110s, so I dived and attacked one of the E/A and after the attack followed him to the top of the cloud layer. By this time the E/A had its port engine on fire and was then going down vertically at over 400 mph. He then disappeared in cloud and I blacked out in straightening out of the pursuing dive.

Pilot Officer Peter Boot DFC's Hurricane was hit in the glycol tank while attacking a He 111, forcing him to land on the Hog's Back, near Guildford. Sergeant Arthur Clowes DFM,

> saw a He 111 at which he had been firing go down in a vertical dive. After rejoining his formation he gave another burst to a He 111 without known result and then dropped below cloud and saw a Ju 88 which he attacked, firing one burst. Four Spitfires appeared and the Ju 88 dived down and crash-landed without apparently waiting for their fire. Pilot Officer G.E. Goodman picked out a He 111 after making initial Squadron attack. He put the engine out of commission with his first burst and saw the bomber crash near Petworth. While he was circling the crash at 500ft it blew up and his aircraft was struck by a fragment which affected his oil pressure. (ORB)

This was not, in fact, a Ju 88, but a 4/KG 55 He 111, which exploded at Upper Frithwold Farm, North Chapel, near Petworth, killing the *Staffelkapitän*, *Hauptmann* Sabler, and his crew.

> Flight Sergeant Berry DFM during the squadron attack saw two of his targets break away from the formation and one of them dived vertically, obviously out of control. Flying Officer H.N.E. Salmon got left behind during the squadron attack so he climbed to 22,000ft and dived on the left wing of the bomber formation; while doing so an Me 110 came into view beneath him. His first burst stopped the port engine and the Me 110

FRIDAY, 16 AUGUST 1940

went into a vertical dive, obviously out of control. He landed to refuel at Redhill and was bombed by a Do 17; he took off and landed at Northolt. Pilot Officer C.M. Stavert went with the squadron in its frontal attack. After diving through cloud he met a He 111 head-on. He fired at it and, emerging below the cloud layer, saw the smoking remains of the twin-engine aircraft immediately below him. (ORB)

This was one of the Heathrow raiders, a He 111 of 6/KG 55, which crashed at Anningtons Farm, Bramber. Three of the crew baled out and were captured, but another crewman was killed and one severely wounded.

During this combat, 1 Squadron claimed 'Four He 111s destroyed, one Ju 88 [*sic*] destroyed, two He 111s probably destroyed, while suffering the loss of one Hurricane only, no pilots', in what was the squadron's 'most successful action in England so far' (ORB).

At 17.10 hrs KG 55 was attacked by 615 Squadron, just inland of Brighton. Squadron Leader Joe Kayll and Sergeant Peter Walley shared a He 111 probably destroyed, Pilot Officer Keith Lofts claimed a He 111 destroyed over Steyning, and Pilot Officer David Evans damaged another. Flight Lieutenant Lionel Gaunce, a Canadian, and Pilot Officer Petrus 'Dutch' Hugo, a South African, attacked another He 111 before being engaged by the Me 110 escorts over Newhaven. Hugo's Hurricane was badly shot up, the pilot being wounded in both legs, although he managed to return to Kenley were the aircraft was considered a write-off. 615 Squadron's 'bag' was completed by Flight Lieutenant James Sanders, who damaged two He 111s.

By 17.15 hrs, Ju 88s, probably the I/KG 51 formation briefed to attack Redhill, escorted by Me 110s, was 'attempting to bomb' (32 Squadron's ORB) Biggin Hill aerodrome at 15,000ft when intercepted over Westerham by Squadron Leader Crossley's Hurricanes.

Flight Lieutenant Peter Brothers, commanding 'B' Flight:

> I was leading Blue Section, in company with Red Section, when I sighted approx. eighty Ju 88s escorted by twenty Me 110s. I dived through the formation of Ju 88s and fired a short burst at two, with no apparent success. I was in a poor position when I broke away and had to give chase. Eventually I caught an Me 110 cruising behind the Ju 88s and fired all my rounds into him from below and behind. His port engine was

smoking badly and he slowly turned to port and dived through the clouds. I followed him and he hit the sea about twelve miles due south of Brighton.

This was a machine of III/ZG 76, the crew of which were fortunate to be rescued by the *Seenotflugdienst*.

Squadron Leader Crossley claimed a Ju 88 destroyed, and the Belgian Pilot Officer Comte Rudolphe de Grunne destroyed an Me 109, while various other 32 Squadron pilots submitted claims for 'probables' and 'damaged' enemy aircraft – all for no loss. By now, the weather was very hazy and south-east England was covered in cloud. Above those clouds over Tunbridge, at 17.20 hrs the eight Spitfires of Kenley's 64 Squadron found Raid 17 – over 100 He 111s and Ju 88s, which had wheeled about and were now heading south, towards France.

Pilot Officer Alexander Laing:

> I was Yellow 1 and Pilot Officer Jones Yellow 2 ... We were vectored above 10/10ths cloud and sighted a large spearhead of He 111s and Ju 88s ... They were escorted by a large number of Me 109s at 22,000ft at the time of sighting and they were on our starboard beam, steering a southerly course. Squadron Leader MacDonell (Red 1) ordered the squadron into sections line astern and we attacked their port flank. Each section went into aircraft line astern and selected one of the many flank sections of three He 111s in close vic, and did a beam attack. Having ordered Yellow 2 into line astern I attacked a section of He 111s in close vic, heading towards their port beam. I opened fire at about 450 yards, giving full deflection on their leader. Immediately I was met with terrific crossfire from the E/A but pressed home the attack till I was within fifty yards of their leader when I broke away underneath them. I gave two seven second bursts in quick succession. As I purposely kept the same deflection all the time I saw the guns of the rear He 111 in No 3 position stop firing and as I approached nearer the formation the bullets from my guns crept forward to the noses of the three He 111s and then started to hit the tail of the leading He 111 and similarly ran the length of that machine's fuselage, stopping the gunners' crossfire considerably and finally smashing the

FRIDAY, 16 AUGUST 1940

Perspex which I saw fly off at fifty yards, just as I broke away. I consider that No 2 He 111 must have got a number of rounds in it also, but did not see any damage done to it as No 3 was in the way. Yellow 2 followed up behind me and did a similar attack.

Pilot Officer Richard Jones:

Yellow 1 did a beam attack on No 3 of enemy vic of three, going south, I followed up and also did a beam attack, giving a long burst. I closed to 100 yards then broke off the attack. Yellow 1 then did another beam attack and I followed up with a No 2 Attack giving long bursts of about eight seconds, closing to 150 yards. As I broke away I saw an E/A emitting black smoke and breaking away from vic.

He 111s were also damaged by Flight Sergeant Ernest Gilbert, Sergeant John Whelan and Squadron Leader Don MacDonell, who also shared the destruction of a Heinkel with Pilot Officer Peter Simpson, whose Spitfire was very badly damaged by return fire but returned safely to base.

Squadron Leader Don MacDonell:

Again, we broke through the cloud at about 8,000ft ... We were about 3,000ft below and behind another large formation of He 111 bombers with the usual formidable fighter escort. But the whole circus had clearly decided that blind bombing was useless and was heading south for France. We were in a hopeless tactical situation ... Again we heard the warning 'Snappers' and the 109s poured down on us, guns blazing and cannons pumping. My No 2 and I were able to knock down one Heinkel which fell away with an engine on fire and parachutes erupting from the crippled aircraft. I attacked another which had closed in to take its place and it began to lag astern with a white spume of glycol from one of its engines and no response from the rear gunner.

The two of us then broke into half-rolls downward and went hell for leather for the cloud cover. Maybe I was too slow ... I was within 1,000ft of the safety of the cloud and had expended all my ammunition when I glanced in my mirror and saw an extremely unwelcome yellow-nosed fighter opening fire with its cannon. I was hit good and proper. There was a lot of smoke, oil and glycol pouring into the cockpit and then an explosion in the engine. Just before we hit the cloud layer, I opened my cockpit hood, released my side panel, and my trusty Spitfire SH-D (P9554) and I parted company as I went over the side.

My parachute opened in the cloud. I felt suspended in a weird world of mist, motionless. I dropped out of the cloud into daylight. I heard a crash which must have been my Spitfire but then I had to concentrate on how best to plan my landing. I had about 2,000ft in hand, was drifting towards a row of bungalows with gardens in front and behind, a wood across the other side of the road, and fields immediately beneath me. I aimed for the fields but drifted too far downwind. I plummeted earthwards, caught the heel of my flying boot in the gutter of a red-tiled bungalow and landed unceremoniously on my bottom in the rose border of the front garden. This shook me a bit. I got up slowly, released my parachute harness and began to gather in the canopy and rigging lines. I realised that I was shaking like a leaf.

What followed was almost comical. No.64 Squadron's CO rang the bungalow's doorbell without response. Then the family emerged from their Anderson shelter in the garden – the man of the house covering 'Bonnie Prince Charlie' with a 12-bore while his daughter searched him and confirmed his identity. A policeman then arrived and took Squadron Leader MacDonell to see the crash-site of his Spitfire – in the grounds of a somewhat eccentric retired naval officer's sizeable property. Then, onwards to Uckfield Police Station, the front office of which was,

> piled with German flying kit – helmets, R/T headsets, flotation waistcoats, flying suits – the lot. We went into the office where a sergeant sat behind a heavy desk. He looked up as we entered 'Not another of the buggers?'
>
> My escort explained who I was and asked me to produce my identity disc. The stunned sergeant apologised profusely, offered me a cup of tea and invited me to join his wife in their sitting room, which was part of the flat they occupied over the

FRIDAY, 16 AUGUST 1940

station. I told my hostess what had happened. She hung on my every word. Then the pick-up arrived from Kenley and I was on my way back to base.

Pilot Officer Richard Jones:

Upon arrival at Kenley, I remember being met by the CO of 64 Squadron, an absolutely charming man and a real gentleman in every sense of the word, Squadron Leader Don MacDonell. He immediately made us new pilots feel at home, who he called his 'Chicks'. We would find our CO a quiet but determined leader and an excellent fighter pilot. He looked after the best interests of all who served under him and he had the respect of all.

To give us battle experience as quickly as possible whenever the time allowed, we were paired off with a senior battle-experienced pilot to practise dog-fighting and yet more dog-fighting to give us both experience and confidence in the Spitfire and combat conditions. We were lucky to have that extra-curricular training, which would have been impossible had we been posted to 64 later on that summer and for obvious reasons.

Meanwhile, the battle in the skies continued.

The RAF fighters had again taken a significant toll of the Me 110 escorts, which became well dispersed. No.601 Squadron was again up from Tangmere, patrolling base below cloud, and, having been airborne for forty minutes, at 17.25 hrs engaged an Me 110 a mile west of the airfield.

Flight Lieutenant Sir Archibald Hope, who was leading the squadron on this occasion:

I saw an E/A below on my left. I turned towards it and it tried to climb up to the cloud. I attacked it from slightly below and to starboard, and after a five second burst it went straight down and crashed outside the military HQ, one-mile west of base. It may well have been damaged before my attack. No return fire.

This Me 110, of 5/ZG 76, crashed and exploded at Shopwyke House, Oving, killing the two-man crew.

BATTLE OF BRITAIN ATTACK OF THE EAGLES

Further to the north-east, at 17.00 hrs, the Hurricanes of 56 Squadron engaged the Do 17s of KG 2 which were inbound north-east of Eastchurch, heading for Hornchurch Sector Station. Flight Lieutenant Steve 'Squeak' Weaver was Red 1 and leading the squadron:

> I attacked a Do 215 [*sic*] from 200/50 yards with an eight second burst from dead astern without apparent effect, although I saw my tracer enter the fuselage. I broke off to avoid collision and saw E/A jettison two bombs. I dived below the clouds as an Me 109 was following me and saw a Do 215, which had already been attacked by Sergeant Whitehead. It was at 2,000ft, doing a climbing turn to escape me.
>
> Using quarter deflection I fired a burst of about six seconds, ending with no deflection at 20/150 yards. E/A's port mainplane and left part of fuselage caught alight, and it dived towards the land and turned back and fell into the sea, bursting into a mass of flames. Sergeant Whitehead and Pilot Officer Wicks witnessed this.
>
> Sergeant Whitehead had doubtless damaged this aircraft before I attacked and would probably have finished it off as he still had ammunition left.

The pair shared destruction of the Me 110. No.56 Squadron claimed a total of two Do 17s destroyed, a probable and one damaged, two Me 109 and a 110 as 'probables', and a 110 damaged.

Flight Sergeant 'Taffy' Higginson, however, who had destroyed the other Do 17, a machine of 3/KG 2 which crashed in flames onto the beach at Whitstable, noticed no return fire but assumed he had been hit when his engine caught fire. Forced to make an emergency landing south of Whitstable, the Welshman was picked up by men of the London Irish Rifles, none the worse for his experience.

As the enemy withdrew, at long last elements of 12 Group's frustrated 19 Squadron found action.

As teatime approached, up at Coltishall Flight Lieutenant Brian Lane DFC, commander of 'A' Flight, flipped a coin with the commander of 'B', Flight Lieutenant Wilf Clouston, a New Zealander, to decide which flight went to tea first; the coin favoured Clouston's pilots, so off they went, leaving 'A' Flight at readiness, awaiting the call for action that never seemed to come. At 17.30 hrs 19 Squadron was recalled to Duxford, so 'A' Flight took off immediately, leaving 'B' to follow-on in due course.

FRIDAY, 16 AUGUST 1940

Flight Lieutenant Lane, who was leading Flying Officer Frank 'Fanny' Brinsden, another New Zealander, Pilot Officer Wallace 'Jock' Cunningham, Flight Sergeant George 'Grumpy' Unwin and sergeants Bernard 'Jimmy' Jennings, Jack Potter and Henry Roden, wrote:

> We took off and circled the aerodrome, climbing for height, then Woody's voice [Wing Commander Alfred Woodhall, Duxford's Station Commander and 'Boss Controller'] came through: 'Climb to 15,000ft. There might be some "trade" for you on your way back.' We set course and climbed up through the sunlit haze and broken cloud.

At 17.30 hrs, thirty miles east of Harwich, over the Thames Estuary, 'A' Flight met the enemy formation previously intercepted by 56 Squadron:

> We flew on for some minutes until I judged we must be near the coast. Then, from behind a bank of cloud, sailed five Heinkels – then another five, and another, and another! A steady stream of aircraft appeared from the cloud ... There must have been at least 150 of them. Heinkels and Me 110 fighters, and way above showed twelve thin white pencils of smoke – the top escort.
>
> The leader of the formation must have seen us a few seconds after I sighted his formation, for the Huns turned out to sea, thin trails of black smoke from their exhausts showing they had opened their throttles wide and were on the run.
>
> 'Keep an eye on those bastards above us,' I ordered. Then, as the humour of the situation struck me, 'My God, what a windy bunch!'
>
> We were overhauling the Huns fast and the rearguard of Me 110s turned back to meet us, blocking our way to the bombers. Damn! There were at least twenty of them.
>
> The old excited feeling fluttered at the pit of my stomach. I remembered getting exactly the same feeling stepping into the boxing ring at school. Thoughts raced through my mind. How could we get to those bombers? I glanced up at the white trails far above us. They hadn't seen us or else thought we were a decoy and wouldn't come down. Ahead the 110s were circling to meet us. I glanced back at Frankie (Brinsden), leading his section behind me, to the left. Could one section hold off the

fighters while the others streaked after the bombers? No – we would have to leave Heinkels and content ourselves with a crack at the fighters.

The leading 110 was abreast of us now, turning to come in behind us. I wheeled left, Frankie taking his section in to meet him while I headed to cut off some of the others. A 110 turned and came straight at me from above, six streams of tracer spurting from his nose, as he opened fire. Hm! Not a very experienced pilot, judging by the range at which he opened fire, and I turned my head to see his tracer going fifty yards behind me. As he flashed past, I stall-turned to come in behind him, the rest of the section breaking away, each picking out an opponent.

I dived after mine and as he turned left I pulled round inside him, got the defection and pressed the firing button. No – dammit – I missed him and he pulled hard round and went underneath me. I turned again in time to see another Spitfire on his tail. A burst of tracer and the Hun went down in a dive – steeper and steeper and, finally plunging vertically downwards, disappeared into the clouds far below.

Turning again, I climbed up towards two more Huns, getting into position behind one of them. As I got there he saw me and began twisting and turning this way and that while I strove to get my sights on and take steady enough aim to fire. At last he was right in the centre of the sight and I opened fire. Blast it! I wasn't out of ammunition yet – must be a stoppage.

It looked as if I was hitting the 110, but he still twisted in front of me and I broke away to get into a better position. As I did so, another Hun came round on my tail and we started circling in what the Germans so aptly call a '*Kurvenkampf*'. The Spitfire had a much better turning circle and as I began to gain on him and come round towards his tail, he broke away into the opposite turn. It was a silly manoeuvre, as it brought me onto his tail almost at once and I fired the rest of my ammunition. He broke away below me and I lost him from sight.

Feeling rather annoyed at having no luck, I dived away towards the clouds. Glancing behind me, the fight appeared to be almost over. Away to the right a 110 was diving homewards,

FRIDAY, 16 AUGUST 1940

a Spitfire turning away from behind him and heading back towards the coast.

This action had been a long time coming for 'A' Flight, and Lane's exasperation at his guns suffering a stoppage can only be imagined. In his log book, he wrote: 'Waded into escort of Me 110s but ruddy cannons stopped on me.' The problem was that 19 Squadron was operating the experimental Spitfire Mk IB, armed with two 20mm cannon but no machine-guns, and it had yet to be worked out how best to mount the cannon in the Spitfire's thin wing section without turning it on its side. Although a chute was intended to eject spent shell cases, in combat the violent manoeuvres involved caused the metal to flex out of shape and line, preventing ejection and causing the cannon to jam. When that happened to both cannon, which it frequently did, with no back-up armament the pilot was defenceless and forced to retire.

Sergeant Potter had 'pursued an Me 110 and fired at very short range from above and saw almost the whole of his starboard engine disappear. He flicked over to port and as he did so a large piece of front section broke away.' When later asked by the Squadron Intelligence Officer whether he thought the claim a certainty, Potter replied 'Well, I knocked the port engine out of the wings, and the nose as far as the windscreen fell out as well, but he might have got home with hell of a draught in his face!'

Flight Sergeant Unwin:

> I attacked one of the Me 110s and gave him a short burst. He half rolled and went down almost vertically. I could not see what happened to him because I was attacked by another. I out-turned him and found myself with a perfect target at close range. My starboard cannon had a stoppage but I fired the remainder of my port cannon's ammunition into the 110. Bits fell off it and he went into a steep dive, during which the tail came off. I followed him down and when I emerged from cloud saw a splash in the sea, which I assumed was him.

Pilot Officer Cunningham also destroyed an Me 110 before his cannon jammed, but, like Flight Lieutenant Lane's, Sergeant Jennings' cannon refused to fire at all.

BATTLE OF BRITAIN ATTACK OF THE EAGLES

Pilot Officer Cunningham: 'I remember mainly Jennings on the R/T bemoaning his jammed 20 mm cannon, full of indignation at the unfairness of life in general!'

Unusually, the Me 110s had no rear gunners, and the Me 109s took no part in the engagement. In his log book, Sergeant Jennings recorded that he suspected the enemy formation to have been practicing, although this was not the case. Sergeant Roden's aircraft returned bullet-holed, but that aside, the Spitfires suffered no loss. Flight Sergeant Unwin claimed a 110 destroyed and a 'probable'; Sergeant Potter and Pilot Officer Cunningham one probable each. The pilots' frustration with their cannon, however, was clear: 'Results would have been at least doubled had we been equipped with either cannon and machine-guns or just eight machine-guns' (ORB). Being based in 12 Group, considering how limited opportunities for action had been to date, this further compounded 19 Squadron's frustration – but at least this action off Harwich represented the unit's first major engagement of the Battle of Britain.

At 17.45 hrs, Manston aerodrome was attacked: 'The station was attacked by eight Me 109s. Hangars and grounded aircraft were machine-gunned. There were no casualties but one Blenheim and one Spitfire were destroyed by fire. Two other Blenheims rendered unserviceable' (ORB).

As quickly as they appeared, the Me 109s vanished, heading back to France low and fast.

To the west, in anticipation of a further thrust between Portland and Portsmouth, the 10 Group Controller scrambled the Spitfires of Warmwell's 152 Squadron to patrol over Southampton, and those of 234 Squadron, based at Middle Wallop, to cover the Isle of Wight. These squadrons were also well-placed to intercept retiring enemy formations – which is exactly what happened in respect of 152 Squadron's engagement, 10 miles south of Southampton at 18.15 hrs.

Pilot Officer Eric 'Boy' Marrs:

> I was Blue 2. When on patrol over Southampton I saw two He 111s about 800ft below, proceeding in a southerly direction. I called Red 1 and dived to attack in order not to lose them in mist. I did stern and quarter attack on rear aircraft, opening fire at 300 yards. Oil poured from the E/A covering my windscreen, spinner and leading edges. The last seen of the E/A was that the propellers appeared to be rotating slowly, with smoke coming from both engines. I broke off the action as I thought the oil may have been from my machine, and as

FRIDAY, 16 AUGUST 1940

this was only ten miles from the Isle of Wight it is considered he failed to get home.

At the same time, five miles south of the Isle of Wight, 234 Squadron ran into the Me 109s of JG 53 which were up on a *Freie Jagd*. The Spitfires were led by the popular Australian Commander of 'A' Flight, Flight Lieutenant Pat Hughes:

> I was patrolling at 16,000ft with eleven aircraft when I saw approx. fifty Me 109s circling 4,000ft above. Section immediately formed line astern and climbed. The E/A formed a circle and I took a deflection shot at the nearest 109, which was on the tail of Blue 3. After a short burst he caught fire and blew up in front of Yellow 2.
>
> I felt a jolt and turned sharply and found another 109 on my tail. He immediately climbed away and pulled up in front of me. I shot him behind the cockpit and he caught fire and crashed into the sea. Then four Ju 87s went by, heading south, and I closed in to attack but as I fired my first burst my tailplane was shot through by a 109 ... The 109 overshot me and I turned onto his tail but had only ¼ second ammunition so had to break off the combat.

It was good shooting by Hughes, who returned his damaged Spitfire safely to base. Me 109s were also claimed destroyed by Pilot Officers Patrick Horton, a New Zealander, and Bob Doe, and the Polish Sergeant Zygmunt Klein; a probable was claimed by Flying Officer Kenneth Dewhurst, who was himself shot down, baling out over Widley. Flying Officer Francis Connor was also shot down and baled out, and was fortunate to be rescued from the sea by the RN. In this action, Spitfires were claimed destroyed by *Hauptmann* Günther von Maltzahn, the *Gruppenkommandeur* of the Guernsey-based II/JG 53, and *Oberleutnant* Kurt Bründle and *Feldwebel* Werner both of 4/JG 53.

Owing to the cloud cover, *Hauptmann* Genst was to record the fact that the majority of bombers returned from their sorties that afternoon with their payloads, having been unable to locate their targets. Yet again, for what the day had achieved, the *Luftwaffe* had suffered heavy losses.

At least eleven Me 109s had been destroyed and three damaged. Two of their pilots had been killed, one being *Hauptmann* Karl Ebbighausen, the

Kommandeur of II/JG 26; two were missing, two were prisoners of war, and four were wounded.

Seven Me 110s had been destroyed and one damaged; four of their crewmen were killed, four were missing, and four captured.

Four He 111s were lost and three damaged; eight of their aircrews had been killed, two were captured and two more were missing; eight were wounded, one of whom died later of his injuries.

Two Ju 88s had been damaged and three crewmen wounded.

Two Do 17s were destroyed, five of their crewmen missing and three killed.

Nine Ju 87s had been shot down and seven damaged; five crewmen were dead, twelve missing, three were captured, and five were wounded.

Going forward, such losses – amounting to at least thirty-five aircraft on this day alone, along with eighty-five aircrew either killed, missing, captured or wounded – were simply unsustainable.

Fighter Command's losses were twenty-five aircraft lost and twenty-two damaged; thirteen pilots were wounded, Pilot Officer Billy Fiske later succumbing to his burns, and five were killed, including Squadron Leader Rodney Wilkinson, CO of 266 Squadron; two pilots were missing.

That night, the *Luftwaffe* sent lone bombers to attack various targets, including airfields and aircraft factories, significantly among them RAF Brize Norton, a training and transport base also accommodating 6 MU, in Oxfordshire, which was attacked by two Ju 88s of an unknown unit. Thirty-two bombs were dropped (presumably most must have been incendiaries, because this figure far exceeds the payload of two Ju 88s). Three petrol bowsers were damaged, a tractor was rendered unserviceable, a Tutor aircraft was damaged, and serious damage was caused to two hangars of 2 SFTS, both of which were gutted by fire. The roof of a barracks was damaged, and the station's electricity and water supply disrupted, and five airmen and a civilian were killed. In what was the largest recorded loss of aircraft on the ground in one action, 2 SFTS suffered thirty-five Airspeed Oxford trainers destroyed, and 6 MU lost eleven Hawker Hurricanes. These were big numbers and showed just what the nocturnal nuisance raids could potentially achieve.

During the day, Coastal Command had lost two Blenheims on the ground at Thorney Island, and that night, Bomber Command lost three Whitleys, a Wellington and three Hampdens. These losses were sufficiently serious to concern Churchill, who pointed out to the CAS that 'While our eyes are concentrated on the results of the air fighting over this country, we must not overlook the serious losses occurring in Bomber Command.' The strength of Bomber Command, so long the focus of pre-war spending, was

FRIDAY, 16 AUGUST 1940

decreasing; on 11 July 1940, Bomber Command comprised forty squadrons, thirty-five of which were operational with 467 aircraft. By 22 August 1940, the figures had dropped to thirty-seven, thirty-one and 436 respectively. Given the broad range of essential tasks allocated to Bomber Command, including attacking the invasion ports, enemy airfields and industrial centres, Churchill was right to express concern. Nonetheless, Churchill also acknowledged that

> During these weeks of intense struggle and ceaseless anxiety Lord Beaverbrook rendered signal service. At all costs the fighter squadrons must be replenished with trustworthy machines. This was no time for red tape and circumlocution, although these have their place in a well-ordered, placid system. All his remarkable qualities fitted the need. His personal buoyancy and vigour were a tonic ... New or repaired aircraft streamed to the delighted squadrons in numbers they had never known before.

Indeed, Churchill was himself 'glad to be able sometimes to lean on him', and made the 'Beaver' a member of his War Cabinet.

On 10 July 1940, Fighter Command comprised fifty-seven squadrons, fifty-four of which were operational with 656 aircraft. By 21 August 1940, there were sixty-one squadrons, fifty-eight being operational with 746 aircraft. In July 1940, the gross output of aircraft was 1,665, of which 496 were fighters. In August, gross output dropped to 1,601, 476 fighters – so in spite of the enemy's best efforts and to the great credit of those essential workers in often vulnerable factories, the output was not appreciably affected. The man responsible for driving this was Beaverbrook (see *The Gathering Storm*, Volume 1); as Churchill said: 'This was his hour', with Dowding adding that, 'No other man in England could have done it.' Noteworthy is the fact that Me 109 production numbered only 220 in July 1940, dropping to 173 the following month. At the crucial time, the *Jagdwaffe* received less than half the aircraft MAP provided Fighter Command. As Bekker wrote, 'How, then, was the aim of "eliminating the enemy's fighter arm" to be achieved?'

Daily Home Intelligence Report, London Region:

> Townswomen's Guilds report jam-making going strong in suburban districts.

Chapter 5

Saturday, 17 August 1940

Once the morning haze disappeared the weather became fine – and yet, ominously, the RDF screens were devoid of any enemy activity. Throughout the day, less than fifty German aircraft were involved in operations against Britain, mostly on reconnaissance flights. Consequently, the number of sorties flown by Fighter Command was lower than on any day since 3 August.

Given the need to make good the losses, Dowding had agreed to make two foreign squadrons operational: 302 (Polish) and 310 (Czech). Initially reluctant owing to the language barrier, Dowding now had no choice but to commit these pilots to battle, many of whom had experience of combat, particularly the Poles, albeit not in modern RAF fighter types. Nonetheless, this was the right decision, and one Dowding would never have cause to regret.

On 1 July 1940, 310 (Czech) Squadron had formed at Duxford, where the Czechs rapidly became popular and earned respect.

Wing Commander Alfred 'Woody' Woodhall, Station Commander, RAF Duxford:

> Most of the Czechs had reported in French uniform, having fought with the French until France fell. Upon arrival they spoke little English and had to be converted onto Hurricanes. They were therefore provided an English Squadron Commander, Squadron Leader Douglas Blackwood, and English flight commanders, namely Flight Lieutenants Gordon Sinclair and Jerrard Jefferies, in addition to an English flying instructor and interpreter. The Czech CO was Squadron Leader Sacha Hess, who was quite famous in Czech air force circles. Much older than the rest, at 45, he was a first-class pilot and a dedicated fighter.
>
> Our first problem was to overcome the language difficulty, so I rang the BBC with the result that the interpreter and

SATURDAY, 17 AUGUST 1940

I spent a day at Broadcasting House where we recorded a series of orders, first in English followed by Czech, covering everything from 'Scramble' to Pancake'. The BBC quickly sent us several copies of these records, and in a very short time the Czechs were conversant with orders in English alone.

[No.]310 Squadron had a spare Hurricane (needless to say the oldest and slowest) which was always at my disposal, and as a result, albeit on the few occasions when I could spare the time from my other duties as Station Commander and Sector Controller, I flew on operations with the squadron as rear-end Charlie.

Squadron Leader Douglas Blackwood: 'I cannot speak highly enough of the Czechs' fighting qualities, although they did not always know what was expected of them; they were very keen on attacking enemy aircraft whenever they saw them, no matter what the circumstances.'

Flight Lieutenant Gordon Sinclair: 'I have nothing but praise for my fellow Czech pilots who were a wonderful bunch of people, totally determined to kill Germans. They went about this task with great enthusiasm and courage, and I found it tremendously comforting in battle to be surrounded by such pilots!'

Corporal Bill Kirk was an orderly clerk attached to 310 Squadron:

> The Czechs were first class and anxious to have a go. It became a tradition for British personnel serving with No 310 Squadron to replace our top tunic buttons with a Czech Air Force example. I was among the personnel sent to form 310, and in our office we processed all the admin from leave passes to Air Ministry orders. Working hours were unspecified, you just went to work until the job was done. I lived in the barrack block at Duxford and we all got on famously with the Czechs. They were always keeping fit, playing volley ball, and were very keen generally.
>
> For us on the ground it was tremendously exciting knowing that our aircraft were going into action, and upon return we all looked anxiously for those Hurricanes with blown gun port patches, indicating that the guns had been fired. It could also be distressing, talking to a chap in the Mess only for him to be

a 'goner' the next day. Our office was almost on the airfield, so we were very close to the pilots and aircraft. They were exciting times.

No.302 (Polish) 'City of Poznan' Squadron had formed at Leconfield on 13 July 1940 under the command of Squadron Leader Jack Satchell. To enable Polish officers to adjust to RAF procedures and while the language difficulties were resolved, the RAF CO and his flight commanders, Flight Lieutenants James Thomson and William Riley were shadowed by Polish officers. On 26 July 1940, the Polish Squadron Leader Mieczyslaw Mumler arrived from the Polish Collecting Centre at Blackpool to shadow Satchell, along with Polish flight commanders Flight Lieutenants Piotr Laguna and Franciszek Jastrzebski. By 17 August 1940, this, the first Polish fighter squadron, would also be operational, and soon see action flying from both Leconfield and Duxford.

Pilot Officer Edward 'Teddy' Morton:

> I received my commission in late June 1940, and was posted to RAF Duxford for supernumerary duties in Operations. The VR letters on my tunic still shone brightly, they were so new. Several of us arrived together, including an elderly pilot officer who was a retired solicitor. We were all introduced to the Station Commander, Wing Commander Woodhall, who noticed that the old lawyer was wearing a Boer War medal ribbon but none from the Great War. When asked where his 1914–18 ribbons were, the old boy replied that he had been too old for active service in that conflict! In view of his obviously extensive life experience, the Wing Commander made him Assistant Adjutant to 19 Squadron, to help the Adjutant write casualty letters.
>
> At that time, the Duxford Sector Controllers were Wing Commander Woodhall, Squadron Leader K.C. Horn (who had commanded a Sopwith Strutter squadron in the Great War and whose brother was a successful Sopwith Camel squadron commander), Squadron Leader Marsden, Squadron Leader Stanley Cooper, and Squadron Leader Livivosk. As dawn broke each day, if on duty at Ops 'B', the Controller would be resting (i.e. asleep and only to be disturbed if necessary). Straight after dawn I would telephone Wing Commander

SATURDAY, 17 AUGUST 1940

Woodhall on his direct line and inform him of the situation over southern England. There was dire trouble if ever 'Woody' wasn't given this brief first!

As an embryonic controller, a 'Wingless Wonder' or 'Penguin', I always made it my business to get to know as many pilots as possible, so as to gain their trust and understand the problems they faced in the air. All of us on the ground, of course, wanted to help them as much as possible.

The WAAF plotters in Duxford's Operations Room were known as 'Woody's Beauty Chorus'.

ACW1 Jill 'Half Pint' Pepper:

In 12 Group there were long periods with little action, so we got plenty of time to chat to the Observer Corps on our headphones. Voices, however, can be very misleading and we often got a shock when meeting the bloke in person!

After Dunkirk things got livelier and we were kept busy on our watches, concentration and calmness being essential to get the plotting right. The planes went up and it was always exciting when we heard 'Tally Ho!' over the intercom. We felt then that we were doing our bit to help stop the bloody Huns. It was sad, though, when some of our aircraft failed to return, even if we did not know the pilots personally.

There were often dances in the big hangar and whenever I hear *In the Mood* I'm back there again and can see the Station Controller, Wing Commander Woodhall, complete with monocle, playing his saxophone with great enthusiasm!

Daily Home Intelligence Report, 17 August 1940:

News of air activities remains the predominant topic of conversation, and the air battles are everywhere regarded as encouraging victories. The attitude towards the war is stiffening, and there is less tendency to compare it with a sporting event. Villages in which German planes have been brought down are proud of this slender association with the exploits of the RAF, and the general feeling in raided areas is 'We can take it'.

BATTLE OF BRITAIN ATTACK OF THE EAGLES

South-Eastern Region (Tunbridge Wells):

> The fact that this Region bore the brunt of yesterday's air attacks has heightened rather than lowered morale, and people are exhilarated by the feeling that they are in the front line.

If the residents of Tunbridge Wells were disappointed by the ominous lack of action on 17 August 1940, the events of the following day would more than compensate ...

Chapter 6

Sunday, 18 August 1940

General Wolfram von Richthofen, commander of VIII *Fliegerkorps*: 'The campaign against England is to proceed energetically, but differently.'

For Hitler, a swift and successful conclusion to the war against Britain was essential, especially with an attack on Russia the following year now embedded in both his mind and strategy. Hitler acknowledged that the most likely means of ensuring a 'short war' was invasion – and therefore the two were inexorably connected. Indeed, the resources and the risks involved in attacking Russia were far greater than those involved in Operation *Seelöwe* – even though Hitler was conscious of the potentially insurmountable difficulties of the invasion plan. Consequently, he had ordered the *Luftwaffe* to overwhelm the RAF – and assured the OKM and OKH that a seaborne invasion would not be launched without mastery of the air – and, so far, it appeared little or no progress had been made towards that essential objective.

By now, it was clear that Fighter Command was not to be swept from the sky with the ease initially predicted by *Reichsmarschall* Göring; indeed, the 'Iron Man' was furious at the apparent lack of progress. Every time the *Luftwaffe* launched attacks on Britain, RAF fighters were there. In fact Spitfires and Hurricanes were everywhere, even in the North and Scotland, far from the main combat area in the south-east. The Me 110, in which Göring placed such great confidence, had been roughly handled in recent days, and the *Stuka* – so terrifying in the Continental battles – was proving extremely vulnerable to RAF fighters, even when escorted. The bomber force's losses were mounting too, and the British always seemed to know when raids were incoming. Given that aerial supremacy enabling *Seelöwe* to proceed was pivotal to Hitler's grand strategy, the *Reichsmarschall* was under great pressure to deliver. Exasperated, Göring cast his net around for someone to blame – and again called his commanders to Carinhall.

The conference began at midday, with the *Luftwaffe* supremo berating those present: the matter should have been decided in a few days but mistakes had led to unacceptable losses. Among those summonsed to Göring's opulent country estate on 18 August 1940 were his two favourite fighter aces: *Major* Werner 'Vatti' Mölders, already decorated with the Knight's Cross and the *Kommodore* of JG 51, and *Major* Adolf 'Dolfo' Galland, *Kommandeur* of III/JG 26; both knew what was coming: the *Reichsmarschall* blamed the fighter pilots for a lack of aggression and failing to protect the bombers. A heated exchange ensued between Göring and the *Luftwaffe Inspektor-General*, Erhard Milch – who defended the *Jagdfliegern* and placed blame firmly at the door of OKL for giving the wrong orders.

At this stage of the battle, Göring was convinced that the best way to defeat Fighter Command was to attack targets within range of the Me 109, which could then shoot down the British fighters – and if the RAF refused to fight in the air, Fighter Command would be attacked on the ground. Again, the *Reichsmarschall*'s thinking was influenced by Schmid's faulty intelligence, based upon exaggerated German combat claims which suggested the *Luftwaffe* was destroying far more RAF fighters than was actually the case. In fact, Fighter Command was numerically stronger than it had been on 1 July 1940, and was four times stronger than Schmid believed. This was why Göring was fixated with the concept of the Me 109 destroying Fighter Command in the air – not on the ground. Had *Luftwaffe* intelligence been accurate, however, Göring would have known that the actual way to defeat his enemy was first to destroy the RDF stations, then flatten the vital Sector Operations Rooms.

It was understandable why the *Kampfgeschwadern* would insist on closer fighter protection, but Galland explains why this was not actually the answer:

> Obviously the proximity and visual presence of the fighters gave the bomber pilots a greater sense of security. However, this was a faulty conclusion, because a fighter can only carry out this purely defensive task by taking the initiative in the offensive. He must never wait until he is attacked, because then he loses the initiative. The fighter must seek battle in the air, must find his opponent, attack and shoot him down. The bomber must avoid such fights, and he has to act defensively in order to fulfil his task: war from the air. In cooperation between bomber and fighter, these two mentalities clash. The words of Richthofen expressed during the First World War, summarising the task of fighters, often came to our lips: 'The fighter pilots have to rove in the area allotted to them in any

SUNDAY, 18 AUGUST 1940

way they like, and when they spot an enemy they attack and shoot him down; anything else is rubbish.'

Indeed, the German fighters had performed well over Dunkirk when unfettered with bomber escorts and able to seek and destroy enemy fighters. The same is true of *Freie Jagd* missions during the Battle of Britain fought to date.

Göring, however, concluded the conference with clear instructions: 'There can no longer be any kind of restriction on any kind of target ... Only I personally reserve the right to order attacks on Liverpool and London.'

In this, Göring had overstepped the mark, because attacks on London could actually only be ordered by Hitler – which rather shows how desperate the *Reichsmarschall* was becoming to force a decision. After the conference, perhaps surprisingly, Göring invested Mölders and Galland with bejewelled Gold Pilot's Medals – but afterwards made plain to the pair of aces that he was totally dissatisfied with the *Jagdwaffe*'s performance to date and demanded greater efforts. Indeed, the *Reichsmarschall*, himself a First World War fighter ace, had his own plan to increase the fighter arm's aggression.

Like the RAF, the outbreak of war had seen *Luftwaffe* fighter units commanded by comparatively mature officers, and this, excepting Mölders' command of JG 51, remained the case. Now, Göring explained that he intended to start replacing the elderly *Kommodoren* with younger men. Galland, aged 28, was to replace 31-year-old *Major* Gottard Handrick as *Kommodore* of JG 26. Galland, however, was sceptical and concerned that being *Kommodore* would mean less flying; not so, the *Reichsmarschall* assured him, and in this he was true to his word. The concept was that the *Kommodore* would lead in the air, so, like the later RAF Wing Leaders, this was a fighting appointment. The other most successful *Gruppenkommandeur* at the time, *Hauptmann* Johannes Trautloft, was also promoted to command JG 54, and now the purges began.

Firstly, Galland's successor as *Kommandeur* of III/JG 26 was *Oberleutnant* Gerhard Schöpfel – another outstanding fighter pilot and more of whom shortly. *Hauptmann* Rolf Pingel replaced Kurt Fischer at the head of I/JG 26; 21-year-old *Oberleutnant* Joachim Müncheberg took over 7/JG 26 from *Oberleutnant* Georg Bayer, who became Galland's Adjutant at *Geschwader* HQ, and soon afterwards *Oberleutnant* Eberhard Henrici took over 1/JG 26. Galland arranged for his *Stabschwarm* to operate from Audembert, near Wissant, where *Oberst* Theo Osterkamp, the *Jagdfliegerführer* based himself.

BATTLE OF BRITAIN ATTACK OF THE EAGLES

In anticipation of a more vigorous and aggressive aerial assault on southern England, Göring also ordered the three Me 109-equipped *Jagdgeschwadern* of *Luftflotte* 3, JG 2, JG 27 and JG 53, to move from their airfields around Cherbourg to the Pas-de-Calais, within *Generalfeldmarschall* Kesselring's *Luftlotte* 2. The *Jagdfliegern* could be under no misapprehension: going forward, south-east England and 11 Group was to be the primary focus of this renewed assault – and, so far as the *Reichsmarschall* was concerned, failure was not an option.

While Göring conferred at Carinhall and made changes to his *Luftwaffe's* Order of Battle, the aerial assault on Britain continued. Sunday, 18 August 1940 would be another day of bitter fighting. Meanwhile, Churchill was at Chequers, composing a speech he would deliver to the House in a couple of days – and which would also be well-remembered by history's 'flickering lamp'.

Squadron Leader Edward Alford GM, Station Armoury, RAF Kenley:

> Air Raid warnings became far more prevalent and all personnel moved quickly and quietly to their appointed places of duty, taking with them steel helmets, anti-gas clothing, respirators and eye-shields, all of which were necessary as no one knew when the 'Chemical Warfare' might start. Today, tomorrow, any day.
>
> One got used to the clear steady voice of the sector controller giving clear unhurried orders over the 'Tannoy' that the routine work of closing windows and doors of buildings, lowering blinds and fixing of anti-gas curtains into position was carried out automatically on receipt of each warning. As the days passed we saw a little more of the arrogant *Luftwaffe* and witnessed several dogfights high above the station as the fighters split up bomber formations and tore them out of the sky, though many times we heard the rattle of Browning guns above the clouds but could see nothing.
>
> Sunday 18 August 1940 started the same as any other day, the squadrons were called to duty and routine work went on at dispersal points and maintenance sections in the normal way.

AC1 Stan Ford was a Flight Mechanic serving on 615 Squadron at Kenley:

> In the morning we had to go over the aircraft and check on everything connected with the engine, and the flight riggers

SUNDAY, 18 AUGUST 1940

would go over what they had to do with the wings, ailerons and flying controls. Then I had to sign the Form 700 [the groundcrew signed off their work on the 700, which the pilot then counter-signed before accepting the aircraft for flight]. Then, with all of that done, we waited until something happened.

Kenley's squadrons, including our 615, used to be on progressive states of readiness: First Readiness, Second Readiness and Third Readiness, coordinated with Biggin Hill and Croydon squadrons. When we were on First Readiness, Croydon would be Second Readiness and Biggin Hill would be Third. When we were on First Readiness the fitter used to sit in the cockpit and on the parachute with the straps over. And if we got a scramble the rigger was on the battery and the fitter in the cockpit would start up. When the pilots came out they jumped in, strapped in and they were off.

Our CO was Squadron Leader Joe Kayll, who said 'I'm Joe Kayll and want to be known as "Joe" and if you speak to me I'm "Joe", nothing else unless someone of higher rank is about,' and so that's what happened. We were known by Christian names on 615 Squadron, the pilots too. We had two French pilots, one was René Mouchotte who we used to call 'Reenee' and the other was Henri Lafonte, called 'Henry'. And another one was a South African pilot called Petrus Hugo, who we called 'Dutch', because with his accent, when he came to the squadron someone said, like the old saying, 'I can't understand him, he's talking double Dutch' – so that's where the name came from.

Sunday, 18 August 1940 started off as just a normal day, quite a sunny day. Anyway, we sort of waited: we were on Readiness that day so we were all ready for a scramble.

Squadron Leader Don MacDonell, commanding 64 Squadron at Kenley, was enjoying some rare time off that fateful Sunday morning:

The morning off was a blessing to all of us. I was back with my Squadron by 1130 hrs and went straight to the Operations Room to see what plots were on the board. There were none: ominous. The *Luftwaffe* usually laid off minor raids before a major build-up. Squadron Leader Anthony Norman, the Sector Controller, confirmed my views and my favourite WAAF plotter gave me an even more generous smile when bringing my coffee.

I got my team together and told them that a full-scale bombing raid was expected ... Kenley and Biggin Hill, both Sector Stations, were likely targets. We sharpened our swords, as it were, and had an early lunch. An hour later we were at readiness. I had only eight Spitfires left.

Squadron Leaders MacDonell and Norman were correct: across the Channel, preparations were being made for further major attacks – and for Kenley, to the discomfort of personnel based there, the day would actually be anything but 'normal'. Indeed, as Frances Cherry, a WAAF cook at Kenley remembered, it would be a 'terrible day'.

From an operational perspective, Sunday, 18 August 1940 began with *Luftwaffe* shipping and weather reconnaissance flights over the North Sea. At 05.20 hrs, the Hurricanes of 257 Squadron left Debden in Essex to operate from the forward base at Martlesham Heath, from where, at 06.22 hrs, 'A' Flight's Yellow Section took off to patrol a southbound convoy off the east coast. Sixty miles south-east of Martlesham, at 3,000ft, Yellow Leader, Pilot Officer Arthur Cochrane, 'chased a Do 17 and had a combat with it. The enemy bomber went straight up into the air and its port undercarriage fell' (ORB). Cochrane reported that 'During his break-away there was a very loud bang and I thought my machine was hit. After coming out of his break-away, the E/A was nowhere to be seen. I then set course for land and base.' Cochrane's Hurricane was actually undamaged; the Do 17 was considered probably destroyed, although more likely it regained base, damaged.

The next three hours were, as Squadron Leader MacDonell felt, ominously quiet. Then, between 11.00 hrs and 11.30 hrs, various lone snoopers reconnoitred 11 Group's airfields. At 08.25 hrs, Squadron Leader 'Prof' Leathart had led his 54 Squadron from Hornchurch to the forward base at Manston, from where, at 10.54 hrs, the Spitfires scrambled 'to investigate unidentified aircraft flying at 25,000ft north-east of aerodrome. Five of the pilots climbed to 25,000ft and saw machine 8,000ft above them. They engaged this machine, identified as an Me 110 [ORB].'

Flight Lieutenant George Gribble and Pilot Officer Colin Gray were first to attack, Gray temporarily setting both engines ablaze and Gribble 'holing the fuselage'. Flight Sergeant Phillip Tew then attacked, the Me

SUNDAY, 18 AUGUST 1940

110's engine again catching fire while the aircraft dived steeply for France. Pilot Officer William Hopkin was fourth into the attack, knocking pieces of the stricken enemy aircraft, and finally Sergeant John Norwell opened fire at sea-level, pulling out of his dive 'only a very few feet above the water'. The Me 110 was last seen 'fully ablaze', but was not seen to crash into the water. The Me 110, of 7(F)/LG 2, was shared between the pilots concerned and accredited as destroyed – which indeed it was: *Oberleutnant* Arnold Werdin was reported missing, and *Oberfeldwebel* Hans Knopf was killed. So perished the first victims of 'The Hardest Day' – and what was about to follow was anything other than quiet.

With the weather set fair, *Luftflotte* 2's HQ in Brussels signalled a flurry of executive orders for the day's raids. KG 1, based around Amiens, was to attack Biggin Hill with sixty He 111s. Kenley was to be hit in audacious fashion: twelve Ju 88s of *Major* Friedrich Möericke's Creil-based II/KG 76, and a further twenty-seven Do 17s of *Major* Theodore Schweitzer's I/KG 76, operating from Beauvais, and Möericke's II/KG 76 were to cross the Kentish coast over Dover and bomb Kenley from high altitude. Then, nine Do 17s of *Hauptmann* Joachim Roth's 9/KG 76, based at Cormieilles-en-Vexin, north of Paris, were to cross the Channel at zero feet before making landfall at Cuckmere Haven, just west of Beachy Head in East Sussex, before hedge-hopping north-east a few miles to Burgess Hill and turning due north for Kenley – some sixty miles inland.

The 9/KG 76 plan, therefore, relied upon surprise by flying undetected beneath the radar screen and bombing from low-level. In the *Luftwaffe*, unlike the RAF, the navigator was the aircraft captain, and so the lead Do 17, in which Roth, the *Staffelkapitän*, flew was piloted by *Oberleutnant* Otto Lamberty. Aboard *Feldwebel* Adolf Reichel's aircraft, the third in the second *Kette* (vic of three), was a passenger, Rolf von Pebel, a *Kriegsberichter*, and another war reporter, Georg Hinze, was to fly with *Oberleutnant* Hermann Magin's lead bomber of the third *Kette*. The highest-ranking officer on the mission, *Oberstleutnant* Dr Otto Sommer, a *Stabsoffizier* gaining operational experience, was to go with *Feldwebel* Johannes Petersen, who flew the first aircraft of the second *Kette*.

The Kenley plan was comparatively complex. First, the Ju 88s of II/KG 76 were approach at high altitude before dive-bombing hangars and other airfield buildings. Then, the heavily escorted high-flying Do 17s of I and II/KG 76 would crater the runway and destroy the airfield's defences. Finally, 9/KG 76 would appear low and fast, in the first such zero-feet raid on England, monopolising on the destructive chaos already achieved to reduce any remaining airfield installations to rubble. Conversely, Biggin Hill was simply to be attacked by successive waves of sixty heavily escorted He 111s of *Generalmajor* Karl Angerstein's KG 1 'Hindenburg', based at Rosiéres-en-Santerre and Montdidier, near Amiens, which would, it was hoped, completely destroy the station.

Although the low-flying 9/KG 76 Do 17s were unescorted, relying upon guile and surprise, the remaining bomber formations were to be closely protected by JG 51, 52 and 54, and ZG 26. From the fighter pilots' perspective, however, the best mission was given to JG 3 and JG 26 – a *Freie Jagd* comprising sixty Me 109s sweeping ahead of the main bomber formations bound for Kenley and Biggin Hill. Unlike many airfields previously attacked, both Kenley and Biggin Hill were Sector Stations, accommodating vital sector operations rooms – although, remarkably, this still remained unknown by *Luftwaffe* intelligence. Nonetheless, this great raid could potentially deliver a body-blow to London's defensive ring.

The weather, however, led to another false start: just before 09.00 hrs, He 111s of KG 1 had taken off on their mission to destroy Biggin Hill but were almost immediately recalled, owing to haze having reduced visibility over south-east England to such a degree that it would compromise 9/KG 76's low-level approach and the dive-bombing of Kenley by II/KG 76's Ju 88s. Frustrated, back at base KG 1 were informed of a two-and-a-half-hour postponement while the rising sun evaporated the problematic haze. At their bases, the aircrew of KG 76 were also held back, as *Unteroffizier* Günther Unger, detailed to fly the second Do 17 in the second 9/KG 76 Kette on the Kenley raid, recalled:

> We spent the whole of the morning kicking our heels by our aircraft. We had stripped off in the marvellous weather and were sunning ourselves ... Gradually we became impatient: were we going to be sent home to our billets today without flying a mission, as had happened so often in the past?

Eventually, reconnaissance aircraft reported that the haze had sufficiently evaporated for the postponed missions to go ahead. KG 1's He 111s were the first to take-off, the whole *Geschwader* making for an impressive spectacle as it met the fighter escorts over the French coast. Things began to go awry for KG 76 almost from the outset, however. Over Calais, 8/10ths cloud at 6,000ft, extending to 10,000ft, meant that the high-flying raiders of KG 76 had to climb above the clouds to meet its fighter escort – but while climbing

SUNDAY, 18 AUGUST 1940

through the cloud the bombers lost formation and were consequently forced to waste crucial time orbiting and re-forming. Six minutes late, the Do 17s of I and III/KG 76 set course for their target – but had already overtaken the Ju 88s of II/KG 76, which should have been five minutes ahead and the first to attack.

Twenty-five miles ahead of the high-flying KG 76 Do 17s and Ju 88s, which were closely escorted by twenty Me 110s of ZG 26, were forty Me 109s of III/JG 26 and JG 3. Fifteen miles behind KG 76 flew the sixty He 111s of KG 1, closely protected by forty Me 109s of JG 54. Meanwhile, fifty miles to the south-west, 9/KG 76 were on time and Kenley-bound, just above the waves, and half way between Dieppe and Beachy Head. Collectively, this was a huge raid, comprising over 250 aircraft – which, excepting the low-level formation, was now showing up on British RDF screens as possibly as many as 350+.

In response, according to Squadron ORBs, the 11 Group Controller scrambled the following fighter squadrons:

> 12.15 hrs: eleven Hurricanes of 32 Squadron from Biggin Hill, to patrol Dover.

> 12.30 hrs: six Hurricanes of 501 Squadron from Hawkinge to patrol the Kentish coast. A section of four followed at 12.40 hrs, four more Hurricanes between 13.00–13.10 hrs, and three more at 13.25 hrs.

> 12.40 hrs: six Spitfires of 54 Squadron to patrol the Canterbury to Maidstone line.

> 12.40 hrs: six Hurricanes of 56 Squadron's 'A' Flight, followed at 12.45 hrs by those of 'B' Flight, from North Weald, also to patrol the Canterbury to Maidstone line.

> 12.45–12.50 hrs: twelve Hurricanes of 615 Squadron from Kenley in anticipation of attack approaching base.

> 12.50 hrs: six Spitfires of 65 Squadron from Rochford to patrol Thames Estuary.

> 12.55 hrs: six Hurricanes of 17 Squadron to intercept enemy raid in Dover area.

At Tangmere, Nos. 43, 601 and 602 Squadrons were held in reserve.

As the two sides converged, one of the two *Kriegsberichter* on the low-level recorded that:

> The mission flown ... will always remain a shining example of the German airmen's spirit. All alone, without being covered by German fighters, the nine Dorniers swept over England at only a few metres height, for the first daring low-level raid against England.
>
> England was so near that we could almost touch it. Sometimes hardly two metres below the wings of our heavily loaded aircraft. After we had jumped the steep coast from sea-level, we were able to study in detail England's coastal defences. We roared so low across the South of England, hedge-hopping over rows of trees and every hedge, that one crew brought back, among the splintered glass of the glazed nose, some leaves from an English tree whose top the machine touched on its wild flight.

Whipping low over the Channel, the Dorniers had been briefly fired upon by the RN, but were there and gone, as they flashed overhead. Passing Beachy Head and the white chalk cliffs of the Seven Sisters, however, having so far approached undetected by RDF, it was the Observer Corps Post K3 at Beachy Head which immediately reported by telephone to Observer Corps HQ in Horsham that the nine Do 17s were inbound, flying north-west, at zero feet. Within minutes, this information had been passed to the Filter Room and Fighter Command HQ, thence to 11 Group's underground Operations Room at Uxbridge, and then to Kenley, whose sector the raid was now fast approaching.

A few minutes before 13.00 hrs, the Hurricanes of 501 Squadron were patrolling over Canterbury, flying in tight vics of three and climbing in a wide spiral. Unfortunately for the Hurricanes, they had been espied by *Oberleutnant* Gerhard Schöpfel, leading III/JG 26 high above. Realising that a lone Me 109 was more likely to succeed in successfully ambushing the RAF fighters, Schöpfel ordered his Me 109s to remain at altitude, and dropped into position. The 27-year-old '*experte*' dropped towards the enemy, achieving total surprise: attacking unseen and out of the dazzling sun, within seconds both 'weavers', crossing to and fro behind their squadron, were dispatched. The remaining Hurricanes, however, flew on – oblivious. Unable to believe his luck, Schöpfel then downed the rearmost aircraft, which was soon plunging earthwards in flames. Still, however,

SUNDAY, 18 AUGUST 1940

501 Squadron continued climbing in tight formation, completely unaware of their comrades' fate, or that death still stalked them.

One of the Hurricanes so far destroyed by Schöpfel was that of the Polish Pilot Officer Franciszek Kozlowski, who baled out seriously wounded, his aircraft crashing at Raynham's Farm, near Whitstable. Another was flown by Sergeant Donald McKay, who baled out slightly wounded over Sturry, Canterbury; Pilot Officer John Bland, however, was killed at Calcott Hill, Sturry. Schöpfel was not finished yet: 'The Englishmen continued on, having noticed nothing. So I pulled in behind the fourth machine and took care of him also, but this time I went in too close.'

Pilot Officer Kenneth Lee: 'I was the fourth Hurricane Schöpfel dispatched. I got a lump of shrapnel in my right calf and the engine caught fire. I baled out sharpish.'

Debris from Lee's stricken Hurricane hit Schöpfel's Me 109, oil covering his windscreen. More than satisfied with the results of the last two minutes – which was an unprecedented achievement in aerial combat at the time – the Me 109 pilot dived away.

As Schöpfel withdrew, more Me 109s fell on the hapless Hurricane formation, but fortunately no more of 501 Squadron were lost. In a different action, though, Pilot Officer Robert Dafforn was shot down over Biggin Hill, baling out of Hurricane R4219, which crashed at Cronks Farm, East Seal; the pilot was unhurt.

More squadrons were scrambled by 11 Group:

> 13.00 hrs: thirteen Spitfires of 610 Squadron from Biggin Hill, to engage bombers approaching from the south.
>
> 13.00 hrs: eight Spitfires of 64 Squadron from Kenley – which 9/KG 76 was fast approaching.
>
> 13.05 hrs: twelve Hurricanes of 111 Squadron from Croydon to patrol base.
>
> 13.15 hrs: six Hurricanes of 1 Squadron from Northolt to patrol base.
>
> 13.15 hrs: ten Spitfires of 266 Squadron from Manston to patrol Rochford.

It became clear to the Station Commanders at Kenley, Wing Commander Thomas Prickman and Squadron Leader Norman, that their airfield was the intended target of the low-level raid still being tracked by the Observer Corps. One fighter squadron in the Sector remained on the ground, which is when 111 Squadron was scrambled from Croydon to 3,000ft, in the hope of meeting the inbound, hedge-hopping, Do 17s. At 13.21 hrs, when the bombers were a minute from target, the Hurricanes sighted the Dorniers and prepared to attack – too late, though, to prevent the airfield being bombed.

Squadron Leader Edward Alford:

> I had just sat down to lunch in the mess and the WAAF waitress placed my meal before me, when we received the 'Preliminary Air Raid Warning' over the Tannoy.
>
> Making a request to the waitress to 'Keep my meal warm until I return,' I left the building and went down to the Station Armoury. The Armourers were already on the roof, had removed the canvas gun covers and were standing ready as they had done so often before. I went through the building to ensure that all was in order and then stood by an ammunition trailer which was concealed under a tree just outside the armourers shop.
>
> During this time the remaining aircraft had been sent into the air, and at about 1310 hrs the 'Attack Alarm' sounded, warning us that it was evident that we were about to be attacked. A Final Warning was given by the Sector Controller at about 1315 hrs as to the direction of approach of the hostile aircraft, and all eyes were fixed in that direction.

As *Hauptmann* Joachim Roth's lead Do 17 arrived over Kenley, however, it was immediately apparent to 9/KG 76's *Staffelkapitän* that the plan had misfired – instead of already having been battered by the dive-bombers and high-flying raiders, the aerodrome was completely intact. Roth had no choice but to press on regardless – and his bombers became the focus of Kenley's defences: four 40-mm Bofors guns were rapid-firing their eight-round magazines, while the heavier pair of 3-inch guns pumped rounds out at a slower rate. The German air gunners responded and the whole airfield became a maelstrom of shot and shell, a cacophony of gun fire and explosions.

Unteroffizier Günther Unger: 'The hail of light flak and machine-gun fire showered around us, the red points of tracer rounds flashing by ... I pushed the aircraft yet lower and went in exactly over the left-hand hangars'.

Squadron Leader Alford:

SUNDAY, 18 AUGUST 1940

The first gun to open fire was a Lewis, sited on top of No 1 Hangar and a few seconds later three formations of three Do 17s swept over the trees at a height of about 50ft. As my Armoury was close to the trees I do not think it could have been seen by the formation which passed over it, and the gunners on the roof of the shop poured a hail of bullets into them. So low were these aircraft that I could see the crew and taking an estimated deflection shot, I let fly with my .45 Webley Revolver, but only had time to fire two shots.

Clutches of bombs dropped from the machines as they swept over the drome and they seemed to 'Porpoise' bounce across the runways, those which exploded sending a 'Geyser effect' of earth into the air. One bomb seemed to penetrate into the ground near the centre of the drome and a pillar of what appeared to be smoke arose from it. This smoke formed into a huge ball approximately 30ft in diameter at a height of about 100ft when it burst into flame and the blast of hot air could be felt from where I was kneeling, at least 400 yards away.

As *Kriegsberichter* Rolf von Pebel, flying in the 9/KG 76 Do 17 of *Feldwebel* Adolf Reichel, wrote:

All hell was let loose on the airfield. The bombs dropped by the first *Kette* left no two bricks of the hangars and control tower standing together. The second *Kette* that followed at a short distance saw how scores of totally surprised and bewildered Englishmen rushed out of their living quarters into the air-raid trenches. Inexorably bombs fell among the seething mass of people. Wooden parts of the barrack units, steel helmets, uniforms, human bodies – all whirled through the air. We of the third *Kette*, roaring through the smoke and dust of the explosions, saw these visions in fractions of seconds and were able to save part of our bombload for targets on the way home.

ACW Frances Cherry:

They came in their droves, all of them at dinner time when everyone was in camp. There was no panic, the sirens went, and all moved pretty damned quick into the shelters ... I was in the wrong place instead of in my allotted shelter. I was once again at sick quarters, having a couple of stitches put on a cut finger, so was in the sick quarters' shelter, which was the only one that had a direct hit. We were buried for almost six hours. Two medical officers lost their lives, one WAAF officer lost her leg, and the rest of us were just bruised and shaken.

AC1 Stan Ford:

All of a sudden there was a terrific roar ... nine Dorniers ... they were right on the ground, more or less, as they were very, very low and dropped bombs on the buildings ... loads of bombs. They dropped some a bit too late for the buildings and they hit the airfield. They skidded, loads of them, and I am standing there by the Dispersal Hut and I thought 'I can't do nothing, if one comes towards me I will jump over it.' Anyway, none came right over there so I was lucky and there were some that didn't detonate. There were three or four that I remember detonated, but all the others didn't. So, I thought to myself, 'Well, that didn't last long.'

Having bombed the hangars, *Oberleutnant* Rudolf Lamberty, Roth's pilot, streaked low across the airfield – but was shocked to see some kind of 'secret weapon' snaking into the air ahead of him – a Parachute and Cable. At 60-ft intervals, the northern side of Kenley airfield was defended by these ingenious but unconventional devices, which shot a rocket 600ft vertically into the air, towing behind it a 480-ft long steel cable. When maximum height was reached, a parachute opened at the top of the cable, suspending it in mid-air – hopeful of snagging the wing of an attacking aircraft. In the event of that occurring, a second parachute opened, at the bottom of the cable, the drag caused by the weapon hopefully causing the pilot to lose control and crash. As the mystifying cable was fired ahead of him, Lamberty pulled up and successfully avoided the contraption – but was then hit by a Bofors round, which tore a hole in the left wing and ignited the fuel tank. As if things could get no worse, it was then that Sergeant William Dymond of 111 Squadron attacked the Do 17 – at a height of just 50ft: 'Attack was delivered from dead astern and E/A had both engines hit and it crashed in a field about three miles NE of Kenley.'

SUNDAY, 18 AUGUST 1940

Other pilots of 111 Squadron also attacked the bombers, including Flight Lieutenant Stanley Connors DFC who had 'led the squadron into attack in line-astern', and was,

> seen flying between three Dorniers in the box and pumping the leader from astern. Green 2, Pilot Officer Simpson followed and one Do 215 [*sic*] was destroyed by these two pilots. Flight Lieutenant Connors was seen to break away safely, but Pilot Officer Simpson suffered damage to his rudder and aileron controls but managed to forced-land on Royal Automobile Club golf course at Woodcote Bank. The break-away had to be upwards owing to the low height of the E/A ... Flight Lieutenant Connors DFC fell in flames and was killed. Yellow 1 ... said that AA fire from the hill south of Kenley had caused the crash. (ORB)

While their aircraft was under attack, two of Lamberty's crew, *Hauptmann* Gustav Peters and *Oberfeldwebel* Valentin Geier, baled out very low – they were lucky to survive with multiple injuries, while *Feldwebel* Hugo Eberhart deployed his parachute immediately upon leaving the aircraft and landed more lightly, suffering only a cut hand. Lamberty and Roth remained aboard, the pilot somehow managing to control the doomed bomber sufficiently to safely crash-land. As the Do 17 passed overhead, though, the twenty-strong detachment of the LDV let fly with rapid rifle fire, after which the bomber lost even more height. Eventually, after a breathless and death-defying couple of minutes since arriving over Kenley's hangars, Lamberty forced-landed his burning bomber at Leaves Green – where both he and his *Staffelkapitän* were captured. Because the bomber crashed immediately after being fired upon by the Home Guard the press actually accredited the kill to the Addington 'Dad's Army' unit.

Having bombed, *Feldwebel* Wilhelm Raab, No.3 in Roth's *Kette*, was about to shoot-up a petrol bowser when the terrifying Parachute and Cable device was fired at, and hit, his aircraft – but fortunately for the German crew the cable failed to find purchase and harmlessly slipped off the wing. Beating it hell-for-leather for home, the bomber was hit by AA fire, severely wounding the navigator and aircraft captain, *Leutnant* Erwin Wittman. Hugging the ground contours of the North Downs, Raab headed for home.

For some reason, *Feldwebel* Johannes Petersen, flying the lead aircraft of the *Kette* to Lamberty's left, flew across Kenley airfield higher than his

BATTLE OF BRITAIN ATTACK OF THE EAGLES

Kameraden – drawing AA fire and being hit by a Parachute and Cable. Out of control, the bomber crashed into a nearby residential bungalow, 'Sunnycroft'; although the five civilians inside who were enjoying their Sunday roast survived, Petersen and his crew, including their passenger *Oberstleutnant* Dr Sommer, were all killed.

The Parachute and Cable had been fired by ACs Knowles and Roberts, both of whom were commended to Fighter Command HQ by their Station Commander – although only AC2 David Roberts was decorated for his actions that day, later receiving the Military Medal.

Kriegsberichter Rolf von Pebel described being on the receiving end of Kenley's defences and 111 Squadron's Hurricanes:

> Our closely flying *Ketten* dispersed. Each separate crew now had four or even more Spitfires [*sic*] and Hurricanes against it. Fast as lightning the bewildering multi-coloured network of tracer trails flashed to and fro, only a few metres above the English soil, above the sprawling suburbs of London, above the villages and towns.
>
> Time and time again the English dived upon homeward flying aircraft. Every time bursts of fire from our rear machine-guns received them. Like a hailstorm beating against a window pane, the machine-gun bullets of the enemy fighters' eight machine-guns hammered into the wings of our machines. Many of our men stayed at their machine-gun posts despite injuries – firing away with their left hands when their right had been hit,

The Do 17 von Pebel was a passenger in was hit, damaging an engine, although *Feldwebel* Reichel successfully evaded further interception and nursed his crippled bomber back across the Channel, crash-landing near Abbeville; von Pebel:

> I heard the corn scraping against the machine. Or was it only the wind whispering past the stopped motor? I closed my eyes. A crash! Was that all? Then came a feeling of drifting, a mad crash, a creaking and grinding. I was knocked down as if by a giant fist. For a moment everything was deathly still, then we all scrambled for the escape hatch. But it obstinately refused to open. The machine might catch fire at any moment!

SUNDAY, 18 AUGUST 1940

Desperately, the three of us hurled ourselves against the hatch in the cabin roof and finally it gave way. In an instant we clambered out.

The Flight Engineer, wounded in both knees, was carefully lifted out of and carried away from the wrecked bomber; there was no fire. The survivors counted 110 bullet-holes in their machine.

Feldwebel Otto Stephani, flying what had been the right-hand bomber of the right-hand *Kette*, was shot-up by three Hurricanes, killing the flight engineer, severely wounding the radio operator and damaging both engines. Limping over the Channel, the surviving crew dumped every non-essential item aboard to lighten the aircraft – including their dead comrade's body. This was only just enough for the damaged bomber to regain France, and crash-land at Calais. There the aircraft captain, *Unteroffizier* Rudolf Grömmer, stopped counting bullet holes in his bomber at 200. The badly wounded radio operator later died.

As the Dorniers attacked Kenley, *Kriegsberichter* Georg Hinze, flying in the right-hand aircraft of the left-hand *Kette*, flown by *Oberleutnant* Hermann Magin and captained by the navigator, *Oberfeldwebel* Wilhelm-Friedrich Illg, was about to experience the shocking violence of war first-hand:

> a machine-gun bullet had ripped open the arm and chest of our pilot and it was the feet of a dying man buckled to the rudder pedals that steered our course. London glided past below us while we were busy getting the pilot from his seat. We fired round after round at the attacking English fighters. Only occasionally could we see anything of the city through the wide-open floor of the bomber, from which the flight engineer had already jettisoned the hatch for the parachute jump that might become necessary.
>
> All this was very exciting but most important to us at that time was to replace the dead pilot [Magin was not yet dead, in fact, but was fatally wounded] with a crew member who could fly the machine and bring us home.

When his pilot was incapacitated, the navigator *Oberfeldwebel* Wilhem-Friedrich Illg grabbed the steering column – at which point the bomber was just 30ft above the ground – and, standing, used the Herculean strength of a desperate man to literally haul the Dornier higher into the air. Bombs were jettisoned and somehow Illg kept the aircraft flying, avoiding the London balloon barrage, and heading for the South Coast – and France.

The Do 17 flown by *Unteroffizier* Günther Unger, who had flown even lower, hugging the ground closer still, as Kenley's defences opened up, was hit by Lewis gun rounds, damaging the bomber's right engine, forcing the pilot to feather it and thereby lose speed. Having dropped his bombs Unger tried to escape, but was intercepted by 111 Squadron's Sergeant Harry Newton. The 20-year-old fighter pilot attacked the Do 17 but was hit by Unger's gunner, *Unteroffizier* Franz Bergmann – setting the Hurricane's fuel tank alight. Newton's cockpit was consumed by flames, even the oxygen in his mask catching fire, but, undeterred, Newton plunged his hands into the flames, grabbed the control column, corrected his course and 'loosed off a long burst in the direction of where I thought the Dornier was'. Then, and only then, did Newton climb his blazing aircraft with a view to baling out, the flames almost consuming him. When the Hurricane's engine cut, Newton rammed the joystick forward and was thrown from the blazing aircraft as it violently pitched forward. As he descended, a squad of soldiers, with fixed bayonets, looked menacingly skywards until the burned Sergeant-Pilot yelled at them to 'Put those bloody things down!' – which, fortunately, they did. Landing near Tatsfield Beacon in Surrey, just fifty yards away his Hurricane's funeral pyre rose skywards. The young pilot was so badly burned, however, that a young girl collapsed and fainted upon seeing him.

The salient point about this particular combat is that, having reached back into the flames instead of first thinking to save himself, Newton's burst of fire hit and damaged Unger's Dornier. Unlike Flight Lieutenant Nicolson's 'signal act of valour' occurring two days previously, there is no ambiguity surrounding Newton's actions – which were, in fact, no less deserving of a VC. Such actions, however, must be witnessed – and the only eyewitnesses to Newton's bravery were Unger and his crew. Indeed, the story only came out when both Squadron Leader Harry Newton AFC (as he became) and *Herr* Günther Unger provided their accounts to British historian Dr Alfred Price. During the Battle of Britain, and indeed throughout the Second World War, countless courageous acts went unrecognised – this was undoubtedly one of them.

No.111 Squadron, which appeared on the scene seconds before the first bombs had fallen, was soon a spent force, however, the surviving pilots' ammunition exhausted. Among them was Sergeant Albert 'Harry' Deacon,

SUNDAY, 18 AUGUST 1940

whose Hurricane was hit by understandably twitchy AA gunners at Kenley while returning to Croydon. Wounded in both legs, he baled out at just 200ft – and was very lucky indeed to survive.

After Sergeant Newton was shot down, Unger continued flying south until he reached the coast, but with an engine out and the other losing power, he ultimately had no option but to ditch in the sea off Le Touquet. The crew survived the crash but messed up inflating their dinghy, which proved impossible. Three hours later, the crew, having been unable to broadcast their position on account of Sergeant Newton's fire destroying their radio, were reaching the end of their endurance, exposure taking its toll. Just when it appeared all was lost, a spotter aircraft found them and minutes later all four men were saved from the Channel by the Boulogne-based minesweeper that was actually searching for another 9/KG 76 crew, that of *Unteroffizier* Bernard Schumacher.

As the Dorniers attacked, Schumacher had been on the formation's right, his aircraft damaged by bomb blasts, AA fire, and shot-up by 111 Squadron. Half-way back across the Channel, with both engines hit and running roughly, the left-hand motor eventually gave up and the Dornier began to lose speed; as Schumacher's Airspeed Indicator had been shot away, the loss of speed was only evident to the pilot as he watched his two comrades' aircraft, flown by Raab and *Unteroffizier* Mathias Maassen, draw away. Ultimately, like Unger, Schumacher had no choice but to ditch, off Étaples. Apart from the flight engineer, who was drowned, the crew took to their dinghy, so were in a better position than Unger's crew, who were actually in the water. Maassen flew on to Boulogne, where he landed and initiated a rescue operation, himself flying as observer in the Fieseler Storch which spotted both Unger and Schumacher's crews in the water. Being more in need, Unger's crew was rescued first, then Schumacher's, from their dinghy. Maassen, who had flown No.2 in Roth's lead *Kette*, then returned to Boulogne and flew his Do 17, which was the least damaged of 9/KG 76's aircraft, back to Cormeilles-en-Vexin.

While Maassen diverted to Boulogne, Raab pressed on for France with his severely wounded navigator *Leutnant* Erwin Wittman aboard – he landed at Amiens and sought urgent medical attention. The first of 9/KG 76's crews to return, Raab and the other survivors counted twenty-six hits to their aircraft as the wounded Wittman was removed to a waiting ambulance. The crew remained confused, however, by the bright lights and small parachutes they had seen – and upon inspection damage was found to the port wing consistent with a cable having dragged along it.

An hour later, Raab took-off and made the twenty-minute flight back to Cormeilles-en-Vexin – where, upon arrival, he was astonished to find that his was the only aircraft to have so far returned. Immediately his aircraft came to a halt, a staff officer boarded the aircraft, subjecting the pilot to a barrage of questions. Then, Raab was sped away for an interview with the *Geschwaderkommodore, Generalmajor* Fröhlich. Raab outlined events, but his description of the 'secret weapon' was greeted with incredulity and ascribed to combat fatigue. Maassen, next to land at Cormeilles-en-Vexin, having successfully initiated and directed the rescue of the two ditched crews, confirmed Raab's account, but was equally mystified by the Parachute and Cable defences.

The last of 9/KG 76's Dorniers to land back in France was that being flown by the navigator, *Oberfeldwebel* Wilhelm-Friedrich Illg. After three circuits, Illg felt sufficiently confident to attempt a landing at St Omer airfield – which, astonishingly, he achieved successfully. For this feat, Illg was immediately promoted in the field to *Leutnant* and awarded the coveted *Ritterkruez*. His pilot, *Oberleutnant* Hermann Magin, died en route to hospital.

9/KG 76 had suffered badly. Only Maassen's Do 17 returned without wounded or dead crewmen aboard. Four of the bombers had been destroyed, two seriously damaged, and the other three, including Maassen's, damaged in some way. Of the forty-aircrew involved, eight had been killed, five were captured, three were wounded, and seven required rescuing from the sea. The survivors of 9/KG 76 wrongly assumed that their chance encounter with the RN off Beachy Head was the cause of their misfortune – when, in fact, the tracking of their progress belongs entirely to the Observer Corps and provides further evidence of the comprehensive thought given to planning Britain's aerial defensive system. Thanks to the Observer Corps' reports, Kenley and Croydon were able to scramble squadrons on the ground minutes in advance of the attack – and Kenley's defences were ready and waiting. The outcome evidenced the fact that even low and fast-flying aircraft were extremely vulnerable to alerted aerial defences. Even so, Kenley was badly damaged – and more was to follow.

Squadron Leader Alford:

> Immediately after the Dorniers had gone, my Sergeant, Sergeant Bull, and I decided to move, from the tarmac apron in front of a hangar, a Hurricane aircraft onto which pieces of charred and burning wood were falling from the roof of the

SUNDAY, 18 AUGUST 1940

hangar, which was well and truly alight. While doing this we were joined by two airmen who loomed up out of the smoke, completely equipped with fire buckets and extinguishers. They were fully prepared to try and do something about the fire but it had by then too great a hold for any hand equipment to be of use. The maximum efforts of all four of us could only just move the aircraft and in desperation I looked for help. From out of the smoke I could just discern a figure of a man who I shouted at to come and help. He was most willing and responsive to my order and to my surprise it was the Station Commander, Wing Commander Prickman. We moved the aircraft to a place of safety and then returned to save two petrol tankers, one of which we could drive away, while the other we had to push.

It was then that, late on target, the high-flying bomber force appeared over Kenley, which had overtaken the Ju 88 dive-bombers of II/KG 76, which should have opened the attack.

AC1 Stan Ford: 'When the second lot came over there was a terrific roar and with all these aircraft there was like a big cloud of aircraft coming over.'

Kenley, already wreathed in smoke and flame, was now subjected to further bombing – although the billowing smoke substantially concealed the target and doubtless contributed to why over 150 bombs missed their target, causing substantial damage to the nearby railway line and civilian properties beyond the airfield.

Having scrambled at 13.00 hrs, twenty-five minutes later Squadron Leader Don MacDonell and his Spitfires of 64 Squadron were 21,000ft over base when the pilots saw bombs exploding among the hangars. Leading his fighters down to 7,000ft, MacDonell ran into the Do 17s of I and III/KG 76, escorted by Me 110s of I/ZG 26. Attacking a 'Do 215' [sic], MacDonell hit both his target's engines, causing it to stall, 'almost vertically and spun slowly down, finally crashing near Biggin Hill'. This aircraft was actually the *Stab* I/ZG 26 Me 110 of the *Gruppenadjutant*, *Oberleutnant* Rüdiger Proske, who deliberately allowed his aircraft to appear out of control before flying off to the south-east, trailing smoke from both engines. Eventually, the Proske was forced to crash-land near the Kentish coast, near Lydd, where he and his *Bordfunker*, *Unteroffizier* Hans Mobius were captured.

Squadron Leader MacDonell then found a Ju 88, into which he emptied his remaining ammunition, which 'slewed to port, and port engine emitted black smoke'. The Ju 88 jettisoned its bombs before being subsequently engaged by a Hurricane. In fact, the raider was engaged by a number of Spitfires and Hurricanes before crashing at Ide Hill, near Sevenoaks, killing the crew. Having claimed – without loss – five enemy bombers destroyed and two damaged, plus an Me 110 destroyed, MacDonell led his Spitfires to land at the Redhill satellite airfield, owing to damage at Kenley – where the runway was cratered and delayed action or unexploded bombs (UXB) littered the airfield.

Squadron Leader Alford:

> Unknown to Sergeant Bull and I, a high-level attack had developed meanwhile, and what we took to be oxygen cylinders exploding in the hangars were in some cases bombs. These, however, fell near the other side of the aerodrome without doing much damage, since they penetrated the soil to a depth of about 15–20ft.
>
> Reports came in from the various sections of damage done etc. and I was informed that several UXBs had been located in various parts of the station. These were carefully marked on a small chart of the station prepared beforehand, and the CO detailed the order in which he wanted them dealt with. The first was a 50KG which fouled the main runway and with Sergeant Bull and my armourers we set out to remove it. The equipment was placed in a 30 Cwt lorry and we drove out, to within about five yards of the bomb. A sandbag traverse was built round it and then a discharger fitted to the No 25 Rheinmetall Fuse, which was located in the side of it.
>
> This had to be left for a few minutes, after which we paid out the wire rope and passed a couple of half-hitches round the bomb at one end, while the other was attached to the towing hook of the lorry. It was then possible to give the bomb a good 'disturbance test' without endangering any personnel. The next operation was to remove the lock ring from the fuse and this done, a piece of string was attached to the eyebolt which formed part of the discharger. This string was paid out to its full length (as long as a piece of string) and with everybody lying flat on the ground we hauled at the other end until a black blob came over the sandbags which we knew to be the fuse. The bomb was then rolled over to remove the Picric Pellets

SUNDAY, 18 AUGUST 1940

and the gaine was unscrewed from the fuse and everything was 'safe' once again.

The disposal of this bomb had just been completed when the warning sounded again and we hustled aboard the lorry and returned to our duty stations at the armoury. However, nothing happened and we were able to deal with other unexploded bombs when the 'All Clear' sounded. One bomb reported to be close to the airmen's dining hall had been marked by red flags and inquisitive personnel were kept away by an armed guard. My Sergeant and I persuaded the sentry that we were 'entitled' to view this bomb and found when we reached it that the 'bomb' was a small type Oxygen bottle, as used in aircraft, and some consternation was caused when Bull rolled it over with his foot – and then picked it up and carried it away under his arm. We dealt with all the UXBs we could before darkness fell and the last two or three had to be finished by the light of an electric torch, and the remaining left until the following morning. The Sergeants' Mess had suffered some damage but the 'Bar' was still 'serviceable' and after a UXB had been removed from the 'Dead Marines' (empties) which were stacked in the yard outside, the Mess Caterer was kept well occupied.

ACW Frances Cherry, who had been in the sick quarter's shelter when it suffered a direct hit:

> By the time we were rescued, most of the fires were out, not one building was left standing, there were huge craters everywhere, and the petrol pumps were still burning. The locals and other people had by this time organised tea and wads, so we all went back to our billets and the boys were all put under canvas, having lost their huts ... The raid took about 15–20 minutes to flatten the whole airfield.

The Ju 88 dive-bombers of II/KG 76, however, which should have attacked first, arrived over Kenley to find it so concealed by smoke that the leader decided to abort and head for the secondary target of West Malling instead – where damage caused was slight.

BATTLE OF BRITAIN ATTACK OF THE EAGLES

RAF Kenley had certainly suffered heavy damage, as the Station ORB recorded:

> Nine aircraft, Dornier and Me 109 [*sic* - the attacking Hurricanes of 111 Squadron must have been mistaken by someone as being Me 109s] took part in first attack (low bombing) and from thirty to fifty in the second (high bombing). Approximately 100 HE bombs were dropped, of which twenty-four were delayed action; twelve were rendered ineffective, the remainder received prompt attention.
>
> Extent of damage: extensive. All hangars, aircraft, sick quarters, officers mess, sergeant's mess Station HQ, Barrack rooms, telephonic system and fire appliances, armoured cars and M.T. [Of the hangars,] 10 destroyed by fire; 6 damaged by bombs and falling debris (3 repairable). 4 Aero engines destroyed by fire. There was no gas.
>
> Casualties: Army personnel: Killed – nil. Wounded: one Officer and one man.
>
> RAF personnel: Killed – one Officer and seven men.
>
> Wounded: seven airmen and one WAAF.
>
> Machine-gunning: the enemy also machine-gunned with all guns while attacking.

Kenley, however, was only out of action for a matter of hours – although the all-important Operations Room, as a precaution against further attacks, was relocated above an empty butcher's shop in nearby Caterham – where it was less vulnerable and remained until 1 November 1940.

Returning to the aerial action over Kenley, it was the Hurricanes of the beleaguered station's own 615 Squadron which next charged into action against the high-flying second wave. The Hurricane pilots would claim one He 111, two Ju 88s, and a Do 17 destroyed, and one damaged Me 109, Ju 88 Do 17 and a 'He 113'. Flying Officer David Looker, though, was attacked by Me 109s, setting his aircraft on fire, although he landed safely at Croydon to be admitted to hospital suffering from shock. Flight Lieutenant Lionel Gaunce, a Canadian, was shot down and baled out near Sevenoaks, slightly burned. Pilot Officer Petrus 'Dutch' Hugo was also attacked by fighters, crash-landing at Orpington and being admitted to hospital with

SUNDAY, 18 AUGUST 1940

wounds to both legs. Sergeant Peter Walley, however, was shot down by an Me 109 and was killed when his Hurricane crashed onto Morden Park Golf Course.

By now, the skies over the North Downs and Kent were a veritable aerial battlefield. Kenley having taken its turn, at 13.27 hrs the sixty He 111s of KG 1, escorted by forty JG 54 Me 109s, ran into attack Biggin Hill. Unlike Kenley, Biggin Hill's defences were hamstrung from engaging the approaching bombers owing to the presence of RAF fighters. Consequently, the Germans enjoyed an unmolested approach to this important target, as another *Kriegsberichter*, Bankhardt, flying with I/KG 1, later described:

> We had expected some flak, but none came, and we continued to our target. The order 'Bombs away!' was given – and down they rained. With a hissing noise our bombs fell away. Now, with a turn to the left, the target could be seen. A giant cloud of black smoke announced that the bombs had struck. A single flak position revealed itself, but nothing came near us. Is this is best the English can do? Or is the *Englische Luftwaffe* already nearing the end of its tether?

Gefreiter Willi Wanderer, KG 1:

> No English fighter, no flak, came near us. Where are the English? That was the thought that went through our heads. Nothing seemed to move and, quite unscathed, we set course for home. I could not even bring my machine-guns into action. Pity – I should have liked to have taken a few pot shots at an Englishman. It was just like an exercise, flying above the sleeping English. Nobody in the *Staffel* had ever experienced such a quiet operational mission. Can it be that the 'Tommies' are finished already?

The raid lasted ten minutes – after which a hush descended on the aerodrome as personnel emerged from their shelters. The injured were attended to as a priority and treated at the Decontamination Centre. So the story goes, a young subaltern who was wounded when a bomb exploded near a Bofors site, killing one of the crew and wounding others, was brought in on a stretcher, along with the survivors of the 9/KG 76 Do 17 brought down at Leaves Green. According to Graham Wallace (see Bibliography), 'Their captain, a young *Leutnant*, stepped forward and spat in the face of the wounded gunner. "We felt like shooting the lot", a WAAF [who was apparently present] told the doctor.' In spite of KG 1's unopposed approach, the damage to Biggin Hill was slight: the empty MT sheds had suffered a direct hit but there was no other damage to installations or aircraft on the ground; two personnel were killed, and three wounded.

Biggin Hill's runway, though, was cratered and many delayed action bombs had yet to explode – it was now that a certain WAAF Sergeant, Joan Mortimer, showed exceptional courage under fire. As the bombs rained down, she had refused to leave her switchboard post, continuing to pass essential messages throughout the raid – despite being located close the Armoury. Then, before the 'All-Clear' wailed, Sergeant Mortimer, of her own initiative, marked all UXBs on the runway with red flags, ensuring safe landings for returning fighters. While engaged in this dangerous and uncertain endeavour, a UXB went off close-by, winding her; undeterred, she continued until the last crater was marked. Afterwards, Sergeant Mortimer assisted Flight Sergeant Joe Hunt in defusing the UXBs, later recalling: 'We had a special tool which we used to short-out the electrical condenser fitted to the German bomb fuses, then the bomb could be lifted clear.' In due course Joan Mortimer was awarded the Military Medal for her bravery, the citation acknowledging her 'exceptional courage and coolness while under attack', which 'had a great moral effect on all those she came into contact with. Her steadfast courage to both remain at her post while under bombardment and undertake action to prevent further aircraft losses was outstanding.' And with that, no one would disagree.

Nearby Croydon airfield was also hit:

> 'A' Hangar damaged by medium sized bomb and incendiary bomb penetrating roof and exploding inside. Two craters on edge of tarmac close by main building. One bomb in middle of main building. One bomb on roadway between guard-room and airmen's cookhouse, adjacent to Purley Way. Two bombs beyond aerodrome boundary, Purley Way side, on playing fields (ORB).

A soldier was killed at Croydon, and a Hurricane of 111 Squadron destroyed in 'A' Hangar and another damaged.

SUNDAY, 18 AUGUST 1940

Having dropped their bombs and wheeled about, however, *Kriegsberichter* Bankhardt and *Gefreiter* Wanderer were about to discover that the '*Englische Luftwaffe*' was far from finished.

According to 54 Squadron, by 12.40 hrs 'the first big attack of the day had developed. At least 600 enemy aircraft – and probably a good many more – were plotted all over Kent. The squadron was unable to approach the main formations but dealt satisfactorily with a large number of stragglers' (ORB).

No.54 Squadron's CO, Squadron Leader James 'Prof' Leathart DSO reported that his Spitfires were variously in action against 'very large formations' between 12.40 hrs and 13.42 hrs, at heights between 15,000–25,000ft:

> Sighting some smoke trails I led the squadron up to 28,000ft in pursuit. I saw three He 113s [*sic*] painted a dark colour and with yellow wing tips. I fired at No 3 of the 'V' who went into a vertical dive and was still in it at 4,000ft when I pulled out. Climbed up again and encountered an Me 109 and shot one of his slats off.
>
> On the way home at 3,000ft I saw AA fire over Tilbury which turned out to be about a mile behind a lone Do 17 ay 1,000ft. I gave him the remainder of my ammunition at 200–100 yards. Bullets entered the wings and fuselage but without apparent effect.

Flying Officer Desmond McMullen split up a formation of twelve Me 109s, one of which he damaged before shooting-up a Do 17. Flight Lieutenant George Gribble claimed an Me 109 destroyed, and Pilot Officer Colin Gray damaged a Do 17. Pilot Officer Alan Campbell and Flight Sergeant Phillip Tew both destroyed Me 109s, the latter having 'had the good fortunate to secure this enemy casualty without firing a shot. E/A was pursuing him and Tew pulled out at a low altitude and the 109 failed to follow and crashed straight into the ground' (ORB). No.54 Squadron had fought over the greater part of Kent, as the enemy withdraw, the sky a confused mass of aircraft. The squadron suffered no casualties in this engagement.

The Hurricanes of 32 Squadron, up from Biggin Hill, also found themselves engaged over the greater part of Kent. Pilot Officer John 'Polly' Flinders reported combats occurring between 13.25 hrs and 13.45 hrs, over Godstone, just west of Biggin Hill, and Canterbury, well to the east:

> I took off from Biggin Hill at 1300 hrs when the Attack Alarm sounded and climbed to 12,000ft, where I met 32 Squadron.

At 1320 hrs about thirty E/A were seen 3,000ft above us, approaching from the SE. While we immediately engaged and broke up, I got onto the tail of a Do 17 and fired four bursts: clouds of black smoke and flame poured from the machine and it went into an almost vertical dive. The engagement took place in the vicinity of Godstone.

I then sighted another aircraft, believed to be a Do 215 [*sic*] at 12,000ft flying east about two miles away and gave chase. He immediately dived towards the ground. At 3,000ft he levelled out and I found that I was gradually closing in. We passed to the north of Malling and over Detling. I was at about 600 yards. A running fight then ensued, the Do pilot doing barrel rolls and half-rolls in an attempt to get rid of me. We were now down to 200ft and as I knew that I had very little ammunition left I refrained from firing until I had a certain target. Two miles north of Canterbury this Do 215 pulled up out of a dive and as he lost speed I closed to 150 yards and got in a good burst. The starboard engine caught fire and the machine dived into the ground and exploded.

The enemy aircraft Flinders had clearly destroyed, however, was actually a 1/ZG 26 Me 110, which crashed and exploded with such force at Rough Common, Harbledown, near Canterbury, that no trace of the crew, *Unteroffizier*s Rudolf Mai and Josef Gebauer, was ever found.

Time and time again 32 Squadron's Hurricanes attacked the raiders as they retired, claiming a total of fifteen enemy aircraft either destroyed or damaged. This tally, however, was not without loss. Pilot Officer John Pain was shot down in flames over Biggin Hill, baling out slightly wounded; having destroyed an Me 110, Flight Lieutenant Humphrey a'Beckett 'Humph' Russell was severely wounded when his cockpit was hit by a cannon shell over Biggin Hill – baling out, during his descent Russell stemmed the flow of blood by coolly applying a tourniquet; Sergeant Bernard Henson's gravity tank was set on fire over Biggin Hill, forcing him to crash-land at Otford, with facial wounds. All three pilots were admitted to hospital where they were reportedly 'doing well' (ORB) later in the day.

Between 13.30 hrs and 13.45 hrs, the fifteen Spitfires of 610 Squadron, which had taken off prior to the raid on their base, were also in action. Squadron Leader Ellis attacked and set a He 111 ablaze which crashed into the Channel off Dungeness. Sergeant Stanley Arnfield claimed two Me 109s

SUNDAY, 18 AUGUST 1940

destroyed, also in flames, and Pilot Officer Kenneth Cox set another on fire which he claimed as destroyed. Flying Officer Fred Gardiner attacked and destroyed an Me 110, while Sergeant Peter Else damaged two Do 17s.

Pilot Officer Brian Rees reported his combats taking place south-east of Biggin Hill:

> I was leading Reserve Section ... we waited until the enemy were in sight of the aerodrome to NW. We took off and immediately split up as we were among the enemy. I chased a Dornier, which was separated from the rest, and delivered two long bursts, his port engine went on fire, smoking very badly, also there were bits flying off. It lost height rapidly, I was following it down when I was attacked from behind, I could not see my attacker but could see tracer as it passed me. I put my propeller in fine pitch and throttled back. My attacker shot past me and I gave it a very long burst at very short range. At about 150 yards. It suddenly turned over and crashed into a wood about ten miles from the aerodrome.

Sergeant Claude Parsons was Red 3 and climbed with 610 Squadron to 31,000ft in order to engage the escorting fighters, the Spitfires pairing off to attack. Parsons then became separated from his leader:

> and saw a formation of Do 17s at about 15,000ft. These E/A immediately went into a defensive circle on seeing me approach. I climbed into the sun and waited for the circle to break up. They broke up after about five minutes. I attacked a Do 17 from the rear, putting the rear-gunner out of action immediately. I then carried out a quarter attack on his port side and finished by firing at the port engine, which stopped running. I broke to the right and carried out a further quarter attack on his starboard side, during which I ran out of ammunition. I made two further quarter attacks and forced the E/A to descend quickly. At 500ft I saw the E/A make a forced-landing in a field on Romney Marsh, near Brookland Station. During my quarter attacks the E/A tried small turns to the left and right, though these decreased when the port engine stopped running. I noticed that immediately the engine stopped the undercarriage went down.

Parsons, however, was mistaken, as so often happened in the air: this was not a Do 17 but an Me 110 of 6/ZG 26, which crash-landed at St Mary's Marsh, Blackmanstone, near Newchurch – the crew, *Leutnant* Hans-Joachim Kästner and *Unteroffizier* alter Kaffenberger, were both captured unhurt.

Pilot Officer Joe Pegge shot-up an Me 109 and watched it spin away, on fire, then attacked a damaged a He 111. Sergeant Horatio Chandler attacked a 'Do 215' [*sic*] over Croydon, both engines of which caught fire following one long burst from his eight machine-guns, the enemy aircraft crashing 'five miles south of Croydon' (ORB). This was most likely, however, the 5/KG 76 Ju 88 which crashed at Ide Hill and which also appears in several other pilots' combat reports, including 615 Squadron's Flight Lieutenant Sanders, 64 Squadron's Pilot Officers Laws, O'Meara and Gilbert, and both Flight Lieutenant Brothers and Pilot Officer Wlasnowolski of 32 Squadron – indicating how one enemy aircraft destroyed could end up multiplied many times over on the balance sheet. Nonetheless, the Spitfires had certainly recorded definite successes – all for no loss.

Over Cranbrook, at around 13.20 hrs, five 65 Squadron Spitfires found and shot up a straggling KG 1 He 111. Flying Officer Jeffrey Quill was leading the formation:

> In 65 Squadron we did not fly the useless formation comprising vics of three, but instead our four sections flew in line astern. This could be rapidly opened out sideways and, like the German line abreast *schwarm*, required much less concentration. 18 August, 1940 however, was a hectic day and we suffered a fatal casualty: Flying Officer Franek Gruszka. The trouble was that our two Poles, Szulkowski and Gruszka, were inclined to go off chasing the enemy on their own, so determined were they. None of us saw what happened to Gruszka, and back at Hornchurch Szulkowski was very upset that his friend was missing.

All that was known was that Flying Officer Franciszek Gruszka was last seen at 14.15 hrs, chasing a German aircraft somewhere between Canterbury and Manston.

Michael Wigmore, an 11-year-old schoolboy, had excitedly watched the air battle overhead:

> A Spitfire's engine was screaming as the plane came down, very close to me. It crashed with a loud thud at a 45° angle and

SUNDAY, 18 AUGUST 1940

immediately burst into flame. It was completely out of control and the pilot made no attempt to pull out of the dive.

The RAF fighter concerned, Spitfire R6713, had crashed into the remote Grove Marshes at Wickhambreaux, near Canterbury. There the aircraft and its pilot – Flying Officer Gruszka – would remain, undisturbed, until 1971, when amateur aviation archaeologists excavated the site. Cutting a very long story short, the pilot was not actually recovered for burial until the RAF did so on 15 April 1974. As of that day, at long last, Flying Officer Gruszka was no longer missing, and on 17 July 1975, was buried with full military honours at Northwood Cemetery.

Flying Officer Franek Gruszka was the second Polish fighter pilot to die in the Battle of Britain, and the first Polish Spitfire pilot to lose his life defending Britain. Of 145 Polish pilots who fought with the RAF during the Battle of Britain, seventy-nine of them, like 238 Squadron's Pilot Officer Michal Steborowski, the first Polish pilot to be killed, on 11 August 1940, and Flying Officer Gruszka served in British squadrons. Sixty-four more flew with the Polish 302 and 303 Squadrons. With them, these men brought experience, an offensive spirit, and a burning desire to one day liberate their homeland. Twenty-nine Polish pilots would lose their lives during the Battle of Britain.

Having led the Hurricanes of 17 Squadron up from Martlesham at 12.56 hrs, Squadron Leader Cedric Williams orbited Manston, then flew down to Dover before being vectored south-east. At 13.35 hrs, ten miles off Dover, Williams reported seeing:

> a huge cluster of E/A numbering at least 150, stepped up from 15,000ft–18,000ft. I made for these and as I approached saw Me 109s at 25,000ft–30,000ft. Yellow Section had previously peeled off from formation to attack Me 109s. On hearing from Red 1 'Bandits behind!' I ordered section to draw off. Green Section was attacked and separated, and I also saw that Blue 2 and 3 were not with me. I then saw three Do 17s well-spaced out, with Nos 2 and 3 of the formation breaking away, outwards. I singled out No 1 and dived on him, giving a short burst in a stern-quarter attack at 400 yards, turning into a stern attack when I gave a long burst at 250 yards. Finally, I gave a short burst into the port engine which caught fire. The E/A dived suddenly and steeply, turning over onto its back, and

went down obviously out of control. I broke away. I saw that I was being attacked by an Me 109 and in making an evasive turn saw three more Me 109s also attacking. A series of tight turns brought me almost to sea-level, and I returned to Dover at zero feet when Blue 2 and Green Section joined me. My aircraft was hit by four bullets, but was only slightly damaged. I did not see Blue 3 after Red and Green Sections broke away.

Blue 3 was Pilot Officer Neville Soloman, who was shot down off the French coast and reported missing. Later, his body washed up on the French coast and was interred at Pihen-les-Guines Cemetery.

Flying Officer Count Manfred Czernin damaged an Me 109 over the Channel, but Sergeant Glyn Griffiths was shot-up and forced-landed at Manston – where his Hurricane was destroyed in a raid minutes later. Sergeant David North-Bomford's Hurricane was also damaged, although he returned safely to base.

At 13.45 hrs, the Hurricanes of 56 Squadron engaged the withdrawing Germans, at 21,000ft over Ashford. Flight Lieutenant Weaver later described the action:

> I was leading No 2 Section and was put into line astern by the squadron leader (Squadron Leader Manton). I observed approximately five Me 110s below us in a defensive circle and singled one out and attacked. I fired for about six seconds, and broke away when smoke and bits poured from the starboard engine. I then observed an Me 110 below me, I chased it down to about 3,000ft, full throttle and 12lbs boost. I eventually closed to 200 yards and as E/A was doing evasive tactics fired short bursts, with and without defection. My guns finished firing, E/A went into a steep right-hand turn and then dived vertically into the ground, bursting into flames, about eight miles south of Ashford on the northern bank of a canal. This was confirmed by both Flight Lieutenant Gracie and Flight Sergeant Higginson.

This Me 110, of 3/ZG 26, crashed and exploded at Bonnington; neither crew-member, *Oberfeldwebel* Willi Stange and *Unteroffizier* Hans Hesse, have ever been found. All five Me 110s, in fact, were destroyed by 56 Squadron, the Hurricane pilots all landing safely at Rochford.

SUNDAY, 18 AUGUST 1940

Having scrambled from Northolt to patrol base at 13.15 hrs, the six Hurricanes of 1 Squadron's 'B' Flight, led by Flight Lieutenant Brian Hillcoat, were 'sent down to Shoreham. When over the South Downs they encountered a formation of sixty Do 17s' (ORB). At 13.40 hrs, Hillcoat led the Hurricanes into the attack at 19,000ft off Dungeness.

Pilot Officer George Goodman:

> I was Blue 3 ... I went ahead of No 1 (Flight Lieutenant Hillcoat) and 2, (Pilot Officer Stavert) and got in a good burst into a straggling Do 17 which started flames from its belly. As soon as flames started catching he opened his bomb doors and let out about eighty squarish metal tins; then a parachute opened out in front of me and fell through my line of fire. I broke away to the right and saw Blue 1 and 2 carry out their attacks. Two more parachutes opened, I suspected them to be dummies, but they held members of the crew. I saw E/A crash into the water, and I then circled a parachute to see if it contained a member of the crew. While doing this an Me 110 appeared at 50ft, heading south. His port engine was emitting some smoke. I got into line astern and after one short burst his port engine caught fire. He carried out swift turns but I noticed no return fire. I got a bead on his starboard engine and got in a good burst. The starboard engine burst into flames when instantly I was hit from behind by an Me 109. I did a swift right-turn and saw this Me 110 crash into the water. In the turn I made half a mile on the 109 and tried to climb in order to bale out, but saw the 109 gaining rapidly on me – so I pulled the plug [emergency boost] and made for home with the E/A gaining slightly until I reached the cliffs near Rye. I did a swift turn in the valley near the town and led the 109 over the shore batteries but they took no action, Me 109 made off for home, and I turned and climbed to 7,000ft and landed at base with my aircraft unserviceable.

The Do 17, which belonged to 8/KG 76 and the crew of which were killed, was shared between Blue Section. The Me 110 involved, of 6/ZG 26, had previously been attacked by 56 Squadron; the pilot, *Feldwebel* Herbert Stange was captured, but his *Bordfunker*, *Unteroffizier* Gerhard Wollin was killed.

BATTLE OF BRITAIN ATTACK OF THE EAGLES

The next RAF fighters to engage the withdrawing German forces were the ten Spitfires of 266 Squadron, up from Manston. Following the death in action of Squadron Leader Rodney Wilkinson two days before, on this day Squadron Leader Desmond Spencer took command and was leading the formation. Spencer, having only converted to modern fighters the previous month, had been serving in a supernumerary capacity, first with 222 Squadron, then in the same capacity with 266 Squadron since 25 July 1940. Initially patrolling Rochford at 10,000ft, the Spitfires were vectored to Dover, where Me 109s were sighted at 13.45 hrs.

Pilot Officer Richard Trousdale (a New Zealander):

> Flying at about 20,000ft over the Channel I saw about ten Me 109s passing us in line astern at about 300 mph, in western direction to attack on our stern. I dived onto an Me 109 100ft below and gave him a deflection shot – all my bursts were deflection – also two astern shots at him. Saw his Perspex collapse and aircraft dived in spiral to the sea. Ended up scrap at 10,000ft, E/A still crashing towards the sea. Visual camouflage yellow wing tips. No E/A fire experienced. Weather hazy up to 10,000ft, clear above.

The enemy fighter was accredited as probably destroyed, and one Me 109 destroyed was claimed by Pilot Officer Wycliff Williams (coincidentally also a New Zealander).

As the Spitfires landed at 14.20 hrs, they had been spotted from on high by *Oberleutnant* Wolfgang Ewald, leading I/JG 52, which was covering the bombers' withdrawal. Because Manston's runways were so covered in craters, the Spitfires were not dispersed but bunched more tightly together than normal. The target was too tempting for Ewald to ignore; he left 3/JG 52 as top cover while he led six Me 109s of 2/JG 52 down to attack. Manston had absolutely no warning as suddenly the Me 109s appeared low and fast, strafing as they went. Fire, however, was returned by Private Joseph Lister of the 6th Border Regiment who let fly with a Bren mounted on an AA tripod – but a 109 curved into position and strafed the Bren gunner. Lister, who was hit multiple times, survived but later suffered amputation of his right leg above the knee; he would later be decorated with the Military Medal for his courage under fire that day.

As suddenly as they had appeared, the 109s were gone – leaving in the wake two of 266 Squadron's Spitfires destroyed by fire and five more

SUNDAY, 18 AUGUST 1940

damaged. Fortunately, the only casualties among the helpless pilots were Sergeant Don Kingaby, who received a slight cut to a finger, and Sergeant William Jones, who was treated for shock. One airman, AC1 Sydney Philbrick, a 23-year-old from Brighton, was killed, and fifteen more injured, 'mostly on the Servicing Flight' (RAF Manston ORB).

Flight Lieutenant Bob Stanford Tuck DFC, commanding 'B' Flight of Pembrey's 92 Squadron, was attending a conference with the Air Fighting Development Unit (AFDU) at Northolt – but at 13.50 hrs found himself in action, alone, against the withdrawing enemy:

> the Raid Alarm was sounded and I learnt that 160 E/A had crossed the coast. Thinking I could be of use I took-off in my Spitfire and flew down to the coast. After patrolling up and down the coast off Beachy Head at 10,000ft for about quarter-of-an-hour, I spotted two Ju 88s that had passed over me at 15,000ft heading SSW or south. I turned onto them and got above. As there was no cloud at the time the two E/A put down their noses and went straight onto the surface of the water on the same course.
>
> I flew straight ahead of them as fast as possible and then turned head-on and fired at No 2 E/A. After passing close over the top of E/A and pulling straight up I observed that he had gone into the water with a terrific splash and disappeared (up until this time I had only been hit in the wings and through left side of the Perspex on the windscreen).
>
> I then flew straight ahead to attack the E/A that was left. Just when I opened fire on this head-on attack I saw a large greeny-bluish flash from the nose of the Ju 88. Immediately following this there was a loud crash on the underneath front of my aircraft. This seemed to tip my tail up and I thought I should hit the water. However, I pulled straight up and left the Ju 88 heading off on the same course leaving a trail of oil on the water. I was now approx. thirty-five–forty miles off Beachy Head at 4,000ft. My airscrew must have been badly damaged as there was excessive engine vibration, and glycol and oil temperatures were very high. I managed to reach the coast but by this time dense fumes were coming from my engine and under the dashboard. I could feel myself being overcome by the fumes so decided to abandon my aircraft.

Eventually jumped at 8,000ft. Could not see whether my aircraft was straight and level or not as flames had blinded me. My aircraft landed half-a-mile away from me in a wood and did no damage.

Spitfire N3040 crashed at Park Farm, Horsmondon, just beyond the boundary of Lord Cornwallis's Plovers Estate. His Lordship's son drove the Spitfire pilot to RAF Biggin Hill, where the only accommodation available was a bed in station sick quarters – next to the young pilot of a Ju 88 shot down nearby that afternoon. After some initial awkwardness on Tuck's part, the pair conversed in detail about their respective war and flying experiences. In a solemn gesture, the German airman presented Tuck with his Iron Cross – to being him luck 'every time you go up'. Tuck, although embarrassed by it, would go on to do so – but reflecting upon the encounter some days later, realised that he had not even asked the enemy pilot his name. Tuck was credited with one Ju 88 destroyed and a probable (although there is no twin-engine enemy aircraft loss of any description in German records corresponding with this combat).

Back at Pembrey, there was a move afoot for 92 Squadron: Flight Lieutenant Brian 'Kingpin' Kingcome and 'A' Flight were to relieve 'A' Flight of 87 Squadron at RAF Bibury in Gloucestershire. Personnel and kit were flown to their new base in three transport aircraft, the remainder travelling by road. Facilities at what was actually Manor Farm, Ablington, were basic, but from there Kingcome's Spitfires, and Tuck's at Pembrey, were to cover the Bristol Channel and West Country – in which a number of aircraft factories were located. After arriving at Bibury there was much for Kingcome to organise: 'A' Flight had to be fully operational by 15.00 hrs the following day.

Meanwhile, even before the Dover Strait was clear of the enemy, to the west *Luftflotte* 3, which had so far played no part in the day's fighting, was unleashing a major assault from the airfields of Normandy and Brittany – and in which the *Stukas* of *Generalmajor* Baron Wolfram von Richthofen were to play a key role. Indeed, the planned attacks would see the greatest number of Ju 87s deployed so far – 109. Whereas the morning's strikes by *Luftflotte* 2 had targeted important 11 Group airfields, *Luftflotte* 3's target selection was again questionable: the four *Gruppen* of Ju 87s were to attack the airfields at Gosport, Ford and Thorney Island – none of which were connected to Fighter Command – and the RDF station at Poling, just inland of the South Coast near Arundel. Thorney Island was the target for twenty-eight Ju 87s of *Hauptmann* Herbert Meisel's I/StG77; twenty-

SUNDAY, 18 AUGUST 1940

eight of *Hauptmann* Alfons Orthofer's II/StG77 were briefed to attack Ford; thirty-one of *Major* Helmut Bode's III/StG 77 would dive-bomb Poling, while twenty-two of *Hauptmann* Walter Siegel's I/StG3 were to hit Gosport. The plan provided for the *Stukas* to cross the Channel in one huge formation – escorted by 157 Me 109s: seventy of JG 27 and thirty-two of I/JG 53 providing close cover, while fifty-five of JG 2 would fly a *Freie Jagd* mission over Portsmouth. At midday, to increase their range, the *Stuka* units moved forward to fly the mission from coastal bases around Cherbourg.

At 14.00 hrs, it became immediately apparent to the defenders that another major threat was incoming, when, simultaneously RDF gave warning of 80+ twenty miles north of Cherbourg, and 20+ to the east. Two minutes later a formation of 10+ was travelling north-west, off Le Havre. It was obvious that these raids were heading for the Solent area, where ten Hurricanes of 601 Squadron were already patrolling Tangmere at 10,000ft – now to be reinforced by further squadrons from both 10 and 11 Groups.

> 14.07 hrs: 213 Squadron scrambled from Exeter with orders to patrol St Catherine's Point.
>
> 14.10 hrs: 152 Squadron left Warmwell for Portsmouth.
>
> 14.12 hrs: 43 Squadron took-off from Tangmere to patrol Thorney Island.
>
> 14.15 hrs: 602 Squadron left Westhampnett to patrol base, and 234 Squadron scrambled from Middle Wallop for the Isle of Wight.

Two Hurricanes of the Fighter Interception Unit (FIU) also scrambled from Tangmere, making a total of sixty-eight Spitfires and Hurricanes bearing down on the enemy, and 235 Squadron of Coastal Command sent up a flight of Blenheims from Thorney Island to bolster the defences. The twelve Spitfires of 609 Squadron were to remain in reserve at Middle Wallop.

As this massive phalanx of German warplanes droned towards the Isle of Wight, the *Staffelkapitän* of 3/JG 2, *Oberleutnant* Helmut Wick, observed: 'Wherever we looked, the sky was filled with aircraft.' When the raid was fifteen miles from the Isle of Wight, *Hauptmann* Siegel's I/StG 3 with II/JG 27's escorting Me 109s broke away towards their Gosport target. As the main raid approached Selsey Bill, the Tangmere Sector Controller, Squadron Leader David Lloyd, ordered 601 Squadron's airborne Hurricanes to that location. Four minutes later the remainder of the *Stukas* arrived over Selsey Bill, when *Hauptmann* Herbert Meisel's I/StG 77 and III/JG 27 proceeded towards Thorney Island. *Major* Helmut Bode's III/StG 77, escorted by I/JG 53, and *Hauptmann* Alfons Orthofer's II/StG 77 and III/JG 27 continued on their way, flying north-east to Ford, which II/StG 77 attacked, while III/StG 77 cruised the short distance to Poling.

As the raid approached Selsey Bill, 43 Squadron and 601 Squadron both engaged. Pilot Officer Hamilton Upton, of 43 Squadron reported his combat as having occurred at 14.20 hrs, 'Off Thorney Island':

> I was Blue 1 astern of Red (leading) and Yellow Sections when enemy was sighted at approx. 7,000ft, 2–3,000ft below us, travelling in a northerly direction over Selsey. On approaching Selsey Bill, Red Leader gave order for line-astern and I attacked with my Section Leader. I approached a Ju 87 and at 200 yards gave a short burst of two or three seconds. It caught fire but I did not follow it down for my attention was diverted by an Me 109 on my starboard side. I turned sharply to the right and gave short deflection burst of four to five seconds – the machine nose-dived straight down into the creek four miles east of Thorney. This machine may have been attacked before, but I did not see anyone attacking. I then circled Thorney Island but was unable to deliver another attack.

This Ju 87, of 1/StG 77, had been previously attacked, by Sergeant Jim Hallowes, also of 43 Squadron, and crashed into Fishbourne Creek. The crew, *Oberleutnant* J. Wilhelm and *Unteroffizier* A. Wörner baled out and were captured.

Pilot Officer Roy Lane, Yellow 2, 43 Squadron:

> About seven Ju 87s were flying in rough line astern to the right so I tried a beam attack but saw no results. I then saw a single Ju 87 diving towards Chichester. I dived after him but could not close very fast, so I fired from 400–350 yards, from astern. The E/A turned right and climbed. I then saw an Me 109 on my tail and turned sharply left to evade the Me 109. I climbed up behind the Ju 87 and opened firer from 180 yards. The E/A commenced a stall turn to the left and I broke off. I saw the Ju 87 diving steeply and it crashed into a field east of Bosham and burst into flames.

SUNDAY, 18 AUGUST 1940

> By this time the E/A had left the district and I was ordered by Control to patrol base. The Me 109 was not camouflaged and showed no inclination to fight beyond threatening my tail.

This Ju 87, of 3/StG 77, crashed at North Barn, Chidham; the crew, *Oberleutnant* D. Lehmann and H. Winiarski both remain missing.

No.43 Squadron would claim eight Ju 87s destroyed and a probable, and an Me 109 destroyed. Acting Flight Lieutenant Frank 'Chota' Carey DFM, commanding 'A' Flight, was shot-up, however, and crash-landed his Hurricane at Holme Street Farm, Pulborough. Wounded in the right knee, the pilot was admitted to hospital and remained out of the battle until 5 October 1940.

No.601 Squadron also intercepted the *Stukas* and their escorts south of Selsey Bill, as Pilot Officer Thomas Grier reported:

> We attacked in line astern, out of the sun. We came in on a steep right-hand turn. I shot a short burst at one Ju 87 who broke away and turned towards the sea, doing violent manoeuvres to evade. I gave him two other bursts and he went into the sea five miles south of Selsey. He went right in, nobody got out. I climbed up again, attacked another, which was coming from land to the sea at 4,000ft. I fastened onto his tail after being attacked by an Me 109 who dived on my tail but broke away after firing. I gave the Ju 87 three separate bursts and it plopped into the sea east of the Isle of Wight. Both these aircraft went right in and left a patch of green on the water but nobody appeared to get out.

This was good shooting by Grier, and in total 601 Squadron would claim six Ju 87s and two Me 109s destroyed, and another Me 109 damaged. Two pilots were lost, however: Sergeant Leonard Guy, who was never seen again, and Sergeant Redvers Hawkings, who was killed, his Hurricane crashing near Pagham. At the material time and place, *Leutnant*s Josef Jansen and Ernst Dülberg, both of 5/JG 27, claimed Hurricanes destroyed. Flight Sergeant Pond's Hurricane was damaged in the fight, as a result of which the engine cut as Pond was finals at Tangmere, causing the aircraft to crash, but fortunately the pilot was unhurt.

The Spitfires of 602 Squadron now engaged the Ford raiders, 'heading off two waves of Ju 87s and following them out to sea' (ORB).

Flight Lieutenant Dunlop Urie, commanding 'A' Flight, was leading 602 Squadron on this sortie and reported that the Spitfires engaged at 14.25 hrs:

> I was Villa Leader ... I saw about sixty Ju 87s manoeuvring to bomb Ford aerodrome at 6,000ft. Seeing no protecting enemy fighters I attacked the Ju 87s. The first wave of thirty Ju 87s was already beginning to attack Ford aerodrome so I attacked the rear aircraft of this formation and five others, employing stern and beam attacks. Squadron had re-formed sections line-astern. I saw my tracer bullets striking in the glasshouse of five of these. Return fire was experienced from one of these and the rear-gunner silenced in three cases. Large pieces of the fuselage were seen to break off one glasshouse of these five.
>
> I then broke off the combat, all my ammunition being expended, and was attacked by two Me 109s or He 113s [*sic*], whose cannon fire hit my aircraft in three places in the fuselage.
>
> I landed at Westhampnett 1439 hrs with undercarriage down but one tyre burst and flaps not working.

Flight Lieutenant Urie's Spitfire, X4110, was so new, having only been received by 602 Squadron that morning, that there had been no time to apply squadron code letters to the fuselage – and now, with a broken back, battered by cannon and machine-gun rounds, it would never fly again. The service life of X4110 with 602 Squadron lasted from 14.15 hrs, when Urie took off, to 14.39 hrs, when the pilot, wounded in both feet, landed – just twenty-four minutes!

No.602 Squadron's Blue 2, Sergeant Basil Whall reported that over 'Ford aerodrome' he:

> attacked first formation of Ju 87s, singling one out which was flying parallel with the coast ... I did four separate beam attacks and saw it land at Poling, apparently intact and pilot captured.
>
> I then followed about ten Ju 87s retreating, about two miles out. Singled out the most convenient and did four beam attacks, closing to fifty yards. I saw this Ju 87 crash into the sea. The rear-gunner of this damaged my machine's wing, I believe with 0.5-inch ammunition.

SUNDAY, 18 AUGUST 1940

I then broke off to return to land but my engine caught fire and I came down right on the edge of the sea. One Ju 87 had a bright blue spinner. Retreating Ju 87s flew very low, skidding all over the place and not yet in any formation.

The first Ju 87 Sergeant Whall shot down landed on Ham Manor Golf Course at Littlehampton – the rear-gunner, *Oberfeldwebel* Geiger, was killed but the pilot, *Oberfeldwebel* Schweinhardt, was captured. Whall forced-landed at Elmer Sands, Middleton.

No.602 Squadron was unable to prevent Ford being seriously damaged, but claimed a toll of the raiders: six Ju 87s destroyed, seven damaged (five by Flight Lieutenant Urie), a probable, and two Me 109s destroyed. Flying Officer Christopher Mount's Spitfire was damaged in the combat, although he returned safely to base, and Pilot Officer Henry Moody was shot-up, landing at Ford with a burst tyre, his Spitfire tipping up on its nose. Flight Lieutenant Peter Fergusson was so badly shot-up by an Me 109, his Spitfire damaged in the port wing and petrol tank, that he collided with the RDF mast and Poling before careering through power cables to crash-land at Norway Farm, Rustington. Surprisingly, the pilot was admitted to hospital suffering only from shock and a strained back.

By 14.30 hrs, III/StG 77 was dive-bombing Poling, II/StG 77 were attacking Ford and I/StG77 was bombing Thorney Island. I/StG 3 was still headed for Gosport. Meanwhile, 152 Squadron was flying east towards the Isle of Wight, ready to cut-off the enemy's line of retreat, and 213 was making haste from Exeter.

At 14.45 hrs, 234 Squadron mixed it with Me 109s over the Isle of Wight. This squadron, recently arrived at Middle Wallop, had suffered heavy casualties on its first major engagement, on 16 August 1940. The following day, Squadron Leader Joseph 'Spike' O'Brien DFC took command, and now led twelve 234 Squadron Spitfires to engage the Me 109 escorts. The CO reported:

> The Squadron ordered to patrol Isle of Wight at 12,000ft. Sighted about twenty Me 109s over the island. Squadron broken up in dogfights. Fired at one Me 109 from astern. It turned slowly on its back and went straight down. Unable to watch result as the other was firing at me.

O'Brien claimed a 'possible'.

BATTLE OF BRITAIN ATTACK OF THE EAGLES

The Australian commander of O'Brien's 'B' Flight, Flight Lieutenant Pat Hughes, was more certain of his results (timed at 14.55 hrs over the island):

> Twenty Me 109s appeared above me in the sun. I climbed towards them and my Section attacked individually. I fired a burst at one Me 109 with no effect at extreme range. I turned and set this aircraft on fire but was immediately attacked by the second one so could not follow it down. He attacked and climbed away and then dived. I followed until he started to pull up and shot him with two bursts of two seconds each. This pilot immediately jumped out and landed on the Isle of Wight and his aircraft crashed there a few seconds later, on fire. When I observed this crash I saw a second cloud of smoke and fire just off the Isle of Wight, which appeared to be the first 109. This combat was observed by Red 3.

Hughes was awarded both Me 109s destroyed. One clearly was *Oberleutnant* R. Möller-Friedrich of 6/JG 2, who baled out and was captured, wounded, his aircraft crashing at Tapnall Farm, near Freshwater on the Isle of Wight.

The end result of 234 Squadron's engagement was six Me 109s claimed as destroyed, two probables and two damaged. While these figures were optimistic, considering the losses suffered by the squadron only two days before, this outcome was undoubtedly a morale-booster – especially as all pilots returned safely to base.

At 14.45 hrs, south of the Isle of Wight the eleven Spitfires of 152 Squadron dived from 4,000ft to attack thirty retiring Ju 87s, flying south at sea-level:

> Red 1, Flight Lieutenant Boitel-Gill, sent one into the sea, attacked three others and was himself attacked, probably by He 113s [*sic*]. Red 2, Pilot Officer Holmes also destroyed a Ju 87. Yellow 2, Sergeant Shepperd, closing to fifty yards, sent another Ju 87 into the sea and then finished his ammunition on another Ju 87 but was unable to see any resulting damage. By this time Me 109s had appeared and White 1, Pilot Officer Cox, having attacked a Ju 87 without result broke away upwards to attack an Me 109 which was on the tail of a Spitfire. Blue 1, Pilot Officer Beaumont, attacked the same Me 109, which

SUNDAY, 18 AUGUST 1940

dived into the sea. White 2, Sergeant Barker, dived behind White 1 at the beginning of the engagement and attacked a Ju 87 from the upper port quarter, closing from 200 – forty yards. The E/A, which was about fiftyft above the sea, dived in. Blue 1, Pilot Officer Beaumont, and Blue 2, Pilot Officer Williams, each destroyed a Ju 87. (ORB)

Pilot Officer Timothy Wildblood, Black 1, succinctly reported: 'The squadron attacked from behind and in the ensuing fight I attacked a Ju 87, saw it dive into the sea, and then attacked another with several other Hurricanes and Spitfires. This one disintegrated.'

Pilot Officer Walter Beaumont's Spitfire was damaged, although the pilot was unharmed and returned safely to Warmwell. There comes a point, however, with so many aircraft involved and crashing hither and thither, that trying to establish from the facts available who shot down who is impossible. Suffice it to say that I and II/JG 27 lost five Me 109s off the Isle of Wight that afternoon, and seven *Stukas* were also swallowed by the waves.

At 14.55 hrs, the Hurricanes of 213 Squadron had crossed the Isle of Wight, over which they were, according to Sergeant Harold Atkinson:

> investigated by a squadron of Spitfires [either 152 Squadron or 234 Squadron] who proceeded to come round from the beam onto our tails, thus not allowing us to carry on our patrol as normal for fear of the Spitfires mistaking us for 109s. I climbed about 2,000ft above the rest of the squadron to keep an eye on the Spitfires. One came right through the sections and on the leader's tail [Flight Lieutenant John 'Jackie' Sing].

By now, 213 Squadron was at 12,000ft, five miles south of Ventnor. Sergeant Atkinson, while waiting for the Spitfire to 'leave us alone':

> I saw a single aircraft 2,000ft below the squadron, heading south. I gave a quick call on the R/T and dived on him. He went down to sea-level and with my extra height I caught up to him within 350–500 yards and gave him one long burst. He started smoking and slow-rolled over into the sea approximately seven miles from Ventnor. I started climbing and turning back to the land, I saw about twenty Me 109s at sea-level. Four of them chased me towards land, but I shook these off by turning and

got a quick burst into another with no apparent effect. They turned round back to the French coast. I had not enough petrol to climb back up to the rest of the formation, so returned after trying to get in touch with my Section Leader.

Sergeant Atkinson – an experienced fighter pilot at 22 – was credited with the Me 109 destroyed, a JG 27 machine. Indicative of the uncertainty of life, however, is that Atkinson himself had just one week left to live.

In such a fast-moving and high stress combat environment, aircraft misidentification was common; of 213 Squadron's sortie over Hampshire on 16 August 1940, Pilot Officer Alexander Osmand wrote in his log book that the Hurricanes had 'Dived onto Spitfires'. Now, Osmand was flying in Flight Lieutenant Sing's formation off Ventnor: 'Patrol Portland – 15,000ft – on to St Catherine's Point – where I was attacked by three Me 109s, which tried to pick me off rear of Squadron. Head-on – got burst in windscreen – glass in my eyes!'

Although unrecorded in any other document, Pilot Officer Osmand noted in his log book that his Hurricane, N2630, VK-E, was damaged. Having had a lucky escape, the young pilot returned safely to RAF Exeter, and wrote about the incident to his fiancée, Miss Marjorie Hodges of Peckham, the following day:

> From my brief and belated note of yesterday you will have learned that I have been slightly in the wars at the moment. I am off the flying and am likely to be for a few days. The damage is really very slight, but in a most painful and disconcerting place. My hand is nothing to worry about and the cut there can be ignored, but the two scratches on my left eye are most bothersome. I went to bed early last night, after suffering a deal of undeserved lionisation, but I had a pretty rotten night. The eye was painful and kept me in a feverish sort of state. However, I got up late in the morning and was a lot better for the long rest. I didn't come up here until just before lunch and I let the Medical Officer have another look at my eye a few moments ago. He isn't worried about it and I asked him how long it was likely to take before I could be passed as fit for flying again. He wants to see it again in the morning, then, if it's coming on OK, he may give me a couple of days off to recuperate. Two days off!

SUNDAY, 18 AUGUST 1940

Pilot Officer Osmand was 213 Squadron's only casualty, and Sergeant Atkinson's Me 109 its only combat claim in this action. The Me 109s had been the German formation's rearguard as it withdrew back across the Channel, and having shot-up Osmand's Hurricane, low on fuel, they too about-turned and headed back to Cherbourg.

In the *Stukas'* wake, voluminous black smoke billowed over RNAS Ford from blazing fuel tanks, the airfield having been seriously damaged. A hangar, the Equipment Stores, Workshops, the Officers' and Men's sleeping quarters all destroyed. During the attack, Leading Wren Steward Nina Marsh, although wounded, had attended to injured colleagues and ensured their evacuation before accepting treatment herself; Wren Cook Irene Marriott, also wounded, organised evacuation of her kitchen before returning to extinguish fires; the devotion to duty of both women would later be recognised by British Empire Medals. Surgeon Lieutenant K. Scott was blown into a trench by an exploding bomb but although wounded and shaken he attended to the casualties in a clearing station he rapidly created amid the flames and smoke. The hut in which Chief Petty Officer P. Cahalane worked imploded on him, but he too prioritised treating other casualties and had to be formally ordered to have his own wounds dressed. Countless other acts of courage took place at Ford that afternoon, and many lives saved – but, owing to the complete lack of warning, the death toll was high: twenty-eight killed, seventy-five wounded. Fourteen aircraft of various types were destroyed, twenty-six more damaged. Had Ford been a Fighter Command sector station, this would have represented a grievous blow to 11 Group – but it was not.

Thanks to the early intervention of 43 and 601 Squadrons, and three Blenheims of 235 Squadron, which had scrambled from Thorney Island before the raid, the airfield there was not as badly hit as Ford and Gosport. According to the 235 Squadron ORB, Pilot Officers Peacock and Wordsworth, and Sergeant Nelson, 'attacked a formation of Ju 88s [*sic*]. Peacock and Wordsworth each shot one down and Sergeant Nelson fired 2,000 shots into a third E/A, results unobserved' (no combat report exists). Nonetheless, thirty-five HE bombs found their mark, fourteen of which were delayed action. Two hangars were hit and damaged by fire, and three aircraft were destroyed, another damaged; five civilians were wounded but nobody was killed.

Gosport had been badly damaged, two hangars had been hit and various buildings wrecked, along with five aircraft written-off and another damaged – but there were no personnel casualties.

BATTLE OF BRITAIN ATTACK OF THE EAGLES

At Poling RDF station, the receiver section had been accurately dive-bombed and one of the huge pylons hit – which put the long-range Chain Home radar out of commission. The Chain Home Low set, which tracked low-flying aircraft, was undamaged, however, and the only casualties were one man suffering from shock and another slightly wounded. Other RDF stations to west and east, however, provided interlocking coverage, so the damage to Poling made no difference. During the attack, WAAF Corporal Avis Hearn was working the switchboard, passing information regarding plots to Fighter Command HQ's Filter Room at Bentley Priory, a vital task she felt unable to abandon – until the Operations Room was hit and her switchboard destroyed. For her courage, Corporal Hearn was later decorated with the Military Medal.

Although Fighter Command claimed thirty-four Ju 87s destroyed, and AA gunners two more, the actual *Stuka* losses were sixteen destroyed and eight damaged – all of StG 77, the Thorney Island raiders of I/StG 77 suffering the heaviest casualties with nine aircraft destroyed and five damaged. I/StG 3, miraculously suffered no losses. Nonetheless, the losses incurred by these *Stukas* of *Fliegerkorps* VIII were sufficient for *Reichsmarschall* Göring to withdraw *Generalmajor* von Richthofen's 220 Ju 87s from the battle. This was undoubtedly a drawback because dive-bombing was more accurate than doing so from high altitude – during the dive-bombing attacks this day, for example, bombs had all fallen on the intended military objectives. It was clear, though, how vulnerable to attack by RAF fighters the *Stukas* were, and what a difficult commitment escorting the slow-moving dive-bombers was for fighters. On this occasion, eight of the escorting fighters were destroyed, while Fighter Command lost five aircraft with eight more damaged (including Pilot Officer Osmand's, which was only documented in his personal log book); two pilots had been killed and four wounded (again including Osmand). It was a good result for the defenders, and the fighters had been well handled by the 10 Group and 11 Group controllers in what was a model of inter-group cooperation.

After *Luftflotte* 3's major afternoon effort, the action now reverted to *Luftflotte* 2 and 11 Group. Having hit the sector stations at Kenley and Biggin Hill, *GeneralFeldmarschall* Kesselring would now strike at those of Hornchurch and North Weald. Fifty-eight Do 17s of KG 2 were briefed to hit Hornchurch, and North Weald would be attacked by fifty-one He 111s of KG 53. The two forces of bombers were to cross the English coast simultaneously, KG 53 north of Foulness, KG 2 over Deal. Again, there would be a huge fighter escort, comprising 140 Me 109s and Me 110s from JG 3, 26, 51 and 54, and ZG 26.

SUNDAY, 18 AUGUST 1940

At 16.20 hrs, RDF detected 20+ over the Pas-de-Calais, between St Omer and Boulogne, and a further force of indeterminable size off Cap-Gris-Nez. Then, at 16.50 hrs, 50+ near Lille. The 11 Group Controller's first reaction was to despatch 501 Squadron to patrol Hawkinge, and 54 Squadron to cover Manston. It was soon apparent that the enemy was bound for targets either side of the Thames Estuary and so defending squadrons were scrambled: 151 to patrol North Weald; 56 Squadron from Rochford to intercept the formation approaching the Blackwater; 257 Squadron, in transit from Martlesham to Debden diverted to patrol Canterbury; 32 Squadron from battered Biggin Hill to head north of Canterbury; 85 Squadron from Debden to patrol base, and 1 Squadron from Northolt to intercept the enemy over Southend. Elements of six other 11 Group squadrons were scrambled to patrol airfields, although they would play no part in the fighting ahead. Interestingly, 11 Group, well-used to perfect cooperation from 10 Group to the west, requested assistance from 12 Group, which despatched Digby's 46 Squadron, already reinforcing the Duxford Sector, to patrol North Weald.

At 16.45 hrs, 151 Squadron's Hurricanes engaged the more northerly enemy force, which was heading for North Weald, five miles off Burnham, as the commander of 'A' Flight, Flying Officer Kenneth Blair, reported:

> I was leading Yellow Section when we intercepted 100+ E/A heading for Chelmsford. The leading section attacked the front of the bombers and turned them around. I then found myself in the middle of the bomber formation, completely surrounded, so I broke away and climbed up to attack the rear of the bomber formation. While climbing a formation of Me 110s started to attack the Hurricanes engaging the enemy formation. I had by this time plenty of height and so dived to attack an Me 110, he saw me, turned and climbed. I fired at him head-on and after closing to 100 yards approx. broke away. He turned over on his back and crashed into the sea. I then attacked another Me 110 which was flying on a straight course – he saw me when I opened fire and started to turn, so I made a quarter attack on him all the way round the turn. Black smoke came from the starboard engine. I was by this time under attack from several Me 109s, so turned over and broke away.
>
> The main formation had become separated from its fighter escort owing to clouds and the friendly fighters were able to attack the bomber formation easily. The Me 110 being about

three to four miles astern and the Me 109s about seven miles aster and higher. I afterwards climbed up in company with a Spitfire and chased the Me 109 aircraft but was unable to catch them, so returned to North Weald.

Flying Officer Blair was credited with one Me 10 destroyed, the other 'severely damaged'.

Flying Officer Richard 'Dickie' Milne, also engaged at 16.45 hrs:

We were brought to readiness due to an impending attack on the aerodrome and took off at 1630 hrs. We climbed to 10,000ft to the east of the aerodrome and had just reached that height below the clouds when immediately in front of us appeared large formations of enemy bombers. They were descending through the clouds via a gap and pointing straight at the aerodrome. There were other Hurricane squadrons waiting and this sight was too much for them. The complete formation turned to port and commenced heading in the opposite direction. When completely round I caught up with the last member of the formation and closed to dead astern position at 200 yards. The bombers were now flying very fast and using full throttle. I encountered fire from the rear-gunner but this was not accurate as I kept the rudder of E/A between us. I opened fire and after a few seconds smoke commenced to come from both motors. I continued firing and was enveloped by the oil and smoke from the E/A. This got thicker and I could only see the wing tips as I came to the end of my ammunition. Tracer ammunition flashed past me and several hits made on my aircraft by Me 110. I half-rolled and evaded the rest of his attack. As I glanced behind I saw the Heinkel explode and huge pieces fly off, but I did not see the final crash as an Me 110 was still paying me attention. After this I saw the craters and smoke of jettisoned bombs both on the land and out to sea. Pilot Officer Ellacombe reports seeing the smoking remains of a bomber in the sea with oil all around the wreckage.

Flying Officer Milne had shot down the He 111 of II/KG 53's *Gruppenkommandeur*, *Major* Tamm, who was killed, along with the rest of his crew, the wreckage seen in the water by Pilot Officer John Ellacombe

SUNDAY, 18 AUGUST 1940

was from this machine. KG 53, however, had not turned about because of the RAF fighters' presence, disconcerting though that doubtless was, but because the cloud was closing in, concealing their target.

In this action Pilot Officer Kenneth Debenham and the Polish Pilot Officer Franciszek Czajkowski also claimed Me 110s destroyed and which crashed into the sea, and North Weald's Station Commander, Wing Commander Victor Beamish DSO AFC, damaged a 'Ju 88'[*sic*] but was shot-up and forced to land at Martlesham Heath; fortunately he was unhurt. Squadron Leader John Gordon, who had only taken command of 151 Squadron on 5 August 1940, was shot down and baled out, badly burned; admitted to Rochford Hospital, 'he is quite OK' (ORB). Pilot Officer John Ramsay, however, was missing; he would remain so until recovered by aviation archaeologist Steve Vizard on 11 August 1983; only then could the 21-year-old Hurricane pilot be buried in consecrated ground and accorded full military honours at Brookwood.

Flight Lieutenant Steve 'Squeak' Weaver of 56 Squadron reported that at 17.20 hrs, 56 Squadron intercepted '200 plus', at 10,000ft over Bradwell:

> I was flying Yellow One, leading No 2 Section. After various vectors I saw a large, escorted, formation of bombers approaching Burnham from the east, north of us. I took the lead and flew under the rear section, selecting the extreme left-hand bomber of the rear section. I fired about ten seconds burst into him and saw him begin to burn and break away from the formation. I broke away violently owing to the escorting fighters behind. I then joined in with escorting Me 110s, firing two or three second burst at several from various angles. No observed effects. My ammunition then ran out. Pilot Officer Mounsden saw the first E/A attacked going down in flames.

The He 111, a machine of 8/KG 53, was flown by *Leutnant* Walter Leber, whose gunners shouted warning of 56 Squadron's appearance before opening fire. Leber could see tracer rounds streaming from the guns of the other *Heinkels* around him – then the temperature of his right-hand motor began rising dangerously. Clearly the cooling system had been hit, so Leber feathered the airscrew and shut the engine down. Unable to maintain formation, the damaged bomber straggled behind and was attacked by a Spitfire pilot, Pilot Officer John Hopkin of 54 Squadron, who wrecked the raider's other engine. With three of his crew too badly wounded to bale out, Leber's only option was to jettison his bombs and make a forced-landing.

All the time, Pilot Officer Hopkin circled the bomber, but chivalrously did not attack, a gesture much appreciated by Leber who safely crash-landed at Small Gains Farm, Foulness, at 17.35 hrs. Those aboard were captured, but the sole crew-member who did take to his parachute later died of his injuries.

It was another highly successful action for 56 Squadron, enemy aircraft also being destroyed by Squadron Leader Manton, Flight Lieutenant 'Jumbo' Gracie, and Flight Sergeant 'Taffy' Higginson, while Flying Officer Innes Westmacott, Pilot Officer Maurice Mounsden and Sergeant Peter Robinson damaged others – all for no loss.

Squadron Leader G.A.L. 'Minnie' Manton, commanding 56 Squadron:

> From those hectic times I remember well one particular incident ... probably because it occurred shortly after I had taken over the squadron following two-and-a-half years at the Air Ministry. Every moment with 56 Squadron, therefore, was new and exciting for me. After only my first or second combat. I was returning to North Weald, trying to gather my wits, when another 56 Squadron Hurricane came alongside and formated on me. The pilot opened his hood, gave me a great grin, a thumbs up and then one finger to indicate that he had made a kill: it was 'Squeak'.

The three Hurricanes of 46 Squadron's Red Section, having scrambled from Duxford at 17.32 hrs, were also in action at 17.45 hrs near Chelmsford. Red 1, Flight Lieutenant Alexander Rabagliati, claimed an Me 110 destroyed and a probable, and Pilot Officer Charles Ambrose damaged three more. At the same time, twelve Spitfires of 54 Squadron were also engaged in the same area, off Clacton:

> The second wave of bombers and their escort – this time about 300 strong – came north and south of the Thames. It looked as if a pincer movement was being evolved with Hornchurch as the objective! Once again the squadron dealt faithfully with the enemy – being able to include some damage on the main formation which might have made things very unpleasant for the station. (ORB)

Ironically, 54 Squadron had not intercepted the Hornchurch raiders but the force intending to target North Weald before turning about.

SUNDAY, 18 AUGUST 1940

Once more, the New Zealander Pilot Officer Colin Gray of 'B' Flight was among 54 Squadron's successful pilots:

> I was leading Green Section when the squadron encountered a large number of E/A. Blue Section engaged a formation of Me 110s alongside the bombers, while I climbed to engage fighters. On emerging from a cloud I saw Red 1 being engaged by a number of Me 110s. I fired at two in turn, in both cases using bursts of three seconds each, from very close range. In both cases the E/A fell in a slow vertical spiral, obviously out of control. I then engaged a third E/A, using slight deflection in an attack from above. I fired the remainder of my ammunition and the E/A turned on its back and fell in a slow, vertical spiral, in the same way as the previous one. I followed this down and saw it crash in a town (Clacton?) and explode.

Pilot Officer Gray was correct: this Me 110, of 4/ZG 26, fortunately missed houses and crashed at Smith's Sandpits, Alton Park Road, Clacton – killing the *Staffelkapitän*, *Hauptmann* Hubert Lüttke, and *Unteroffizier* Herbert Brillo.

In what was 54 Squadron's fourth sortie of the day, in addition to Pilot Officer Gray's Me 110 destroyed and two probables, the Spitfire pilots claimed two more Me 110s destroyed, two probables, a Do 17 destroyed, and two He 111s damaged.

At 17.35 hrs, Squadron Leader Peter Townsend's 85 Squadron, up from Debden, was ordered to intercept Raid 51, which was incoming over Folkestone. While proceeding there, at 17.39 hrs, when eight miles north of Chelmsford, Squadron Leader Townsend sighted the North Weald raiders fifteen miles to the east:

> Owing to the numerical superiority of the enemy, the squadron was unable to deliver any method of attack and the battle developed into individual dogfights. The main action took place at approximately eight to twelve miles east of Foulness Point.
>
> Squadron Leader Townsend attacked one Me 110 with full deflection shot, five second burst, while doing a left-hand turn, and the enemy aircraft heeled over, spiralling vertically downwards out of control from 10,000ft. Pilot Officer English

and Sergeant Howes saw it go down and corroborate the opinion that the pilot must have been killed. He then attacked an Me 109 and the aircraft caught fire after a three second burst and spun down in flames. He was then attacked by another Me 109 but without difficulty manoeuvred on its tail, the pilot baled out and the machine broke up in the air. He then attacked another Me 109 ineffectively and then with ammunition exhausted, returned to Debden.

Pilot Officer English (Red 2) followed Squadron Leader Townsend in the attack on twenty Me 110s, tackled two Me 110s which dived ahead of him. He gave one long burst, saw tracer entering the wing, and silenced the rear-gunner. Sergeant Howes (Red 3), while Red 1 and 2 were attacking, climbed to 9,000ft and attacked an Me 110 and saw it crash into the water. He then climbed and made a number 2 attack on one of several Me 110s circling, which burst into flames. He then climbed to 15,000ft and tackled straggling Do 17, which went down out of sight with thick smoke streaming from it.

Flight Lieutenant Hamilton (Yellow 1) attacked a He 111 with a five second burst, and on breaking away it dropped its undercarriage, smoke poured from the fuselage and two engines and E/A went gliding slowly down to sea. He then attacked an Me 110 which dived down with both engines on fire.

Pilot Officer Marshall (Yellow 2) followed Yellow 1 in pursuit of the Me 110 but broke away to engage a He 111 three miles away and opened fire at 250 yards. Pieces broke away from the E/A which was in a cloud of white vapour, and flying into this Pilot Officer Marshall's wing cut off the tail unit of the E/A. Despite a damaged aircraft minus a wingtip, he landed safely at Debden.

Sergeant Ellis (Yellow 3) destroyed one Me 109 and damaged an Me 110. He used his cine-gun throughout this combat.

Sergeant Walker-Smith (Blue 3) delivered a frontal attack on an Me 110, 150 yards above it. The E/A glided down to hit the sea forty miles out. After firing several ineffective bursts on another aircraft he made a similar frontal attack. This time the Me 110 broke up, one baling out into the sea.

Pilot Officer W.H. Hodgson (Blue 4) during the dogfight climbed to 12,000ft and dived on a Do 17 which went diving

SUNDAY, 18 AUGUST 1940

down, white smoke pouring from its engines. He then turned on the tail of an Me 109 by a steep climbing turn, and after a short burst the E/A dived vertically into the sea. He then climbed to 20,000ft to a circle of Me 110s, made a snap shot at one, and then dived onto another, making the E/A's starboard wing smoke.

Pilot Officer Gowers (Green 1) attacked a Ju 87 [*sic*] from dead astern with a five second burst, followed by a seven second burst, and the E/A was almost completely blotted out by black smoke and dived towards the sea.

Pilot Officer Lockhart (Green 2) attacked an Me 110 and silenced the rear-gunner.

Pilot Officer Lewis DFC (Green 3) encountered twelve Me 110s circling at 12,000ft, one of which proceeded to dive on a Hurricane down below, and in so doing presented a plain view in his sights at 150 yards. Two short bursts caused it to smoke and dive at a steep angle.

Pilot Officer Hemingway (Blue 2) followed Flight Lieutenant Lee DSO DFC (Blue 1) who chased a lone Ju 88 [*sic*] but broke away to attack a circling formation of Ju 88s [Me 110s]. He attacked a Ju 88 but was himself attacked by two Ju 88s in close formation. His engine was hit, his cockpit filled with oil and glycol, and his aircraft went into a spin. He pulled out at 7,000ft and set course for land, but his engine stopped and he had to bale out. After being one-and-a-half hours in the sea he was picked up by Lightship 81 boat twelve miles east of Clacton. He was then landed at Felixstowe by MTB and returned to Debden the next day [at the time of writing in March 2023, Group Captain Hemingway is the only known Battle of Britain airman alive, aged 102].

This was quite a bag for 85 Squadron, although it is inevitable the claims were exaggerated because, as we have seen, a single enemy aircraft could (and did) end up attacked and claimed by several pilots, all acting independently, and therefore becoming multiplied many-fold on the score sheet.

There was, however, a sad loss for 85 Squadron: Flight Lieutenant Richard 'Dickie' Lee DSO, DFC – the godson of none other than Lord Trenchard, the 'Father of the Royal Air Force' himself, failed to return. Lee was last seen by Squadron Leader Townsend and Flying Officer Gowers ten miles north-east of Foulness Point, chasing three Me 109s well ahead of him.

At 17.50 hrs, Squadron Leader Hill Harkness's 257 Squadron also engaged the northerly raiders.

Sergeant Alexander Girdwood was Red 3, following his Flight Commander, Flight Lieutenant Hugh Beresford (Red 1):

> While following Red Leader at a height of 12,000ft, we came upon a section of He 111s flying in a big bomber formation. Red 1 made an astern attack on one of the He 111s. When he broke off firing I closed in and fired until it started to smoke and go down. As I broke away, bullets entered my cockpit, which exploded and caught fire. After a struggle I managed to bale out and as I fell I succeeded in pulling the rip cord and in untwisting the lines which wound round my legs. After that I was nearly strangled by the lines which got entangled round my neck. A toe of my right foot was fractured by a bolt which was forced into it by a bullet. I received some burns and bruises. Subsequently I found that the He 111 had crashed near Foulness just below my own plane. Two of the wounded German airmen were brought to the same hospital at Foulness as myself.
>
> I have the impression that the He 111 may have been slowed up and forced slightly out of the formation by a puff of AA fire.

Sergeant Girdwood, who was 257 Squadron's only casualty in the action, shared destruction of the He 111 with Flight Lieutenant Beresford. Pilot Officer David Hunt claimed a 'Ju 87' probable, although as none were present this must have been an Me 109, and Pilot Officers Gerald Maffett and Arthur Cochrane each damaged 'Do 215s'.

The final squadron to engage over the Thames Estuary, at 18.15 hrs, was 1 Squadron, up from Northolt. The CO, Squadron Leader David Pemberton, reported that:

> I was leading No 1 Squadron and when over Southend at 21,000ft on emerging through a cloud layer we saw, and were attacked by, nine to twelve Me 109s. One continued its dive past me and I followed it. I gave it a two second burst from about 250 yards, which made him go down, and the E/A hedge-hopped through Kent. I withheld my fire for some

SUNDAY, 18 AUGUST 1940

time in the hope that he would go down, but when it started to regain some height I gave him a short burst at 500ft when the aircraft crashed in flames between Tenterden and Cranbrook.

This was an Me 109 of 8/JG 3, the pilot of which, *Obergefrieter* Walter Bäsell being killed when his fighter crashed at Blue House Farm, Milebush. It was the only combat fought by 1 Squadron that evening.

Having failed to bomb North Weald aerodrome and having offloaded thirty-two bombs on Shoeburyness, causing damage to civilian property and loss of life, the raiders withdrew.

Further south, having thus far escaped interception, by 17.45 hrs the Hornchurch-bound Do 17s of KG 2 were north of Herne Bay and heading straight for their target – when the Hurricanes of 32 Squadron appeared on the scene. According to the 32 Squadron ORB, Squadron Leader Mike Crossley DFC led the charge, which 'broke up the formation'. The Me 109s of III/JG 26 rained down from on high, however, counter-attacking. Having destroyed an Me 109, Squadron Leader Crossley was shot down, baling out unhurt over Gillingham; Sergeant Leonard Pearce was hit by a 109 over Canterbury and baled out slightly wounded, but Pilot Officer de Grunne took to his parachute over Ruckinge, badly burned. The action was not all one-sided, though: Flight Lieutenant Peter Brothers, Pilot Officer Alan Eckford, and the Polish Pilot Officers Boleslaw Wlasnowolski and Karol Pniak all claimed Me 109s destroyed, two in the latter's case, Blue 2, who reported:

> I saw on the same height two Me 109s. I attacked the one which was nearer me from a distance 250 yards. I gave him first short burst. He was quite surprised. I drew nearer and gave him two two second bursts. Just after I saw Me 109 in black smoke and flames. He was diving in south-east direction. I climbed to the height of 13,000ft. I saw two Hurricanes which were fighting with five Me 109s. I attacked one which was near from back of Hurricane. He saw me because I attacked ¾ from above. At once he turned in my direction and began to dive ... I turned in his direction and after several seconds shot near him. I gave first burst from 300 yards. After next several bursts he was burning. I left him at 7,000ft. He was turning in the south direction. When I came back I saw one Me 109 was diving in the south direction but he was too far. I came home.

One of these Me 109s was that of 7/JG 26's *Oberleutnant* Walter Blume, whose aircraft was set on fire; the pilot crashed at Kingston and was captured, badly wounded. The other 109 was flown by *Leutnant* Gerhard Müller-Dühe, who was killed when his fighter crashed at Chilham.

Flight Lieutenant George Stoney was leading his section of 501 Squadron's Hurricanes to attack the Do 17s when, like 32 Squadron, the Hurricanes were bounced by high-flying Me 109s – this time of II/JG 51. As his section broke, Stoney continued towards the bombers – until hacked down by *Hauptmann* Josef 'Joschko' Fözö, *Kommandeur* of I/JG 51, who later described the man he had ambushed as 'A very brave man, he was the only English fighter in the whole area. It was easy to dive down and open fire. He fell like a stone.' Flight Lieutenant Stoney was killed when his Hurricane crashed at Chilham. Many years later, Air Vice-Marshal Harry Hogan, 501 Squadron's CO throughout the Battle of Britain, remembered that 'Stoney's was a great loss. He was an exceptional officer and definitely destined for air rank.' The squadron's two Polish pilots, Flying Officer Stefan Witorzenc and Pilot Officer Pavel Zenker, avenged their Flight Commander's death by shooting down two Me 109s over Whitstable: *Hauptmann* Horst Tietzen, a 'Spaniard', the *Staffelkapitän* of 5/JG 51and the fourth top-scoring German fighter pilot at the time, and *Leutnant* Hans-Otto Lessing, both of whom were killed.

The German fighters had done a splendid job of protecting KG 2, only one Do 17 being damaged, which returned to base with a wounded crewman aboard. Like North Weald, cloud obscured Hornchurch, and so the Dorniers too wheeled about and headed home. KG 53, however, had lost four He 111s and one damaged, and ten fighters had been destroyed. The defenders were cock-a-hoop, believing at the time that stiff fighter opposition and AA fire had turned the raiders about.

In total on this day, the *Luftwaffe* had flown 970 sorties, and lost sixty-nine aircraft destroyed or damaged beyond economic or practical repair; ninety-four German aircrew were killed, forty were captured and twenty-five were wounded. From this point onwards the hard-hit *Stukas* played no further part in the aerial assault against England. The forces committed by Fighter Command were much stronger than the enemy expected: Air Chief Marshal Dowding's pilots flew 927 sorties, losing thirty-one fighters, ten pilots killed, twenty wounded; 11 August 1940 had seen the highest number of Spitfire and Hurricanes pilots killed throughout the entire Battle of Britain – twenty-five, its place in history perhaps being 'The Worst Day'; 15 August 1940 had seen both sides fly more sorties than any other day, the *Luftwaffe* launching

SUNDAY, 18 AUGUST 1940

raids along a 500-mile front which saw the daylight defeat of *Luftflotte* 5, becoming 'The Greatest Day' to the British but 'Black Thursday' to the Germans. The British historian Dr Alfred Price, writing in 1974, decided that 18 August 1940 was 'The Hardest Day', given that as 100 German aircraft had been destroyed or damaged, and likewise 136 RAF machines: 'On no other day during the Battle of Britain would either side suffer a greater number of aircraft put out of action.' 18 August 1940, therefore, deserves its place in history – although the killing was not quite over...

Among pilots undergoing training at 6 SFTS, Little Rissington, in Gloucestershire, was one Sergeant Bruce Hancock. Hendon-born Bruce, a former Boy Scout would be affectionately remembered by his family as 'the jolly, carefree, one', attending the town's Algernon Road and William Ellis School before joining the staff of Johnston Evans, a local estate agent. On 1 December 1938, Bruce joined the RAFVR, learning to fly at Hendon. After general mobilisation on 3 September 1939, he undertook mandatory 'square bashing' at an initial training wing, then successfully completed elementary flying training. On 15 June 1940, Bruce was posted to 6 SFTS. On the night of 18 August 1940, Sergeant Hancock was to practice 'circuits and bumps', solo, and fly from nearby RAF Windrush. It was to be his last exercise with 6 SFTS, as the following day Bruce was to be commissioned and posted to an operational training unit, on the last leg of his path to a bomber squadron. That final, routine, flight was to be undertaken in a yellow-painted and unarmed Anson, and at RAF Windrush a row of Glim Lamps had been laid out, to assist pilots' landings and orientation. The problem was that it was not just unarmed, friendly, Ansons active over the Cotswolds that night ...

Across the Channel, bitter though the fighting had been during daylight, not all enemy bomber units had participated. *Luftflotte* 2's KG 27 *Boelcke*, based at Dinard, near St Malo on the north-western coast of Brittany, had not been engaged by day, and now certain elements of the unit prepared for the usual solo nuisance raids on England after dark. One such crew belonged to 5/KG 27, tasked with bombing RAF Brize Norton, just one of around forty RAF airfields in Oxfordshire – and subject to a devasting attack two nights before. Although Brize was not a Fighter Command airfield it was a large aerodrome, so given their recent success, unsurprisingly the Germans returned to the same target on the night of 18 August 1940.

The pilot of the He 111 concerned (*Werke Nummer* 1408) was *Oberfeldwebel* Alfred Dreher, a 30-year-old from Schwabisch Hall; as mentioned earlier, in German aircraft the observer/navigator is the captain, in this case 22-year-old *Unteroffizier* Herbert Rave who, together with the 20-year-old flight-engineer and air gunner *Unteroffizier* Richard Schmidt, hailed from Hamburg. Before the flight, the radio operator, 27-year-old *Unteroffizier* Ewald Cohrs, from Lüneburg, had written home to his sister, Gertrude. Unusually in such a letter, which typically downplays the dangers faced, Cohrs described the inherent hazards of nocturnal operations, how the stress arising denied him of sleep, and how he craved home leave – all primary evidence of the strain under which enemy aircrews were operating. Collectively, this was an experienced crew, in fact, having previously survived both the Polish and French campaigns.

Wartime was, of course, the time of the 'Black Out', with domestic properties, service installations and streets alike cloaked in darkness, no visible light being permitted, for fear of assisting the navigation of enemy aircraft. RAF Brize Norton, however, lay just five miles to the south-east of RAF Windrush, from where, to Rave and his crew, the Glim Lamps of the latter must have literally shone like beacons in the night. It is actually inconceivable, considering the successful attack on Brize only two evenings before, and given the extent of the enemy's assault on RAF airfields for the past five days, that this night-time training, with ground illumination and Ansons with navigation lights switched on, went ahead. Inevitably, the He 111, obviously aware that the Glim Lamps represented a flare path for night landings, was drawn to Windrush – and the opportunity for destruction presented.

That night, LAC James Walding was Duty Medical Orderly, occupying a tent on Windrush airfield and watching the ongoing flying. The Duty Pilot's green flare, fired from his Very pistol, had soared aloft, signalling the waiting Anson pilots to take-off and begin their exercise. The time was 22.50 hrs, Double Summer Time, and night-time proper was rapidly falling. Suddenly, explosions shook the ground, as the He 111's bombs found their mark, straddling the brightly lit flare path. Then, the Germans' machine-guns opened up, raking the airfield. By now, all but one of the Ansons was safely down – only Sergeant Hancock remained airborne, making his approach in Anson N9164, still 'lit up like a Christmas tree', as Walding later recalled. Behind him lurked the He 111, which Walding could see closing quickly on the Anson from astern. The Heinkel's nose-gun opened fire on the defenceless trainer which, Walding noted, had now extinguished its navigation lights. Still pouring fire on the Anson, the bomber rapidly overhauled its slower target. According to other eye-witnesses, having doused his lights, Sergeant Hancock banked to port, causing the He 111 to

SUNDAY, 18 AUGUST 1940

overshoot, then, just as the raider passed immediately overhead, the Anson suddenly reared up, crashing into the German. Walding remembered 'a blinding flash', and a 'fiery blob falling to earth'.

Both aircraft, in fact, crashed just two miles or so south-west of Windrush airfield, the He 111, ablaze, at Blackbitch Farm, Aldsworth, near Northleach – killing all aboard instantly. In the next field lay the wrecked Anson – in which LAC Walding and colleagues found the lifeless, and virtually unmarked, body of Sergeant Hancock.

To James Walding, there was no doubt that on that dreadful night he had witnessed a 'signal act of valour' worthy of a Victoria Cross. Like the case of Pilot Officer Bird (see Volume 2, *The Breaking Storm*), however, it could never be *conclusively* proven that the collision occurred because Sergeant Hancock deliberately rammed his assailant, or whether, perhaps wounded, he had pulled up and collided with the Heinkel. A hand-written minute in Sergeant Hancock's Casualty File, dated 26 August 1940, records that 'Sergeant Hancock was killed while night-flying, and … was shot down by enemy aircraft' – but anecdotal evidence exists from his elder brother Jim, that Bruce had previously told him personally that should he ever be airborne in an unarmed aircraft and contact an enemy aircraft, he would ram it.

We cannot be completely certain of what actually happened, but on balance the available evidence does support the view that Sergeant Hancock rammed his tormentor. This was certainly the view reported by *The Times* and *Guardian*, Hendon's local read, on 23 August 1940, which headlined 'Local RAF Hero: Unarmed Sergeant Rammed Enemy Bomber', naming Sergeant Hancock – which was unusual at the time, given the Air Ministry's clear policy of not identifying individuals in the press. Similarly, another newspaper declared 'Rammed Enemy Bomber: Heroic RAF Pilot's Name Revealed', again identifying Sergeant Hancock, and reported:

> Reliable spectators on the ground believe that the Heinkel, which was on a night-bombing raid, intercepted the Anson, and finding it was an unarmed machine, chased it, firing with machine-guns. When he was found unable to regain his base, Sergeant Hancock, it is believed, resolved to bring down the enemy aircraft. He turned the Anson and rammed the Heinkel, bringing both machines to earth. The planes were completely smashed and the occupants of both – there were five Germans in the Heinkel – were killed.

Sergeant Hancock left behind a young widow, Annie Jayne Sophie 'Cissie' Hancock. The wedding had taken place at St John's, the Parish Church of West Hendon, but sadly, less than five months later, on 23 August 1940, Bruce Hancock's funeral was held there, the same church at which he had also been Christened and confirmed. Afterwards, Bruce was buried nearby, at Hendon Park Cemetery.

Clearly, Sergeant Bruce Hancock's heroism was recognised and appreciated by many, but, like Pilot Officer Bird, because he was not serving with one of the Fighter Command or associated units accredited as having fought in the Battle of Britain, there would be no Battle of Britain Clasp awarded. Nor would any posthumous gallantry medal be forthcoming.

Over at RAF Kenley that night, work was ongoing to clear up the mess, as Squadron Leader Edward Alford recalled:

> It was nearing midnight when the Station Defence Officer Flight Lieutenant Kilby, told me that he had received a request from the local police to go and see what could be done about unexploded bombs which had fallen outside the area of the station. On arrival at the Police station we were confronted with detailed reports as to the position of these bombs, but it was then explained to the Police Sergeant that they would have to be attended to by the local Bomb Disposal Squads as we had first to clear up the station. It was about 0130 hrs when we returned to the station and I climbed the stairs of the Mess to my room, where I had to use a little brute force to open the door, as it was jammed slightly by blast. When I did get it open I found that the ceiling plaster was all over the floor and my bed. However, that did not deter me from sleep and after shaking the blankets clear of debris, I turned in and was soon in the 'Arms of Morpheus'.

Squadron Leader Alford was, for sure, among countless exhausted men and women that night, all lucky to have survived the 'Hardest Day'. Indeed, also at Kenley, Squadron Leader Don MacDonell, CO of 64 Squadron, remembered that 'we were bloody tired', adding that 'The BBC put out the number of enemy aircraft claimed as shot down. It was a tremendous score and though it was exaggerated it was a great morale booster to us and the public rejoiced.' To the 54 Squadron diarist, it had been 'A great day'.

There would be no respite …

Reflections

In the handful of days covered in this book, much happened. The *Luftwaffe* launched its Eagle Attack, which suffered a false start owing to adverse weather and miscommunication. 'The Greatest Day' on 15 August 1940 had seen *Luftflotte* 5 neutralised, and 18 August 1940 had seen the *Stuka* defeated and withdrawn from the battle. The inadequacy of *Luftwaffe* air intelligence led to poor target selection, with much effort being expended against airfields unconnected with Fighter Command, although successful blows had been struck against the sector stations of Kenley and Biggin Hill. *Luftwaffe* losses, and its failure to force a quick decision, however, infuriated Göring, who demanded closer protection of his bombers from the fighter force – forgetting the lessons of the First World War in which the fighter pilot achieved far more when allowed to operate as a hunter. Although figures submitted by intelligence chief 'Beppo' Schmid indicated that Fighter Command was much weakened, in reality this was not so, and RAF fighters aplenty consistently intercepted the raiders – much to the *Luftwaffe*'s surprise and frustration. The weather was a constant frustration, cloud inconveniently concealing targets, preventing successful attacks – and time was running out. With the invasion scheduled for 15 September 1940, the *Luftwaffe* had less than a month to defeat Fighter Command and achieve the conditions necessary for Operation *Seelöwe* to go ahead. Clearly, however, Fighter Command was not an inadequate force equipped with obsolete aircraft, so easily swept aside in the past by the *Luftwaffe* – and from here-on Fighter Command, especially 11 Group, would become the focus of Göring's wrath – who urged his commanders and crews to even greater efforts.

In the two previous volumes we have seen how Fighter Command controllers frequently reacted to threats using very small formations, of sections of three or flights of six, rarely a whole squadron, in order to preserve limited resources and provide a flexible defence. This was also because pre-war training had revolved around such formations. With increasingly larger enemy formations incoming, this book has seen controllers respond with whole squadrons – and lots of them, putting up a robust defence. Air Chief Marshal Dowding's strategy of not concentrating his strength in the South had paid dividends on 15 August 1940, when northern-based squadrons routed *Luftflotte* 5. No.10 Group, to the West, worked perfectly with 11 Group, providing reinforcements against raids on the Portsmouth and Southampton areas, and likewise 11 Group provided support in actions over Portland and Weymouth Bay. No.12 Group, however, remained frustrated at a lack of action and on 15 August 1940 a row broke out between 12 Group and 11 Group when 19 Squadron, based in 12 Group's Duxford Sector, arrived too late to prevent Martlesham Heath, a forward coastal airfield in 11 Group, being bombed. Arguably, on this occasion 12 Group was requested too late, so the criticism was unfair – but it was the start of what would soon become a full-blown row with significant consequences for Air Chief Marshal Dowding and Air Vice-Marshal Park in particular. Nonetheless, it would be wrong to think that there was no cooperation between 11 and 12 Groups from that point onwards. On 18 August 1940, for example, a number of 12 Group squadrons scrambled to support 11 Group in repelling the raids bound for Hornchurch and North Weald, although only one section of 46 Squadron found and engaged the enemy. The fact was, the whole situation was unprecedented and to a degree Fighter Command – and the *Luftwaffe* – were both learning in real time.

In forthcoming days, the fighting would increase in intensity as 11 Group's aerodromes found themselves increasingly under attack – and the situation would become critical …

Acknowledgements

As always, I must thank Martin Mace for general support, friendship, undertaking essential research at The National Archives, and much else besides.

As ever, the Pen & Sword team were a pleasure to work with.

Andy Long's knowledge of the Defiant aircraft was helpful, and likewise assistance with archival research. Mike Hatch of the MOD Air Historical Branch was most efficient in responding to my various queries, which was much appreciated.

Linda Duffield, Tony Adams et al of the Kenley Revival Project have done a terrific job of recording and sharing interviews from certain survivors of Kenley's Battle of Britain, and I am indebted to all for that work, which has really helped bring the events of 18 August 1940 to life.

Tony and Trish Osmand provided treasures from the family archive in respect of Tony's father, Flight Lieutenant Alexander Osmand, who flew Hurricanes during the Battle of Britain with 213 Squadron but was sadly later killed in action in the Far East during 1943. The letters exchanged between Tony's parents are moving and atmospheric indeed, and exactly the kind of material sought to provide an extra dimension to the work.

Chris Myers was helpful regarding the Staffordshire Home Guard and KG 100 raid on Castle Bromwich Aeroplane Factory, and Robin Gilbert kindly obtained the Reverend Dagger's notes. Me 110 expert John Vasco kindly provided certain photographs, otherwise unobtainable.

That this eight-volume work will provide a lasting reference for The Battle of Britain Memorial Trust and National Memorial to The Few is motivational, and I would especially thank the Trust's Chairman, Richard Hunting CBE, Honorary Secretary Group Captain Patrick Tootal OBE DL, Trustee Wing Commander Andy Simpson MBIM RAFVR(T), and Malcolm Triggs and Becca Collier-Cook for help with promoting 'Battle of Britain: The People's Project'.

During a career spanning forty years I was privileged to know many of The Few and other survivors, all now sadly deceased, along with Dr Alfred Price, my old friend and mentor – I remain grateful to all for their long support, interviews, correspondence and permissions to quote from their own works, in certain cases.

Finally, I must thank my family, especially Sue, and friends for essential support and, indeed, tolerance!

Bibliography

The National Archives

The National Archives at Kew is the main repository for primary source documents; the following documents were consulted during the course of research for this book.

Operations Record Books
AIR27/2018	'A' Flight, 1 Photographic Reconnaissance Unit
AIR27/2015	'B' Flight, 1 Photographic Reconnaissance Unit
AIR27/589	1 Squadron
AIR27/32	3 Squadron
AIR27/202	15 Squadron
AIR27/252	19 Squadron
AIR27/317	26 Squadron
AIR27/360	32 Squadron
AIR27/441	43 Squadron
AIR27/447	44 Squadron
AIR27/460	46 Squadron
AIR27/554	50 Squadron
AIR27/503	53 Squadron
AIR27/511	54 Squadron
AIR27/528	56 Squadron
AIR27/554	59 Squadron
AIR27/598	66 Squadron
AIR27/624	72 Squadron
AIR27/629	73 Squadron
AIR27/640	74 Squadron
AIR27/655	77 Squadron
AIR27/664	79 Squadron
AIR27/681	82 Squadron
AIR27/712	87 Squadron

BATTLE OF BRITAIN ATTACK OF THE EAGLES

AIR27/776	97 Squadron
AIR27/801	101 Squadron
AIR27/807	102 Squadron
AIR27/813	103 Squadron
AIR27/841	107 Squadron
AIR27/857	110 Squadron
AIR27/866	111 Squadron
AIR27/882	114 Squadron
AIR27/969	141 Squadron
AIR27/984	145 Squadron
AIR27/1025	152 Squadron
AIR27/1298	210 Squadron
AIR27/1315	213 Squadron
AIR27/1340	217 Squadron
AIR27/1360	219 Squadron
AIR27/1365	220 Squadron
AIR27/1371	222 Squadron
AIR27/1385	224 Squadron
AIR27/1442	235 Squadron
AIR27/1445	236 Squadron
AIR27/1453	238 Squadron
AIR27/1471	242 Squadron
AIR27/1498	249 Squadron
AIR27/1511	253 Squadron
AIR27/1526	257 Squadron
AIR27/1553	264 Squadron
AIR27/1558	266 Squadron
AIR27/1941	500 Squadron
AIR27/1949	501 Squadron
AIR27/1964	504 Squadron
AIR27/2059	600 Squadron
AIR27/2068	601 Squadron
AIR27/2028	604 Squadron
AIR27/2088	605 Squadron
AIR27/2093	607 Squadron
AIR27/2102	609 Squadron
AIR27/2106	610 Squadron
AIR27/2112	612 Squadron
AIR27/2123	615 Squadron

BIBLIOGRAPHY

AIR27/2126   616 Squadron
AIR27/2263   928 Squadron

Pilots' Combat Reports
AIR50/1   1 Squadron
AIR50/4   3 Squadron
AIR50/9   17 Squadron
AIR50/10   19 Squadron
AIR50/16   32 Squadron
AIR50/18   41 Squadron
AIR50/19   43 Squadron
AIR50/20   46 Squadron
AIR50/21   54 Squadron
AIR50/22   56 Squadron
AIR50/24   64 Squadron
AIR50/25   65 Squadron
AIR50/26   66 Squadron
AIR50/31   73 Squadron
AIR50/32   74 Squadron
AIR50/33   79 Squadron
AIR50/36   85 Squadron
AIR50/37   87 Squadron
AIR50/40   92 Squadron
AIR50/43   111 Squadron
AIR50/62   145 Squadron
AIR50/63   151 Squadron
AIR50/64   152 Squadron
AIR50/83   213 Squadron
AIR50/84   219 Squadron
AIR50/85   222 Squadron
AIR50/89   234 Squadron
AIR50/91   238 Squadron
AIR50/92   242 Squadron
AIR50/96   249 Squadron
AIR50/100   257 Squadron
AIR50/105   266 Squadron
AIR50/165   601 Squadron
AIR50/166   602 Squadron
AIR50/167   603 Squadron

AIR50/171	609 Squadron
AIR50/173	611 Squadron
AIR50/172	610 Squadron
AIR50/175	615 Squadron
AIR50/176	616 Squadron

Casualty Files

AIR81/1393	Sergeant G. Atkinson, 151 Squadron.
AIR81/1449	Pilot Officer M.A. King, 249 Squadron
AIR81/1320	Flying Officer R.S. Demetriadi
AIR81/1401	Flying Officer H. McD Goodwin
AIR81/2609	Flight Lieutenant H.M. Ferriss
AIR81/1463	Flight Lieutenant J.B. Nicolson
AIR81/1473	Pilot Officer W.M.L. Fiske
AIR81/2628	Flying Officer F. Gruszka
AIR81/2638	Sergeant D.A.S. McKay
AIR81/2694	Pilot Officer F. Kozlowski
AIR81/2659	Pilot Officer J.D. Bland
AIR81/2661	Pilot Officer K.N.T. Lee
AIR81/2688	AC2 A. Jones
AIR81/1428	ACW2 M.H. Hudson et al
AIR81/1426	Squadron Leader T.G. Lovell-Gregg
AIR81/2652	Sergeant H.S. Newton
AIR81/1451	LAC G.D. Hulse
AIR81/1445	Corporal G. Bage
AIR81/2718	Multiple RAF personnel casualties, RAF Detling, 13 August 1940
AIR81/1428	Multiple RAF personnel casualties, RAF Driffield, 15 August 1940

Miscellaneous

AIR22/296	Personnel: Casualties, Strength and Establishment of the RAF.
AIR28/64	RAF Biggin Hill Operations Record Book
AIR28/178	RAF Croydon Operations Record Book
AIR28/345	RAF Hawkinge Operations Record Book
AIR28/512	RAF Manston Operations Record Book
AIR28/526	RAF Martlesham Heath Operations Record Book
AIR28/419	RAF Kenley Operations Record Book
AIR28/509	RAF Lympne Operations Record Book
AIR28/815	RAF Tangmere Operations Record Book

BIBLIOGRAPHY

AIR28/907   RAF West Malling Operations Record Book
WO98/8/730   VC citations, including Flight Lieutenant J.B. Nicolson, 249 Squadron
WO208/
3331/792   PoW repatriation debrief, Flight Lieutenant V. Parker, 234 Squadron

Pilot's Flying Log Books

Flight Lieutenant B.J.E. Lane DFC, 19 Squadron (AIR4/58)
Pilot Officer J.F.D. Elkington, 1 Squadron
Pilot Officer DMC Crook DFC, 609 Squadron (AIR4/21)
Pilot Officer R.L. Jones, 19 and 64 Squadron
Pilot Officer M.D. Wainwright, 64 Squadron
Pilot Officer A.G. Osmand, 213 Squadron
Flight Sergeant G.C. Unwin, 19 Squadron
Sergeant B.J. Jennings, 19 Squadron

German Documents

OKW Directives for Invasion of the UK, Operation *Seelöwe*, Summer and Autumn 1940, Bundesarchiv
Luftflotte 2 and 3 records, available via Digital History Archive (see website detailed below)
German fighter combat claims can be found in the OKL records of the *Chef für Ausz. und Dizsiplin Luftwaffe-Personalamt LP(A)V* (available via various online sources)
German loss records can be found in the *Oberfehlsaber der Luftwaffe Genst. Gen. Qu/6 Abteilung/40.g. Kdos.I.C*, records, preserved by the Imperial War Museum.

Unpublished Sources

Correspondence, papers and interviews, Dilip Sarkar Archive.
Original manuscript of *Spitfire Pilot*, Flight Lieutenant D.M. Crook DFC.
The Memories and Thoughts of the Late Reverend J.H.K. Dagger, Battle of Britain Padre: RAF Exeter 1940–41 (Courtesy of his son M Christopher Dagger).

Pilot's Flying Log Book, Squadron Leader P.C. Pinkham AFC.
Pilot's Flying Log Book, Pilot Officer A.G. Osmand.
Pilot's Flying Log Book, Pilot Officer D.M.C. Crook DFC.

Published Sources

Adams, P., *Hurricane Squadron: 87 Squadron at War 1939–1941*, Air Research Publications, New Malden, 1988

Aders, G. and Held, W., *Stuka: Dive-Bombers-Pursuit Bombers-Combat Pilots, A Pictorial Chronicle of German Close-Combat Aircraft to 1945*, Schiffer Publishing Ltd, Pennsylvania, USA, 1989

Aders, G. and Held, W., Chronik: Jagdgeschwader 51 'Mölders', Motor Buch Verlag, Stuttgart, 2009

Addison, P. and Crang, J.A. (eds.), *The Burning Blue: A New History of the Battle of Britain*, Pimlico, London, 2000

Addison, P. and Crang, J.A. (eds.), *Listening to Britain: Home Intelligence Reports on Britain's Finest Hour – May to September 1940*, Vintage Books, London, 2011

Alexander, Kristen, *Australia's Few and the Battle of Britain*, Pen & Sword, Barnsley, 2015

Allen, Wing Commander H.R., *Fighter Squadron: A Memoir 1940–42*, Granada, London, 1982

Anon, *The Battle of Britain: August–October 1940*, Ministry of Information on behalf of the Air Ministry, London, 1941

Anon, *The Battle of Britain*, Air Ministry Pamphlet 156, Issued by the Department of the Air Member for Training, August 1943

Anon, *The Rise & Fall of the German Air Force 1939–45*, Air Ministry Pamphlet 248, Public Record Office, London, 2001

Ashworth, C., *RAF Coastal Command: 1936–1969*, PSL, Sparkford, 1992

Bekker, C., *The Luftwaffe War Diaries*, Corgi Books, London, 1972

Bekker, C., *Hitler's Naval War*, Corgi, London, 1976

Bishop, E., *The Battle of Britain*, George Allen & Unwin Ltd, London, 1960

Bowyer, M.J.F., *2 Group RAF: A Complete History, 1936–1945*, Faber & Faber, London, 1974

Calder, A., *The People's War: Britain 1939–45*, Pimlico, London, 2008

Caldwell, D., *JG26: Top Guns of the Luftwaffe*, Orion Books, New York, 1991

Caldwell, D., *The JG26 War Diary: Volume One, 1939–42*, Grub Street, London, 1996

BIBLIOGRAPHY

Campion, G., *The Good Fight: Battle of Britain Propaganda and The Few*, Palgrave-Macmillan, London, 2010

Cannandine, D. (ed.), *The Speeches of Winston Churchill*, Penguin, London, 1990

Churchill, W.S., *The Second World War, Vol. II, Their Finest Hour*, Cassell & Co, London, 1949

Clapson, M., *Britain in the Twentieth Century*, Routledge, Abingdon, 2009

Collier, B., *The Defence of the United Kingdom*, HMSO, London, 1957

Cox, S. and Probert, H. (eds.), *The Battle Re-Thought: A Symposium on the Battle of Britain*, Airlife, Shrewsbury, 1991

Cox, S., 'RAF & *Luftwaffe* Intelligence Compared' in Handel, M.I. (ed.), *Intelligence & Military Operations*, Frank Cass, Abingdon, 1990

Dean, Sir Maurice, *The Royal Air Force in Two World Wars*, Cassell, London, 1979

Deere, Air Commodore A.C., *Nine Lives*, Hodder Paperback Ltd, London, 1959

Deighton, L., *Fighter: The True Story of the Battle of Britain*, Triad/Panther Books, St Albans, 1979

Dierich, W., *Kampfgeschwader 'Edelweiss': The History of a German Bomber Unit, 1939–45*, Purnell Book Services Ltd, London, 1975

Dierich, W., *Chronik: Kampfgeschwader 55 'Greif'*, Motorbuch Verlag, Stuttgart, 2012

Donnelly, M., *Britain in the Second World War*, Routledge, London, 1999

Donnelly, L., *The Other Few: The Contribution Made by Bomber and Coastal Aircrew to the Winning of the Battle of Britain*, Red Kite, Walton-on-Thames, 2004

Dowding, ACM Lord H.C.T., *Dispatch: The Battle of Britain*, The London Gazette, London, 1946

Fleming, P., *Invasion 1940*, Rupert Hard-Davis, London, 1957

Foreman, J., *RAF Fighter Command Victory Claims of World War Two, Volume One*, Air Research Publications, Red Kite, Walton-on-Thames, 2003

Forrester, L., *Fly For Your Life: The Story of RR Stanford Tuck DSO, DFC and Two Bars*, The Companion Book Club, London, 1956

Galland, A., *The First and the Last: Germany's Fighter Force* in the Second World War, Fontana, London, 1954

Gleed, Wing Commander I.R., *Arise to Conquer*, Victor Gollanz Ltd, London, 1942

Green, W., *Aircraft of the Battle of Britain*, MacDonald & Co (Publishers) Ltd and Pan Books Ltd, London, 1969

Handel, M.I. (ed.), *Intelligence and Military Operations*, Frank Cass, Abingdon, 1990

Henshaw, A., *Sigh for an Merlin: Testing the Spitfire*, Crécy Publishing, Manchester, 1996

Hough, R. and Richards, D., *The Battle of Britain: The Jubilee History*, Hodder & Stoughton Ltd, London, 1990

Humphreys, R., *Dover at War 1939–1945*, Alan Sutton, Stroud, 1993

James, T.C.G., *The Battle of Britain*, Frank Cass, London, 1990

Johnstone, AVM A.V.R., *Spitfire into War*, William Kimber & Co Ltd, London, 1986

Jones, Wing Commander I. *Tiger Squadron*, Award Books, New York, 1966

Jones, Professor R.V., *Most Secret War: British Scientific Intelligence 1939–45*, Hamish Hamilton, London, 1978

Kesselring, Field Marshal A., *The Memoirs of Field-Marshal Kesselring*, Greenhill Books, London, 1997

Kershaw, I., *Hitler: 1936–1945, Nemesis*, Penguin, London, 2001

Legg, R., *Battle of Britain Dorset*, Dorset Publishing Company, Wincanton, 1995

Lewin, R., *Ultra Goes to War*, Hutchinson & Co Ltd, London, 1978

Lisiewicz, Squadron Leader M. (ed.), *Destiny Can Wait: The Polish Air Force in the Second World War*, William Heinemann Ltd, London, 1949

MacDonell, Air Commodore A.R.D. (MacDonell L. and MacKay A., – eds.), *From Dogfight to Diplomacy: A Spitfire Pilot's Log 1932-1958*, Pen & Sword, Barnsley, 2005

Mason, F.K., *Battle Over Britain*, Aston Publications, Bourne End, 1990

Mason, P.D., *Nicolson VC: The full and authorised biography of James Brindley Nicolson*, Geerings of Ashford Ltd, Ashford, 1991

Middlebrook, M. and Everitt, C., *The Bomber Command War Diaries: An operational reference book 1939–1945*, Midland Counties Publications, Hinckley, 1996

Morgan, E. and Shacklady, E., *Spitfire: The History*, Key Publishing, Stamford, 1987

Muggeridge, M. (ed.), *Ciano's Diary 1939–1943*, William Heinemann Ltd, London, 1947

Orange, V., *Park: The biography of Air Chief Marshal Sir Keith Park*, Grub Street, London, 2001

Orange, V., *Dowding of Fighter Command: Victor of the Battle of Britain*, Grubb Street, London, 2008

BIBLIOGRAPHY

Overy, R., *The Air War 1939-1945*, first edition, Europa Publications Ltd, London, 1980

Overy, R., *The Battle of Britain*, Penguin, London, 2004

Overy, R., *Goering: The Iron Man*, Bloomsbury Revelations, London, 2021

Pope, R., *War & Society in Britain 1899-1948*, Longman, Harlow, 1991

Price, A., *Spitfire at War*, Ian Allen Ltd, Shepperton, 1974

Price, A., *Battle of Britain: The Hardest Day, 18 August 1940*, MacDonald & Jane's Publishers Ltd, London, 1979

Prien, J., *Jagdgeschwader 53: A History of the 'Pik As' Geschwader, March 1937–May 1942*, Schiffer Publishing Ltd, Sedona, Arizona, USA, 1997

Priestley, J.B., *Postscripts*, William Heinemann Ltd, London, 1940

Quill, J.K., *Spitfire*, Arrow Books, London 1985

Ramsay, W. (ed.), *The Battle of Britain: Then & Now, Mk V Edition*, Battle of Britain Prints International Ltd, London, 1986

Ramsay, W. (ed.), *The Blitz Then & Now, Volume I*, Battle of Britain Prints International Ltd, London, 1989

Richards, D., *RAF Bomber Command in the Second World War: The Hardest Victory*, Penguin, London, 2001

RAFHS, *Air Intelligence: A Symposium*, RAFHS, London, 1997

Rootes, A., *Front Line County: Kent at War, 1939-45*, Robert Hale Ltd, London, 1980

Roskill, Captain S.W., *The War at Sea 1939–45: Volume 1*, HMSO, London, 1954

Rohwer, J and Hunnelchen G., *Chronology of the War at Sea*, Ian Allen Ltd, London, 1972

Sarkar, D., *The Final Few*, Amberley Publishing, Stroud, 2015

Sarkar, D., *Letters from The Few: Unique Memories From the Battle of Britain*, Pen & Sword, Barnsley, 2020

Sarkar, D., *Battle of Britain 1940: The Finest Hour's Human Cost*, Pen & Sword, Barnsley, 2020

Sarkar, D., *Sailor Malan: Freedom Fighter*, Pen & Sword, Barnsley, 2021

Schenk, P., *Operation Sealion: The Invasion of England*, Greenhill Books, Barnsley, 2019

Shirer, W.L., *The Rise and Fall of the Third Reich*, Simon & Schuster, New York, 1960

Smith, M., The RAF, In Addison, J. and Crang, J.A. (eds.), *The Burning Blue: A new History of the Battle of Britain*, Pimlico, London, 2000

Townsend, Group Captain P., *Duel of Eagles: The Classic Account of the Battle of Britain*, Weidenfeld & Nicolson, London, 1990

Trevor-Roper, H.R. (ed.), *Hitler's War Directives 1939-45*, Pan Books, London, 1966
Vasco, J.J. and Cornwell, P.D., *Zerstörer: The Messerschmitt 110 and its Units in 1940*, JAC Publications, Norwich, 1995
Vasco, J., *Bombsights Over England: The History of Erprobungsgruppe 210 Luftwaffe Fighter-Bomber Unit in the Battle of Britain*, JAC Publications, Norwich, 1990
Wakefield, K., *The First Pathfinders: The Operational History of Kampfgruppe 100, 1939–1941*, Crécy Books, Somerton, 1992
Warner, G., *RAF Biggin Hill: The Immortal Story of One of the Battle of Britain's Most Famous Fighter Stations*, Putnam & Co Ltd, London, 1969
Willis, J., *Churchill's Few: The Battle of Britain Remembered*, Guild Publishing, London, 1985
Wheatley, R., *Operation Sealion*, Oxford University Press, Oxford, 1958
Wright, R., *Dowding and the Battle of Britain*, Corgi, London, 1970
Ziegler, F.H., *The Story of 609 Squadron: Under the White Rose*, MacDonald, London, 1971

Websites

The National Archives: https://www.nationalarchives.gov.uk
Commonwealth War Graves Commission: https://www.cwgc.org
Battle of Britain Memorial Trust: https://www.battleofbritainmemorial.org
Battle of Britain: The People's Project: https://www.battleofbritainthepeoplesproject.com
Dilip Sarkar: https://www.dilipsarkarauthor.com
Digital History Archive: https://www.digitalhistoryarchive.com
Kenley Revival Project: https://www.kenleyrevival.org
Battle of Britain London Monument: https://www.bbm.org.uk

Films

Although produced for either propaganda purposes or popular culture, the following films can provide an idea of the timeframe this book concerns:
The Lion Has Wings, directed by Michael Powell, Adrian Brunel and Brian Desmond Hurst (London Films, 1939).
Target for Tonight, directed by Harry Watt (Crown Film Unit, 1941).
A Yank in the RAF, directed by Henry King (Twentieth Century-Fox, 1941).

Mrs Miniver, directed by William Wyle (Metro-Goldwyn-Mayer, 1942).
The First of the Few, directed by Leslie Howard (British Aviation Pictures, 1942).
Battle of Britain, directed by Guy Hamilton (Spitfire Productions, 1969).

Television

The World at War, directed by David Elstein (ITV, 1973).

Other Books by Dilip Sarkar

Spitfire Squadron: No 19 Squadron at War, 1939–41
The Invisible Thread: A Spitfire's Tale
Through Peril to the Stars: RAF Fighter Pilots Who Failed to Return, 1939–45
Angriff *Westland: Three Battle of Britain Air Raids Through the Looking Glass*
A Few of the Many: Air War 1939–45, A Kaleidoscope of Memories
Bader's Tangmere Spitfires: The Untold Story, 1941
Bader's Duxford Fighters: The Big Wing Controversy
Missing in Action: Resting in Peace?
Guards VC: Blitzkrieg 1940
Battle of Britain: The Photographic Kaleidoscope, Volumes I–IV
Fighter Pilot: The Photographic Kaleidoscope
Group Captain Sir Douglas Bader: An Inspiration in Photographs
Johnnie Johnson: Spitfire Top Gun, Part I
Johnnie Johnson: Spitfire Top Gun, Part II
Battle of Britain: Last Look Back
Spitfire! Courage & Sacrifice
Spitfire Voices: Heroes Remember
The Battle of Powick Bridge: Ambush a Fore-thought
Duxford 1940: A Battle of Britain Base at War
The Few: The Battle of Britain in the Words of the Pilots
Spitfire Manual 1940
The Sinking of HMS Royal Oak: In the Words of the Survivors (re-print of Hearts of Oak)
The Last of the Few: Eighteen Battle of Britain Pilots Tell Their Extraordinary Stories
Hearts of Oak: The Human Tragedy of HMS Royal Oak
Spitfire Voices: Life as a Spitfire Pilot in the Words of the Veterans
How the Spitfire Won the Battle of Britain
Spitfire Ace of Aces: The True Wartime Story of Johnnie Johnson

OTHER BOOKS BY DILIP SARKAR

Douglas Bader

Fighter Ace: The Extraordinary Life of Douglas Bader, Battle of Britain Hero (re-print of above)

Spitfire: The Photographic Biography

Hurricane Manual 1940

River Pike

The Final Few: The Last Surviving Pilots of the Battle of Britain Tell Their Stories

Arnhem 1944: The Human Tragedy of the Bridge Too Far

Spitfire! The Full Story of a Unique Battle of Britain Fighter Squadron

Battle of Britain 1940: The Finest Hour's Human Cost

Letters from The Few: Unique Memories of the Battle of Britain

Johnnie Johnson's 1942 Diary: The War Diary of the Spitfire Ace of Aces

Johnnie Johnson's Great Adventure: The Spitfire Ace of Ace's Last Look Back

Sailor Malan – Freedom Fighter: The Inspirational Story of a Spitfire Ace

Spitfire Ace of Aces – The Album: The Photographs of Johnnie Johnson

The Real Spitfire Pilot

The Real Hurricane Pilot

Bader's Big Wing Controversy: Duxford 1940.

Bader's Spitfire Wing: Tangmere 1941

Spitfire Down

Forgotten Heroes of The Battle of Britain

Faces of The Few

Spitfire Faces

Arise to Conquer: The Real Hurricane Pilot (introduction, commentary and photographs supplied to a new edition of Wing Commander IR Gleed DSO DFC's wartime memoir)

Free French Spitfire Hero: The Diaries of and Search for René Mouchotte (with Jan Leeming)

Battle of Britain: The Finest Hour in Cinema

Battle of Britain: The Movie (contributor to and publisher of the now late Robert Rudhall's original edition (2000), and editor and substantial contributor to 2022 revised edition)

Faces of HMS Royal Oak: The 'Mighty Oak' Disaster at Scapa Flow

Battle of Britain – Volume 1: The Gathering Storm – Prelude to the Spitfire Summer of 1940

Battle of Britain – Volume 2: The Breaking Storm – 10 July 1940 – 12 August 1940

Index

Aalborg, 28, 53, 67, 76
Acklington, 58, 63
Adler Tag, xiii, 2–3, 7, 16, 18
Akroyd, Sergeant Harold, 93
Alford, Squadron Leader Edward, 184, 192, 200, 202, 240
Altendorf, *Leutnant*, 16
Ambrose, Pilot Officer Charles, 230
Andover, 15, 25–6, 104
Angerstein, *Generalmajor* Karl, 188
Appleby, Pilot Officer Michael, 21–2, 43
Armitage, Flight Lieutenant Dennis, 111–12
Arnfield, Sergeant Stanley, 113, 161, 208
Arras, 3, 7
Ashford, 37, 55, 112, 130, 212
Atkinson, Pilot Officer Harold, 21, 45, 147, 223–5
Atkinson, Sergeant George, 34, 248
Ayerst, Pilot Officer Peter 'Decoy', 46
Azores, 2

Bader, Squadron Leader Douglas, 27, 47
Badger, Squadron Leader John 'Tubby', 40, 95, 136

Bage, Corporal George, 115, 248
Bankhardt, *Kriegsberichter*, 205, 207
Bannister, Sergeant Oswald, 75
Bartlett, Sergeant Leonard, 78
Barton, Flying Lieutenant Robert 'Butch', 96, 136, 147
Batt, Sergeant Gordon, 10
Bayer, *Oberleutnant* Georg, 183
Bazley, Flight Lieutenant Sydney, 133
Beachy Head, 45, 77, 86, 187, 189–90, 200, 215
Beamish, Wing Commander Victor, 154–6, 229
Beaumont-le-Roger, 7
Beaumont, Flying Officer Stephen, 145–6
Beaumont, Pilot Officer Walter, 222–3
Beggs, Sub-Lieutenant Henry, 34, 112
Bentley Priory, 226
Beresford, Flight Lieutenant Hugh, 25, 234
Bergmann, *Unteroffizier* Franz, 198
Berlin, 50, 53
Berry, Flight Sergeant Fred, 80, 137–8, 162
Beyer, *Leutnant* Franz, 34

INDEX

Biggin Hill, 34, 53, 90, 110, 112, 115–16, 125, 133, 157, 163, 185–9, 191, 201, 205–209, 216, 226–7, 241
Bird, Pilot Officer Alec, 46, 239–40
Blackwood, Squadron Leader Douglas, 176–7
Blair, Flying Officer Kenneth, 85, 227–8
Bland, Pilot Officer John, 191, 248
Blume, *Oberleutnant* Walter, 236
Blyth, 58, 63
Boddington, Sergeant Michael, 42
Bode, *Major* Helmut, 124, 217–18
Boitel-Gill, Flight Lieutenant 'Bottle', 92–3, 222
Bognor Regis, 11
Boot, Pilot Officer Peter, 162
Boulogne, 5, 156, 199, 227
Bowen, Pilot Officer Nigel, 133
Boyd, Flight Lieutenant Robert, 143, 160
Brand, Air Vice-Marshal, 89
Bretnütz, *Hauptmann* Heinz 'Pietzch', 154
Brinkman, *Leutnant* Heinrich, 35
Brinsden, Flying Officer Frank 'Fanny', 169
Brize Norton, 174, 237–8
Brossler, *Oberleutnant* Bruno, 43
Brothers, Flight Lieutenant Peter, 163, 210, 235
Brown, Pilot Officer Peter, 27
Brown, Flight Lieutenant Mark 'Hilly', 79, 81
Browne, Pilot Officer Dennis, 81
Bruder, *Unteroffizier* Ernest, 133
Bründle, *Oberleutnant* Kurt, 173
Brzezina, Flight Lieutenant Stanislaw, 4
Bulldog, HMS, 10
Bülowius, *Generalmajor* Alfred, 91
Busch, *Oberstleutnant* Hermann, 58

Calais, 5, 18, 77, 84, 126, 129, 133, 160, 188, 197
Cale, Pilot Officer Francis, 112
Campbell, Pilot Officer Alan, 207
Campion, Sergeant Alfred, 29
Cap Blanc Nez, 3, 53
Carey, Flight Lieutenant Frank 'Chota', 219
Carnall, Sergeant Ralph, 131
Carter, Pilot Officer Peter, 73
Casson, Pilot Officer Lionel 'Buck', 71
Castle Bromwich Aeroplane Factory (CBAF), 29–31
Chandler, Sergeant Horatio, 39, 210
Cherbourg, 4, 7, 53, 107–108, 136, 139, 157, 184, 217, 225
Cherry, ACW Frances, 186, 193, 203
Chichester, 10, 143, 218
Christans, *Hauptmann*, 20
Church Fenton, 26, 52, 68, 90, 96
Churchill, Prime Minister Winston, 30, 125, 174–5, 184
Clark, Squadron Leader David de Brassey, 35
Claus, *Oberleutnant* Georg, 108–109
Cleaver, Flying Officer Gordon, 94
Clouston, Flight Lieutenant Wilf, 168
Clowes, Sergeant Arthur, 81, 162
Clyde, Flying Officer William, 94

Coastal Command, 3, 5, 18–19, 28, 47–8, 77, 125, 129, 137, 174, 217
Cochrane, Pilot Officer Arthur, 186, 234
Cohrs, *Unteroffizier* Ewald, 238
Collard, Flying Officer Peter, 37–8
Comely, Pilot Officer Peter, 102
Connors, Flight Lieutenant Stanley, 96, 120–1, 130, 195
Cowley, Sergeant James, 102
Cox, Pilot Officer Kenneth, 113, 209, 222
Cox, Sergeant David, 5, 82
Craig, Sergeant John, 6, 96, 130
Crook, Pilot Officer David, 22–3, 42–4, 103, 105–106, 249
Crossley, Flight Lieutenant Mike, 78, 116, 121, 133, 157, 163–4, 235
Crowley-Milling, Pilot Officer Denis, 47
Croydon, 5–6, 77, 86–7, 90, 95, 116–23, 129–30, 158, 185, 191–2, 199–200, 204, 206, 210, 248
Cunningham, Pilot Officer Wallace 'Jock', 117, 169, 171–2
Currant, Pilot Officer Christopher 'Bunny', 65
Czernin, Flying Officer Count Manfred, 212

Daedalus, HMS, 137, 146
Dafforn, Pilot Officer Robert, 53, 161, 191
Darley, Squadron Leader Horace, 21, 105
David, Pilot Officer Denis, 24
Davies, Sergeant Leonard, 34
Davis, Flight Lieutenant Carl, 94
Deacon, Sergeant Albert 'Harry', 198
Debden, 4, 136, 186, 227, 231–3
Debenham, Pilot Officer Kenneth, 84, 229
Deere, Flight Lieutenant Al, 55, 113–15
Denmark, 28
Detling, 18–19, 31, 87, 208, 248
Dewar, Squadron Leader Johnny, 11, 96–8, 126
Dewhurst, Flying Officer Kenneth, 109, 173
Dickoré, Hauptmann Karl-Friedrich, 91, 110
Dieppe, 4, 7, 189
Doe, Pilot Officer Bob, 106, 109, 173
Dorset, 23, 102–103
Doulton, Pilot Officer Michael, 15, 93–4
Dover, 18–19, 33–4, 36–7, 39–40, 46, 52–6, 77, 82–6, 110–12, 127, 129, 133–5, 156, 187, 189, 211–12, 214, 216
Dowding, Air Chief Marshal, xi, 50, 57, 76, 124–5, 128, 155, 175–6, 236, 242
Dreher, *Oberfeldwebel* Alfred, 237
Du Vivier, Pilot Officer Reginald,
Duckenfield, Group Captain Ron,
Dülberg, *Leutnant* Ernst, 219
Dundas, Flying Officer John, 22, 42–3
Dundas, Group Captain Sir Hugh 'Cocky', 70
Dunkirk, 27, 89, 156, 183
Dupree, Sergeant Oswald, 75–6

INDEX

Duxford, 136, 168–9, 176–9, 227, 230, 242
Dymond, Sergeant William, 6, 87, 119, 130, 194

Eade, Sergeant Arthur, 111–12
'Eagle Day', 2, 28–32, 50
Eastchurch, xi, 2–6, 19, 31, 77, 84, 86, 88–9, 168
Ebben, *Unteroffizier* Willi, 17
Ebbighausen, *Hauptmann* Karl, 132, 173
Eberhart, *Feldwebel* Hugo, 195
Eckford, Pilot Officer Alan, 235
Edge, Flight Lieutenant Gerry, 130
Edge, Flying Officer Alexander, 105
Efner, *Unteroffizier* Ernest, 122
Elkington, Pilot Officer John 'Tim', 80–1, 137–9, 249
Ellacombe. Pilot Officer John, 84, 112, 228
Ellis, Squadron Leader John, 157, 160–1, 208
Else, Sergeant Peter, 209
Evans, Pilot Officer David, 55, 163
Evans, Sergeant George, 106
Ewald, *Oberleutnant* Wolfgang, 214
Exeter, 11–12, 15, 20, 24, 33, 41, 45, 53, 90, 96, 98, 126, 136, 146, 217, 221, 224

Falmouth, 107
Farnborough, 7, 11, 31
Feary, Sergeant Alan, 42
Fergusson, Flight Lieutenant Peter, 221
Ferriss, Flight Lieutenant Henry, 6, 88, 130–1, 248
Fink, *Oberst* Johannes 'Papa', 3–4, 7

Fiedler, *Oberleutnant* Horst, 120
First World War, 12, 182–3, 241
Fisher, Flying Officer Antony, 96
Fisher, Flying Officer Basil, 96
Fiske, Flying Officer William 'Billy' Meade Lindsley, 9–10, 15, 141–3, 174, 248
Flamborough Head, 68, 70–3
Flinders, Pilot Officer John 'Polly', 116, 123, 207–208
Folkestone, 37–9, 46, 53–6, 86, 114, 133, 135, 231
Fopp, Sergeant Desmond, 78
Ford, AC1 Stan, 184, 194, 201
Ford, 216–21, 225
Fowlmere, 19, 78, 82, 136
Fözö, *Oberleutnant* Josef 'Joschko', 133, 236
Frank, *Oberst* Walter, 43
Fröhlich, *Generalmajor*, 200
Fuch, *Major* Adolf, 3
Fuchs, *Obertleutnant* Karl, 17

Galland, *Major* Adolf, 3
Gardiner, Flying Officer Fred, 209
Gardner, Pilot Officer Peter, 39, 133
Gaunce, Flight Lieutenant Lionel, 163, 204
Gayner, Pilot Officer John, 37
Gebauer, *Unteroffizier* Josef, 208
Geier, *Oberfeldwebel* Valentin, 195
Gibson, Flight Lieutenant John, 54
Gilbert, Flight Sergeant Ernest, 10, 83, 165, 210
Gleed, Flight Lieutenant Ian 'Widge', 98–9
Glienke, *Obertleutnant* Joachim, 16
Glowacki, Sergeant Anton, 85
Glyde, Flying Officer Richard, 11

Goddard, Flight Lieutenant Henry, 73
Goodman, Pilot Officer George, 162, 213
Goodwin, Pilot Officer Barrie, 44, 248
Goodwin, Flying Officer Henry MacDonald, 22, 44, 248
Gordon, Squadron Leader John, 34, 88, 112, 229
Göring, *Reichssmarschall* Hermann, xiii, 2, 11–12, 16, 50, 124, 181–4, 226, 241
Gorrie, Pilot Officer David, 140
Gosport, xi, 137, 144, 146, 216–17, 221, 225
Götz, *Leutnant* Hans, 12
Gowers, Flying Officer, 233
Gracie, Flight Lieutenant 'Jumbo', 17, 212, 230
Graham, Flight Lieutenant Ted, 58
Graham, Pilot Officer Leslie, 129
Grandy, Squadron Leader John, 96, 147–8, 153–4
Gray, Pilot Officer Colin, 113, 115, 135, 186, 207, 231
Gray, Pilot Officer Donald, 160–1
Greenshields, Sub-Lieutenant Henry la Fone, 110–111, 133, 160
Gribble, Flight Lieutenant George, 55, 115, 135, 186, 207
Grice, Pilot Officer Douglas 'Grubby', 79
Grier, Pilot Officer Thomas, 219
Griffin, Sergeant John, 73
Griffiths, Sergeant Glyn, 212
Grömmer, *Unteroffizier* Rudolf, 197
Groth, *Hauptmann* Erich, 91
Gruszka, Flying Officer Franciszek, 210–11, 248
Gugelhuber, *Obergefreiter* Otto, 16
Guschewski, *Unteroffizier* Max, 105
Guy, Sergeant Leonard, 25, 94, 219

Haack, *Oberfeldwebel* E., 23
Habisch, *Leutnant* Alfred, 122
Hahn, *Leutnant* Siegfried, 107
Haigh, Sergeant Cyril, 106
Hallings-Pott, Wing Commander J., 46
Hallowes, Sergeant Jim, 25, 139, 218
Hardy, Pilot Officer Richard 'Dick', 107–109
Hamann, *Unteroffizier* Horst, 16
Hancock, Sergeant Bruce, 237–40
Handrick, *Major* Gotthard, 18, 183
Hanson, Flying Officer David, 78
Harkness, Squadron Leader Hill, 7–8, 25, 234
Harnett, Flying Officer Thomas, 75
Harper, Flight Lieutenant William, 78, 81
Haselmayer, *Unteroffizier* H., 23
Havercroft, Flight Sergeant Ralph 'Titch', 26, 45
Hawkings, Sergeant Redvers, 219
Hawley, Sergeant Frederick, 89
Helber, *Unteroffizier* Rudolf, 55
Henshaw, Alex, 30
Hesse, *Unteroffizier* Hans, 212
Higgingson, Flight Sergeant 'Taffy', 168, 212, 230
Hight, Pilot Officer Cecil, 106
Hillcoat, Flight Lieutenant Harry, 136

INDEX

Hillcoat, Flight Lieutenant Brian, 213
Hintze, *Oberleutnant* Otto, 77–8, 116
Hinze, *Kriegsberichter* Georg, 187, 197
Hogan, Squadron Leader Harry, 122, 157, 161, 236
Hohagen, *Leutnant* Erich, 133
Hope, Flight Lieutenant Sir Archibald, 13–14, 93–4, 142, 167
Hopkin, Pilot Officer John, 229–30
Hornchurch, 4, 89, 112–13, 129, 135–6, 158, 168, 186, 210, 226, 230, 235–6, 242
Hornsea, 71–2
Horton, Pilot Officer Patrick, 173
Howell, Flight Lieutenant Frank, 22, 103–104
Hughes, Acting Flight Lieutenant David, 12–13
Hughes, Flight Lieutenant Pat, 109, 173, 222
Hugo, Pilot Officer Petrus 'Dutch', 163, 185, 204
Hulbert, Sergeant Donald, 8
Humpherson, Pilot Officer John, 122
Hunt, Flight Sergeant Joe, 206
Hunt, Pilot Officer David, 234
Hunter, Air Commodore Henry, 74
Huth, *Oberstleutnant* Joachim, 3

Illg, *Oberfeldwebel* Wilhelm-Friedrich, 197–8, 200
Isle of Wight, 10, 25, 40–1, 44, 90, 104, 127, 136, 140, 144–6, 172–3, 217, 219, 221–3

Janke, *Hauptmann* Johannes, 28
Jansen, *Leutnant* Josef, 219
Jastrzebski, Flight Lieutenant Franciszek, 178
Jay, Pilot Officer Trevor, 11, 102
Jennings, Sergeant Bernard 'Jimmy', 169, 171, 249
Jeschonnek, *Generaloberst* Hans, 2
Johnston, Pilot Officer James, 34, 112
Johnstone, Squadron Leader Alexander 'Sandy', 26, 143, 157
Jones, Corporal G.W., 141
Jones, Pilot Officer Richard, 10, 165, 167
Jones, Professor R.V., 29, 31
Jones, Flight Lieutenant Parry, 47
Jones, Sergeant William, 132, 215

Kästner, Leutnant Hans-Joachim, 210
Kayll, Squadron Leader Joe, 157, 163, 185
Kaufman, *Feldwebel* Werner, 173
Keil, *Hauptmann* Anton, 53
Kemen, *Unteroffizier* Gerhard, 40
Kenley, 10, 18, 33, 37, 45, 53, 55, 110, 115–16, 125, 134, 157, 163–4, 167, 184–92, 194–205, 226, 240–1, 248
Kent, 19, 28, 39, 77, 84, 89, 110, 136, 157, 187, 201, 205, 207, 234
Kern, *Hauptmann* Wilhelm, 104
Kesselring, *Generalfeldmarschall* Albert, 3, 7, 32, 52, 123, 184, 226
Keymer, Sergeant Michael, 37
Kilner, Sergeant Joseph, 18

263

Kingaby, Sergeant Don, 215
Kingcome, Flight Lieutenant Brian 'Kingpin', 216
King, Squadron Leader Eric 'Whizzy', 96, 147, 152–6
King, Pilot Officer Martyn Aurel, 248
Kirk, Corporal Bill, 177
Klein, Sergeant Zygmunt, 173
Knopf, *Oberfeldwebel* Hans, 187
Korte, *Oberstleutnant* Hans, 44
Kozlowski, Pilot Officer Franciszek, 191, 248
Kratz, *Oberleutnant* Rudolf, 68, 74, 76
Kretzer, *Obergefreiter* Ludwig, 119, 122

La Fone, Sub-Lieutenant Henry, 110, 133, 159
Labusch, *Unteroffizier* Fritz, 25
Lacey, Sergeant James 'Ginger', 85, 161
Laguna, Flight Lieutenant Piotr, 178
Laing, Flying Officer Alexander, 83, 135, 164
Lake, Pilot Officer Donald, 75
Lambie, Pilot Officer William, 75
Lane, Pilot Officer Roy, 95, 218
Lane, Flight Lieutenant Brian, 136, 168–9, 249
Laricheliere, Pilot Officer Joseph, 15, 97, 147
Law, Pilot Officer Kennith Schadtler, 65
Leathart, Squadron Leader James 'Prof', 112, 186, 207
Leber, *Leutnant* Walter, 229–30

Lee, Pilot Officer Kenneth, 191
Lee, Flight Lieutenant Richard 'Dickie', 233
Lehmann, *Oberleutnant* D., 219
Lehner, *Unteroffizier* Willy, 107
Leonhard, *Leutnant* Karl, 108–109
Liensberger, *Hauptmann* Horst, 11–12, 16, 91
Little, Sergeant Ronald, 21
Llewellyn, Sergeant Reginald, 15, 33
Lock, Pilot Officer Eric 'Sawn Off', 60, 62
Loebel, *Oberstleutnant* Walter, 67
Loerzer, General Bruno, 12
Lofts, Pilot Officer Keith, 37–8, 54–5, 163
Looker, Flying Officer David, 204
Lovell, Flight Lieutenant Tony, 60, 67
Lovell-Gregg, Squadron Leader, 98, 102–103, 126, 248
Luftflotte 2, 3, 12, 16, 31, 41, 50, 52, 56, 77, 110, 187, 216, 226, 237, 249
Luftflotte 3, 7, 19, 31, 41, 50, 91, 109, 184, 216, 226
Luftflotte 5, 50–1, 56–7, 67, 77, 124–5, 241–2, 237
Lympne, xi, 28, 53, 56, 248

Maassen, *Unteroffizier* Mathias, 199–200
Mable, Pilot Officer Sidney, 37
MacDonell, Squadron Leader Don, 10, 82–3, 134–5, 157, 164–7, 185–6, 201–202, 240
MacGregor, Squadron Leader Hector, 15, 136, 146

INDEX

MacPherson, Flight Sergeant Robert, 37
Magin, *Oberleutnant* Hermann, 187, 197, 200
Mai, *Unteroffizier* Rudolf, 208
Maidstone, 84–6, 112–13, 115, 122, 189
Maffett, Pilot Officer Gerald, 234
Makrocki, *Hauptmann* Wilhelm, 16
Malan, Squadron Leader A.G. 'Sailor', 4–5, 27
Mann, Sergeant Jack, 10, 135
Mann, Pilot Officer Harold, 79–80
Manston, 4, 16, 18, 31, 34–6, 40, 46–7, 53, 56, 77, 89, 110, 112, 129, 132, 134, 157–8, 172, 186
Manton, Squadron Leader, 186, 191, 210–12, 214–15, 227, 230, 248
Marrs, Pilot Officer Eric 'Boy', 93, 172
Marsh, Sergeant Henry 'Tony', 21
Martlesham Heath, 77, 79, 82, 88, 186, 229, 242, 248
Marx, *Leutnant* Horst, 119, 122–3
Matthews, Flying Officer Peter, 80, 162
Mayer, *Unteroffizier* Richard, 35
Mayers, Pilot Officer Howard, 14
McArthur, Flight Lieutenant James, 22, 105
McGrath, Pilot Officer John, 94
McGregor, Flight Lieutenant Gordon, 130
McKay, Sergeant Donald, 191, 248
McKellar, Flight Lieutenant Archie, 63, 65
McIntyre, Pilot Officer Athol, 6, 96
McLean, Squadron Leader J., 46
McMullen, Flying Officer Desmond, 55, 115, 135, 207
McNab, Squadron Leader Ernest 'Archie', 86–7
McNay, Sergeant Alexander, 71–3
Meisel *Hauptmann* Herbert, 216, 218
Middle Wallop, 4, 10, 20–1, 31, 42–4, 47, 90–1, 96, 103–106, 109, 172, 217, 221
Midhurst, 9
Milch, Erhard, 182
Miller, Pilot Officer Rogers Garland, 22
Millington, Pilot Officer William, 63
Mills, Sergeant Jack, 8–9
Milne, Pilot Officer Richard 'Dickie', 6, 84, 228
Mitchell, Flying Officer Lancelot, 7–8
Mitchell, Pilot Officer Harry, 41
Möericke, *Major* Frederick, 187
Mölders, *Major* Werner 'Vatti', 182–3
Möller-Friedrich, *Oberleutnant* R., 222
Montgomery, Pilot Officer Cecil, 37
Mortimer, WAAF Sergeant Joan, 206
Mortimer-Rose, Pilot Officer Edward, 107, 109
Moody, Pilot Officer Henry, 143, 221
Morgan, Flight Lieutenant Thomas Dalton, 8–9
Morton, Pilot Officer Edward 'Teddy', 178

Mounsdon, Pilot Officer Maurice, 130
Mount, Flying Officer Christopher, 221
Müller, *Obertleutnant* Helmut, 16
Mumler, Squadron Leader Mieczyslaw, 178
Müncheberg, *Oberleutnant* Joachim, 183
Münchmeyer, *Leutnant* Wolfgang, 25

Neil, Pilot Officer Tom, 152, 154
Newberry, Flying Officer John, 105
Nicolson, Flight Lieutenant James Brindley, 96, 147–9, 152–6, 198, 248–9
Norman, Squadron Leader, 186, 191
Norris, Sergeant Philip, 21, 39
North-Bomford, Sergeant David, 212
Northolt, 7–8, 25, 77, 91, 136–7, 157–8, 163, 191, 213, 215, 227, 234
North Weald, 4, 6, 77–8, 80, 112, 130, 136, 154, 189, 226–31, 235–6, 242
Norwell, Sergeant John, 187

O'Brien, Squadron Leader Joseph 'Spike', 221–2
Observer Corps, 19, 25, 37, 179, 190, 192, 200
Odiham, 7, 11, 31
Olive, Flight Lieutenant Gordon, 18, 37, 157–8
Oliver, Squadron Leader Dennis, 19
Orthofer, *Hauptmann* Alfons, 217–18
Ortner, *Leutnant* Helmut, 25, 121
Osmand, Pilot Officer Alexander, 20–1, 98, 224–6
Ostaszewski-Ostoja, Flying Officer Piotr 'Osti', 22, 104, 109

Pain, Pilot Officer John, 122, 208
Pargiter, Major-General R.B., 67
Park, Air Vice-Marshal, 47, 50, 57, 82, 89, 125, 242
Parker, Pilot Officer Vincent, 107–108
Parrott, Pilot Officer Peter, 27
Parsons, Pilot Officer, 28
Parsons, Sergeant Claude, 39, 209–10
Pas-de-Calais, 2, 47, 126, 184, 227
Passy, Pilot Officer Cyril, 65
Pearce, Sergeant Leonard, 120, 235
Pegge, Pilot Officer Joe, 210
Pemberton, Squadron Leader David, 136, 157, 161–2, 234
Pepper, ACW1 Jill,
Peters, *Hauptmann* Gustav, 195
Petersen, *Feldwebel* Johannes, 187, 195–6
Philippart, Pilot Officer Jacques, 97
Photographic Reconnaissance Unit (PRU), 28
Pigg, Flying Officer Oswald St John, 60
Pilger, *Hauptmann* Otto, 77
Pingel, *Hauptmann* Rolf, 183
Pinkham, Squadron Leader Phillip, 19, 136
Pittman, Pilot Officer Geoffrey, 78
Pond, Flight Sergeant Arthur, 14, 25, 94, 219

INDEX

Portland, 11–15, 19–21, 24, 26, 41, 52, 89–92, 97–103, 124, 136, 146, 172, 224, 242
Potter, Sergeant Jack, 169, 171–2
Prickman, Wing Commander Thomas, 191, 201
Priller, *Oberleutnant* Josef 'Pips', 133
Proske, *Oberleutnant* Rüdiger, 201
Putt, Flight Lieutenant Alan, 54
Pyman, Flying Officer Lee, 37, 40, 159

Quill, Flying Officer Jeffrey Kindersley, 36–7, 158–9, 210

Raab, *Feldwebel* Wilhelm, 195, 199–200
Rabagliati, Flight Lieutenant Alexander, 230
Ramsay, Pilot Officer John, 229
Rave, *Unteroffizier* Herbert, 238
Rayner, Flight Lieutenant Roderick 'Roddy', 98
Rees, Pilot Officer Brain, 39, 209
Reichel, *Feldwebel* Adolf, 187, 193
Restemeyer, *Hauptmann* Werner, 58, 67
Rieckhoff, *Oberstleutnant* Herbert, 53
Riley, Flight Lieutenant William, 178
Ritchie, Pilot Officer Thomas, 143
Roach, Pilot Officer Robert, 89, 112, 132
Robbins, Sergeant Robert, 115
Roberts, Wing Commander David, 20
Robinson, Sergeant Peter, 93, 103, 230
Rochford, 16–17, 19, 31, 33–4, 37, 53, 56, 84, 129, 157, 189, 191, 212, 214, 227, 229
Roden, Sergeant Henry, 169, 172
Roth, *Hauptmann* Joachim, 187, 192, 194–5, 199, 210
Royal Aircraft Establishment, 7
Rozwadowski, Pilot Officer Mieczyslaw, 85, 112
Rubensdörffer, *Hauptmann*, 18, 82, 116, 119–20, 122–4
Russell, Squadron Leader Humphrey 'Humph', 116, 120, 208

Satchell, Squadron Leader Jack, 178
Saul, Air Vice-Marshal Richard, 57, 67
Savill, Sergeant Joseph, 6
Schlaffer, *Oberleutnant* Urban, 160
Schank, Gefrieter, 35
Schmid, *Oberst* Joseph 'Beppo', 2, 57–8, 182, 241
Schnoor, *Obertleutnant* Emil, 16
Schöpfel, *Oberleutnant* Gerhard, 183, 190–1
Schulz, *Feldwebel* Karl, 106
Schumacher, *Unteroffizier* Bernard, 199
Schümichen, *Unteroffizier* Werner, 16
Schweinhardt, *Oberfeldwebel*, 220–1
Schweitzer, *Major* Theodore, 187
Scott, Pilot Officer Donald, 72–4, 76
Seabourne, Sergeant Eric, 10
Sealand, 46
Seelöwe, Operation, xii, 2, 48–9, 181, 241, 249

Selsey Bill, 25, 39, 89–90, 94, 96, 103, 109, 116, 137, 139–40, 217–19
Shanahan, Sergeant Martin, 81
Shoreham, 9, 90, 95, 213
Siegel, *Hauptmann* Walter, 217
Simon, *Gauleiter* Gustav, 48
Simpson, Pilot Officer Peter, 10, 134–5, 165, 195
Smart, Flight Officer Tommy, 18
Smith, Flight Lieutenant Rod, 6
Smythe, Pilot Officer Rupert, 40
Soden, Pilot Officer John, 133
Soloman, Pilot Officer Neville, 212
Sommer, *Oberstleutnant* Dr Otto, 187, 196
Southampton, 19, 24–5, 31, 47, 92, 94, 104, 136, 147–9, 152, 154–5, 157, 172, 242
Spencer, Squadron Leader Desmond, 214
St Leger, 3
St Omer, 3, 48, 77, 156, 200, 227
Stage, *Oberfeldwebel* Willi, 212
Stange, *Feldwebel* Herbert, 213
Station Gosport, 146
Steding, *Unteroffizier* Hans, 35
Steigenberger, *Feldwebel* Otto, 55
Stephani, *Feldwebel* Otto, 197
Stevens, Pilot Officer Leonard, 78
Stoeckl, *Oberst* Alois, 43
Stoney, Flight Lieutenant George, 53, 236
Stumpff, *Generaloberst*, 50, 77
Szcesny, Pilot Officer Henryk, 4

Tangmere, 4, 7–10, 12, 24–6, 40, 45, 90–1, 93–4, 136–7, 139–43, 145–6, 167, 189, 217, 219, 248

Taylor, Sergeant Norman, 94
Temme, *Obertleutnant* Paul, 9
Tew, Sergeant Phillip, 135, 186, 207
Thiel, *Feldwebel* Jonny, 44
Thompson, Squadron Leader John 'Tommy', 5–6, 87, 95, 116, 118–19, 122–3, 130–1
Thomson, Flight Lieutenant James, 178
Thorney Island, 95, 174, 216–18, 221, 225–6
Tietzen, *Hauptmann* Horst 'Jacob', 55, 133, 236
Topham, Sergeant John, 75
Trautloft, *Hauptmann* Johannes, 183
Trousdale, Pilot Officer Richard, 132, 214
Trubenbach, Major *Hans*, 84
Truran, Pilot Officer Anthony, 55
Tuck, Flight Lieutenant Robert 'Bob' Stanford, 26, 44–5, 215
Twyford, 94, 106

Unger, *Unteroffizier* Günther, 188, 192, 198–9
Unwin, Flight Sergeant George 'Grumpy', 169, 171–2, 249
Upton, Pilot Officer Hamilton, 140, 218
Urie, Flight Lieutenant Dunlop, 220–1

von Bulow, *Obertleutnant* Harry, 7
von Chamier-Glisczinski, *Oberst* Wolfgang, 77
von Cramon-Traubadel, *Major* Hans Jürgen, 91
von Hahn, *Oberleutnant* Hans, 108

INDEX

von Maltzahn, *Hauptmann* Günther, 173
von Pebel, *Kriegsberichter* Rolf, 187, 193, 196
von Richthofen, General Wolfram, 24, 181–2, 216, 226
von Waldau, *Generalmajor* Otto Hoffman, 2

Walker, Pilot Officer James, 131
Walker, Pilot Officer William, 155–6
Wallace, Sergeant Thomas, 87, 95–6, 121, 130–1
Walley, Sergeant Peter, 163, 205
Wanderer, *Gefreiter* Willi, 205, 207
Ward, Squadron Leader The Hon. Edward, 141–2
Warmwell, 10, 12, 20–1, 90, 92–3, 96, 103, 136, 145, 217, 223
Warner, Flight Lieutenant William, 112–13, 161
Watling, Pilot Officer William, 26, 45
Weaver, Flight Lieutenant Steve 'Squeak', 17–18, 157, 168, 212, 229
Webb, Flying Officer Paul, 160
Weitkus, *Major* Paul, 3
Welford, Pilot Officer Harry, 65
Werdin, *Oberleutnant* Arnold, 187
Wemhöner, *Unteroffizier* Hans, 19
Werner, *Unteroffizier* Johann, 120
West Malling, 4, 87–8, 115–16, 131, 136, 203, 249

Whall, Sergeant Basil, 220–1
Walley, Sergeant Peter, 205
Whelan, Sergeant John, 165
Whitstable, 4, 168, 191, 236
Wildblood, Pilot Officer Timothy, 223
Wilhelm, *Oberleutnant* J., 218
Wilkinson, Squadron Leader Rodney, 110, 112, 129, 132–3, 174
Williams, Pilot Officer Wycliff, 214
Windrush, 237–9
Winiarski, *Oberleutnant* H., 219
Winter, Pilot Officer Douglas 'Snowy', 59–60
Witorzenc, Flying Officer Stefan, 54, 236
Wittman, *Leutnant* Erwin, 195, 199
Wlasnowalski, Pilot Officer Boleslaw, 78–9
Wolfien, *Major* Günther, 58
Wollin, *Unteroffizier* Gerhard, 213
Woodhall, Wing Commander Alfred 'Woody', 169, 176, 178–9
Woods-Scawen, Pilot Officer Charles, 8–9, 94–5, 140
Wörner, *Unteroffizier* A., 218
Worrall, Squadron Leader John, 116, 121, 133, 157

Zenker, Pilot Officer Pavel, 236
Zurakowski, Pilot Officer Janusz, 105, 109